Beginning Windows Phone 7 Development

■ ■ ■

Henry Lee
and
Eugene Chuvyrov

Apress®

Beginning Windows Phone 7 Development

Copyright © 2010 by Henry Lee & Eugene Chuvyrov

ISBN-13 (pbk): 978-1-4302-3216-2

ISBN-13 (electronic): 978-1-4302-3217-9

Printed and bound in the United States of America 9 8 7 6 5 4 3 2 1

President and Publisher: Paul Manning
Lead Editor: Ewan Buckingham
Development Editor: John Osborn
Technical Reviewer: Stefan Turalski
Editorial Board: Steve Anglin, Mark Beckner, Ewan Buckingham, Gary Cornell, Jonathan Gennick, Jonathan Hassell, Michelle Lowman, Matthew Moodie, Duncan Parkes, Jeffrey Pepper, Frank Pohlmann, Douglas Pundick, Ben Renow-Clarke, Dominic Shakeshaft, Matt Wade, Tom Welsh
Coordinating Editor: Jennifer L. Blackwell
Copy Editor: Mary Ann Fugate
Compositor: MacPS, LLC
Indexer: Brenda Miller
Artist: April Milne
Cover Designer: Anna Ishchenko

Distributed to the book trade worldwide by Springer Science+Business Media, LLC., 233 Spring Street, 6th Floor, New York, NY 10013. Phone 1-800-SPRINGER, fax (201) 348-4505, e-mail orders-ny@springer-sbm.com, or visit www.springeronline.com.

For information on translations, please e-mail rights@apress.com, or visit www.apress.com.

Apress and friends of ED books may be purchased in bulk for academic, corporate, or promotional use. eBook versions and licenses are also available for most titles. For more information, reference our Special Bulk Sales–eBook Licensing web page at www.apress.com/info/bulksales.

The source code for this book is available to readers at www.apress.com.

To Erica, my beautiful wife, for her love and support.
Thank you for always being there for me.

—Henry Lee

To Marianna—my friend, my wife, my muse—and to
my parents for their gift of unconditional love.

—Eugene Chuvyrov

Contents at a Glance

Contents

About the Authors

 **Henry Lee** is the founder of NewAgeSolution.net and is passionate about technology. He works with various Fortune 500 companies, delivering mobile applications and rich Internet applications. He recently formed a startup company called ToeTapz.com, focusing his energy on delivering mobile applications in Windows Phone 7, Android, and iPhone. In his spare time, he dedicates his effort to help his .NET community by delivering sessions at technology events. He enjoys talking with other technologists about current trends in technology and sharing business insights with fellow colleagues. Often you will find Henry at a local cigar bar, enjoying a cigar and a drink, trying to come up with the next big mobile application.

 **Eugene Chuvyrov** is an independent .NET consultant in beautiful Jacksonville, Florida. He was lucky enough to start working with Microsoft technologies when he graduated from college in 1998, and has been consistently delivering a positive return on investment to the clients that engage him. His most recent venture is an online event marketing startup, packedhouseevents.com, which extends event creation, marketing, and electronic payments to anybody with Internet access. Eugene also facilitates the meetings of the Jacksonville Software Architecture Group, where he enjoys networking and learning from smart people.

As soon as Eugene heard the news that a new mobile platform (Windows Phone 7) was being released by Microsoft, he was immediately intrigued. It was hard to resist the temptation of wide-open possibilities to create smartphone applications using his favorite IDE and all the latest cloud and functional programming–based technologies. This passion, combined with a cigar with Henry at a local cigar bar, resulted in the book you now hold in your hands. He sincerely hopes you find it useful!

About the Technical Reviewer

 **Stefan Turalski** is a nice chap who is capable of performing both magic and trivial things, with a little help from code, libraries, tools, APIs, servers, and the like. Wearing many hats, he has experienced almost all aspects of the software life cycle, and is especially skilled in business analysis, design, implementation, testing, and QA. His main area of interest is quite wide and could be summarized as emerging technologies, with a recent focus on .NET 4, mobile development, functional programming, and software engineering at large.

Before he realized that he enjoys criticizing other people's work more, Stefan published several technical articles, mainly about .NET technology, SOA, and software engineering. For the last ten or so years, he has built solutions ranging from Perl scripts, through embedded systems and web sites, to highly scalable C++/Java/.NET enterprise-class systems. Feel free to contact him at stefan.turalski@gmail.com.

Acknowledgments

We would like to express our love and gratitude to our wives for letting us ignore dog walking, dishwashing, and housecleaning chores to write this book—but most of all for providing love and support during the rough times, which encouraged us to finish this book. We would also like to thank Joe Healy for providing technical support and giving us access to the Windows Phone 7 prototype phone, which helped tremendously in writing this book.

We are also grateful to Apress for giving us the opportunity to write about what we love to do and share it with the world. The staff at Apress made this book possible by spending many days and nights reviewing and editing the book to meet the tight deadline. Ewan Buckingham provided us with this unique opportunity to share our knowledge. Thank you, Ewan, for believing in us. Stefan Turalski has given us consistent in-depth technical guidance and commentary—thank you for ensuring that we use industry best practices at all times. John Osborn made our book understandable not only to the two of us, but to the rest of the world as well. Thank you, John; we are much better writers now because of you! Mary Ann Fugate performed very timely copyedit checks and ensured that all the references and grammar made sense—thank you, Mary Ann.

However, this book would have never come to fruition if it weren't for our coordinating editor, Jennifer Blackwell. Jennifer encouraged us when we needed encouragement, provided guidance when we were lost, and made us see the light at the end of the tunnel at all times. For that, we are extremely grateful!

Introduction

We decided that we should write a book about something we enjoy doing to share with our fellow developers to fulfill their dreams. This is how our journey started. When the startup company NewAgeSolution.net was founded, the company emphasized delivering compelling rich Internet applications using Silverlight. The company enjoyed great success, with eight employees, delivering amazing Silverlight applications that you can read about in a Microsoft case study (www.microsoft.com/casestudies/Case_Study_Detail.aspx?CaseStudyID=4000006798).

Then Microsoft invited many of the Silverlight partners to join the Windows Phone Partner program, and after attending the Windows Phone partner conference in Redmond at the Microsoft campus, we truly believed that the age of the smartphone had begun. It was a natural progression for us to tackle Windows Phone, since Silverlight is one of the primary development platforms, and we were able to utilize all the knowledge that we had gained over the years.

Windows Phone is our passion and our daily life, The Windows Phone market is big, and we want to share our dream with you by showing you how to successfully develop a Windows Phone application so you can also deploy your dream to the Marketplace.

Who This Book Is For

This book assumes that you have basic C# and .NET knowledge. This book will provide you with basic fundamentals and skills that you will need to be successful in developing a Windows Phone application. You do not need previous experience in developing a mobile application—the only thing you need is a desire to learn new technology.

What You Need to Use This Book

In order to write Windows Phone applications and to test out the examples in this book, you'll need to download the tools listed here. All of these are available at no charge from Microsoft. You'll find additional information on how to install and use these tools in Part 1 of this book.

- **Windows Phone Developer Tools RTW** (http://download.microsoft.com/download/1/7/7/177D6AF8-17FA-40E7-AB53-00B7CED31729/vm_web.exe)

- **Zune Software** (www.zune.net/en-us/products/software/download/)

- **Windows Phone 7 UI Design and Interface Guide** (http://go.microsoft.com/fwlink/?LinkID=183218)

- **Windows Phone 7 Marketplace Certification Requirements** (http://go.microsoft.com/?linkid=9730558)

- **Microsoft SQL 2008 R2 Express** (www.microsoft.com/express/Database/)

- **Azure Tools for Visual Studio 1.2 June 2010**
  (`http://download.microsoft.com/DOWNLOAD/1/F/9/1F96D60F-EBE9-44CB-BD58-88C2EC14929E/VSCLOUDSERVICE.EXE`)

- **Azure SDK June 2010**
  (`www.microsoft.com/downloads/en/details.aspx?FamilyID=21910585-8693-4185-826e-e658535940aa&displaylang=en`)

- **Windows Azure Platform Training Kit September—for the latest update, please check at** `www.microsoft.com/windowsazure/windowsazure`.
  (`www.microsoft.com/downloads/en/details.aspx?FamilyID=413E88F8-5966-4A83-B309-53B7B77EDF78&displaylang=en`)

How This Book Is Organized

The book contains nineteen chapters broken into two major parts. In Part 1, we will walk you through the development life cycle of the application. You will go from coding the simplest possible "Hello World"–style Windows Phone 7 application to building a full-blown, modern n-tier application that uses both the Windows Phone development platform and the unique cloud services that support it. The section concludes with step-by-step instruction on how to gain certification from Microsoft and offer an application to the public through the Windows Phone Marketplace.

In Part 2, you will learn how to use specific features of Windows Phone devices in your applications, including the accelerometer, location service, application bar, reactive extensions, application hub integration, application life cycle events, isolated storage, Silverlight, XAML, skinning controls, web browser controls, media elements, photos, push notifications, internalization, and security. While each of its chapters is a tutorial, you can also use Part 2 as a reference. Each chapter will focus on a single phone feature and provide step-by-step instructions on how to incorporate it into your application.

Where to Find Sources for the Examples

The source code of all of the examples is available at `www.apress.com/book/view/1430232161`.

Send Us Your Comments

We value your input. We'd like to know what you like about the book and what you don't like about it. You can send us comments via e-mail to `feedback@apress.com`. When providing feedback, please make sure you include the title of the book in your note to us.

We've tried to make this book as error-free as possible. However, mistakes happen. If you find any type of error in this book, whether it is a typo or an erroneous command, please let us know about it. Please e-mail the problem to `support@apress.com`. Your information will be validated and posted on the errata page to be used in subsequent editions of the book. The corrigenda can be viewed on the book's web page at `http://www.apress.com`.

Contacting the Authors

You can contact us directly at the following e-mail addresses:

Henry Lee: `Henry.Lee@NewAgeSolution.net`

Eugene Chuvyrov: `echuvyrov@msn.com`

The Essentials of Windows Phone 7 Application Development

In Part 1, you will be introduced to the full development life cycle of a Windows Phone 7 application: installing and understanding the tools and SDKs; deploying database and service layers to the Azure cloud; creating a connected Windows Phone application; debugging and catching errors; and finally deploying your application to the Marketplace. These skills are essential for developing a successful application. In Part 1, the focus is on building the application, getting familiar with development tools like Visual Studio for Windows Phone and Microsoft Expression Blend for Windows Phone, and learning to interact with the Windows Phone developer portal, rather than special phone features such as the GPS radio or accelerometer. We'll turn to those in Part 2.

CHAPTER 1

■ ■ ■

Introducing Windows Phone 7 and the Windows Phone Platform

This is an exciting time for developers, as the smartphone race has begun between the major players, like Microsoft's Windows Phone, Apple's iPhone, and Google's Android. As a developer, you are faced with this amazing opportunity to develop a mobile application that can be sold to millions of consumers worldwide using any of the platforms (Windows Phone, iPhone, and Android). By 2014 the Gartner report predicts that the smartphone market will boom and there will be billions of dollars at stake. This could well be the next big "dot com boom" that everyone's been waiting for.

The Marketplace for Windows Phone, where consumers can purchase applications, is virtually untapped as the market will open to the public on November of 2010, and you will have a chance to publish an application that is first to the market. You might consider downloading Zune software from `www.zune.net/en-US/products/software/download/downloadsoftware.htm` to view the current Marketplace. Once you have downloaded the Zune software and fired it up, click marketplace ➤ APPS links, and you will be able to see all the Windows Phone applications currently published, as shown in Figure 1–1. You will learn more about the Marketplace in Chapter 5.

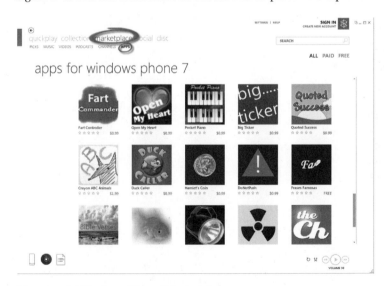

Figure 1–1. Windows Phone Marketplace

There are hundreds of ideas for applications still waiting to be discovered and developed by you. Take a look at QuotedSuccess, DuckCaller, and a MobileBaseball game developed and published to the market, as shown in Figure 1–2. Which of these will be among the first Windows Phone hits to catch fire with consumers and sell millions of units?

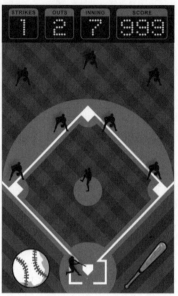

Figure 1–2. Windows Phone applications

What application will you be developing? We've written this book to help and guide you through the steps it takes to write and launch a successful application to the Marketplace. So what are we waiting for? Let's get started by diving into what Windows Phone has to offer to developers like you.

Windows Phone Overview

Microsoft Windows Phone is a great consumer phone because it has all of the features to which users have become accustomed with the Apple iPhone and Android-powered smartphones, like the Motorola Droid and HTC Incredible. These features include multitouch, a beautiful user interface (UI) that implements a new modern design Microsoft has named Metro, social networking services like Facebook, and support for popular e-mail accounts such as Yahoo, Hotmail, Google, and AOL, or, if you are a corporate user, Microsoft Exchange. Uniquely, the phone ships with a version of Microsoft Office that you can use to read, edit, save, and synch any Word files, Excel spreadsheets, and other Office formats, making it a great phone for those who use Office at home or in the office. Windows Phone can also integrate with Xbox LIVE, making it a great choice for gamers.

Microsoft Windows Phone uses the Zune software to sync installed applications, pictures, music, and back up and flash operating system updates. As a developer, you'll also use Zune in conjunction with Visual Studio to debug your applications on a real device, as you'll learn in Chapter 4.

Microsoft also introduces the concept of a **hub** with the Windows Phone: a People hub where users can store all of their contacts and social networking connections, a Music hub where consumers can listen to, download, and purchase music, and an App hub, also known as the Marketplace, which you will be most interested in, since you will be publishing the application you create.

Having a phone that's a hit with consumers is important because the consumer marketplace is where the greatest opportunities for applications that you write are to be found. One of the great things about Windows Phone is that Microsoft imposes the hardware specifications on the phone manufacturer, making it easy for you to develop an application without worrying about writing special codes for the specific devices. For any future release of the phone, you are guaranteed that the application you write today will work regardless of the brand of the phone.

Naturally, you want to know what language you'll need to master for your work. For Windows Phone, the language of choice today is C#; Visual Basic (VB) programmers will have to wait. Although Microsoft has said it will support that popular language on the phone, the company had not yet announced a timeline when this book was written. As for an application development framework, you have two choices: Silverlight or XNA. Silverlight and XNA both use core .NET Framework. You will learn more about the two frameworks later in this chapter, but first let's take a closer look at the hardware features you can expect on a Windows Phone.

Windows Phone Hardware Specifications

Knowing what's included in the Microsoft Windows Phone hardware specifications will help you prepare for the special needs of projects you'd like to attempt. Table 1–1 lists the minimum hardware requirements any Windows Phone manufacturer must meet, and also includes suggestions as to how they can impact developers like you.

Table 1–1. Windows Phone Minimum Hardware Requirements

Hardware Feature	Description
Must display at WVGA (800 x 480)	Having to worry about only one single screen resolution makes it easy to develop an application.
4-point-multi-touch capable	This is unique to the Windows Phone, and you can use this feature to create four-player games. There is definitely room for innovation for using this particular feature.
DirectX 9 hardware acceleration	This means the phone will have a graphical processing unit allowing graphically intense tasks in the application to be offloaded to the graphics chips of the phone. This will help you create very smooth and responsive applications and games. This also means 3D games are possible as well.
GPS	You will be able to create location-aware applications. See Chapter 14 to learn about location services and learn to use Bing Maps and plot GPS data on the map.
Accelerometer	This feature will measure the change of the acceleration in the phone. The accelerometer can be used in games or in creating utility applications, like a level. See Chapter 6 to learn more about this feature.
Compass	Detect north, south, east, and west.
Light	Can be used for flashlight for the camera.
Digital Camera	For taking a picture and sharing it on Facebook and other social networking sites. Learn more about this feature in Chapter 16.
Hardware controls: back, start, and search buttons	Every phone will have three buttons on the front of the phone. Keep in mind that you will be required to use back buttons for going backward in your application, otherwise having separate back buttons in the application can confuse the user. Learn more about integration with the hardware buttons to the application lifecycle in Chapter 10.
Support data connections: cellular network and Wi-Fi	This feature allows you to connect to the Internet. You can create web services and consume them from your applications, or you can consume third-party APIs like Twitter or Facebook in your application.
256 MB of RAM and 8GM flash storage	Keep in mind that your application can use only 90MB of memory unless the device has more memory than 256. If your application does not respect this, the application will fail the certification process at the Marketplace. See Chapter 5 for more details.
	Also 8GB of flash memory used for storage is shared among other applications, so if you are saving any kind of static data into the Isolated Storage, you must check for the space available and handle the exception appropriately. See more details on this in Chapter 13.

At the time this book was written in United States, AT&T had announced it would carry Samsung's Focus, LG's Quantum, and HTC's SurroundTM. And T-Mobile had announced it would carry HTC's HD7. For those who have other cell phone providers, Dell said it planned to ship its Venue Pro. You can find more information on the release of these phones at `www.microsoft.com/windowsphone/en-us/buy/7/phones.aspx`.

In the next section, you will learn how the software behind these great consumer phones also provides a great development platform for developers.

Windows Phone Application Platform

Microsoft did not invent any new languages or frameworks for the Windows Phone application platform. The company simply adapted its existing frameworks. This means that you will be able to program using C# (VB is not supported at the time this book was written) with .NET Framework. What .NET provides is a common base class library that every Microsoft .NET programmer will be familiar with, including support for multithreading, XML, Linq, collections, events, data, exceptions, IO, service model, networking, text, location, reflection, globalization, resources, runtime, security, and diagnostics. On top of core .NET Framework, the Windows Phone application platform consists of two major frameworks: Silverlight and XNA. You'll use Silverlight primarily for business applications and simple 2D games. Silverlight uses the Extensible Application Markup Language (XAML) that is declarative markup language for creating compelling UI. The designers will have tremendous flexibility in creating UI for Windows Phone using familiar tools like Adobe Illustrator, Photoshop, and Microsoft Expression Design to create vector-based UI that can be easily exported to XAML. XNA is primarily used for creating games, and the framework comes with a game engine that allows you to create loop-based games and also provides a 3D engine, allowing you to create 3D games.

In the following sections, you will learn more in detail about the main components of the Windows Phone application platform: Silverlight, XNA, tools, and cloud services.

Silverlight for Windows Phone

The interesting thing about Silverlight is that Silverlight is used in the web technology that is browser plug-in that enables rich Internet application content just like Flash technology. Silverlight provides you with a sandboxed experience, and the limitation of Silverlight with respect to the underlying operating system is clearly borderline. Within a Silverlight application, you cannot access any native operating systems unless through provided APIs, if any. This architecture of Silverlight makes it very compelling security-wise to be used in Windows Phone, because Windows Phone provides the same restriction of only providing APIs to developers and limiting access to the native operating system.

Also Silverlight uses XAML, which can be used to declare vector-based graphics and create animations. Any designer familiar with vector-based applications, like Adobe Illustrator and Microsoft Expression Design, can easily create highly visual elements in vector and can be exported out to XAML. This means the designers have full control over the layout, look and feel, and graphical assets, making Silverlight an extremely powerful choice for creating consumer-oriented applications. Also XAML provides a powerful data binding feature to the controls making it ideal for creating business oriented applications.

XNA for Windows Phone

Like Silverlight, XNA is not a new technology. XNA is used in creating Xbox games, using managed code. It is a natural choice for creating games since Windows Phone has Xbox LIVE integration, allowing XNA-based Xbox games to be easily posted over to Windows Phone. The only thing Xbox game developers have to worry about is screen resolution, which can easily be adjusted and fixed.

XNA provides a rich framework perfect for game developments, like a game loop engine, 2D and 3D engines, and the ability to manage game assets like models, meshes, sprites, textures, effects, terrains, and animations.

Tools

You can download the tools you need for developing Windows Phone applications from `http://create.msdn.com/en-us/home/getting_started`. Also on this Getting Started page, you will find rich documentation and tutorials. Also consider downloading the UI Design and Interaction Guide to understand the Metro design guidelines that Microsoft encourages you to use in developing applications.

Visual Studio

If you do not have a paid version of Visual Studio 2010 on your development machine, then the development tool that you have downloaded from Microsoft will install a free version of Visual Studio 2010 Express for Windows Phone as show in Figure 1–3. Visual Studio is absolutely necessary because it can be used to design, debug, create projects, package and automatically generate package manifests. It also includes a phone emulator on which to test the results of your work. In Chapter 5, you will learn to debug and run the emulator from Visual Studio, and in Chapter 5 you will use Visual Studio to create a package for publication to the App Hub.

Figure 1–3. Microsoft Visual Studio 2010 Express for Windows Phone

Expression Blend

You will need Expression Blend if you want to develop compelling applications using Silverlight for Windows Phone as show in Figure 1–4. Typically Expression Blend is used by designers, and many of the Expression Blend functionalities are similar to Adobe Illustrator, Photoshop, or Expression Design. Also from Expression Blend you can import any Illustrator, and Photoshop files, and if you are using Expression Design, you can export Expression Design file directly to an XAML file.

Expression Blend also provides a way to create animation sequences. Although you can achieve in creating animation in Visual Studio using XAML, it would be very difficult to write complex XAML code to represent complex graphics or animation sequences. It is best to leave complex graphics and animations to Expression Blend.

Figure 1–4. Microsoft Expresion Blend 4 for Windows Phone

Windows Phone Emulator

The Windows Phone emulator as seen in Figure 1–5 is integrated to Visual Studio that simulates a real device. However, there are things you cannot do in the emulator, like test the accelerometer, GPS, compass, FM radio, SMS, e-mail, phone calling, contact list, camera, and other features that require a physical device.

There is, however, a technique called Reactive Extensions, covered in Chapter 18, which you'll be able to use to simulate the data feed you can expect on a real phone. For example, you'll learn how, using Reactive Extensions, you can simulate the accelerometer and GPS readings so that you can work with the emulator without the need of the device.

Figure 1–5. Windows Phone emulator

Documentation and Support

There are many ways you could get help while you are developing your application if you get stuck on a problem. You can visit http://create.msdn.com/en-us/home/getting_started, and you will find the Windows Phone 7 Training Kit that might contain how-tos on specific technology you are having problems with. You can go to http://forums.silverlight.net/forums/63.aspx, where you can ask about Silverlight for Windows Phone–related questions, or if you have other related Windows Phone questions, you can visit http://social.msdn.microsoft.com/Forums/en-US/windowsphone7series. Also the Windows Phone development team puts out many useful blogs that you can follow at http://windowsteamblog.com/windows_phone/b/wpdev/. Of course, you also have Windows Phone documentation, found at MSDN http://msdn.microsoft.com/en-us/library/ff402535(VS.92).aspx.

Cloud Services

Working with a Windows Phone application that requires saving the data to a database is a tricky thing. The first big problem is that you do not know how popular your application will be, and if it becomes popular, you might suddenly find millions of users using your application and saving the data to its database at a rate that would require an enterprise-level solution. Not just database you would need to worry you also need to consider the web service that can provide APIs to your application to save to the database since Windows Phone applications cannot directly connect to the database.

This is where the Microsoft Azure cloud comes into your solution. Microsoft Azure provides Windows Azure service for deploying services (WCF, Windows service) and SQL Azure for the database that allows you to scale infinitely as your demand grows larger. You will learn more about the Microsoft Azure cloud in Chapter 3.

There are also Bing Maps services that you can use freely. Bing Maps is free only if you are developing a Windows Phone application. Along with Bing Maps services, Microsoft provides Bing Maps controls in Silverlight that you can use in Windows Phone. You will learn about Bing Maps and location services in Chapter 14.

Push notification services are hosted in the cloud as well, which allows you to push messages to the phone, which is a very powerful messaging mechanism. You can learn more about this in Chapter 17. Xbox LIVE services also reside in the cloud, which you can take advantage of in your application. This topic will not be covered in this book, however.

You learned a bit about Windows Phone and the Windows Phone platform in the foregoing sections. In the following sections, you will learn about the beginning to the end of Windows Phone application development.

Metro Design

Microsoft is targeting Windows Phone 7 toward busy professionals, and to provide compelling UI, Microsoft came up with Metro design. Metro design derives from the transportation industry typography and visual designs where busy professionals constantly scan and go, and because of this, Metro design puts heavy emphasis on simple and clean designs.

Metro design follow five principles. First principle emphasize on clean, light, open, fast to eliminate clutter, and typography, as consumers will be using the phone to read e-mail, SMS, Facebook, and Twitter while on the go. The second principle of Metro design puts the focus on content, where the design premise must gear toward presenting the content. The third principle focuses on seamless integration of hardware and software. The fourth principle puts an emphasis on gestures, where the design enables a world-class multitouch user experience. Lastly, the Metro design concept focuses on an application that is soulful and alive, where information that matters most to the user is presented in such a way that it is easily accessible at the click of the touch. You can find out more about Metro design by downloading the document provided by Microsoft at
http://go.microsoft.com/fwlink/?LinkID=183218.

Application Development Life Cycle

Understanding the application life cycle will help you understand what you will need to prepare much more in-depth discussion including certification process is covered in Chapter 5. Figure 1–6 illustrates a high-level view of the life cycle of an application.

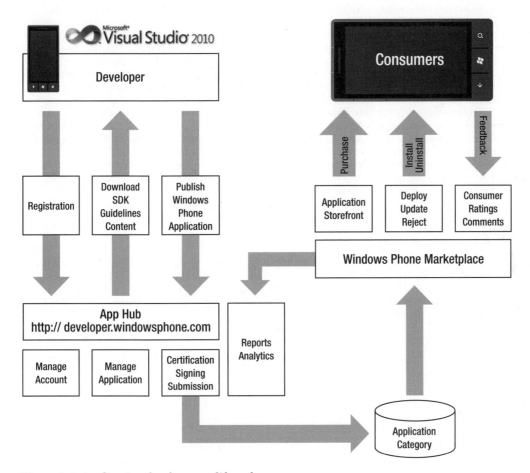

Figure 1–6. Application development life cycle

As a developer, you will start out at the App Hub registering with your Windows Live ID (create it if you do not have one). Once signed up at the App Hub, you can register your physical device so you can debug in the real device. Remember that you can add up to three devices. Using Visual Studio and/or Expression Blend, you will be creating your application and debugging using the emulator or the device you registered. Once the application is created, you need to submit the application to the certification process.

In order to ensure that your application will pass the Marketplace certification process, it would be a good idea for you to read and understand the application certification document found at http://go.microsoft.com/?linkid=9730558. As part of the certification process, your application will go through a series of validations against the application and content policies, packaging, code, phone feature disclosure, language, and images requirements. Your application will also get tested on reliability, performance, resource management, phone functionality uses, and security. The certification process is in place to help promote quality applications to consumers, to protect consumers from malwares, and protect Microsoft services. You will learn much more in detail about Marketplace certification in Chapter 5.

Once the application passes the certification process, it will be deployed to the Marketplace and downloaded and used by the consumer. The consumer will use your application and provide ratings and comments, and reports can be generated by you from the App Hub to show how your application is performing in the Marketplace. Based on the feedback you receive, you can choose to deploy an updated version that contains bug fixes and new features to users. Your ultimate goal is to create a compelling application that you know consumers will use and publish to the Marketplace. The Marketplace will cost $99 annually, which will give you access to the Windows Phone Marketplace and the Xbox 360 Marketplace. In the Windows Phone Marketplace, you can submit an unlimited number of paid applications and you can submit five free applications. Additional submissions will cost $19.99. In the Xbox 360 Marketplace, you can submit up to ten games.

You will be able to observe any Marketplace activities through the report provided, like comments, ratings, and how many sold, so that you can effectively improve sales and marketing efforts.

When your application is bought by consumers, Microsoft will take 30% and you get to keep 70%. Also you get your money deposited directly to your bank, and your account will be activated to receive money only when you make your first sale of $200.

Summary

You have embarked on the journey of developing an application for the Windows Phone Marketplace, which is untapped and ready to be explored by developers like yourself. You can be part of a billion-dollar global market, where you have a chance to develop an application that can be sold to millions.

In this chapter, you learned about the general overview of Windows Phone features, hardware specifications, the development platform, and the Marketplace. In later chapters, you will learn in greater detail about the features and the platform mentioned in this chapter. In Chapter 2, you will learn to build your first Windows Phone application by using tools like Visual Studio, Expression Blend, and the Windows Phone controls.

CHAPTER 2

■■■

Building Windows Phone 7 Applications

This chapter will prepare you with everything you will need to get started with Windows Phone 7 development. You will learn about the Windows Phone emulator, Visual Studio 2010, and Microsoft Expression Blend 4. You will also learn to use these tools to create your first Windows Phone application.

Before you can write your first application, you first need to download and install the tools. In the next section, we'll show you how.

Preparing Your Development Machine

At the time of writing this book, Windows Phone 7 developer tool beta version 1.0 was used. The latest Windows Phone developer tool can be downloaded from `http://developer.windowsphone.com/windows-phone-7/`. The Windows Phone developer beta tools (`vm_web.exe`) will install the following:

- *Any commercial version of Visual Studio 2010 or free version of Visual Studio 2010 Express for Windows Phone*: Programmer's development IDE.

- *Windows Phone emulator*: Used to run and test the Windows Phone application.

- *Silverlight for Windows Phone*: Silverlight Framework for Windows Phone based on Silverlight 3 technology. See Chapter 1 for the subtle difference between Silverlight 3 and Windows Phone Silverlight framework.

- *Microsoft Expression Blend for Windows Phone*: Can be used to design user interfaces.

- *XNA Game Studio 4*: Tools for developing games.

Once you have installed Windows Phone developer beta tools, you can start to build your first Windows Phone application in the next section.

Building Your First Windows Phone 7 Application

In this section, you'll build a simple "HelloWorld" application using Silverlight framework. Creating the application will provide you with an opportunity to use Visual Studio 2010 Express for Windows Phone, the Windows Phone 7 Emulator, and some Windows Phone Silverlight controls. Also later in this chapter, you will learn to use Blend to design Silverlight controls. The final application is displayed in

Figure 2–19 at the end of this chapter. A click of its OK button will display the words "Hello World" in a text box. But before you can get started, you must first create a Visual Studio 2010 project.

Creating a Windows Phone Project

To get started, you first fire up Visual Studio Express 2010 and create a project.

1. To launch Visual Studio 2010 Express, select Windows Start ➤ All Programs ➤Microsoft Visual Studio 2010 Express ➤ Microsoft Visual Studio 2010 Express for Windows Phone.

2. Create a new project by selecting File ➤ New ➤ Project on the Visual Studio menu, as shown in Figure 2–1.

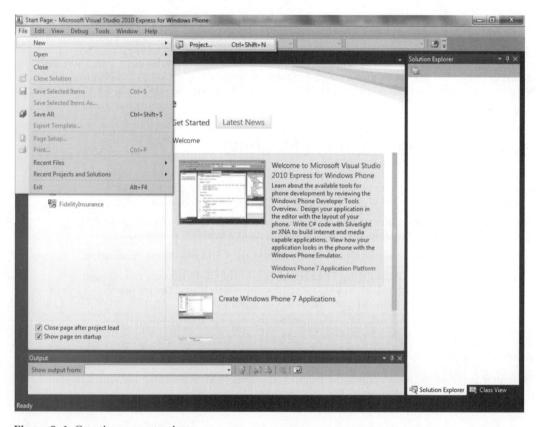

Figure 2–1. *Creating a new project*

3. From among the three C# templates that Visual Studio displays on its New Project dialog page, select the Windows Phone Application Visual C# template, as shown in Figure 2–2.

■ **Note** There are three different Windows Phone Visual Studio project templates. The Windows Phone Application template is a template for one-page applications. The Windows Phone List Application template uses ListBox control and page navigation framework to create applications with multiple pages. The Windows Phone Class Library template can be used to create a class library that can be referenced by other Windows Phone projects.

4. For the purposes of this exercise, change the Name of the new project to "HelloWorld," by changing the text in the Name box, as shown in Figure 2–2. Also you can change the location where the project will be saved by changing the path in the Location box.

Figure 2–2. Creating a new Silverlight Windows Phone application

5. Finally, select OK on the New Project dialog, and Visual Studio 2010 will build your project, whose elements are displayed in Figure 2–3.

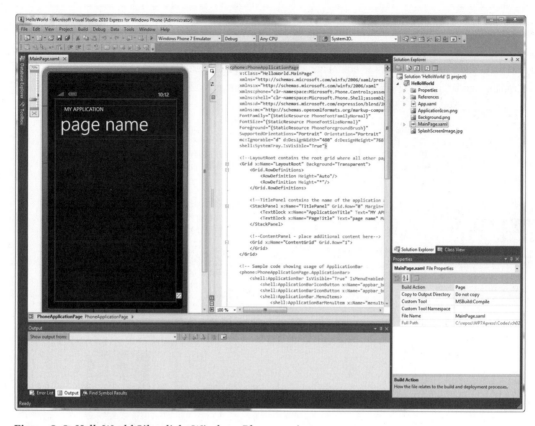

Figure 2–3. *HelloWorld Silverlight Windows Phone project*

By default two TextBlock controls will be placed in Windows Phone, and you can see this in design view on the far left in Figure 2–3.

With a phone project ready to roll, it's time to bring the application to life by adding some functionality and creating a user interface. We'll start with the interface, adding some controls to its blank design surface for users to press and in which the application can display text.

Using Your First Windows Phone Silverlight Controls

The next step is to add Silverlight controls to the HelloWorld Windows Phone application we created in the previous steps. You will learn to set the properties of the controls so that the controls can size and position automatically in both Portrait and Landscape mode of Windows Phone.

1.   In the Windows Phone Design view window, click MY APPLICATION TextBlock.
     In the Properties windows at the lower right corner of the Visual Studio IDE,
     change the Text property from "MY APPLICATION" to "HelloWorld App."
     Notice that the new text now appears on the Design surface, as shown in Figure
     2–4.

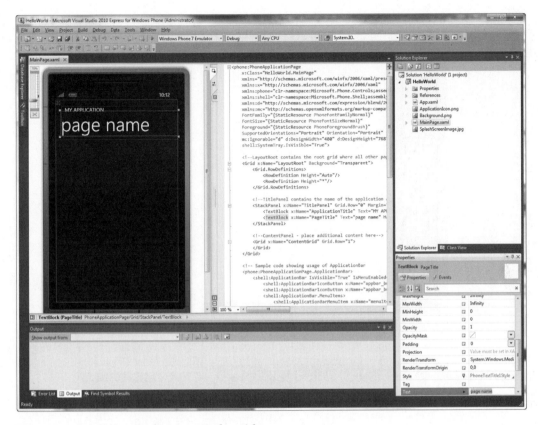

Figure 2–4. *Renaming application window title*

2. Now open the Visual Studio Toolbox, which we'll use to find some controls for the HelloWorld user interface. If you can't find the Toolbox, select View Toolbox on the Visual Studio menu. The result of either step, when successful, is to display a list of controls in a vertical panel on the left side of the Visual Studio IDE, as shown in Figure 2–5.

Figure 2–5. *Visual Studio Toolbox containing Windows Phone controls*

The Visual Studio Toolbox contains Windows Phone controls that ship with the Windows Phone developer tools. You'll be using them throughout the book to build increasingly sophisticated user interfaces. You can add any of these to your user interface by dragging one to the Windows Phone Design surface in Visual Studio.

3. To create the interface for the HelloWorld application, let's first add a TextBox to display some text. To do so, drag a TextBox control from the Toolbox to the designer surface directly below the page title TextBlock. When the TextBox control is successfully placed on the phone's designer surface, the TextBox control will be automatically selected. In the Properties window (if you cannot find the Properties Window go to View ➤ Properties Window), change the following TextBox properties.

   a. Set Width and Height to Auto.

   b. Set HorizontalAlignment to Stretch.

   c. Set VerticalAlignment to Top.

   d. Resize the TextBox width so that there is enough room to its right for an OK button.

   e. Set Name to txtMessage.

20

When you properly follow steps a, b, c, and d, you should see the following XAML in the XAML editor area.

```
<TextBox Height="Auto" Margin="0,55,166,0" Name="txtMessage" Text="TextBlock"
VerticalAlignment="Top" HorizontalAlignment="Right" Width="290" />
```

You set Horizontal Alignment to Stretch in step b because you want the TextBox to automatically stretch to fill the extra space created when you rotate the phone emulator to landscape orientation. Width and Height are set to Auto because we want the TextBox to automatically change its size when Font size increases or decreases. Setting Vertical Alignment to Top will always position the textbox aligned to the top. You will be able to access the textblock control in code by referring to its Name, "txtMessage".

4. Now, let's add the application's OK button to the user interface. To do so, drag and drop a Button control from the Toolbox and drop it to the right of the TextBox. Change the button properties in Properties Window.

   a. Set Button Content to OK.

   b. Set HorizontalAlignment to Right.

   c. Set VerticalAlignment to Top.

   d. Set Name to btnOk.

When steps a, b, and c are properly followed, you should see the following XAML in the XAML editor area. Setting the button's horizontal alignment to Right will always align button position to the right side.

```
<Button Content="OK" Height="72" HorizontalAlignment="Right" Margin="308,31,0,0"
Name="btnOk" VerticalAlignment="Top" Width="160" />
```

5. Your layout should be done. In XAML view, look for the grid containing the controls you just added. It should look similar to this:

```
<Grid x:Name="ContentGrid" Grid.Row="1">
    <TextBox Height="Auto" Margin="0,55,166,0" Name="txtMessage" Text="TextBlock"
VerticalAlignment="Top" HorizontalAlignment="Right" Width="290" />
    <Button Content="OK" Height="72" HorizontalAlignment="Right" Margin="308,31,0,0"
Name="btnOk" VerticalAlignment="Top" Width="160" />
</Grid>
```

6. Figure 2–6 shows the final layout after adding TextBox and Button controls.

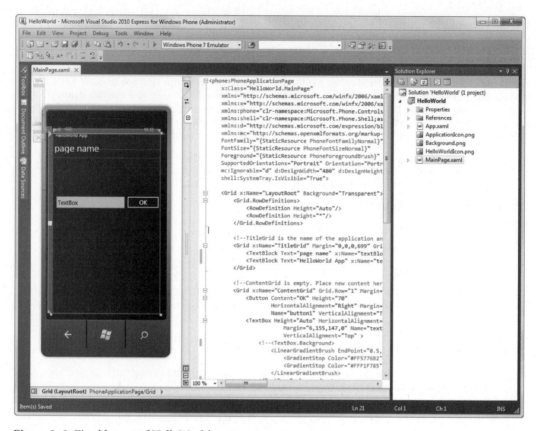

Figure 2–6. Final layout of HelloWorld app

Writing Your First Windows Phone Code

In this section, we will be writing C# code that will handle the button click event that will populate the TextBlock named "textBlock1" with "hello World!"

1.   To add behavior to the OK button, double-click the OK button on the Design surface of your project. Visual Studio will display MainPage.xaml.cs where you can see the btnOk_Click method is automatically added. You will add proper code in the next step to handle the button click event.

```
using System.Windows;
using Microsoft.Phone.Controls;

namespace HelloWorld
{
    public partial class MainPage : PhoneApplicationPage
    {
        public MainPage()
```

```
        {
            InitializeComponent();
            // Setting SupportOrientations will control the behavior
            // of the page responding properly to the rotation of the
            // phone. So if you rotate the phone to the landscape
            // your page will change to landscape view.
            SupportedOrientations = SupportedPageOrientation.PortraitOrLandscape
;
        }

        private void btnOk_Click(object sender, RoutedEventArgs e)
        {

        }
    }
}
```

2. In `MainPage.xaml` you will notice that the button `Click` event handler is automatically added to OK button.

```
<Button Content="OK" Height="70"
        HorizontalAlignment="Right" Margin="0,155,-4,0"
        Name="button1" VerticalAlignment="Top" Width="160" Click="button1_Click" />
```

3. In `MainPage.xaml.cs` replace the button1_click method with the following code.

```
private void button1_Click(object sender, RoutedEventArgs e)
{
    txtMessage.Text = "Hello World!";
}
```

Running Your First Silverlight Windows Phone Application

Your Hello World application is complete. Now it's time to build the application and run it in the Windows Phone 7 emulator.

1. To build the solution, select Build ➤ Build Solution on the Visual Studio menu.

2. To run the application, select Debug ➤ Start Debugging.

3. When the emulator appears, click OK and you will see "Hello World!" as shown in Figure 2–7.

Figure 2–7. Hello World in Windows Phone 7 Emulator

    4.   Click the rotate control on the Windows Phone 7 emulator, as shown in Figure 2–8.

Figure 2–8. Clicking Windows Phone 7 Emulator rotate control

Notice in the landscape view that the TextBox is automatically resized, stretched out to make full use of the landscape orientation of the device, as shown in Figure 2–9.

Figure 2–9. Hello World landscape view

5.   Stop the application debugging by selecting Debug ➤ Stop Debugging.

■ **Tip** The Windows Phone 7 emulator can take a long time to start, so you want to avoid closing it down whenever possible. If you need to stop an application in the middle of a debugging run, it's better to use the Visual Studio Debug ➤ Stop Debugging command instead of completely closing down the Windows Phone 7 emulator. Using this technique, the next time the application debugging starts, the project will be loaded into the emulator without first waiting for the emulator to be started.

Customizing Your First Windows Phone Application

In the following code walkthrough, you'll learn how to customize the Windows Phone 7 application icon that is displayed to the user, and how to change the application's name.

1.   In the Solution Explorer, right-click the HelloWorld project and select Add ➤ Existing Item…, as shown in Figure 2–10.

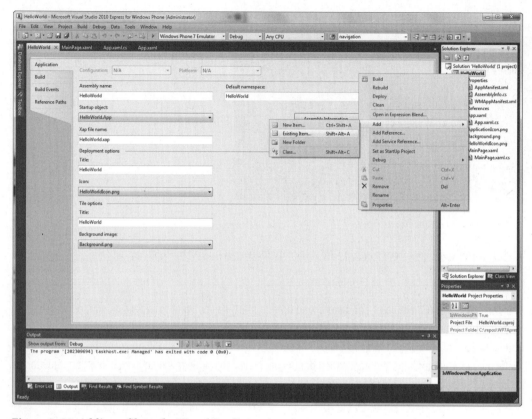

Figure 2–10. Adding a file to the Visual Studio project

2. Go to where you unzipped the sample codes and choose
    \Codes\Ch01\Assets\HelloWorldIcon.png. The Windows Phone 7 application
    icon can be any .png file with 62 x 62. By default, when the Windows Phone
    application project is created, the ApplicationIcon.png is used.

3. Right-click the HelloWorld project ➤ Choose Properties.

4. Click the Application tab.

5. In Deployment options ➤ Change the Icon to HelloWorldIcon.png.

6. Change the Title to HelloWorld. Changed properties can be seen in Figure 2–11.

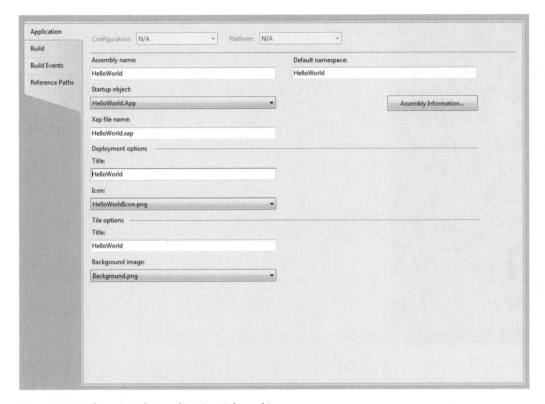

Figure 2–11. Changing the application title and icon

7. Hit F5 to run the application.

8. When the application starts in the Windows Phone 7 emulator, hit the back button on the emulator, as shown in Figure 2–12.

Figure 2–12. Windows Phone 7 back button

9. You will see the list of applications installed on the emulator including HelloWorld, as shown in Figure 2–13.

Figure 2–13. Windows Phone 7 application list

Styling Your Application

Either Visual Studio or Microsoft Expression Blend 4 can be used to design XAML-based Silverlight interfaces. Microsoft Expression Blend 4 provides tools for the graphical manipulations, and animations for creating more complex controls than Visual Studio. You will look at the basics of Blend and how Blend makes it easy to style controls.

1. Open Microsoft Expression Blend 4, and select Windows Start ➤ All Programs ➤ Microsoft Expression Blend ➤ Microsoft Expression Blend 4 for Windows Phone, as shown in Figure 2–14.

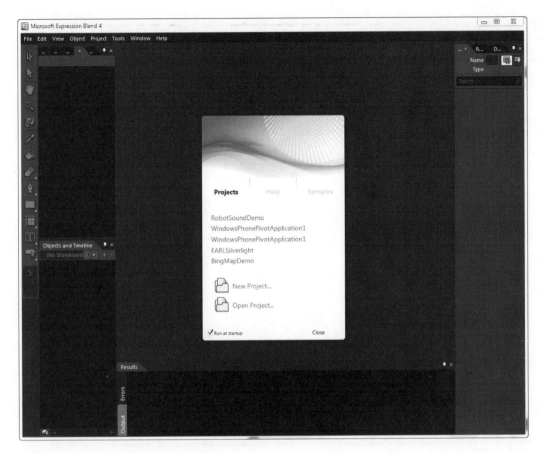

Figure 2–14. Microsoft Expression Blend 4

2. Click "Close" when you are prompted with the project type selector.

3. In Blend 4, go to File ➤ Open Project/Solution. Browse to the HelloWorld solution you created in the previous steps, as shown in Figure 2–15.

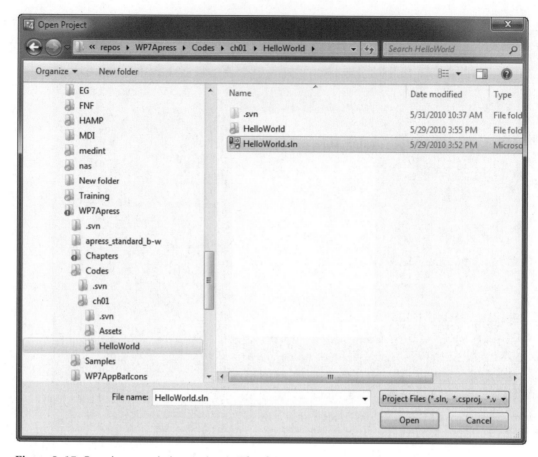

Figure 2–15. Opening an existing project in Blend 4

4. When the project opens, click the TextBox. Notice that in the Properties window you will see various properties that can be changed. If you do not see the Properties window, open it by going to Window ➤ Properties, as shown in Figure 2–16.

Figure 2–16. Properties window in Blend 4 when the control is selected

5. In the Properties window's Brushes category, select Background ➤ choose
    Gradient brush. Notice that the color editor now has ability to set the gradient
    color of the TextBox's background color.

6. Choose the first gradient color of blue at 21% and second color of yellow at 64%,
    as shown in Figure 2–17.

Figure 2–17. Applying gradient background to TextBox in Blend 4

7. Go to Project ➤ Run Project.

8. When Change Device Selection window shows, choose Windows Phone 7 Emulator, as shown in Figure 2–18.

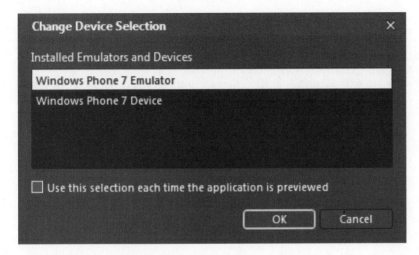

Figure 2–18. Change Device Selection window in Blend 4

9. Click OK and the HelloWorld application will start, as shown in Figure 2–19.

Figure 2–19. HelloWorld after stylized in Blend 4

Summary

In this chapter, you learned how to set up your Windows Phone development environment. You built a simple Windows Phone 7 application using Visual Studio 2010, interacted with the phone emulator, and then used Microsoft Expression Blend to style the application.

In the next chapter, you will learn to build an application that can interact with Microsoft SQL Azure in order to store the data.

CHAPTER 3

■ ■ ■

Using Cloud Services As Data Stores

Today we hear lots of buzz on cloud computing technology, and it is definitely exciting technology that you should tune into, because the cloud truly empowers you as the developer to focus on building an application and off-loading the infrastructure needs to the cloud.

Suppose you have developed an application where businesses can take a picture of invoices and track the money spent like QuickBooks. In Windows Phone, you can easily use the isolated storage covered in Chapter 13. The problem with isolated storage is that the storage space is tied to the phone, and it can differ from manufacturer to manufacturer, and, most importantly, many users will store music, videos, and documents, which can quickly consume the storage space on the phone. A good solution would be to save the invoices information on the database, and to do this, you would need a web service that will interact with the database so that the phone can save the invoices, as shown in Figure 3–1.

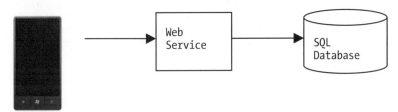

Figure 3–1. *Common 3–tier architecture*

In order to deploy the solution depicted in Figure 3–1, you need to solve a number of problems. First, you need to consider what type and how many servers to buy to host the web service and database. Once you do, you'll have to purchase and maintain them yourself, or pay a hosting service to do the job for you. But this doesn't solve the problem of what you will do to scale up your application if it becomes so popular that millions of consumers want to download and use it, or if you experience periodic surges in use at, say, the end of each month. Finally, how will you provide for disaster recovery and backup of the database to ensure your service does not go down and disappoint users?

To plan ahead for the huge number of users your application might attract, a more robust architecture must be considered. One example is shown in Figure 3–2, where the load balancer can help accommodate massive concurrent calls to the service and take care of the scenario where if any of the service goes down, the load balancer will automatically point the request to available service. On the database side, you have to provide both an active and a passive database in case the main database—the active one—goes down and a switch to the currently passive database becomes necessary. Then you have to worry about disk space, so you will need a storage area network (SAN). Figure 3–2 is your typical Enterprise-grade deployment scenario that will provide reliability, scalability, maintenance, and performance, but it will cost you lots of money and networking complexities.

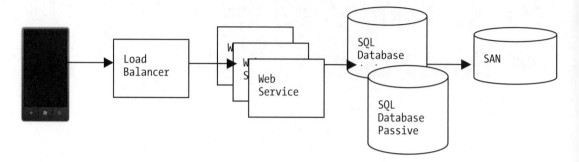

Figure 3–2. Enterprise-level n-tier deployment scenario

Worrying about implementing Figure 3–2 architecture seems to be overkill for the tiny invoice application you might be creating, but you do not want to lose the potential that it might be bought by millions who might love the application. To resolve this dilemma, Microsoft provides Azure service, which takes care of every single detail of the infrastructure architecture that you otherwise have to worry about and simply gives peace of mind to work only on developing the application that can scale to millions of users at a very affordable price. Also Microsoft Azure gives peace of mind with a Service Level Agreement of 99.95 uptime, which is equivalent to 4.38 hours downtime per year or 43.2 minutes of downtime per month.

In the remaining sections of this chapter, you will learn to create a simple note-taking application. The application, which we've named Notepad, will implement the n-tier architecture described in Figure 3–2. With the Notepad application, you will be able to create, read, update, and delete notes. The application will consist of three main components: a Windows Phone client (UI), a web service (middle tier) that provides the APIs the UI will use to access a central database, and finally the database itself, which will store the notes the user writes.

Introducing the MVVM Pattern

In developing the Notepad phone application, you will be using the increasingly popular Model-View-ViewModel (MVVM) pattern. MVVM is a design pattern that provides a clear separation between the UI, the application logic, and the data of an application. The models maintain the data, the views display the data or provide the UI for user interaction, and the view-model acts as the controller or brain that handles the events that affect either the data or the view. See Figure 3–3, which illustrates the elements of the MVVM pattern and their relationships.

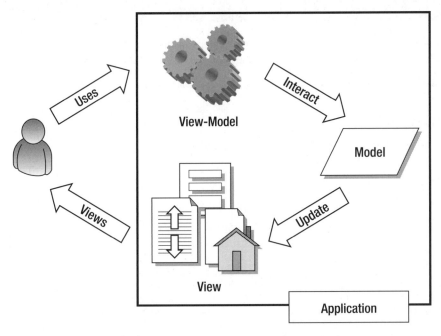

Figure 3–3. *The MVVM pattern*

Introducing Microsoft Azure and SQL Azure

Azure is the name of Microsoft's cloud services, which developers can use to deliver applications at scale for various workloads and devices. Microsoft Azure provides a runtime framework for applications that currently supports .NET 3.5 and .NET 4.0, as well as load balancers, operating systems, servers, storage, and networking, leaving you to worry only about building the application.

Microsoft Azure provides three services: Windows Azure, SQL Azure, and Windows Azure AppFabric. For building a consumer-facing Windows Phone application, you will be more interested in Windows Azure, which can host web and web service applications, and SQL Azure for the database. Windows Azure AppFabric is more of an Enterprise solution that provides Enterprise Service Bus patterns typically popular in the business process application.

In the following section, you will start first by learning to work with SQL Azure in order to save the notes in the database.

Creating a Cloud Database

The first step is to create an SQL Azure database to store the notes a user creates with this application. Think of SQL Azure as a hosted database in the cloud where you do not have to worry about the infrastructure. With your familiar knowledge in working with a Microsoft SQL server, you will be able to work in SQL Azure. NotepadService, which you will be creating in the next section, will connect to this database by using Entity Framework to create, read, update, and delete records from the database.

ENTITY FRAMEWORK

The Entity Framework is an object-relational mapping (ORM) tool that allows you to generate objects based on the tables in a database, taking care of the interaction to the database that otherwise you have to code yourself; the Entity Framework will save you lots time.

Creating an SQL Azure Database

You will be creating a database in SQL Azure in order perform create, read, update, and delete operations for the Notepad application.

Signing Up for SQL Azure

You will learn to create an SQL Azure account in the following steps.

1. Open a browser of your choice.

2. Go to www.microsoft.com/windowsazure/ to sign up and buy the Windows Azure service account. Follow the direction provided by Microsoft in order to purchase and acquire the service account in order to continue with the following steps. You can use Microsoft Azure each month for free (25 hours of computing time, 500 MB storage, 10,000 storage transactions, 1 GB database, and 500 MB data transfer); this promotional offer might end soon, though.

3. Go to http://sql.azure.com/ and sign in using the account you created in Step 1.

4. Once signed in, click the SQL Azure menu tab on the left side. When the Windows Azure page loads, you will see the project that you created during the registration process in Step 1. See Figure 3–4, which corresponds to this step.

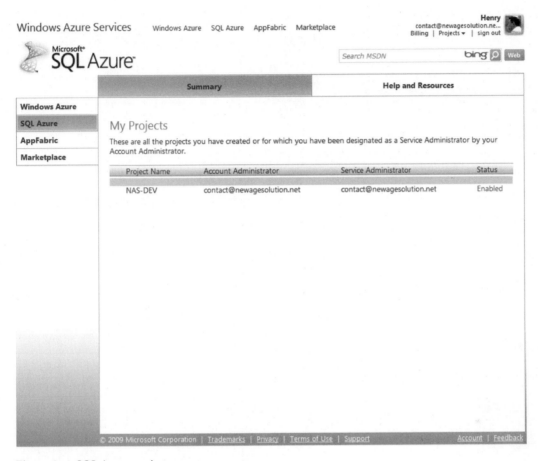

Figure 3–4. SQL Azure main screen

Connecting to the SQL Azure Project

After you register and purchase your Azure service account, you can now log in to an SQL Azure portal.

1. Click the project hyperlink NAS-DEV. In your case, you should click the name of the project that corresponds to the one you created in the "Signing up for SQL Azure" section.

2. Click the I Accept button on the Terms of Use page, as shown in Figure 3–5.

Figure 3–5. SQL Azure Terms of Use screen

Creating an SQL Azure Database

Here you will be creating an SQL Azure database with a username and password.

1. On the Create Server page, enter "NotepadAdmin" as the administrator username and "P@ssword" as the administrator password. Retype the password, and choose North Central US on the Location drop-down. See Figure 3–6 for the inputs. Note that for the location, you would want to choose the region where you are closest for optimal performance. If you are planning to deploy the application to a specific region, then you would want to select the appropriate region here.

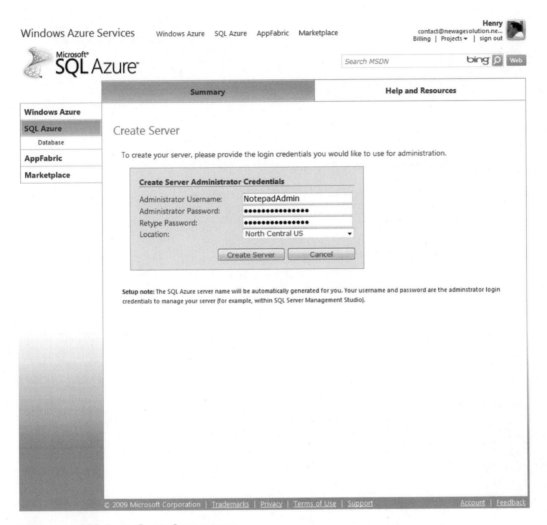

Figure 3–6. SQL Azure Create Server screen

2. Click the Create Server button and you will see Figure 3–7. Take note of the
    server name assigned to your SQL Azure database as you will need this
    information to connect using SQL Server Management Studio in Step 20.

***Figure 3–7.** SQL Azure Server Administration screen*

3. Click Create Database. When the pop-up window appears, enter "NotepadDB" as the name of your database, choose "Web" on the "Specify an edition" drop-down menu, and choose "1GB" on the "Specify the max size" drop-down menu, as shown in Figure 3–8. Now click the Create button.

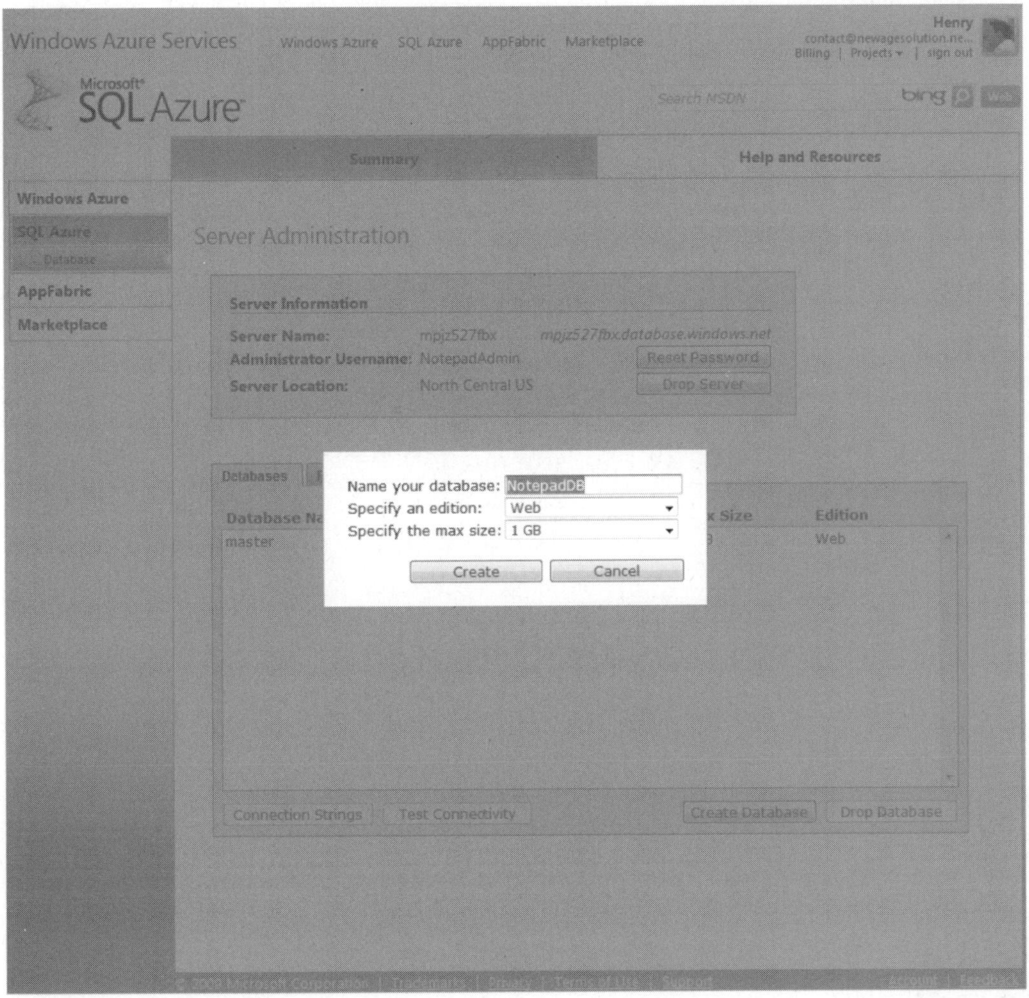

Figure 3–8. SQL Azure create database screen

Configuring the SQL Azure Firewall

In the next steps, you will learn to properly configure the SQL Azure firewall so you can connect to the database. By default SQL Azure denies all access to the database until you add specific IP.

1. Notice that NotepadDB now appears in the list of databases on the Databases tab. Now click the "Firewall Settings" tab, where you will add your IP to the firewall in order to access the SQL Azure database that you just created from the Microsoft SQL Management Console application to perform various database-related tasks.

2. Select "Allow Microsoft Services to access to this server" check box, which will allow programs like Microsoft SQL Management consoles to connect directly to the SQL Azure database, as shown in Figure 3–9.

Figure 3–9. SQL AzureFirewall Settings

3. Click the Add Rule button, and when the popup appears, enter "MyComputer" into the Name text box. Notice that the popup displays your IP address, which you should now copy and paste into the IP Range text boxes, as shown in Figure 3–10.

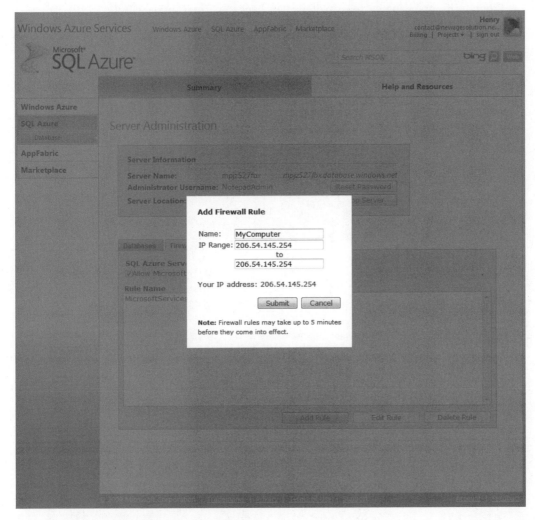

Figure 3–10. SQL Azure Add Firewall Rule screen

4. Click the Submit button. Notice that firewall rules can take up to five minutes to go in effect.

Testing the SQL Azure Database Connection

In this section, you will learn to test to make sure all the configuration steps are performed properly and you can connect to the database.

1. Let's test to see if you can properly connect. Click the Databases tab.

2. From the list of databases, select NotepadDB, click the "Test Connectivity" button, and the pop-up window will appear, as shown in Figure 3–11.

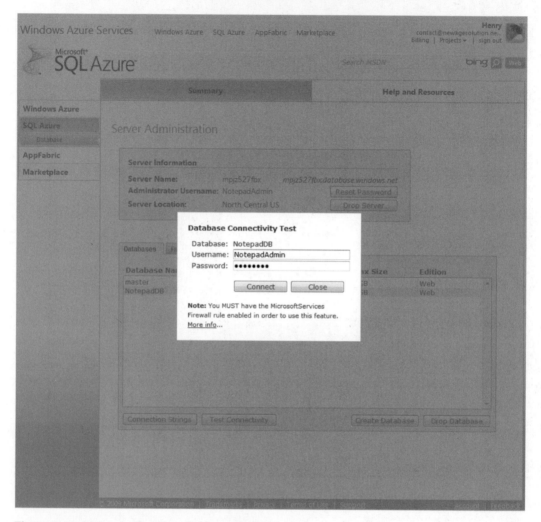

Figure 3–11. SQL Azure Database Connectivity Test

3. Enter "NotepadAdmin" and "P@ssword" (or your own versions of these) into the Username and Password boxes and click the Connect button. You may choose to use your own username password of your choice.

4. Click the Connect button and you will see a "Successfully connected to the database" message.

5. Click the Close button to return to the main page behind.

Creating a Database in SQL Azure

In the following section, you will learn to create database tables in NotepadDB, which is hosted directly in SQL Azure using the Microsoft SQL Server Management application.

Using SQL Server Management Studio to Connect to the Cloud Database

You will be connecting directly to the SQL Azure database NotepadDB you created in the foregoing steps using the SQL Management application.

1. You want to make sure that you can connect to SQL Azure directly from SQL Management Studio in order to perform various database operations. If you do not have SQL Management Studio installed, you can download the free SQL Server 2008 R2 Express (www.microsoft.com/express/database/). Open SQL Server Management Studio by going to Start ➤ Programs ➤ Microsoft SQL Server 2008 R2, as shown in Figure 3–12.

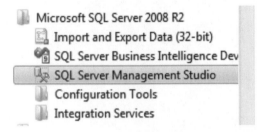

Figure 3–12. SQL Server Management Studio from the Windows menu

2. In the Connect to Server window, put the server name you obtained from Step 7 into the Server name text box, put NotepadAdmin and P@ssword into the Login and Password text box, and click the Connect button, as shown in Figure 3–13.

Figure 3–13. SQL Server Management Studio Connect to Server screen

3. Once you are connected successfully to your SQL Azure database, SQL Server
    Management Studio will display an Object Explorer window on the left side of
    its IDE, as shown in Figure 3–14. Expand the Databases folder and you will find
    NotepadDB, which you just created, listed there, also shown in Figure 3–14.

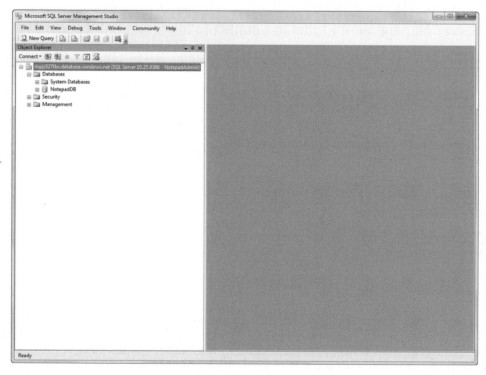

Figure 3–14. SQL Server Management Studio Object Explorer

Creating SQL Azure Database Tables

Once you are connected to NotepadDB, you can create the tables you'll use to store and manage the
notes your users will create and save. You will be creating the database schema shown in Figure 3–15.

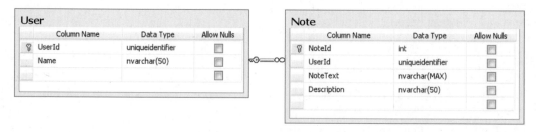

Figure 3–15. NotepadDB database schema

4. Right-click NotepadDB from the Object Explorer window, and from the context menu choose New Query.

5. You will be executing SQL scripts in the query window in order to create tables in NotepadDB.

6. To the newly opened query window, enter or cut and paste the following database script.

```
USE [NotepadDB]
GO

CREATE TABLE [dbo].[User]
(
        [UserId] [uniqueidentifier] NOT NULL,
        [Name] [nvarchar](50) NOT NULL,
    CONSTRAINT [PK_User] PRIMARY KEY ( [UserId] )
)
Go

CREATE TABLE [dbo].[Note]
(
        [NoteId] [int] IDENTITY(1,1) NOT NULL,
        [UserId] [uniqueidentifier] NOT NULL,
        [NoteText] [nvarchar](max) NOT NULL,
        [Description] [nvarchar](50) NOT NULL,
    CONSTRAINT [PK_Note] PRIMARY KEY CLUSTERED ( [NoteId] )
)
GO

ALTER TABLE [dbo].[Note]
        WITH CHECK ADD CONSTRAINT [FK_Note_User] FOREIGN KEY([UserId])
        REFERENCES [dbo].[User] ([UserId])
GO

ALTER TABLE [dbo].[Note] CHECK CONSTRAINT [FK_Note_User]
GO
```

7. Notice that when you expand the tables from NotepadDB in Object Explorer, you will see two tables: Note and User, as shown in Figure 3–16.

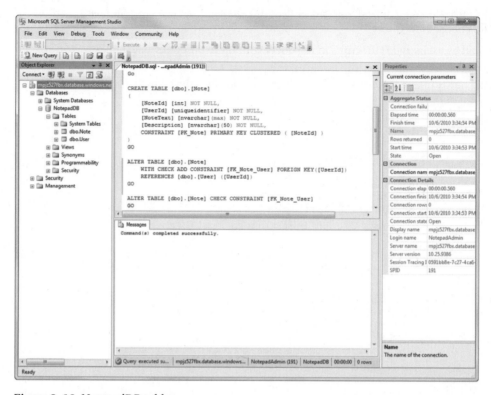

Figure 3–16. NotepadDB tables

Now you have the live database in SQL Azure ready to be used by your web service that you will be creating in next section. You will be creating a web service using Windows Communication Foundation (WCF). The web service layer provides managed APIs the phone application can use to access the database.

Creating a Cloud Service to Access the Cloud Database

You will be creating a WCF service called NotepadService that will be consumed by the Windows Phone Notepad application. Think of NotepadService as the layer that provides managed APIs to the Notepad application. NotepadService will utilize the Entity Framework to generate object models based on the database tables, and it will also generate a persistence layer that performs the database operations, which otherwise you would have to code yourself. Finally, the steps will provide you with instructions on creating and deploying NotepadService to Windows Azure. You will be creating a WCF Azure service and running it from your machine, and then you will learn to package and deploy the project to the Azure cloud, where you will be able to configure to have multiple services run if your application demand increases.

Creating a Windows Azure Project

You will be creating a Windows Azure NotepadService project in Visual Studio in the following steps. In order to create Azure services, you would need to download Azure tools and SDK from www.microsoft.com/windowsazure/windowsazure/default.aspx.

1. Create a new Windows Phone Application by selecting File ➤ New Project on the Visual Studio command menu. Select the Cloud installed template on the left, and choose Windows Azure Cloud Service from the list on the left, as shown in Figure 3–17. Name the Azure service "NotepadService" and click OK.

Figure 3–17. Windows Azure Cloud Service project

2. You will be prompted to select the type of role. Notice here that if you want to host the web project, you would need to select ASP.NET Web Role. For Notepad WCF service, you will need to select WCF Service Web Role, as shown in Figure 3–18, and click the arrow pointing to the left. In Cloud Service Solution, you will see WCFServiceWebRole, and if you hover your mouse over the item, you will see that a little pencil icon appears. Click the pencil icon and change the name to NotepadServiceRole, as also shown in Figure 3–18.

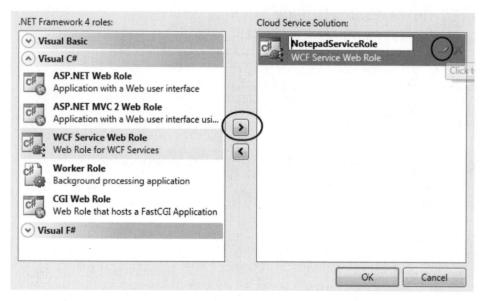

Figure 3–18. Selecting WCF Service Web Role

Generating an Object Model to Access the Cloud Database

Now that we have basic plumbing for implementing a WCF service, it is a good time to implement a persistence layer that allows you to interact with the database. Entity Framework will act as an object-relational mapping tool that will take database tables and create equivalent object models and many of the tedious tasks of coding methods, like add, delete, update, and search, which can be easily handled by Entity Framework.

When you complete this section, you will be creating two object models, User and Note, which you can work directly in the code. Also Entity Framework will provide the ability to save these models directly back to the database.

In the following steps, you will learn to add an Entity Framework item to the project and then connect to NotepadDB in SQL Azure and generate object models.

1. Right-click the NotepadServiceRole project found in Solution Explorer, and choose Add ➤ New Item.

2. Click the Data from Installed Templates list, choose ADO.NET Entity Data Model, and name the model NotepadService.edmx, as shown in Figure 3–19.

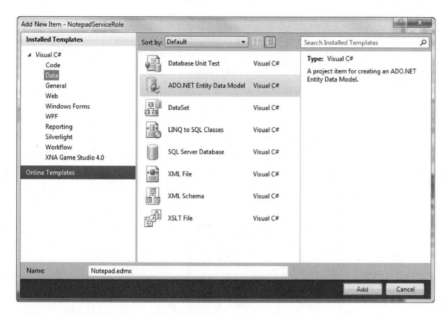

Figure 3–19. *Adding Entity Framework*

3. You will be prompted with the Entity Data Model Wizard, as shown in Figure 3–20. Click the Next button.

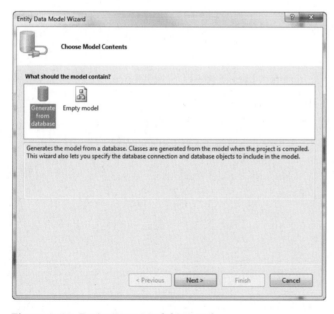

Figure 3–20. *Entity Data Model Wizard*

4. Click the "New Connection..." button, and when Choose Data Source appears, select Microsoft SQL Server from the list, as shown in Figure 3–21. Click the Continue button.

Figure 3–21. Choose Data Source window

5. You will be prompted with a Connection Properties window. In the service name, put the SQL Azure server name that you acquired from the previous steps and enter "NotepadAdmin" and "P@ssword" as your username and password. Then from the "Select or enter database name" drop-down, select NotepadDB, as shown in Figure 3–22.

Figure 3–22. Connection Properties window

6. Click the OK button, and you will return to the Entity Data Model Wizard window. Select Yes, include the sensitive data in the connection string radio button, and click the Next button.

7. If you expand the tables, you will see the two tables (Note and User) that you created previously. Select both of the tables, as shown in Figure 3–23.

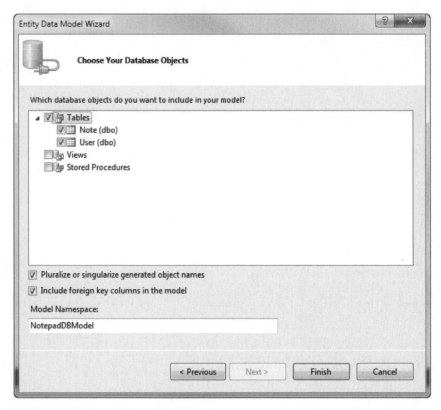

Figure 3–23. Choosing the database objects

8. Take the default option for everything else, click the Finish button, and you will return to the Visual Studio project and see Notepad.edmx, which contains two object models: User and Note, as shown in Figure 3–24.

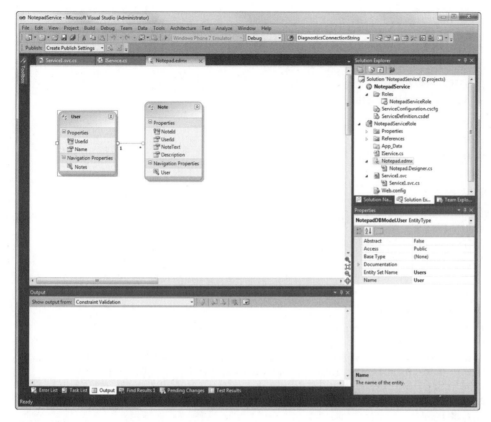

Figure 3–24. Entity model Notepad.edmx

You now have User and Note object models that you can work with in your NotepadService. In the next section, you will be preparing NotepadService, which will implement simple create, read, update, and delete operations using the entity model that you generated in this section.

Implementing a WCF Service to Access the SQL Azure Database

Now that you have an entity model of User and Note, you can implement NotepadService, which will add, update, delete, and search notes. In this section, you will learn to implement a WCF service and also learn to use Entity Framework to interact with the SQL Azure database.

Coding the WCF Contract

In order to create a WCF service, you must first define a WCF service contract. The following steps will guide you through how to do this. If everything was successfully done, you should see a Solution Explorer in Visual Studio that resembles Figure 3–25.

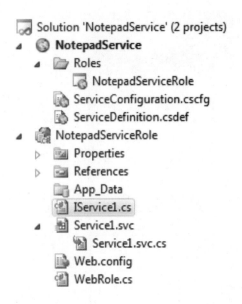

Figure 3–25. NotepadService project in Solution Explorer

Open `IService.cs` and replace the content with the following code. The WCF contract will contain a way to add, delete, update, and search the note in NotepadDB. Notice here the namespace of `System.ServiceModel`, which allows you to add attributes `ServiceContract` and `OperationContract`, which must be defined in order to create a WCF service.

```
using System.ServiceModel;
using System.Collections.Generic;
using System;

namespace NotepadServiceRole
{
    [ServiceContract]
    public interface IService1
    {
        [OperationContract]
        Guid AddUser(Guid userId, string userName);

        [OperationContract]
        NoteDto AddNote(Guid userId, string notedescription, string noteText);

        [OperationContract]
        void UpdateNote(int noteId, string noteText);

        [OperationContract]
        void DeleteNote(Guid userId, int noteId);

[OperationContract]
```

```
        List<NoteDto> GetNotes(Guid userId);

        [OperationContract]
        NoteDto GetNote(Guid userId, int noteId);

    }
}
```

In the next section, you will be creating a data contract that will be sent to the client through the service.

Coding the DataContract

Before you implement the service contract, you will need to define two data transfer objects to map to the entity object. Although we can expose the entity generated by the Entity Framework directly to the WCF service, it is not a recommended practice because the Entity Framework exposes information not necessary for the client. For example, information like foreign key, primary key, and any Entity Framework–related information that is in the Note and User objects has no meaning to the client. Also when the Entity Framework object is serialized, it will include all this unnecessary information, causing the serialized objects coming through the Internet to get huge, and since we are working with the Windows Phone over wireless or Wi-Fi transmission, you will want information sent over the wireless to be small.

1. To NotepadServiceRole add the UserDto.cs class with the following code. Notice the namespace that we will be using, System.Runtime.Serialization, which allows you to add DataContract and DataMember attributes that allow the WCF service to serialize this object to be sent over the service to the client.

```
using System.Runtime.Serialization;

namespace NotepadServiceRole
{
    [DataContract]
    public class UserDto
    {
        [DataMember]
        public int UserId { get; set; }

        [DataMember]
        public string Name { get; set; }
    }
}
```

2. To NotepadServiceRole add the NoteDto.cs class with the following code.

```
using System.Runtime.Serialization;

namespace NotepadServiceRole
{
    [DataContract]
    public class NoteDto
    {
        [DataMember]
        public int NoteId { get; set; }
```

```
        [DataMember]
        public string Description { get; set; }

        [DataMember]
        public string NoteText { get; set; }

    }
}
```

Coding the Service

In the following steps, you will implement the NotepadService WCF contract defined in the foregoing section. You will be using the Entity Framework to access the SQL Azure database.

Open Service1.svc.cs in the NotepadServiceRole project, and add the code blocks spelled out in the following sections.

Coding AddUser Method

AddUser will add a new user to the database. Notice that you are instantiating NotepadDBEntities, which is the Entity Framework–generated context that connects to the SQL Azure NotepadDB.

```
        public Guid AddUser(Guid userId, string userName)
        {
            using (var context = new NotepadDBEntities())
            {
                context.AddToUsers(new User()
                    {
                        UserId = userId,
                        Name = userName,
                    });
                context.SaveChanges();

                return userId;
            }
        }
```

Coding AddNote Method

Notice here in AddNote method after instantiating NotepadDBEntities, you are creating the Note entity that you generated in the foregoing steps using the Entity Framework Wizard. Once the note is saved, you are mapping to NoteDto to be sent to the client.

```
        public NoteDto AddNote(Guid userId, string notedescription, string noteText)
        {
            using (var context = new NotepadDBEntities())
            {
                Note note = new Note()
                    {
                        Description = notedescription,
                        UserId = userId,
```

```
                NoteText = noteText,
            };
        context.AddToNotes(note);
        context.SaveChanges();

        return new NoteDto()
            {
                NoteId = note.NoteId,
                Description = note.Description,
                NoteText = note.NoteText,
            };
    }
}
```

Coding UpdateNote Method

In order to update the note, first you need to instantiate the entity context that connects to NotepadDB, and then you must query for the note that you are going to update. Once the note is retrieved, you will then update the properties and save changes.

```
public void UpdateNote(int noteId, string noteText)
{
    using (var context = new NotepadDBEntities())
    {
        var note = context
                        .Notes
                        .Where(n => n.NoteId.Equals(noteId)
                            ).Single();
        note.NoteText = noteText;
        context.SaveChanges();
    }
}
```

Coding DeleteNote Method

When deleting the note, the note must be retrieved first and then the retrieved note will be added to the DeleteObject of the Notes collection. Then save the changes where the delete will be performed by the Entity Framework.

```
public void DeleteNote(Guid userId, int noteId)
{
    using (var context = new NotepadDBEntities())
    {
        var note = context
                        .Notes
                        .Where(n => n.NoteId.Equals(noteId)).Single();
        context.Notes.DeleteObject(note);
        context.SaveChanges();
    }
}
```

Coding GetNotes Method

GetNotes will bring all the notes associated with the specific userId. You will be using a technique called Linq to Entity that closely resembles the SQL statement. And inside the Linq to Entity, you will be performing translation of the Note entity to NoteDto. This is a very useful technique for mapping an entity object to a data transfer object.

```
public List<NoteDto> GetNotes(Guid userId)
{
    using (var context = new NotepadDBEntities())
    {
        var notes = (
                    from eachNote in context.Notes
                    where eachNote.UserId == userId
                    orderby eachNote.Description ascending
                    select new NoteDto
                    {
                        NoteId = eachNote.NoteId,
                        Description = eachNote.Description,
                        NoteText = eachNote.NoteText,
                    }
                    ).ToList();

        return notes;
    }
}
```

Coding GetNote Method

GetNote will query a single user note from the database.

```
public NoteDto GetNote(Guid userId, int noteId)
{
    using (var context = new NotepadDBEntities())
    {
        var notes = (
                    from eachNote in context.Notes
                    where eachNote.NoteId == noteId
                            && eachNote.UserId == userId
                    select new NoteDto
                    {
                        NoteId = eachNote.NoteId,
                        Description = eachNote.Description,
                        NoteText = eachNote.NoteText,
                    }
                    ).SingleOrDefault();

        return notes;
    }
}
```

Testing Azure WCF NotepadService on Your Machine

You will be testing NotepadService on your machine so that when you connect to NotepadService from the Windows Phone Notepad application, you will be able to debug and step through NotepadService when the service call is made from the Notepad application.

Press F5 and you will notice that the Development Fabric window appears with Internet Explorer. Development Fabric simulates the Azure service environment in your machine. Notice that when you expand NotepadService you see NotepadServiceRole, which is the WCF service that you coded in the foregoing steps. When NotepadService is deployed, you will see one instance of the service deployed, as shown in Figure 3–26. Do not stop the service, as you will be referencing the service from the Notepad application.

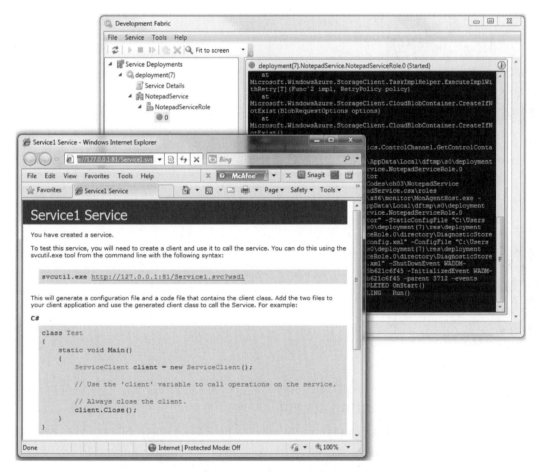

Figure 3–26. *Development Fabric simulating the Azure Service environment*

In the previous steps, you created the NotepadDB database in SQL Azure and NotepadService hosted locally using Development AppFabric to simulate Windows Azure. In the following section, you will be consuming NotepadService from the Notepad application, and ultimately when the service works properly, you will be deploying NotepadService to Windows Azure.

Building a Phone Client to Access a Cloud Service

The Notepad application will allow you to add notes and retrieve the notes that will be saved to the cloud database NotepadDB. You will be building the Notepad application that will consume NotepadService, the WCF Azure service that you created previously, and you will verify at the end that the notes are properly saved to SQL Azure NotepadDB. When it's finished, the UI for the Notepad application will resemble Figure 3–27.

Figure 3–27. *Notepad application*

Creating a Windows Phone Project

To set up the Notepad project, follow the steps you've used for previous examples in this book.

1. Open Microsoft Visual Studio 2010 on your workstation.

2. Create a new Windows Phone Application by selecting File ➤ New Project on the Visual Studio command menu. Select Silverlight for Windows Phone from Installed Templates, and then select the Windows Phone Application template on the right when the list appears, as shown in Figure 3–28. Name the application "Notepad" and click OK.

Figure 3–28. Creating a Windows Phone Application project

Building the User Interface

You will be building the user interface using XAML in Visual Studio. For building simple controls, it is faster to work with XAML code. First you will build two user controls, NoteListUsercontrol, which will display the list of the notes that the user can select to display and edit, and UserRegistrationUserControl, where the user can register so that the notes can be saved to NotepadDb in the cloud.

Building UserRegistrationUserControl

UserRegistrationUserControl is displayed the first time when the user starts the Notepad application, and thereafter the user registration information will be saved to the isolated storage application settings (isolated storage will be covered in detail in Chapter 13).

1. Right-click the Notepad project and choose Add ➤ New Item.

2. From the Add New Item window, choose Windows Phone User Control and name the control UserRegistrationUserControl.xaml, as shown in Figure 3–29. Click the Add button.

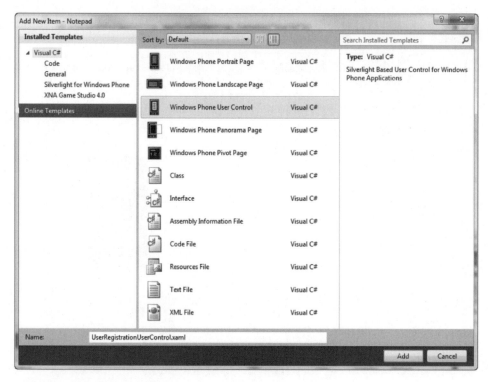

Figure 3–29. Creating UserRegistrationUserControl

3. Open UserRegistrationUserControl.xaml, which you just added from Solution Explorer, replace the content with the following XAML code, and you will see a control that will resemble Figure 3–30 in Visual Studio design view.

Figure 3–30. UserRegistrationUserControl design view

Declaring the UI Resources

Take default namespaces as shown in the following code.

```
<UserControl x:Class="Notepad.NoteListUserControl"
    xmlns="http://schemas.microsoft.com/winfx/2006/xaml/presentation"
    xmlns:x="http://schemas.microsoft.com/winfx/2006/xaml"
    xmlns:d="http://schemas.microsoft.com/expression/blend/2008"
    xmlns:mc="http://schemas.openxmlformats.org/markup-compatibility/2006"
    mc:Ignorable="d"
    FontFamily="{StaticResource PhoneFontFamilyNormal}"
    FontSize="{StaticResource PhoneFontSizeNormal}"
    Foreground="{StaticResource PhoneForegroundBrush}"
    d:DesignHeight="480" d:DesignWidth="480">
```

Adding Components for UserRegistrationUserControl

You will be adding a Register button, a UserName label, and a TextBlock to capture the username.

```
<Grid x:Name="LayoutRoot" Background="{StaticResource PhoneChromeBrush}">
        <Button Content="Register" Height="72" HorizontalAlignment="Left"
                Margin="118,260,0,0" Name="btnSave" VerticalAlignment="Top"
                Width="160" Click="btnSave_Click" />
        <TextBox Height="72" HorizontalAlignment="Left"
                Margin="118,154,0,0" Name="txtUserName" Text=""
                VerticalAlignment="Top" Width="337" />
        <TextBlock Height="30" HorizontalAlignment="Left"
                Margin="17,177,0,0" Name="textBlock1"
                Text="UserName: " VerticalAlignment="Top" />
</Grid>
```

Building NoteListUserControl

NoteListUserControl displays the list of notes that the user created. The control will be prompted when the user clicks the View/Edit button from the MainPage.

1. Right-click the Notepad project and choose Add ➤ New Item.

2. From the Add New Item window, choose Windows Phone User Control and name the control NoteListUserControl.xaml. Click the Add button.

3. Open NoteListUserControl.xaml, which you just added from Solution Explorer, replace the content with the following XAML code, and you will see a control that will resemble Figure 3–31 in Visual Studio design view.

Figure 3–31. NoteListUserControl design view

Declaring the UI Resources

Take default namespaces as shown in the following code.

```
<UserControl x:Class="Notepad.NoteListUserControl"
    xmlns="http://schemas.microsoft.com/winfx/2006/xaml/presentation"
    xmlns:x="http://schemas.microsoft.com/winfx/2006/xaml"
    xmlns:d="http://schemas.microsoft.com/expression/blend/2008"
    xmlns:mc="http://schemas.openxmlformats.org/markup-compatibility/2006"
    mc:Ignorable="d"
    FontFamily="{StaticResource PhoneFontFamilyNormal}"
    FontSize="{StaticResource PhoneFontSizeNormal}"
    Foreground="{StaticResource PhoneForegroundBrush}"
    d:DesignHeight="480" d:DesignWidth="480">
```

Adding Components for NoteListUserControl

You will be adding a ListBox control that will be bound to the Notes, which is a collection of NoteDto that will be coming from the NotepadViewModel object that you will be implementing later. And each ListBoxItem will contain a TextBlock that is bound to NoteDto's Decription property.

```
    <Grid x:Name="LayoutRoot" Background="{StaticResource PhoneChromeBrush}">
        <ListBox Height="458" HorizontalAlignment="Left" Margin="10,10,0,0" Name="lstNotes"
                VerticalAlignment="Top" Width="460"
 SelectionChanged="lstNotes_SelectionChanged"
                ItemsSource="{Binding Notes}">
            <ListBox.ItemTemplate>
                <DataTemplate>
                    <StackPanel>
                        <TextBlock Text="{Binding Description}" />
                    </StackPanel>
                </DataTemplate>
            </ListBox.ItemTemplate>
        </ListBox>
    </Grid>
</UserControl>
```

Building MainPage

MainPage will contain the user controls NoteListUserControl and UserRegistrationUserControl, which you just created, and the buttons Add, AddNew, Delete, and View/Edit, which will allow the user to add, insert, and delete the notes.

Declaring the UI Resources

The namespaces you see in the following code snippet are typically declared by default when you first create a Windows Phone project. In particular, the namespaces xmlns:phone="clr-namespace:Microsoft.Phone.Controls; assembly=Microsoft.Phone" allow you to add common Windows Phone controls to the application main page.

Also you will be adding xmlns:uc="clr-namespace:Notepad", which will allow you to add BooleanToVisibilityConverter, which implements converting value from the Boolean to Visibility that is set on the controls.

```
<phone:PhoneApplicationPage
    x:Class="Notepad.MainPage"
    xmlns="http://schemas.microsoft.com/winfx/2006/xaml/presentation"
    xmlns:x="http://schemas.microsoft.com/winfx/2006/xaml"
    xmlns:phone="clr-namespace:Microsoft.Phone.Controls;assembly=Microsoft.Phone"
    xmlns:shell="clr-namespace:Microsoft.Phone.Shell;assembly=Microsoft.Phone"
    xmlns:d="http://schemas.microsoft.com/expression/blend/2008"
    xmlns:mc="http://schemas.openxmlformats.org/markup-compatibility/2006"
    xmlns:uc="clr-namespace:Notepad"
    mc:Ignorable="d" d:DesignWidth="480" d:DesignHeight="768"
    FontFamily="{StaticResource PhoneFontFamilyNormal}"
    FontSize="{StaticResource PhoneFontSizeNormal}"
    Foreground="{StaticResource PhoneForegroundBrush}"
    SupportedOrientations="Portrait" Orientation="Portrait"
    shell:SystemTray.IsVisible="True">
```

Building the Main Page and Adding Components

In MainPage, you will be adding Add, Delete, AddNew, and View/Edit buttons to work with the notes. Two TextBlocks, txtNotes, and txtNoteName, are added to display the note name and the note content. txtNote and txtNoteName are bound to SelectedNote.NoteText and SelectedNote.Description. The SelectedNote property comes from the NotepadViewModel object, which gets bound to the context of MainPage so that any control in MainPage can bind to any properties of the NotepadViewModel object.

And there are two user controls that you will be adding that you created in previous steps. Visibility of these user controls is controlled by the ShowNoteList and NeedUserId properties found in NotepadViewModel. When the user clicks the View/Edit button, ShowNoteList will be set to true, causing NoteListUserControl, bound to the ShowNoteList property, to appear to the user.

When the user first starts the application and does not have the user ID stored in the application settings, NeedUserId will be set to true in NotepadViewModel, causing the UserRegistrationUserControl to appear.

Adding BoolToVisibilityConvert

Notice that you will be adding a custom converter that will convert the Boolean value received from NotepadViewModel to Visibility enumeration in order to hide and unhide the controls. You will be coding BoolToVisibilityConvert in later.

```
<UserControl.Resources>
    <uc:BoolToVisibilityConverter x:Key="BoolToVisibilityConverter" />
</UserControl.Resources>

<Grid x:Name="LayoutRoot" Background="Transparent">
    <Grid.RowDefinitions>
        <RowDefinition Height="Auto"/>
        <RowDefinition Height="*"/>
    </Grid.RowDefinitions>

    <StackPanel x:Name="TitlePanel" Grid.Row="0" Margin="12,17,0,28">
        <TextBlock x:Name="ApplicationTitle" Text="Notepad"
                   Style="{StaticResource PhoneTextNormalStyle}"
                   HorizontalAlignment="Left" Margin="12,0,0,0" Width="89"/>
    </StackPanel>

    <Grid x:Name="ContentPanel" Grid.Row="1" Margin="12,0,12,0">
        <Button Content="Add" Height="72" HorizontalAlignment="Left"
                Margin="-8,10,0,0" x:Name="btnSave" VerticalAlignment="Top" Width="99"
                Click="btnSave_Click" />
        <Button Content="Delete" Height="72" HorizontalAlignment="Left"
                Margin="71,10,0,0" x:Name="btnDelete" VerticalAlignment="Top" Width="125"
                Click="btnDelete_Click" />
        <Button Content="AddNew" Height="72"
                Margin="176,10,128,0" x:Name="btnAddNew" VerticalAlignment="Top"
                Click="btnAddNew_Click" />
        <Button Content="View/Edit" Height="72" HorizontalAlignment="Left"
                Margin="306,10,0,0" Name="btnEdit" VerticalAlignment="Top" Width="160"
                Click="btnViewEdit_Click" />
        <TextBox x:Name="txtNote" TextWrapping="Wrap"
                 Margin="10,163,8,8" AcceptsReturn="True"
                 Text="{Binding Path=SelectedNote.NoteText}"/>
        <TextBlock x:Name="lblNoteName" HorizontalAlignment="Left" TextWrapping="Wrap"
                   Text="Note Name:" VerticalAlignment="Top" Margin="32,114,0,0"/>
        <TextBox x:Name="txtNoteName" TextWrapping="Wrap"
                 VerticalAlignment="Top" Margin="143,91,8,0"
                 Text="{Binding Path=SelectedNote.Description}"/>
        <uc:NoteListUserControl x:Name="ucNoteList"
                Visibility="{Binding ShowNoteList, Converter={StaticResource
BoolToVisibilityConverter}}" d:IsHidden="True" />
        <uc:UserRegistrationUserControl x:Name="ucUserRegistration"
                Visibility="{Binding NeedUserId, Converter={StaticResource
BoolToVisibilityConverter}}" d:IsHidden="True"  />
    </Grid>
</Grid>
```

In the next section, you will be adding events for the controls that you built in foregoing steps.

Coding MainPage

In Solution Explorer, open `MainPage.xaml.cs` and replace the code there with the following C# code blocks that will implement the UI interacting with the user to add, delete, view, and edit notes, and also to register the user for the first time.

Specifying the Namespaces

Begin by listing the namespaces the application will use.

```
using System.Windows;
using Microsoft.Phone.Controls;
```

Code Constructor

In the constructor of `MainPage`, you will be setting `DataContext` of the user controls to the `NotepadViewModel` instance. When `DataContext` of `ucNoteList` and `ucUserRegistraton` is set to `NotepadViewModel`, the controls within the user controls' values will be controlled by the properties of `NotepadViewModel`.

```
public MainPage()
{
    InitializeComponent();

    this.DataContext = NotepadViewModel.Instance;
    ucNoteList.DataContext = NotepadViewModel.Instance;
    ucUserRegistration.DataContext = NotepadViewModel.Instance;
}
```

Coding the Save Button Event

When the user clicks the Add button, the `SaveNote` method from the `NotepadViewModel` instance will be called. Any direct calls to NotepadService will be handled from `NotepadViewModel`, leaving the handling of the web service call complexity centralized to `NotepadViewModel`. This is a great abstraction technique, allowing you to easily maintain the application.

```
private void btnSave_Click(object sender, RoutedEventArgs e)
{
    if (!string.IsNullOrEmpty(txtNote.Text))
    {
        NotepadViewModel.Instance.SaveNote(txtNoteName.Text, txtNote.Text);
    }
}
```

Coding the ViewEdit Button Event

When the ViewEdit button is clicked, the `ShowNoteList` property in `NotepadViewModel` will be set to true, which will trigger `NoteListUserControl` to appear. `ShowNoteList` will be set to true only if there are Notes to be selected.

```
private void btnViewEdit_Click(object sender, RoutedEventArgs e)
{
    if (!string.IsNullOrEmpty(txtNote.Text))
    {
        NotepadViewModel.Instance.SaveNote(txtNoteName.Text, txtNote.Text);
    }
}
```

Coding the AddNew Button Event

When the AddNew button is clicked, SelectedNode in NotepadViewModel will be set to null, triggering the txtNote and txtNoteName contents to be set to empty because they are bound to SelectedNote. Although you can directly set the Text fields of txtNote and txtNoteName to an empty string, we are abstracting this particular task to NotepadViewModel because when the user selects the specific user note from NoteListUserControl, the txtNote and txtNoteName content will be automatically changed because they are bound to SelectedNote.

```
private void btnAddNew_Click(object sender, System.Windows.RoutedEventArgs e)
{
    NotepadViewModel.Instance.SelectedNote = null;
}
```

Coding the Delete Button Event

When the Delete button is clicked, the DeleteNote method from the NotepadViewModel instance will be invoked, SelectedNode will be set to null, and txtNote and txtNoteName will be set to an empty string automatically because they are bound to SelectedNode.

```
private void btnDelete_Click(object sender, System.Windows.RoutedEventArgs e)
{
    NotepadViewModel.Instance.DeleteNote();
}
```

Coding the BoolToVisibilityConvert

You will learn to create a custom converter that implements IValueConverter, which can be used during the binding in the control where the bound value can be converted to any value that the control will understand. BoolToVisibilityConvert will convert Boolean value bound to the control Visibility to Visibility enumeration so that the controls can hide and unhide.

1. Right-click the Notepad project and choose Add ➤ Add New Item.

2. When the Add New Item window pops up, choose Class and name the class BoolToVisibilityConvert, as shown in Figure 3–32. Click the Add button.

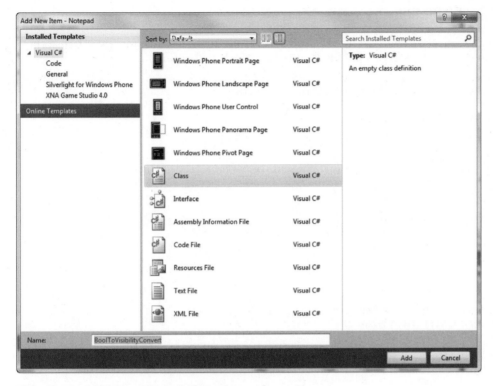

Figure 3–32. Adding BoolToVisibility *class to the project*

3. Open BoolToVisibilityConvert.cs and paste the code blocks spelled out in the following sections.

Specifying the Namespaces and Applying IValueConverter Interface

The namespace System.Windows.Data will allow you to declare the IValueConverted interface for the BoolToVisibilityConverter class.

```
using System;
using System.Windows;
using System.Windows.Data;

namespace Notepad
{
    public class BoolToVisibilityConverter : IValueConverter
    {
```

Implementing IValueConvert

In order to use the converter in the XAML to convert bound value to the control property or transform to other value, you need to implement the Convert and ConvertBack methods.

```
        public object Convert(object value, Type targetType,
object parameter, System.Globalization.CultureInfo culture)
        {
            bool boolValue;

            if (bool.TryParse(value.ToString(), out boolValue))
            {
                return boolValue ? Visibility.Visible : Visibility.Collapsed;
            }
            else
            {
                // By default it will always return Visibility.Collapsed
                // even for the case where the value is not bool
                return Visibility.Collapsed;
            }

        }

        public object ConvertBack(object value, Type targetType,
object parameter, System.Globalization.CultureInfo culture)
        {
            Visibility visibilityValue = Visibility.Collapsed;

            try
            {
                visibilityValue = (Visibility)Enum.Parse(typeof(Visibility),
(string)value, true);
                return visibilityValue;
            }
            catch (Exception)
            {
                // if fails to conver the value to Visibility
                // it will return Collapsed as default value
                return visibilityValue;
            }

        }
    }
}
```

Adding Reference to NotepadService

Before you code NotepadViewModel, add a web service reference to the NotepadService WCF service that will be hosted in Azure.

1. Right-click the References folder found under the Notepad project in Solution Explorer, and choose Add Service Reference.

2. You will be prompted with the Add Service Reference window. In Address put `http://127.0.0.1:81/Service.svc`, and put `NotepadServiceProxy` in the Namespace text box. Click the Go button and NotepadService information is retrieved. You will see Service1 in the Services box.

3. When you expand Service1, you will see `IService`. Click `IService` and the Operations box will be populated with NotepadService, which you created in the foregoing steps, as shown in Figure 3–33. Click the OK button.

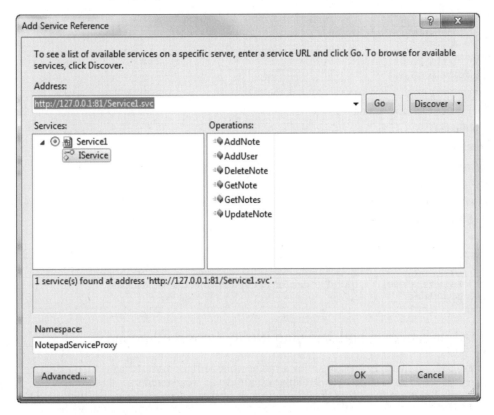

Figure 3–33. Adding service reference to NotepadService

Coding NotepadViewModel

`NotepadViewModel` is considered the controller of this application, and it controls the events and the data that will manipulate the UI. You can think of it as the brain of the application.

1. Right-click the Notepad project, and choose Add ➤ Add New Item.

2. When the Add New Item window pops up, choose Class and name the class `NotepadViewModel`. Click the Add button. Your Solution Explorer should resemble Figure 3–34.

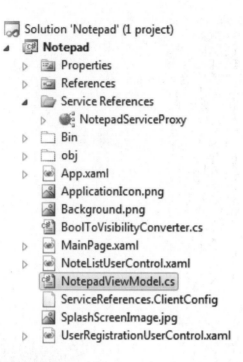

Figure 3–34. Notepad project items in Solution Explorer

3. Open NotepadViewModel.cs, found under the Notepad project, and paste the following c# codes.

Specifying the Namespaces and Applying INotifyPropertyChanged

The namespace Notepad.NotepadServiceProxy allows you to work with the web service NotepadService you referenced. System.IO.IsolatedStorage will allow you to save the registered user ID so that the application will know what notes to work with in the database. System.ComponentModel will allow you to implement the INotifyChanged interface that can raise the property changed events, allowing the controls that are bound to properties like Notes, SelectedNotes, ShowNoteList, and NeedUserId to respond to the changes. System.Linq will allow you to query to objects with syntax that resembles the SQL statement.

```
using System;
using System.Windows;
using System.IO.IsolatedStorage;
using System.ComponentModel;
using Notepad.NotepadServiceProxy;
using System.Collections.ObjectModel;
using System.Linq;

namespace Notepad
{
```

```
/// <summary>
/// Settings class is singleton instance that will contain various application
/// configuration that will be used by all the controls of the application.
/// </summary>
public sealed class NotepadViewModel : INotifyPropertyChanged
{
```

Initializing the Variables

There are many variables that will be added to NotepadViewModel that will control the behavior of the UI controls. Please refer to the comment in the following code for an explanation of what significance the properties have for the UI controls.

```
        // For creating Singleton instance
        public static NotepadViewModel Instance = new NotepadViewModel();

// For calling Notepad web service
        private ServiceClient _svc;

        // Populated when the user registers firstime
        // and the value is saved to the isolated storage
        public Guid UserId
        {
            get
            {
                if (IsolatedStorageSettings.ApplicationSettings.Contains("UserId"))
                {
                    return (Guid)IsolatedStorageSettings.ApplicationSettings["UserId"];
                }
                else
                {
                    return Guid.Empty;
                }
            }
            set
            {
                if (IsolatedStorageSettings.ApplicationSettings.Contains("UserId"))
                {
                    IsolatedStorageSettings.ApplicationSettings["UserId"] = value;
                }
                else
                {
                    IsolatedStorageSettings.ApplicationSettings.Add("UserId", value);
                }

                // Raise property changed event to alert user registration control
                // so that if the UserId is empty user registration screen
                // will be prompted for the user to register.
                //
                // To see how raise property changed event works with control Binding
                // see Binding attributes on ucUserRegistration control in MainPage.xaml
                this.RaisePropertyChanged("UserId");
                this.RaisePropertyChanged("NeedUserId");
```

```csharp
        }
    }
// Checks to see if the UserId exist in the isolated storage
    // and make sure UserId is not an empty Guid
    public bool NeedUserId
    {
        get
        {
            return !IsolatedStorageSettings.ApplicationSettings.Contains("UserId")
                || (Guid)IsolatedStorageSettings.ApplicationSettings["UserId"]
== Guid.Empty;
        }
    }

    // ShowNoteList is bound to NoteListUserControl in the MainPage
    // and it will hide if false and else unhide if true.
    private bool _showNoteList = false;
    public bool ShowNoteList
    {
        get
        {
            return _showNoteList;
        }

        set
        {
            _showNoteList = value;
            this.RaisePropertyChanged("ShowNoteList");
        }
    }

    // SelectedNote is populated from NoteListUserControl
    // when the user selects the note from the list box.
// SelectedNote is then used in MainPage by txtNote and
// txtNoteName to populate to textbox content.
    private NoteDto _note;
    public NoteDto SelectedNote
    {
        get
        {
            return _note;
        }

        set
        {
            _note = value;
            this.RaisePropertyChanged("SelectedNote");
        }
    }

    // Collection of NoteDto is populated by calling GetNotes service call
// and all user notes will be contained in this collection.
    private ObservableCollection<NoteDto> _notes;
    public ObservableCollection<NoteDto> Notes
```

```
{
    get
    {
        return _notes;
    }

    set
    {
        _notes = value;
        this.RaisePropertyChanged("Notes");
    }
}
```

Adding the Constructor

In the constructor, you will be adding event handlers for the service calls. GetNotesCompleted will return all the user notes. AddNote, UpdateNote, and DeleteNote will add, update, and delete the note and return successfully if no error occurs, otherwise the error will be reported back to the callbacks. In the constructor ServiceClient, web service proxy, will be initialized and the RebindData method that makes the call to the GetNotes method will populate the Notes property.

```
private NotepadViewModel()
{
    _svc = new ServiceClient();
    _svc.GetNotesCompleted += new
EventHandler<GetNotesCompletedEventArgs>(_svc_GetNotesCompleted);
    _svc.AddNoteCompleted += new
EventHandler<AddNoteCompletedEventArgs>(_svc_AddNoteCompleted);
    _svc.UpdateNoteCompleted += new
EventHandler<AsyncCompletedEventArgs>(_svc_UpdateNoteCompleted);
    _svc.AddUserCompleted += new
EventHandler<AddUserCompletedEventArgs>(_svc_AddUserCompleted);
    _svc.DeleteNoteCompleted += new
EventHandler<AsyncCompletedEventArgs>(_svc_DeleteNoteCompleted);

    if (this.NeedUserId)
    {
        this.Notes = new ObservableCollection<NoteDto>();
    }
    else
    {
        this.RebindData();
    }
}

// To rebind the data GetNotes will be called to retrieve
// all the user notes and resetting Notes value.
public void RebindData()
{
    _svc.GetNotesAsync(this.UserId);
}
```

Adding SaveNote, AddUser, DeleteNote

Here you will be using the Linq to Object technique to query the Notes property to check if noteName exists. If the note exists, UpdateNote will be called, otherwise AddNote will be called. The AddUser method will make a service call to add the user. DeleteNote will call the DeleteNote service.

```
public void SaveNote(string noteName, string noteText)
{
    // Search the user notes and see if the note already exist
    var note = (from eachNote in this.Notes
                where eachNote.NoteText.Equals(noteText,
StringComparison.InvariantCultureIgnoreCase)
                select eachNote).SingleOrDefault();

    if (note == null)
    {
        _svc.AddNoteAsync(this.UserId, noteName, noteText);
    }
    else
    {
        _svc.UpdateNoteAsync(note.NoteId, noteText);
    }

    this.SelectedNote = note;
}

public void AddUser(Guid userId, string userName)
{
    if (this.NeedUserId)
    {
        _svc.AddUserAsync(userId, userName);
    }
}

public void DeleteNote()
{
    _svc.DeleteNoteAsync(this.UserId, this.SelectedNote.NoteId);
}
```

Adding NotepadService Eventhandlers

The following code will handle callbacks for NotepadService calls.

AddNoteCompleted

When the note is added successfully, SelectedNote will be set with the result returned from the call.

```
private void _svc_AddNoteCompleted(object sender, AddNoteCompletedEventArgs e)
{
    if (e.Error == null)
    {
        this.SelectedNote = e.Result;
    }
```

```
            this.RebindData();
        }
        else
        {
            MessageBox.Show("Failed to add the note. Please try again!");
        }
    }
```

GetNotesCompleted

The returned result will contain all the user notes and will be set to the Notes property.

```
    private void _svc_GetNotesCompleted(object sender, GetNotesCompletedEventArgs e)
    {
        if (e.Error == null)
        {
            this.Notes = e.Result;
        }
        else
        {
            MessageBox.Show("Failed to get the notes. Please try again!");
        }
    }
```

UpdateCompleted

When the updated note is completed, RebindData is called, which will trigger the UI element txtNote, txtNoteName to be updated in MainPage.

```
    private void _svc_UpdateNoteCompleted(object sender, AsyncCompletedEventArgs e)
    {
        if (e.Error == null)
        {
            this.RebindData();
        }
        else
        {
            MessageBox.Show("Failed to update the note. Please try again!");
        }
    }
```

AddUserCompleted

If the user registration is successful, the UserId property will be set with the return result saving it to the isolated storage.

```
    private void _svc_AddUserCompleted(object sender, AddUserCompletedEventArgs e)
    {
        if (e.Error == null)
        {
            // Set the UserId only when AddUser service call
            // was made successfully
```

```
                    this.UserId = e.Result;
                }
                else
                {
                    this.UserId = Guid.Empty;
                    MessageBox.Show("Failed to add user please try again!");
                }
            }
        }
```

DeleteNoteCompleted

When the delete note call is successful, SelectedNote will be set to null so that txtNote and txtNoteName will be set with an empty string in MainPage, and RebindData is called to update the properties.

```
        private void _svc_DeleteNoteCompleted(object sender, AsyncCompletedEventArgs e)
        {
            if (e.Error == null)
            {
                this.SelectedNote = null;
                this.RebindData();
            }
            else
            {
                MessageBox.Show("Failed to delete note please try again!");
            }
        }
```

Coding INotifyPropertyChanged Interface

Here you will be coding the implementation of the INotifyPropertyChanged event that will be called whenever the Notes, ShowNoteList, NeedUserId, and SelectedNote properties are changed.

```
        // Implement INotifyPropertyChanged interface
        public event PropertyChangedEventHandler PropertyChanged;
        private void RaisePropertyChanged(string propertyName)
        {
            PropertyChangedEventHandler propertyChanged = this.PropertyChanged;
            if ((propertyChanged != null))
            {
                propertyChanged(this, new PropertyChangedEventArgs(propertyName));
            }
        }
    }
}
```

Testing the Application Against NotepadService Deployed Locally

Before you begin, make sure that NotepadService is running Development Fabric, otherwise press F5 to start NotepadService as shown in the foregoing steps. Then press F5 on the Notepad Windows Phone project. You will see the application as shown in Figure 3–27. Enter the username and register, and add the notes so that we can confirm that the notes are saved to NotepadDB in SQL Azure.

Open up your SQL Server Management Studio by following the steps provided in the previous sections, type in the following SQL statement, press F5, and you will see the notes and the user data saved to NotepadDB.

```
select * from [User]
select * from Note
```

When the SQL statement is executed, you should see the data you added in the Results window, as shown in Figure 3–35.

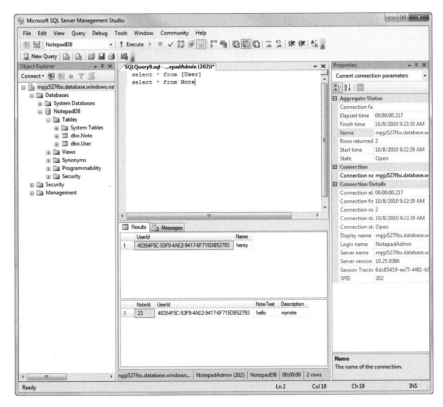

Figure 3–35. Querying NotepadDB

In the next section, you will learn to deploy NotepadService directly to Windows Azure, and you will be modifying the Notepad application to consume the web service located in Windows Azure instead of from the local machine.

Deploying the Service to Windows Azure

By deploying to Windows Azure, you will have a redundant, fault-tolerant service that you can scale out if you need to meet the demands of heavy usage. You will learn how simple it is to configure the service and deploy.

Preparing for Windows Azure NotepadService

You will be creating a Windows Azure service host in order to deploy WCF NotepadService to a Windows Azure platform.

Signing Up for Windows Azure and Creating a Project

1. Open the browser of your choice.

2. Go to www.microsoft.com/windowsazure/ to sign up and buy the Windows Azure service account. Follow the directions provided by Microsoft in order to purchase and acquire the service account in order to continue with the following steps.

3. Go to https://windows.azure.com/ and sign in using the account you created in Step 1.

Connecting to the Windows Azure Project

1. Once you've signed in, click the Windows Azure menu tab on the left side. When the Windows Azure page loads, you will see the project that you created during the registration process (see Step 1). See Figure 3–36, which will correspond to this step.

Figure 3–36. Windows Azure project list

2. Click the project hyperlink NAS-DEV. In your case, you should click the name of the project that corresponds to the one you created in Step 1.

Creating Windows Azure NotepadService

1. When the page loads, if you previously created services, you will see the list of the services, as shown in Figure 3–37. Let's create a new service that will host your WCF service by clicking the "+ New Service" link on the left side of the page.

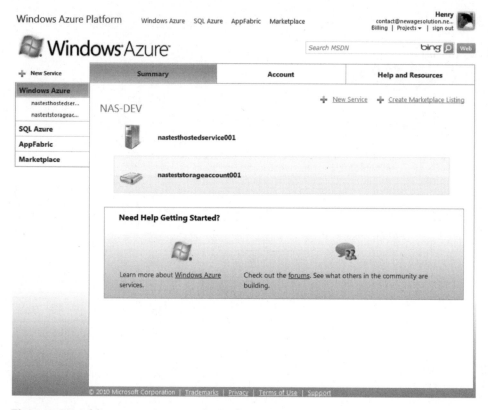

Figure 3–37. Adding a new Azure service to the project

When the next page loads, you will be given an option to choose either "Storage Account" or "Hosted Services." Choose "Hosted Services." See Figure 3–38 for the options you will see displayed.

Figure 3–38. Choosing Hosted Services

2.   When the Service Properties dialogue shown in Figure 3–39 displays, enter
     "NotepadService" as the Service Label and "This is the WCF service for the
     Windows Phone 7 Notepad demo application," as the Service Description. Now
     click the Next button to display the Hosted Service Dialogue on the page.

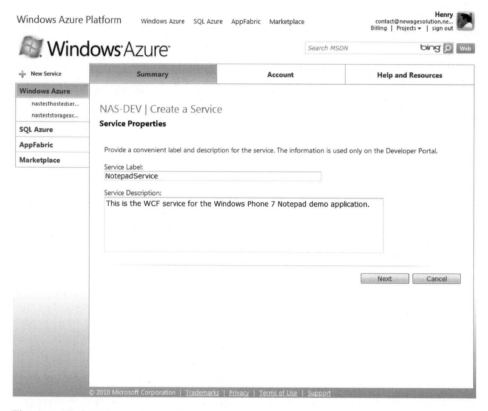

Figure 3–39. Creating Azure service

Configuring Windows Azure NotepadService

Now you're ready to configure the service that you created in the previous section.

1. When the Hosted Service dialogue displays, enter "NotepadService" as the Public Service Name of the Public Hosted Service URL name. Click the Check Availability button to make sure the service name is not taken by someone else.

2. In the Hosted Service Affinity Group section of the Hosted Service dialogue, you have two options to choose from. Typically, relating the affinity among other services allows you to run the services in the same region in order to optimize performance.

   a. If you are creating multiple services that will interact with other services in the same region, then you will want to choose "Yes" and choose the existing Affinity Group from the drop-down.

b. If you create a new Affinity, you can associate to this affinity when you are creating other services. Choose "No" as you will not be creating multiple services that will require the services to be in the same region, and then select the "Anywhere in US" option from the drop-down.

See Figure 3–40 for appropriately filled information. Notice here that for the region you would want to choose the region that you are close to for optimal performance. If you are planning to deploy the application targeting a specific region, then you would want to make sure to choose the appropriate region here.

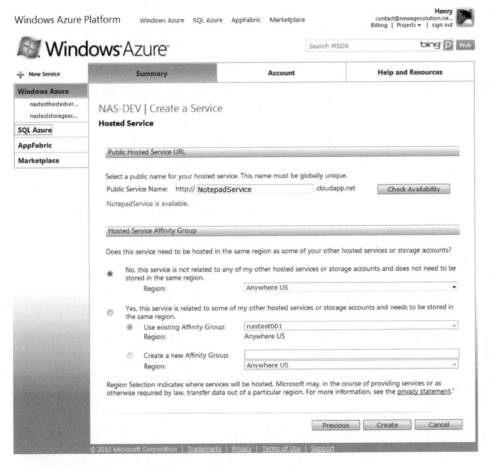

Figure 3–40. Configuring the Azure service

3. Click the Create button and you will see Figure 3–41. Now you are ready to deploy the WCF application that you created in the foregoing section. Notice here that you will be able to deploy first to staging to test your WCF and then deploy to production. This is a very nice feature in that you will be able to test the application running against a real cloud-based service without first deploying to production.

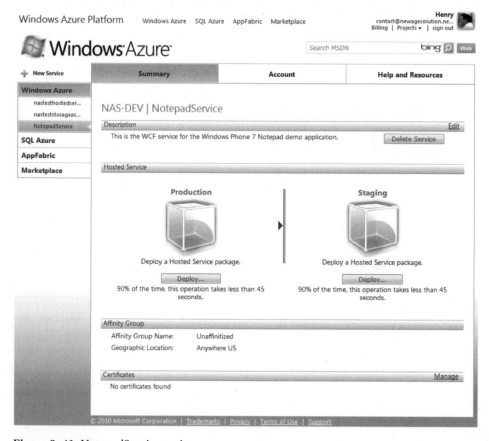

Figure 3–41. NotepadService main screen

Keep this browser open as you will be coming back and deploying the packages.

Deploying NotepadService to Windows Azure

In the foregoing steps, you prepared the NotepadService host, and now it is time for you to deploy NotepadService so that you can consume the Azure service from the phone. We will be deploying the service to staging first. Staging is where you test your service before going to production. This is a very convenient way of making sure your service works before deciding to go live.

Compiling and Publishing NotepadService

We will need a compiled binary so we can deploy to the Windows Azure host.

1. Go to your NotepadService project, stop the project if it is running, right-click the NotepadService project, and choose Publish.

2. The Publish Cloud Service window will appear. Choose Create Service Package Only, as shown in Figure 3–42.

Figure 3–42. *Create a NotepadService package for Windows Azure*

3. Click the OK button and you will notice that Windows Explorer will open with a directory where you will see two files: NotepadService.cspkg is the compiled binary of NotepadService and ServiceConfiguration.cscfg is the configuration file used by Windows Azure. Take note of the directory path as you will be uploading these files to Windows Azure.

Deploying NotepadService.cspkg and ServiceConfiguration.cscfg to Windows Azure

You will be deploying the packages created in the previous steps to Windows Azure.

1. Go to your browser where the NotepadService host main screen is, as shown in Figure 3–41.

2. Click the "Staging Deploy…" button.

3. In the Application Package section, click the Browse button and select NotepadService.cspkg. In Configuration Settings, click Browse to select ServiceConfiguration.cscfg, and choose Automatic for Select OS Upgrades. It is best to have Azure upgrade the OS automatically because each upgrade will include security patches and framework updates. In "Choose a label for this deployment," put "Version 1.0.0". It is best to label the service you are deploying using the version scheme to overcome any future confusion of what is deployed to the Azure service. You should see a screen that resembles Figure 3–43.

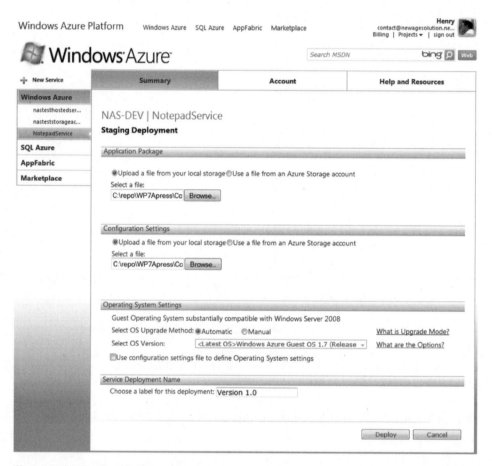

Figure 3–43. Staging Deployment screen

4. Click Deploy. The main screen page will be loaded, as shown in Figure 3–44.

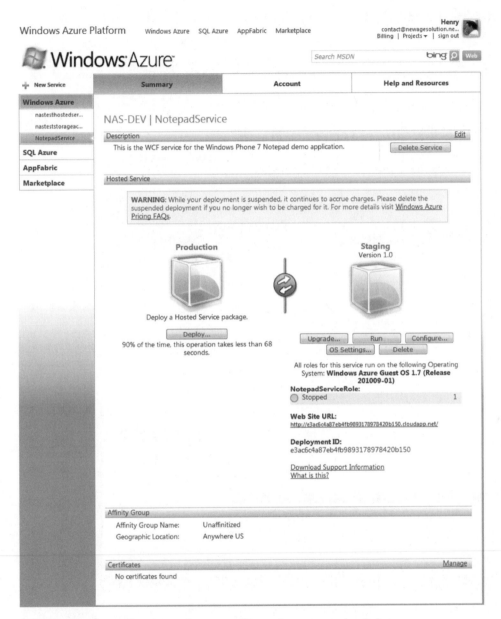

Figure 3–44. NotepadService main screen after packages are uploaded

5. Click Run to run NotepadService. This step will take a while, as long as five minutes. When the service is ready, you will see the Ready status. Notice here that there is a temporary web site URL, which now you can use in your Notepad phone application.

Testing the Notepad Application Against NotepadService Azure Service

In the foregoing steps, you deployed NotepadService to the Windows Azure host. You will be changing the Notepad phone configuration to point to the web service that is hosted in Windows Azure and test in the same way you tested against when the service was deployed locally to your machine.

1. Go to Visual Studio with the Notepad project.

2. In Solution Explorer under the Notepad project, open `ServiceReferences.ClientConfig`. Change the endpoint address from 127.0.0.1:81 to the URL that you received when you deployed to staging in previous steps. See Figure 3–45 with the changed endpoint address.

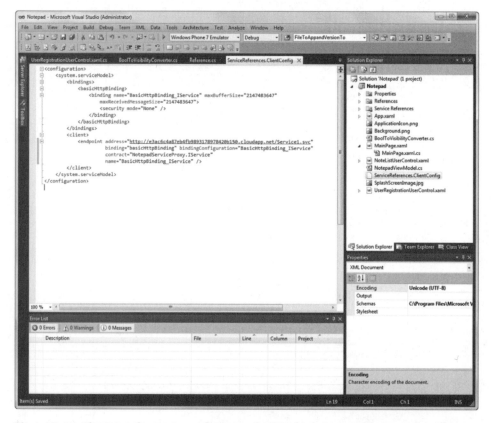

Figure 3–45. Changing the service endpoint to the Windows Azure address

3. Make sure that NotepadService is in Ready status, and then press F5 to run your Notepad phone application in the emulator. Follow the previous steps to test the Notepad application—it should exhibit exactly the same behavior, except that now you are running your Notepad application against the Windows Azure service.

Summary

In this chapter, you learned to build a Windows Phone application that makes use of Microsoft's Windows Azure service to store data to an SQL server in the cloud. Your application is now scalable and fault-tolerant, and can accommodate a large number of users. You learned how simple it is to create the service and the database in the Azure cloud and how Microsoft Azure gives you the power to build an application without having to worry about creating your own complex IT infrastructure to support it.

In Chapter 4, you will learn to catch exceptions and debug and test Windows Phone applications. It will teach you critical skills for you to be successful in building a Windows Phone application.

CHAPTER 4

■■■

Catching and Debugging Errors

As you develop Windows Phone applications, you must learn how to equip them to handle a number of exceptions that are unique to smartphones. Unlike a desktop computer, a Windows Phone is loaded with devices over which you have little direct control, including GPS, an accelerometer, Wi-Fi, isolated storage, and a radio. A user can decide to turn off an onboard device to save power at any time; isolated storage can run out of space, and a resource such as a cell tower, GPS satellite, or WiFi router might not be available. To identify and fix unexpected exceptions in an application, you need to know how to use the powerful debugging facilities of Visual Studio. And to assure yourself that you have dealt with all of the bugs your application is likely to encounter, you need to know how to test your applications on a real device.

In this chapter, you will learn to master the critical debugging and troubleshooting skills using Visual Studio IDE, which you can also use to debug any application, including web applications (ASP.NET), and Windows applications.

The following sections are divided into three major topics. We'll walk you through a series of tutorials covering general exception handling in Windows Phone, Visual Studio debugger features, and testing using the emulator and the real device.

Debugging Application Exceptions

In this section, you will learn how to find and deal with two exceptions that are common to Windows Phone applications. The first is the navigation failed exception, which can be thrown when a main page is loaded; the second deals with the web service call that is consumed by the application.

The ErrorHandlingDemo application that you'll use contains two projects, a Windows Phone project and the Calculator web service project, which has an Add method that adds two numbers and returns the result to the caller. Being able to debug and handle web service call exceptions will be critical especially if you are planning to work with external services like Microsoft Bing Maps services, covered in Chapter 14.

When you finally debug and fix all the issues in the application, you will see the result shown in Figure 4–1.

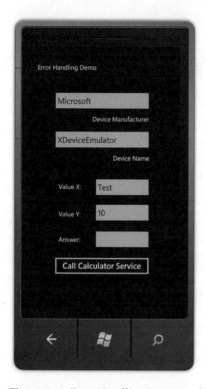

Figure 4–1. ErrorHandlingDemo application

Debugging Page Load Exceptions

The ErrorHandlingDemo application contains bugs that will cause exceptions to be thrown when the application's main page is loaded. In this section, you will learn how to find and fix such problems in Visual Studio.

Catching an Exception

Whenever an application throws an exception, Visual Studio will stop execution at the line where it's thrown. To observe this behavior, let's run the application and take a closer look using the Visual Studio IDE.

Fire up Visual Studio, select File➤Open, and browse to the following file, which you can download from the site for this book:

`{unzippeddirectory}\ch04\ErrorHandlingDemo\Start\ErrorHandlingDemo.sln`.

Once the solution file is loaded, press F5 to run it.

Notice the raised exception message in Figure 4–2, which points to the code that has caused `ArgumentOutOfRangeException` to be thrown. From `DeviceExtendedProperties` you can obtain Windows Phone 7 system information, and only the following keys—`DeviceManufacturer`, `DeviceName`,

DeviceUniqueId, DeviceTotalMemory, ApplicationCurrentMemoryUsage, and ApplicationPeakMemoryUsage—will be available. And when you try to query the system information DName that does not exist, the application throws ArgumentOutOfException.

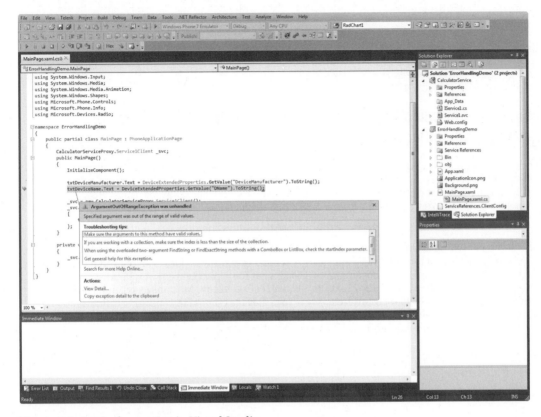

Figure 4–2. A raised exception in Visual Studio

Querying Exception Object Values with Immediate Window

Whenever an application running in Visual Studio pauses at a line where an exception has been thrown, you always have an opportunity to observe its variables in Visual Studio's Immediate Window.

Immediate Window is a most useful debugging feature because it allows you to evaluate any statement when the code execution pauses at the breakpoint. If you do not see the immediate window when the breakpoint is hit, you can go to Debug ➤ Windows ➤ Immediate to bring up the Immediate Window, as shown in Figure 4–3.

1. With ErrorHandlingDemo still paused in the debugger, go to the Immediate Window, type in DeviceExtendedProperties.GetValue("DeviceName") to query the object value, and press Enter. You will see the result printed in an Immediate Window, as shown in Figure 4–3.

Figure 4–3. Query object value in Immediate Window

Catching an Unhandled Exception in RootFrame_NavigationFailed or Application_UnhandledException

Unhandled exceptions in a Windows Phone application will be caught by one of two main methods: RootFrame_NavigationFailed, and Application_UnhandledException. RootFrame_NavigationFailed catches unhandled exceptions thrown while a page is being loaded; Application_UnhandledException catches exceptions thrown in all other cases.

1. Press F5 to continue debugging from the breakpoint in the previous section.

The debugger will next break inside RootFrame_NavigationFailed in App.xaml.cs as shown in Figure 4–4. Notice that in App.xaml.cs you will find various Windows Phone application–related events such as Application_Launching, Application_Activated, Application_Deactivated, Application_Closing, RootFrame_NavigationFailed, and Application_UnhandledException. As far as exceptions are concerned, only two events will be of interest. RootFrame_NavigationFailed captures unhandled exceptions when the Windows Phone page fails to load. In ErrorHandlingDemo, unhandled exceptions occur when MainPage tries to load and throws ArgumentOutOfException.

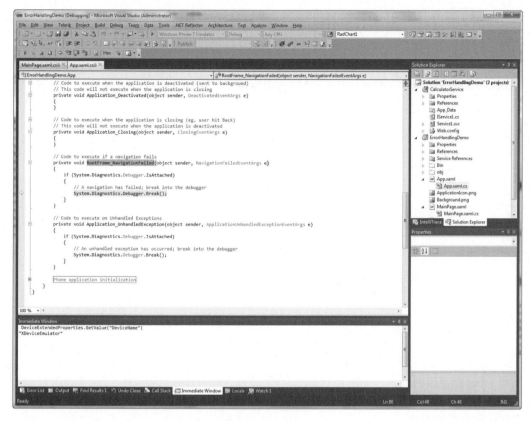

Figure 4–4. Breakpoint at `RootFrame_NavigationFailed`

2. With your mouse, hover over `NavigationFailedEventArgs` e and you will be able to drill into the object value and see the `e.Uri` that contains the page that caused the error during the load, as shown in Figure 4–5.

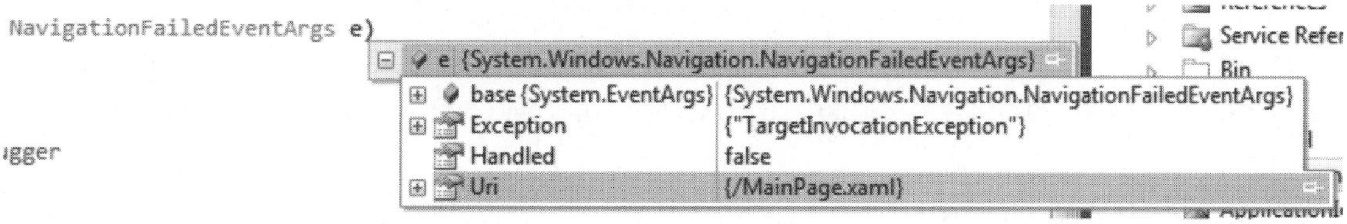

Figure 4–5. `NavigationFailedEventArgs.Uri`

3. Press F5 to continue debugging, and you will notice that code execution next breaks in the `Application_UnhandledException` method. All exceptions that are not handled specifically by a `try-catch-finally` block will ultimately end up in this method.

Handling an Exception RootFrame_NavigationFailed

When an exception is thrown in the `MainPage` of an application, the exception will be caught by the `RootFrame_NavigationFailed` method, and this is where you want to handle it in order to stop the exception from bubbling up to the `Application_UnhandledException` method.

In `ErrorHandlingDemo`, replace the `RootFrame_NavigationFailed` method with following code. Notice the use of `MessageBox` in the code to display the proper error with stack trace and set `e.Handled` to `true`, which will stop the breakpoint to move to the `Application_UnhandledException` method.

```
// Code to execute if a navigation fails
private void RootFrame_NavigationFailed(object sender, NavigationFailedEventArgs e)
{
    if (System.Diagnostics.Debugger.IsAttached)
    {
        // A navigation has failed; break into the debugger
        System.Diagnostics.Debugger.Break();
    }

    MessageBox.Show(
string.Format("Page {0} failed to load because of with error: {1}",
e.Uri.ToString(), e.Exception.StackTrace));
    e.Handled = true;
}
```

Fixing the Error in the Code

In the previous section, you added a `MessageBox` display in case any other page fails to load, and in the following steps, you will be fixing the actual cause of the exception in `MainPage`. But first, let's fix the error in `MainPage.xaml.cs`.

Fix the error in `MainPage.xaml.cs` by replacing

```
txtDeviceName.Text = DeviceExtendedProperties.GetValue("DName").ToString()
```

with

```
txtDeviceName.Text = DeviceExtendedProperties.GetValue("DeviceName").ToString().
```

Debugging a Web Service Exception

`ErrorHandlingDemo` contains the `CalculatorService` web service project, where the service will be hosted locally and consumed by the demo application. The code is written so that the application will throw the exceptions that you will be fixing.

Catching a Web Service Exception

You will be stepping through the breakpoints in order to understand the behavior of the thrown exception.

Before you begin, we need to make sure that both the Windows Phone project and the web service project start simultaneously when you Press F5.

1. Right-click the ErrorHandlingDemo solution in Solution Explorer and choose the property. The solution property page Window shown in Figure 4–6 will display.

2. Select the Multiple startup projects option, and CalculatorService and ErrorHandlingDemo projects' Actions are set to Start.

3. Also put two breakpoints in MainPage.xaml.cs, as shown in Figure 4–6, at the line txtAnswer.Text = e.Result.ToString() and _svc.AddAsync(txtX.Text, txtY.Text).

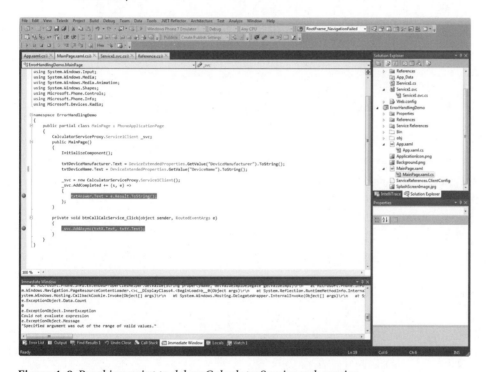

Figure 4–6. Breaking point to debug CalculatorService web service

4. Press F5 and you will see the application show in Figure 4–1 in the emulator, and you will notice the WCF Test Client starts as well, as shown in Figure 4–7. The WCF Test Client will host the CalculatorService, allowing you to step into the web service call.

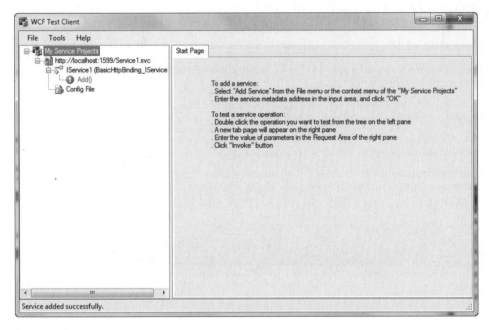

Figure 4–7. WCF test client

5.   From the emulator, press the Call Calculator Service button.

Notice that the Visual Studio catches InvalidCastException thrown from the CalculatorService project, as shown in Figure 4–8.

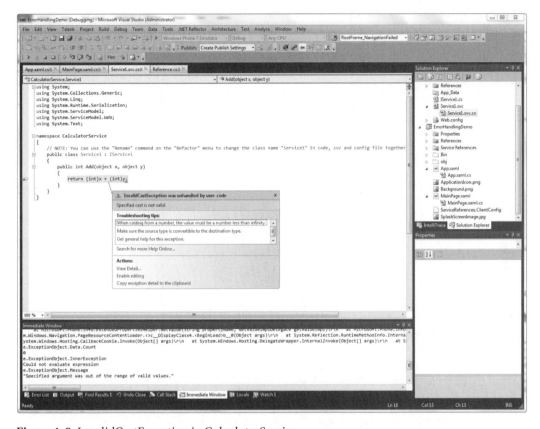

Figure 4–8. InvalidCastException in CalculatorService

6. When you hover over x value you will notice that it contains Test, which cannot be converted to integer causing InvalidCastException.

7. Press F5 to continue, and Visual Studio breaks at Reference.cs, which is the web service proxy class that was generated against WSDL from Visual Studio (see Chapter 3 for more detail on how to consume web services).

8. Press F5 again, and the execution will break on the line txtAnswer.Text = e.Result.ToString() found in MainPage.xaml.cs.

9. In Immediate Window, type in e.Error and you will notice that e.Error is not empty. When the web service returns any kind of error, e.Error will not be empty, and when you try to access e.Result that contains web service call, the result will throw an exception.

10. Press F5 again, and you will notice the exception thrown in the e.Result property, as shown in Figure 4–9.

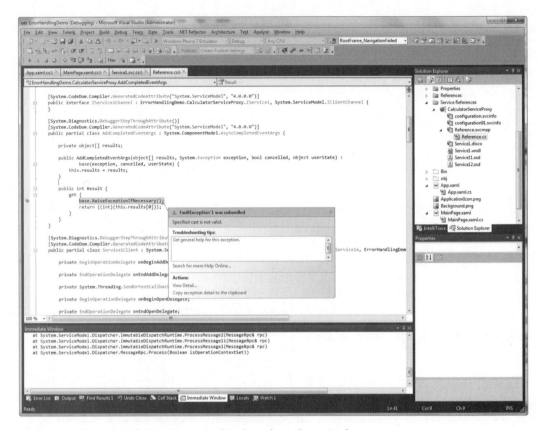

Figure 4–9. Exception thrown in e.Result when the web service has an error

11. Press F5, and the exception will be finally caught in
    `Application_UnhandledException`.

Fixing the CalculatorService Exception

After stepping through the breakpoints, you now have enough information to fix the exception.

First let's check the values received from the caller in `CalculatorService`. Replace `Service1.svc.cs` codes with the following snippet. The `CheckValue` method will make sure that the received value is not null and it converts the value to the integer.

```
public int Add(object x, object y)
{
    int xValue = CheckValue(x);
    int yValue = CheckValue(y);

    return xValue + yValue;
}
```

```
private int CheckValue(object value)
{
    int convertedValue = -1;
    if (value == null)
    {
        throw new ArgumentNullException("value");
    }
    else if (!int.TryParse(value.ToString(), out convertedValue))
    {
        throw new ArgumentException(
string.Format("The value '{0}' is not an integer.", value));
    }

    return convertedValue;
}
```

In `MainPage.xaml.cs` replace the `AddCompleted` event delegate with following codes. You will be checking to make sure `e.Error` is empty before retrieving `e.Result`, and if `e.Error` is not empty, then you will be throwing the proper error message.

```
_svc.AddCompleted += (s, e) =>
    {
        if (e.Error == null)
        {
            txtAnswer.Text = e.Result.ToString();
        }
        else
        {
            MessageBox.Show(
string.Format("CalculatorService return an error {0}",
e.Error.Message));
        }
    };
```

Testing the Application

You've finished debugging and fixing the application exceptions, and now you will be able to properly run the application and handle exceptions.

Press F5 and you will see Figure 4–1; notice now that `txtDeviceManufacturer` and `txtDeviceName` are properly populated during the `MainPage` load. When you change `txtX` to an integer and click the `Call Calculator Service` button, `txtAnswer` will be populated with the result received from the web service.

Registering a Windows Phone Device for Debugging

Testing an application on a Windows Phone device is a lot more work than using the Windows Phone emulator, because it involves registering your device, physically connecting it to your computer via a USB cable, and running Zune software in the background on your workstation. Here are the steps you need to follow to set up a phone as your debugging platform.

First, you must apply for a Windows Phone Marketplace account at the Windows Phone developer portal.

1. If you don't yet have a Windows Phone account, go to
    `http://developer.windowsphone.com/` and sign up.

Microsoft will review your application and activate your account. If you have not yet installed Zune software, you can download the latest Zune software from `www.zune.net/en-us/products/software/download/default.htm`.

2. Once you're approved, click the Windows Start menu on your workstation and select All Programs ➤Zune to start the Zune software, whose Welcome page is shown in Figure 4–10.

Figure 4–10. Zune software

■ **Note** The Windows Phone 7 device is based on the Zune, which is a Microsoft product and iPod competitor for playing video and audio. A Windows Phone uses Zune software to update a Windows Phone 7 system, and Zune must be running in order to deploy an application to a device. Also you can use Zune software to back up your device.

3. Connect your Windows Phone device to your developer workstation using a USB cable.

4. To confirm that your device is properly connected and recognized by the Zune software, click the phone icon at the bottom left corner of the Zune Welcome screen, as indicated by the arrow in Figure 4–11.

Figure 4–11. *Clicking the phone icon in Zune software*

5. When you click the phone icon, the Zune software will display detailed information about your device, as shown in Figure 4–12.

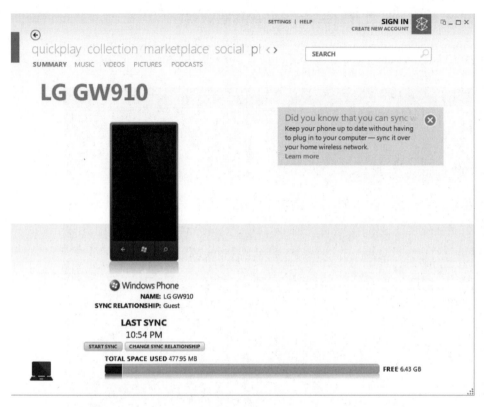

Figure 4–12. Windows Phone device detail page in Zune

Now you are ready to actually register your device.

6. Go to the Windows Start menu, select All Programs ➤Windows Phone Developer Tools, and select Windows Phone Developer Registration, as shown in Figure 4–13.

Figure 4–13. Windows Phone developer registration

A Windows Phone developer registration form will display, as shown in Figure 4–14.

7. Enter the ID and password that you used to register for a Windows Phone Marketplace account in Step 1.

Figure 4–14. Windows Phone developer registration

To confirm that your phone is properly registered, go to `http://developer.windowsphone.com/` and log in.

Once logged in, click Account and select DEVICE REGISTRATION from left side menu, as shown in Figure 4–15. You should see a list of the devices you have registered.

Figure 4–15. Device registration page

In the following section, you will learn tips and tricks to make your life easier when you begin to debug and test using a real device.

TIPS AND TRICKS: DEBUGGING ON A DEVICE

Here are a few things that you should keep in mind to make your life easier and save you time when you're debugging an application on a live Windows Phone.

1. When debugging it is best to disable screen time-out, especially if you are debugging through a complex program that takes a long time. On the Windows Phone device, go to Settings ➤ Lock & Wallpaper and set the screen time-out to never. Remember to come back to reset the screen time-out to other than never so you don't waste your battery.

2. When you try to debug in the Windows Phone 7 device, you will get the error message shown here. And when you click No, you will see an "Access Denied" message in your Error List window. This is because your device is locked due to time-out. To avoid this problem during the debugging, you would want to disable time-out on the device by following Step 1. To resolve this issue, simply unlock your device and restart in debug mode in Visual Studio.

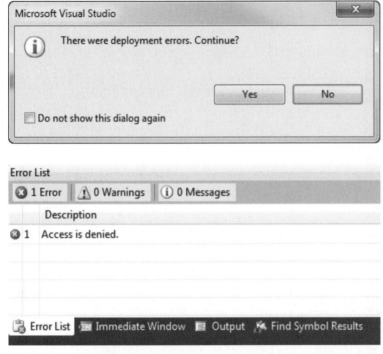

3. When the Zune application is not started, you will receive the error "Zune software is not launched. Retry after making sure that Zune software is launched" in the Visual Studio Error List Window.

Handling Device Exceptions

In the following section, you will learn to capture device-specific exceptions. You will be using the accelerometer device as an example to properly handle unexpected exceptions by catching `AccelerometerFailedException`. `AccelerometerFailedException` can occur if the accelerometer device on the phone is broken. Also the exception can occur if the device throws unexpected error caused internally by Microsoft Window Phone framework. Figure 4–16 displays the basic UI of the CatchDeviceExceptionDemo project that you will be building.

Figure 4–16. *CatchDeviceException UI*

Creating the CatchDeviceExceptionDemo Project

To set up the CatchDeviceExceptionDemo project, follow the steps you've used for previous examples in this book.

1. Open Microsoft Visual Studio 2010 Express for Windows Phone on your workstation.

2. Create a new Windows Phone Application by selecting File ➤ New Project on the Visual Studio command menu. Select the Windows Phone Application template, name the application "CaptureAccelerometerData," and click OK.

3. In order to use the accelerometer, add an assembly reference to `Microsoft.Devices.Sensors` by right-clicking the `References` folder in Solution Explorer, and choose `Microsoft.Devices.Sensors` from the Add Reference window, as shown in Figure 4–17.

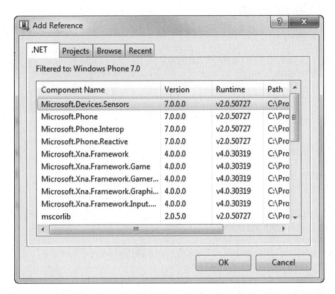

Figure 4–17. Adding reference to `Microsoft.Devices.Sensors`

Building the User Interface

You will be building the user interface using the XAML in the Visual Studio. For building simple controls, it is faster to work with the XAML code. Go to Solution Explorer, open `MainPage.xaml,` and replace the XAML you find there with the following code.

Declaring the UI Resources

The namespaces you see in the following code snippet are typically declared by default when you first create a Windows Phone project. In particular, namespaces `xmlns:phone="clr-namespace:Microsoft.Phone.Controls; assembly=Microsoft.Phone"` allow you to add common Windows Phone controls to the application main page.

```
<phone:PhoneApplicationPage
    x:Class="CatchingDeviceExceptionsDemo.MainPage"
    xmlns="http://schemas.microsoft.com/winfx/2006/xaml/presentation"
    xmlns:x="http://schemas.microsoft.com/winfx/2006/xaml"
    xmlns:phone="clr-namespace:Microsoft.Phone.Controls;assembly=Microsoft.Phone"
    xmlns:shell="clr-namespace:Microsoft.Phone.Shell;assembly=Microsoft.Phone"
    xmlns:d="http://schemas.microsoft.com/expression/blend/2008"
    xmlns:mc="http://schemas.openxmlformats.org/markup-compatibility/2006"
    mc:Ignorable="d" d:DesignWidth="480" d:DesignHeight="768"
    FontFamily="{StaticResource PhoneFontFamilyNormal}"
    FontSize="{StaticResource PhoneFontSizeNormal}"
    Foreground="{StaticResource PhoneForegroundBrush}"
    SupportedOrientations="Portrait" Orientation="Portrait"
    shell:SystemTray.IsVisible="True">
```

Building the Main Page and Adding Components

Create two buttons to start and stop the accelerometer.

```xml
<!--LayoutRoot is the root grid where all page content is placed-->
<Grid x:Name="LayoutRoot" Background="Transparent">
    <Grid.RowDefinitions>
        <RowDefinition Height="Auto"/>
        <RowDefinition Height="*"/>
    </Grid.RowDefinitions>

    <!--TitlePanel contains the name of the application and page title-->
    <StackPanel x:Name="TitlePanel" Grid.Row="0" Margin="12,17,0,28">
        <TextBlock x:Name="ApplicationTitle" Text="CatchingDeviceExceptionsDemo"
Style="{StaticResource PhoneTextNormalStyle}"/>
    </StackPanel>

    <!--ContentPanel - place additional content here-->
    <Grid x:Name="ContentPanel" Grid.Row="1" Margin="12,0,12,0">
        <Button Content="Start Accelerometer" Height="72" HorizontalAlignment="Left"
Margin="84,45,0,0" Name="btnStartAcc" VerticalAlignment="Top"
Width="284" Click="btnStartAcc_Click" />
        <Button Content="Stop Accelerometer" Height="72" HorizontalAlignment="Left"
Margin="84,123,0,0" Name="btnStopAcc" VerticalAlignment="Top"
Width="284" Click="btnStopAcc_Click" />
    </Grid>
</Grid>

</phone:PhoneApplicationPage>
```

Once you have loaded the XAML code, you should see the layout shown in Figure 4–18. In the next section, you will be coding the application.

Figure 4–18. CatchDeviceExceptionDemo design view

Coding the Application

In Solution Explorer, open `MainPage.xaml.cs` and replace the code there with the following code C# code blocks.

Specifying the Namespaces

Begin by listing the namespaces the application will use. Notice our inclusion of `Microsoft.Devices.Sensors` that will allow us to start and stop Windows Phone's accelerometer.

```
using System.Windows;
using Microsoft.Phone.Controls;
using Microsoft.Devices.Sensors;
```

Initializing Variables

The variable _acc, Accelerometer object, will be used to start and stop.

```
Accelerometer _acc;

    public MainPage()
    {
        InitializeComponent();
        _acc = new Accelerometer();
    }
```

Implementing Accelerometer Start and Stop Behavior

Implement a button event for stopping and starting the accelerometer. Notice that you are catching AccelerometerFailedException, which can be raised during the start and stop of the accelerometer. In the exception property, you will find ErrorId and Message that contains specific error code and description that could explain why the error was raised

```
private void btnStartAcc_Click(object sender, RoutedEventArgs e)
    {
        try
        {
            _acc.Start();

            _acc.ReadingChanged += (s1, e1) =>
                {
                    // Do something with captured accelerometer data
                };
        }
        catch (AccelerometerFailedException ex)
        {
            string errorMessage = string.Format(@"
                    Accelerometer threw an error with ErrorId {0}
    during the start operation
                    with error message {1}
                    ", ex.ErrorId, ex.Message);
            MessageBox.Show(errorMessage);
        }
    }

    private void btnStopAcc_Click(object sender, RoutedEventArgs e)
    {
        try
        {
            _acc.Stop();
        }
        catch (AccelerometerFailedException ex)
        {
            string errorMessage = string.Format(@"
                    Accelerometer threw an error with ErrorId {0}
```

```
during the stop operation
                        with error message {1}
                        ", ex.ErrorId, ex.Message);
            MessageBox.Show(errorMessage);
        }
    }
```

Testing the Finished Application

To test the finished application, press F5. The result should resemble the screenshot shown in Figure 4–16. The only thing you will not be able to test is being able to raise AccelerometerFailedException, which can be raised only if the accelerometer device fails. But the demo will give you a good idea of how you should be handling the device-related exception if it ever occurs.

Summary

In this chapter, you learned how catch and handle errors in an application and unexpected errors thrown by a Windows Phone. You also learned how to use Visual Studio's powerful debugging features to troubleshoot and fix defects, regardless of whether you're running an application in the emulator or on a real device.

In Chapter 5, you will learn to package, publish, and manage a Windows Phone application for distribution through the Windows Phone Marketplace.

CHAPTER 5

■ ■ ■

Packaging, Publishing, and Managing Applications

Every developer dreams of developing an application that everyone loves to use and becoming an instant millionaire. You will have that chance when you develop your own application and then packaging, distributing, and selling it to millions of Windows Phone users worldwide through the Windows Marketplace . In order for you to submit your application to the Windows Phone Marketplace you will need to pay $99 per year.

At the Windows Phone Marketplace you have three options for distributing your application.

- You can sell your application at fixed cost that you specify and earn 70% on each sale you make.

- You can distribute your application for free up to five free applications and subsequent applications will cost $19.99 to submit. When you do decide to distribute your application for free you would want to consider incorporating Windows Phone 7 Ad SDK so you can earn money from the advertising. Using Microsoft Advertising service you can produce targeted advertising for your application to display. For example if you are creating health related application then you might considering choosing advertising categories from sports, life style and/or health categories. You have to keep in mind though that you are allowed to select only three categories.

- You can distribute your application as a trial application using the Market Trial API to reduce the number of features available in the application so that users can download the application and try it first before making a purchase.

To package and publish your application to the Windows Phone Marketplace your application must abide by the rules of the Windows Phone Marketplace. In following sections, you will learn in great detail about what you need to do in order to successfully deliver your application to the Windows Phone Marketplace.

Windows Phone Application Publishing Lifecycle

When you develop a Windows Phone application you distribute to Windows Phone Marketplace through the Windows Phone developer portal. Figure 5–1 shows you the overview interaction of the developer to the developer portal to the Windows Phone Marketplace to the consumers.

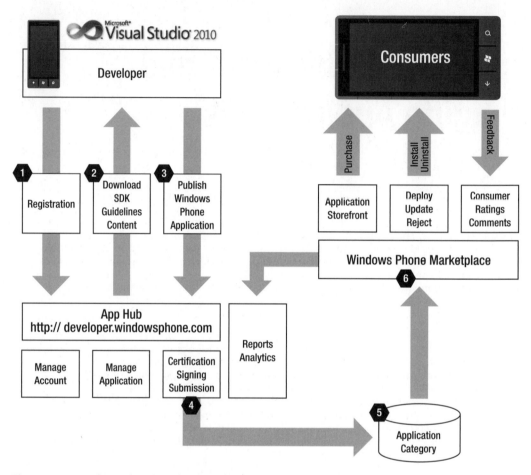

Figure 5–1. *Windows Phone application publishing lifecycle*

First (1) you must register as a developer with the Windows Phone portal and there will be $99 fee that you would need to pay. Your identity will be verified and you will be issued a certificate that the Windows Marketplace will use to sign your application. In addition, your bank account will be verified so that your earning can be deposited there. Next (2), if you haven't already done so, you'll need to download the SDK tools you need to develop in Visual Studio. After you've created your application (3) you will submit it to the portal for validation and certification (4) so Microsoft can assure the application abides by the Windows Phone Marketplace rules. Once your application becomes eligible, it will be signed using the certificate you received during registration (5), and then published to the Windows Phone Marketplace (6).

Once the application is published, users will be able to buy, download and install it from the Widows Phone Marketplace portal. There, users can also rate it and comment on its virtues and flaws, providing you with feedback that you can use to improve it. The Marketplace will provide you with downloads and sales information as well.

In the followings sections you will be learning great deal about the certification requirements and the process that will guide you through so that your application can pass through and be submitted to the Windows Phone Marketplace.

Windows Phone Application Certification Requirements

In the battle of smartphones between (iPhone, Android and Windows Phone), the applications available on each smartphone will play critical role to winning the consumers to use the phone. Windows Phone Marketplace puts in place the rules and process to ensure that the published applications are high in quality. You can download Windows Phone 7 application certification requirements from http://go.microsoft.com/?linkid=9730558. The following list describes the idea behind the rules and the process imposed on publishing the application to Windows Phone Marketplace:

1. **Applications are reliable** – You will be dealing with the consumers who will be picky and any hint of the instability in the application will cause the consumers not only talk bad about the application but the brand behind the phone. So Microsoft will enforce the best practices for creating reliable application.

2. **Applications make efficient use of resources** – Your application must make efficient use of the pone resources and make sure does not have any adverse effect on performance. For example the battery life can be drained quickly if you continue to use the location service or the accelerometer because you forgot to turn it off after to use in the application and the user is continuing to use your application not aware that location service and accelerometer is still running.

3. **Application does interfere with the phone functionality** – The user must be notified before modifying any phone settings or preferences.

4. **Applications are free of malicious software** – The application must be safe to install and use.

In following sections, the summary of main points will be presented so that you can be aware of the content of the certification documents. Remember that the following sections describing the certification requirements are based on version 1.3 and Microsoft could modify and release newer version. So check back with the developer portal http://developer.windowsphone.com.

Application Policies

This section will cover policies that will help protect the Windows Phone Marketplace and the consumers using the Windows Phone application bought from the marketplace.

Windows Phone application binary (XAP file)

You must compile your application in release mode from Visual Studio and it will produce a file with a .xap file extension. A ZAP file is nothing more than a ZIP file with a different extension name. In in fact, if you change the extension name of your XAP file from .xap to .zip, you will be able to extract its file content. You should be aware of following facts.

For installation over the air, the XAP file must be no larger than 20 MB.

1. Must disclose additional data package to be downloaded if greater than 50 MB and notify the user that there might be additional charges depending on how the data package is downloaded.

2. Maximum size of a XAP is 400 MB and a XAP greater than 20 MB can only be installed through Zune, or over Wi-Fi.

What your application must not do

This section will summarize what your application cannot do that is described in the Application Policies section.

Cannot sell, link or promote mobile voice plans.

1. Cannot distribute, link or direct the users to alternate marketplace.

2. Your application cannot taint the security or functionality of Windows Phone devices or Windows Phone Marketplace.

What your application must do

This section will summarize what your application must do.

1. Your application must be functional.

2. Your trial application (if submitted as trial) must reasonably include the feature subsets of the fully functional application.

3. If your application includes / displays advertising, the advertising must abide by http://advertising.microsoft.com/creative-specs.

4. If your application enables chat, instant messaging, or person to person communication and allows the user to create account the user must be verified of at least 13 years old.

5. If your application sells music, the application must include Windows Phone music Marketplace (if available). If the content of the music is purchased elsewhere the application must include its own playback media play.

Location Service

Following requirements will deal with the location service (GPS).

1. Location must be obtained using Microsoft Location Service API (Notifications the subject of Chapter 17).

2. Cannot override, ignore and circumvent Microsoft toast or prompts related to the Location Service API (Location Services are covered later in Chapter 14).

3. Cannot override a user's choice to disable location services on the phone.

4. Must have enable and disable option of the Location Service used in the application.

5. If the location data is published other service or other person. Must fully disclose how the Location Service information will be used, permission to use the location information obtained, user has the option to opt in and out, and there must be visual indicator whenever the information is transmitted. Also must provide privacy policy statement regarding the location service information usage.

6. Security must be in place to protect the location data obtained.

Push Notification Service (PNS)

Following section summarizes the policies relating to the push notification.
Must provide opt in and out option to use the service.

1. Cannot excessively use PNS that can cause a burden to Microsoft network or Windows Phone device.

2. PNS cannot be used to send mission critical that could affect life or death.

Content Policies

Your application must conform to the content restriction of the Windows Phone Marketplace. If the application you developed already has the ratings from ESRB, PEGI and USK, you need to submit the certificate of the ratings. Keep mindful of licensed materials, logo, name and trademarks. The content must not be illegal or suggest harms. Any hate related contents are not allowed. Any promotion of sales and illegal under local law of alcohol, tobacco, weapons and drugs are not allowed. Any x-rated contents are not allowed. Any realistic violence content will not be allowed. Any excessive use of the profanity will not be allowed.

Keep in mind that this section is highly subjective and Microsoft will have final saying at the end. Best suggestion would be to take practical approach and ask yourself if your application will be safe to be used and viewed by the minor.

Application Submission Validation Requirements

In order to package and submit an application for certification, you must make sure that following requirements are met.

Packaging Requirements

When you are getting ready to create a XAP, it is best to use Visual Studio and to compile the binaries in Release Mode, which will produce the XAP file and take care of the many requirements identified in the certification document. Below requirements are things you should make sure to look into because they are easy to overlook them.

XAP file cannot be greater 400 MB.

1. Application icon must be 62 x 62 of PNG file type.

2. Application tile image must be 173 x 173 of png file type.

3. Must have the application title.

Code Requirements

There will be coding requirements that your application will be subjected to. Following list described those requirements

Application must use documented APIs only found at http://msdn.microsoft.com/en-us/library/ff626516(VS.92).aspx.

1. PInvoker and COM interoperability is not allowed.

2. Application must be compiled in release mode.

3. Windows Phone assemblies cannot be redistributed.

4. When using a method from `System.Windows.Controls` APIs in `Microsoft.Xna.Framework.Game` or `Microsoft.Xna.Framework.Graphics` cannot be called.

Phone Feature Use Disclosure

When the user purchases the application from the Windows Phone Marketplace the marketplace will display what phone features the application will be using. This is done through by submission of the application manifest file for Windows Phone (`http://msdn.microsoft.com/en-us/library/ff769509(VS.92).aspx`). The phone features added to application manifest is typically added and removed automatically by Visual Studio so this is not something you would normally be concerned with. But you must be aware to make sure during your packaging process to check to make sure the features listed in the application manifest are something that you are using in your application and correctly represented.

Language Validation

Supported languages are English, French, Italian, German and Spanish. Depends on where you are submitting your application you must properly localize your application for at least one of the supported languages.

Images for Windows Phone Marketplace

Your application must be submitted with the images and screenshots that will be displayed to the user in the Windows Phone Marketplace. Microsoft recommends that you use 262 DPI.

Required small mobile application tile 99 x 99 (PNG) and large mobile application tile 173 x 173 (PNG).

1. Required large PC application tile 200 x 200 (PNG).

2. Optional background art 1000 x 800 (PNG).

3. Required screenshot 400 x 800 (PNG).

Application Certification Requirements

Once the application is submitted for the certification process it will be tested against series of certification requirements. Following sections will summarize those requirements.

Application Reliability

This section will deal with certification requirements that deal with application reliability. Application must run on all Windows Phone 7 devices.

1. Application must handle all raised exception and must not crash the application unexpectedly.

2. Application must not hang and become unresponsive to the user input. If the application is processing time consuming process the visual element must provide progress bar with ability to cancel the progress.

Performance and Resource Management

This section will describe requirements that deal with performance and resource management issue of the application.

Application must launch first screen within 5 seconds after the application is launched. 5 second rule also applies even after the application is closed or deactivated and then restarted.

1. Application must respond to the user input in 20 seconds after launch. 20 second rule also applies even after the application is closed or deactivated and then restarted.

2. When Windows Phone Back button is pressed from first screen will exit the application. If the Back button is pressed from other then the first screen it must return to the previous page. In games if the Back button is pressed it should pause the game with context menu displayed and if the Back button is pressed again it will exit the pause.

3. Application cannot use more than 90MB of RAM. If the device has more than 256 MB the application can use more than 90 MB.

Phone Functionality

The application cannot prevent the use of phone's functionalities or hang when making a call, answering incoming call, ending a call, sending and receiving SMS or MMS messages.

Security

The application must not contain any virus and malware. Application must implement type-safe code as described in unsafe code and pointers (`http://msdn.microsoft.com/en-us/library/t2yzs44b(v=VS.80).aspx`). And finally the application must not run security critical code as described in security changes in the .Net Framework 4 (`http://msdn.microsoft.com/en-us/library/dd233103(v=VS.100).aspx`). Security is covered in greater detail in Chapter 19.

Technical Support Information

The application must include the application name, version, and technical support information.

Submitting Your First Windows Phone Application to the Windows Phone Marketplace

In above sections, you learned a great deal about how to pass through the Windows Phone Marketplace's validation and certification process by understanding the rules and process set forth to protect the consumer and the marketplace. Now you will be learn to deploy your first Windows Phone application to the marketplace so you can start making millions. Let's start first by learning to package the application for submission.

Package the application

To package the application you will use Visual Studio. For this demo you will use the Notepad project that you created in Chapter 3.

Open the Notepad solution found in the directory where you unzipped the source code that accompanies this book; the solution is found at [unzipped directory]\Codes\ch03\Notepad\Notepad.sln. Double click on the solution and Visual Studio will open Notepad solution.

1. When you see Visual Studio as seen in Figure 5–2 below click on Notepad solution found in the Solution Explorer and then select Release mode from the dropdown found in the menu.

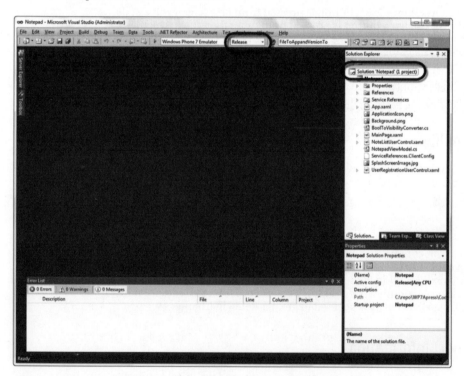

Figure 5–2. Compiling the phone application in Release mode

2. Press F6 to build the solution in Release mode.

3. When the build is done, you'll find the binaries under bin\release directory where the project file is located. To find out where the project file is, click on the Notepad project from the Solution Explorer. In the Properties window that appears you will see the project path in Project Folder property, as seen in Figure 5–3 below.

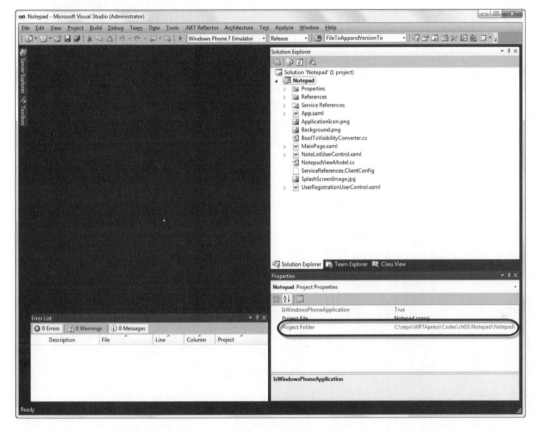

Figure 5–3. Project Folder property

4. In side of [your project folder]\bin\release you will find Notepad.xap which you will be using in next section to submit to the Windows Phone Marketplace.

Submit the application

From the above you compiled Notepad application and created Notepad.xap file. In this section you will be deploying the application.

Open your browser of choice and go to http://developer.windowsphone.com and sign into the portal.

1. You will see menu at the top called "my dashboard." Hover over the menu choose "child menu Windows Phone." When the page loads and if this is your first time submitting you application you will see Figure 5–4 shown below.

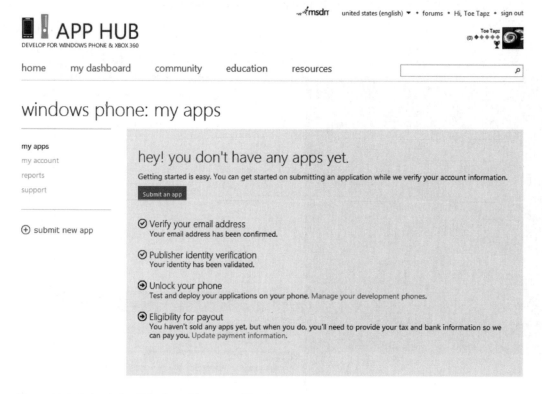

Figure 5–4. Submitting Windows Phone application: my apps page.

2. Click the "submit new app" button and the upload page will load as show in Figure 5–5 below.

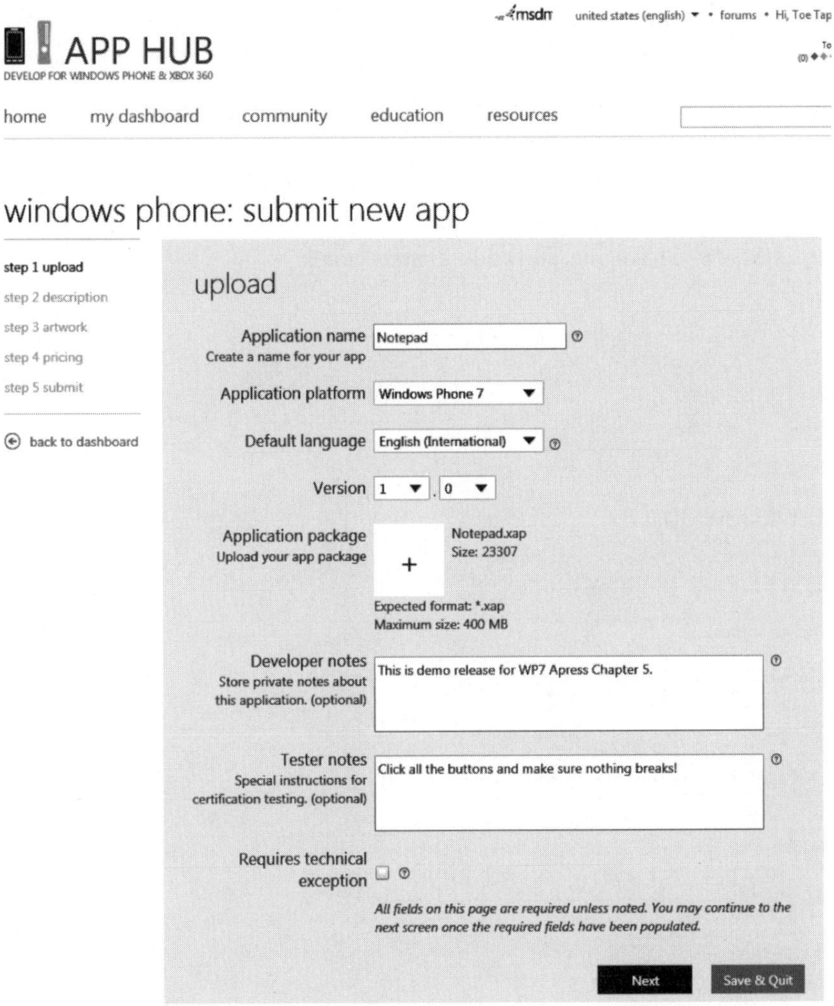

Figure 5–5. Submitting Windows Phone application: upload page

3. From upload page enter Application name, choose Application platform Windows Phone 7, English as Default language, choose initial version, click on Application package and browse to where Notepad.xap is found and select the xap file. Put developer note for yourself and Tester note to provide special instruction. See Figure 5–4 above when you completed the step and click Next button.

4. The description page shown in Figure 5–6 will load. Fill out the description dialogue by completing the following steps:

- Choose a category from the Category from dropdown menu that is appropriate for your application.

- Choose a Sub-category

- Add Detailed a description, and add a Featured app description, a single sentence that will catch a user's eye at the marketplace.

- Add key words that will be used during the search by the user at the marketplace.

- Add a legal URL if you have one, and add a contact email.

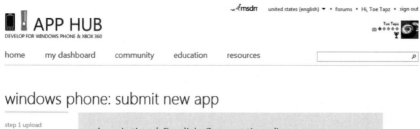

Figure 5–6. Submitting Windows Phone application: Description page

5.   The artwork page will load. You will be uploading large and small application tile, large pc application tile, and screenshots. The screen resolution is defined in the certification requirements document. Your screen should resemble Figure 5–7 below. The images that are used to upload in this step can be found in [directory where source code is unzipped]\Codes\ch05. Click Next button to continue.

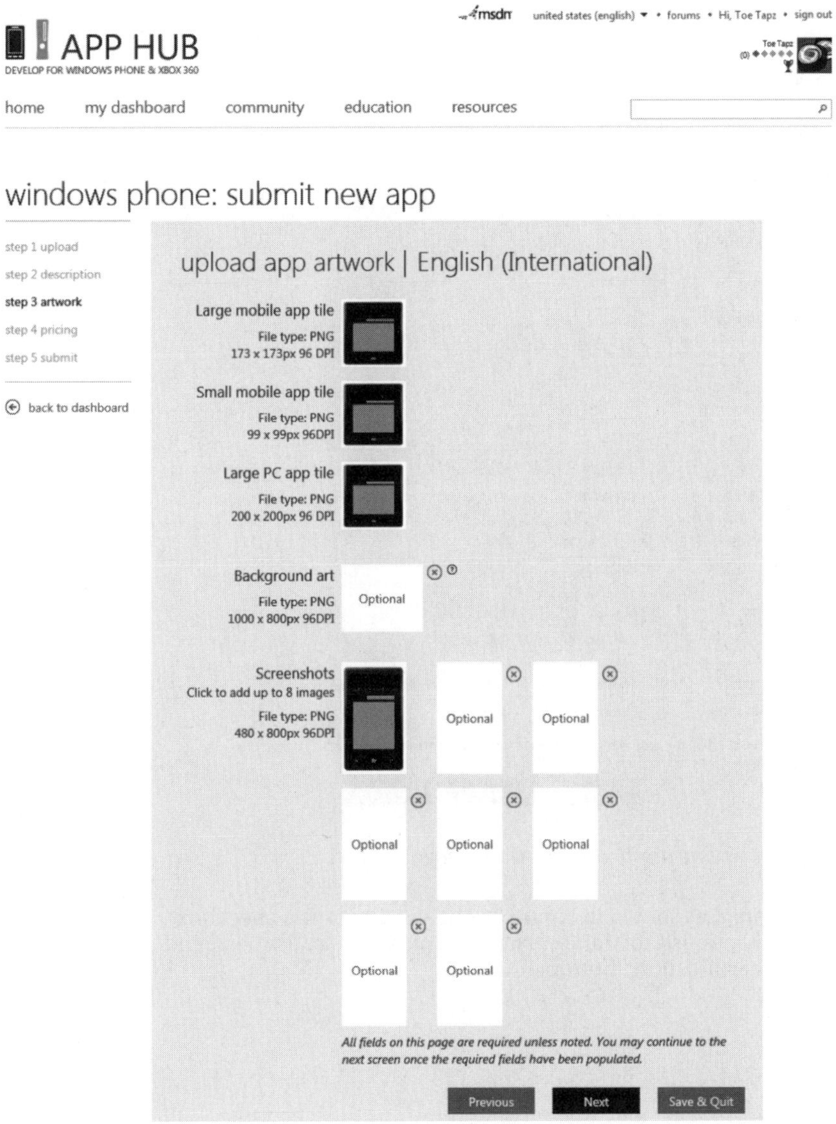

Figure 5–7. Submitting Windows Phone application: artwork page

6. The pricing page shown in Figure 5–8 will load. Choose currency and select application price. If you are targeting worldwide market select Worldwide distribution. Also if the application is trial application select Trial supported application. Your screen should resemble Figure 5–8 below. Click Next button to continue.

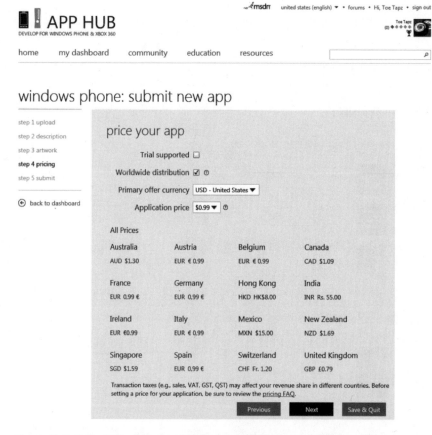

Figure 5–8. Submitting Windows Phone application: pricing page

7. The submit page will load as shown in Figure 5–9 below. Check the checkbox labeled "Automatically publish to Marketplace after passing certification" and click the "Submit for certification" button.

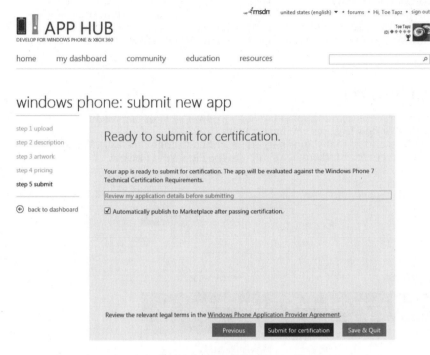

Figure 5–9. Submitting Windows Phone application: submit page

8. You will be returning to my apps page and you will see the application that you just submitted with testing in progress status as show in Figure 5–10 below.

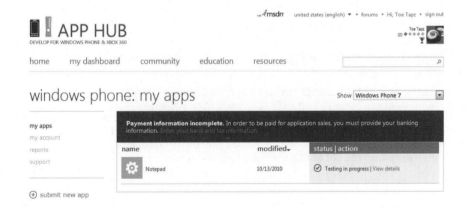

Figure 5–10. Submitted application with Testing in progress status

Congratulations. You have successfully submitted your Windows Phone application to the worldwide market of Windows Phone users for the price of 99 cents. If your application successfully passes through the certification process you will be notified by email. If your application fails the certification process you will be able to see the report of why your application failed and you will have option to resubmit.

Updating your application

In this section, you will learn to redeploy your application with a newer version that might contain fixes to the bugs users have reported or new features you have added.

When you log in to App Hub and go to my apps page as described in above sections. You will see your application that is published to the Marketplace similar to the Figure 5–11 below.

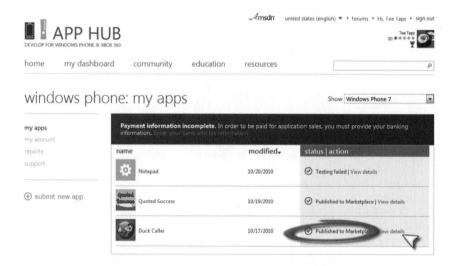

Figure 5–11. *Updating the application published to the Marketplace*

1. Click on the View Details link as show in Figure 5–11. You will find this link next to the application that you want to redeploy.

2. On next screen you will see Action dropdown and from the dropdown select Submit application update as show in Figure 5–12. Notice that Action dropdown contains other options like being able to change the price, removing the application from the Marketplace, and add completely different version of the same application in which case the consumers must buy the product again and where as with the update the consumers will get free update.

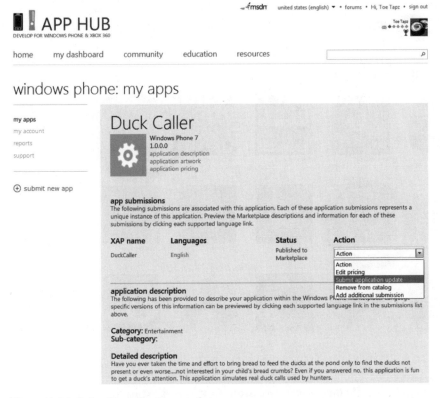

Figure 5–12. Submit application update

3. The remaining steps are exactly the same as those for submitting a new application to the Marketplace, as described in previous section. An update must go through the certification process again.

Finding your application in the Marketplace

In this section you will learn to find your application and view ratings and comments. You will be using Zune software that you download from http://www.zune.net/en-US/products/software/download/downloadsoftware.htm.

1. Install your downloaded Zune software.

2. Open up your Zune software found in your machine at Start ➤ All Programs ➤ Zune.

3. Follow the steps to configure Zune if it is first time use.

4. Once you are on the main page of Zune click on marketplace link and then click on the APPS link as shown in Figure 5–13.

Figure 5–13. Finding your application in the Marketplace using Zune

5. You can either search for your application or navigate to the category look for your application.

Summary

In this chapter, you learned a great deal about the Windows Phone Marketplace's certification requirements. And then you learned to package the application in Visual Studio to produce the xap file and submitted the application through the Windows Phone development portal for the certification process.

In the following chapters, you will begin to learn about the specific features of the Windows Phone. In Chapter 6, you will learn about the accelerometer that is very useful in programming games in order to use the phone like steering wheel. You will learn about using the accelerometer to detect the orientation of the phone or capture the phone shakes.

PART 2

■■■

Using Windows Phone 7 Technologies

In Part 2, you learn how to incorporate features of a standard Windows Phone and the Windows Phone platform into your applications, including the accelerometer, application bar, Windows Phone controls, location service, media elements, photos, push notifications, Reactive Extensions, browser controls, internationalization, trial applications, security, and integration with the Windows Phone OS. These are core features of Windows Phone that make the platform fun to work with and also give you access to features that can make your application stand out from the crowd.

Each chapter introduces a core feature of the phone and shows you, step-by-step—and with tested code examples—how to use it in your own applications. You will also gain an understanding of how these core features are being used in the real world, which, we hope, will inspire you to build great applications of your own.

CHAPTER 6

■■■

Working with the Accelerometer

An accelerometer has many practical uses for applications that depend on the movements of a Windows Phone in three-dimensional space. With data from an accelerometer, you can steer a simulated car in a driving game or fly a plane in a flight simulator. Capturing a motion such as a shake, a punch, a swing, or a slash and mixing accelerometer data with a physics engine can be used to create Wii-like games. Just for fun, you can build novelty applications to amaze your friends, such as a light saber simulation that makes Star Wars–like sounds as you swing your phone in the air. An accelerometer can even be used for business applications, like a level to use when you hang a picture frame. Under the covers, the controllers for games that run on consoles like the Wii remotes are nothing more than accelerometers wrapped in buttons and plastic.

The accelerometer in a Windows Phone measures the device's movements in space, or more precisely its acceleration along three axes—x, y, and z—relative to the Earth's gravitational pull, which is perpendicular to the ground (9.8 m/sec^2). Think of Newton's apple. When you drop an apple, it will fall toward the earth, and the force that pulls it can be calculated using that well-known high school science formula, Force = mass * acceleration. In a Windows Phone, the accelerometer can tell you the orientation of the phone with respect to the earth's gravitational force.

In this chapter, you will learn how to use the Windows Phone accelerometer to write applications that respond to the phone's orientation and movement. In the first example, you will learn to capture data from the accelerometer and to interpret the x, y, and z values. In a second demo, you will learn to use readings from the accelerometer to move a ball in 2D space.

Understanding Orientation and Movement

When you hold a Windows Phone in your hand with its display facing you, think of it as occupying the origin of a three-dimensional graph with its z axis pointing toward you (a positive direction), its y axis pointing down (a negative direction), and its x axis pointing toward the right (a positive direction). Figure 6–1 shows how these three axes are positioned relative to the device as you hold it facing toward you in your hand.

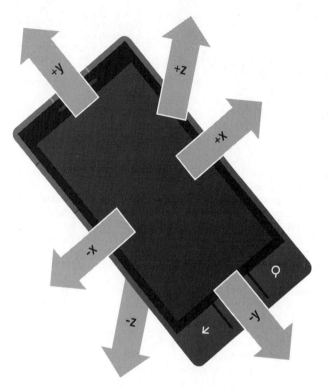

Figure 6–1. Accelerometer axis direction when you hold it in your hand facing toward you

To illustrate the accelerometer reading of the (x, y, z) = (0, -1, 0) means putting the phone on the table, standing up with the phone buttons facing downwards, with the front of the phone facing toward you, as shown in Figure 6–2.

If you were to rotate the phone in Figure 6–2 to the right 90 degrees, so that the Windows Phone control buttons are to the right, as shown in Figure 6–3, and the expected accelerometer readings will be (x, y, z) = (-1, 0, 0).

If you took the phone in Figure 6–2 and rotated it to the right 180 degrees, (x, y, z) would be (0, 1, 0), as shown in Figure 6–4.

If you were to rotate the phone in Figure 6–4 to the right 90 degrees, as shown in Figure 6–5, (x, y, z) would be (1, 0, 0).

If you were to put the phone flat on the table with the phone facing up, as shown in Figure 6–6, (x, y, z) would be (0, 0, 1).

If you put the phone facing down on the table, as shown in Figure 6–7, (x, y, z) would be (0, 0, 1).

Figure 6–2. *(x, y, z) = (0, -1, 0)*   *Figure 6–3.* *(x, y, z) = (-1, 0, 0)*   *Figure 6–4.* *(x, y, z) = (0, 1, 0)*

Figure 6–5. *(x, y, z) = (1, 0, 0)*   *Figure 6–6.* *(x, y, z) = (0, 0, -1)*   *Figure 6–7.* *(x, y, z) = (0, 0, 1)*

Calculating Distance

The so-called Euclidean distance algorithm is a useful way to calculate a distance between two points in three-dimensional space. This is a very useful equation that allows you to detect sudden movements such as the shaking of the phone.

If (Ox, Oy, Oz) is a previous accelerometer value and (Nx, Ny, Nz) is a new one, you can calculate Euclidean distance as follows.

$$EuclideanDistance = \sqrt{(Nx - Ox)^2 + (Ny - Oy)^2 + (Nz - Oz)^2}$$

Calculating Pitch and Roll

With obtained accelerometer readings you will have a pretty good understanding of the current orientation of the phone as seen in foregoing section, but using the accelerometer data, you can obtain much more information to understand how the phone is tilted on the x, y, and z axes. This information can be very useful if you are planning to create airplane simulation games or racing games that use the accelerometer to control the direction of moving objects. Think of it as using a phone like joystick by detecting the tilt motion.

When you hold the phone vertically, with the screen facing you, both the pitch and roll angles are 0 degrees, as shown in Figure 6–8.

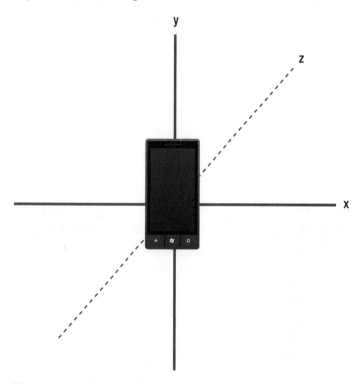

Figure 6–8. *Pitch and roll angles of 0 degrees*

Now if you tilt the phone slightly to the right, you will be able to calculate the pitch (ρ) and roll (φ) angles shown in Figure 6–9. Also there is another angle of interest, which would be theta, the angle respect to the z axis, which is not shown in Figure 6–9.

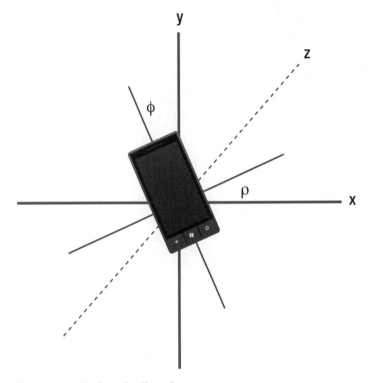

Figure 6–9. *Pitch and roll angles*

In order to calculate pitch (ρ), roll (φ), and theta angles you will need the following equations, where Ax, Ay, and Az are the accelerometer values for x, y, and z.

$$\rho = arctan\left(\frac{Ax}{\sqrt{Ay^2 + Az^2}}\right)$$

$$\varphi = arctan\left(\frac{Ay}{\sqrt{Ax^2 + Az^2}}\right)$$

$$\theta = arctan\left(\frac{\sqrt{Ax^2 + Ay^2}}{Az}\right)$$

You'll use both Euclidean distance and pitch and roll calculations in the examples that follow.

Introducing SDK Support for Accelerometers

In order to use the Windows Phone accelerometer, you'll need to reference the `Microsoft.Devices.Sensors` namespace, which contains the `Accelerometer` class. Among its members is the `ReadingChanged` event, which constantly updates the x, y, and z coordinates of the device as event arguments `e.X`, `e.Y`, and `e.Z`, with a `Timestamp` that can be used to calculate velocity, acceleration, and other values.

There are two things that you must remember about the accelerometer device. First is that heavy use of the accelerometer will use up the battery of the phone, and thus you must remember to turn it on only when it is needed and turn it off when done. Second, the accelerometer runs on a thread that is completely separate from the thread on which the current UI runs. This means that you must use `Deployment.Current.Dispatcher.BeginInvoke` to update the UI, otherwise you will receive "Invalid cross thread exception."

Retrieving Accelerometer Data

You will begin by building a simple application that captures the accelerometer data. The accelerometer data consist of acceleration data in x, y, z directions and time in which the acceleration data was captured. Figure 6–10 displays the basic UI of the accelerometer data captured. In order for this demo to work, you must deploy the project to an actual Windows Phone device—please refer to Chapter 4 for deploying to the device. If you do not have a Windows Phone device, you might consider using Reactive Extension to simulate the accelerometer behavior. Reactive Extension will not be covered in this chapter, but you can refer to Chapter 18 for more detail on how to create simulation in order to work with the accelerometer in the emulator.

Figure 6–10. CaptureAccelerometerData demo

You will build the demo in three steps. First, you'll need to create a Visual Studio project. Next you will build the project's user interface, and then you'll finish up by adding the code the application needs to retrieve and display data from the accelerometer.

Creating the CaptureAccelerometerData Project

To set up the CaptureAccelerometerData project, follow the steps you've used for previous examples in this book.

1. Open Microsoft Visual Studio 2010 Express for Windows Phone on your workstation.

2. Create a new Windows Phone Application by selecting File ➤ New Project on the Visual Studio command menu. Select the Windows Phone Application template, name the application "CaptureAccelerometerData," and click OK.

3. In order to use the accelerometer, add an assembly reference to `Microsoft.Devices.Sensors` by right-clicking the `References` folder in Solution Explorer and choose `Microsoft.Devices.Sensors` from the Add Reference window, as shown in Figure 6–11.

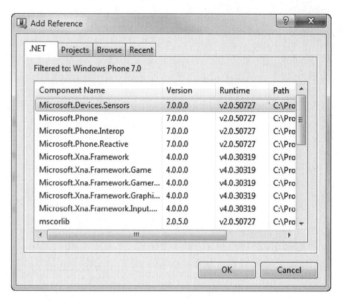

Figure 6–11. *Adding a reference to* `Microsoft.Devices.Sensors`

Building the User Interface

You will be building the user interface using the XAML in the Visual Studio. For building simple controls, it is faster to work with the XAML code. Go to Solution Explorer, open `MainPage.xaml`, and replace the XAML you find there with the following code.

Declaring the UI Resources

The namespaces you see in the following code snippet are typically declared by default when you first create a Windows Phone project. In particular, the namespaces `xmlns:phone="clr-namespace:Microsoft.Phone.Controls; assembly=Microsoft.Phone"` allow you to add common Windows Phone controls to the application main page.

```
<phone:PhoneApplicationPage
    x:Class="CaptureAccelerometerData.MainPage"
    xmlns="http://schemas.microsoft.com/winfx/2006/xaml/presentation"
    xmlns:x="http://schemas.microsoft.com/winfx/2006/xaml"
    xmlns:phone="clr-namespace:Microsoft.Phone.Controls;assembly=Microsoft.Phone"
    xmlns:shell="clr-namespace:Microsoft.Phone.Shell;assembly=Microsoft.Phone"
    xmlns:d="http://schemas.microsoft.com/expression/blend/2008"
    xmlns:mc="http://schemas.openxmlformats.org/markup-compatibility/2006"
    FontFamily="{StaticResource PhoneFontFamilyNormal}"
    FontSize="{StaticResource PhoneFontSizeNormal}"
    Foreground="{StaticResource PhoneForegroundBrush}"
    SupportedOrientations="Portrait" Orientation="Portrait"
    mc:Ignorable="d" d:DesignWidth="480" d:DesignHeight="768"
    shell:SystemTray.IsVisible="True">
```

Building the Main Page and Adding Components

Now create the components you need to display the x, y, z values, and the time reading that your application captures from the accelerometer. You'll also want to add components to display the pitch, roll, and theta values of the device, which you will calculate and use to understand how the phone is oriented. Finally, you also need buttons to start and to stop the accelerometer, which are also specified in this snippet.

```xml
<Grid x:Name="LayoutRoot" Background="Transparent">
    <Grid.RowDefinitions>
        <RowDefinition Height="Auto"/>
        <RowDefinition Height="*"/>
    </Grid.RowDefinitions>

    <StackPanel x:Name="TitlePanel" Grid.Row="0" Margin="24,24,0,12">
        <TextBlock x:Name="ApplicationTitle" Text="CaptureAccelerometer Data"
Style="{StaticResource PhoneTextNormalStyle}"/>
    </StackPanel>

    <Grid x:Name="ContentGrid" Grid.Row="1">
        <TextBlock Name="txtX" Text="TextBlock"
                    Margin="160,56,12,0" FontSize="20"
                    Height="31" VerticalAlignment="Top" />
        <TextBlock Name="txtY" Text="TextBlock"
                    Margin="160,119,12,556" FontSize="20" />
        <TextBlock Name="txtZ" Text="TextBlock"
                    Margin="155,181,12,490" FontSize="20" />
        <TextBlock Name="txtTime" Text="TextBlock"
                    Margin="155,244,12,427" FontSize="20" />
        <Button Content="Start" Height="72"
                Name="btnStart" Width="160"
                Margin="36,514,284,119" Click="btnStart_Click" />
        <Button Content="Stop" Height="72"
                Name="btnStop" Width="160"
                Margin="207,514,113,119" Click="btnStop_Click" />
        <TextBlock FontSize="40" Margin="66,34,331,614"
                    Name="lblX" Text="X" />
        <TextBlock FontSize="40" Margin="66,97,331,552"
                    Name="lblY" Text="Y" />
        <TextBlock FontSize="40" Margin="66,159,346,489"
                    Name="lblZ" Text="Z" />
        <TextBlock FontSize="40" Margin="12,222,331,422"
                    Name="lblTime" Text="Time" />
        <TextBlock FontSize="20" Margin="160,285,7,386"
                    Name="txtPitch" Text="TextBlock" />
        <TextBlock FontSize="22" Margin="0,283,370,365"
                    Name="textBlock3" Text="Pitch" TextAlignment="Right" />
        <TextBlock FontSize="20" Margin="160,345,7,326"
                    Name="txtRoll" Text="TextBlock" />
        <TextBlock FontSize="22" Margin="0,343,370,305"
                    Name="textBlock4" Text="Roll" TextAlignment="Right" />
```

```
        <TextBlock FontSize="20" Margin="160,408,7,263"
                   Name="txtTheta" Text="TextBlock" />
        <TextBlock FontSize="22" Margin="0,406,370,242"
                   Name="textBlock6" Text="Theta" TextAlignment="Right" />
    </Grid>

</phone:PhoneApplicationPage>
```

Once you have loaded the XAML code, you should see the layout shown in Figure 6–12. In the next section, you will be adding events to the updating of the UI with captured accelerometer data.

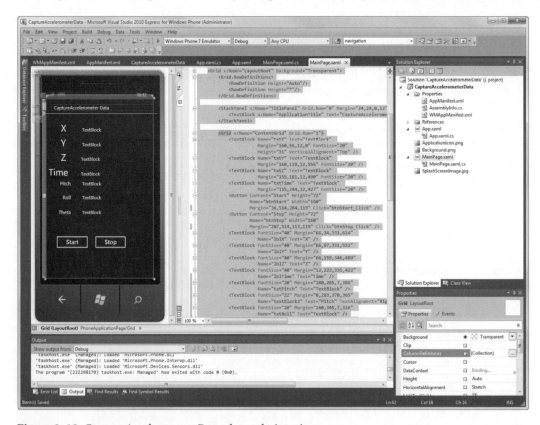

Figure 6–12. CaptureAccelerometerData demo design view

Coding the Application

In Solution Explorer, open MainPage.xaml.cs and replace the code there with the following C# code blocks that will implement the UI updates using accelerometer data.

Specifying the Namespaces

Begin by listing the namespaces the application will use. Notice our inclusion of
Microsoft.Devices.Sensors that will allow you to start and stop Windows Phone's accelerometer.

```
using System;
using System.Windows;
using Microsoft.Phone.Controls;
using Microsoft.Devices.Sensors;
namespace CaptureAccelerometerData
{
    public partial class MainPage : PhoneApplicationPage
    {
```

Initializing Variables

The variable _ac, an Accelerometer object, will be used to start and stop, and retrieve x, y, z and time.
Also notice the inclusion of the ReadingChanged event, which you'll draw on to send captured
accelerometer data to your UI.

```
Accelerometer _ac;

        public MainPage()
        {
            InitializeComponent();

            _ac = new Accelerometer();
            _ac.ReadingChanged += new
EventHandler<AccelerometerReadingEventArgs>(_ac_ReadingChanged);
        }
```

Capturing and Displaying Accelerometer Data

Notice here that you cannot directly change the UI elements upon receiving the accelerometer data
because the accelerometer data comes from a different thread than the current UI thread. If you try to
change the UI elements directly here you will get an "Invalid cross-thread access" error, as shown in
Figure 6–13. In order to overcome this problem, you must use the Dispatcher in the current UI thread, as
shown in the following code.

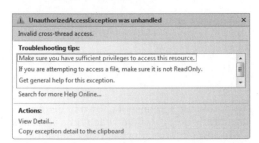

Figure 6–13. Invalid cross-thread access error

```csharp
        private void ProcessAccelerometerReading(AccelerometerReadingEventArgs e)
        {
            txtTime.Text = e.Timestamp.ToString();
            txtX.Text = e.X.ToString();
            txtY.Text = e.Y.ToString();
            txtZ.Text = e.Z.ToString();
            txtPitch.Text = RadianToDegree((Math.Atan(e.X / Math.Sqrt(Math.Pow(e.Y, 2) +
Math.Pow(e.Z, 2))))).ToString();
            txtRoll.Text = RadianToDegree((Math.Atan(e.Y / Math.Sqrt(Math.Pow(e.X, 2) +
Math.Pow(e.Z, 2))))).ToString();
            txtTheta.Text = RadianToDegree((Math.Atan(Math.Sqrt(Math.Pow(e.X, 2) +
Math.Pow(e.Y, 2))/ e.Z))).ToString();
        }
```

Implementing Start and Stop of Accelerometer

Implement the button event for stopping and starting the accelerometer. Notice here that you must anticipate the possible error that might occur when you are trying to start or stop the accelerometer.

```csharp
private void btnStart_Click(object sender, RoutedEventArgs e)
        {
            try
            {
                _ac.Start();
            }
            catch (AccelerometerFailedException)
            {
                MessageBox.Show("Acceleromter failed to start.");
            }
        }

        private void btnStop_Click(object sender, RoutedEventArgs e)
        {
            try
            {
                _ac.Stop();
            }
            catch (AccelerometerFailedException)
            {
                MessageBox.Show("Acceleromter failed to stop.");
            }
        }
    }
}
```

Testing the Finished Application

To test the finished application, press F5. The result should resemble the screenshot shown in Figure 6–10, and you will see that the x, y, z, and time text blocks are constantly being updated each time you click the Start button. Remember that to run the application on a Windows Phone 7 device, you must choose the "Windows Phone 7 Device" option shown in Figure 6–14.

Figure 6–14. *Choosing a Windows Phone 7 device before running the application*

Using Accelerometer Data to Move a Ball

In this second demo, you will learn to use the captured accelerometer data to do something more useful: moving the image of a ball as you tilt the phone left, right, forward, and back. This demo has many uses in helping you understand how to translate the user input of the accelerometer data and apply it to UI elements. Figure 6–15 displays the basic UI of the MoveBallDemo.

Figure 6–15. MoveBallDemo UI

Creating the MoveBall Project

To set up the CaptureAccelerometerData project, follow the steps you've used for previous examples in this book.

1. Open Microsoft Visual Studio 2010 Express for Windows Phone on your workstation.

2. Create a new Windows Phone Application by selecting File ➤ New Project in the Visual Studio command menu. Select the Windows Phone Application template, name the application "MoveBallDemo," and click OK.

3. In order to use the accelerometer, add an assembly reference to `Microsoft.Devices.Sensors` by right-clicking the `References` folder in Solution Explorer and choose `Microsoft.Devices.Sensors` from the Add Reference window, as shown in Figure 6–11 above.

Building the User Interface

You will be building the user interface using the XAML in Visual Studio. For building simple controls, it is faster to work with the XAML code. Go to Solution Explorer, open `MainPage.xaml`, and replace the XAML you find there with the following codes.

Declaring the UI Resources

The namespaces you see here are typically declared by default when you first create the Windows Phone project, and the namespaces like `xmlns:phone="clr-namespace:Microsoft.Phone.Controls;assembly=Microsoft.Phone"` will allow you to add common Windows Phone controls.

```
<phone:PhoneApplicationPage
    x:Class="MoveBallDemo.MainPage"
    xmlns="http://schemas.microsoft.com/winfx/2006/xaml/presentation"
    xmlns:x="http://schemas.microsoft.com/winfx/2006/xaml"
    xmlns:phone="clr-namespace:Microsoft.Phone.Controls;assembly=Microsoft.Phone"
    xmlns:shell="clr-namespace:Microsoft.Phone.Shell;assembly=Microsoft.Phone"
    xmlns:d="http://schemas.microsoft.com/expression/blend/2008"
    xmlns:mc="http://schemas.openxmlformats.org/markup-compatibility/2006"
    FontFamily="{StaticResource PhoneFontFamilyNormal}"
    FontSize="{StaticResource PhoneFontSizeNormal}"
    Foreground="{StaticResource PhoneForegroundBrush}"
    SupportedOrientations="Portrait" Orientation="Portrait"
    mc:Ignorable="d" d:DesignWidth="480" d:DesignHeight="768"
    shell:SystemTray.IsVisible="True">
```

Building the Main Page and Adding Components

The UI consists of Start and Stop buttons for stopping and starting the accelerometer and a ball that moves as the Windows Phone is tilted left, right, forward, and backward.

```
    <Grid x:Name="LayoutRoot" Background="Transparent">
        <Grid.RowDefinitions>
            <RowDefinition Height="Auto"/>
            <RowDefinition Height="*"/>
        </Grid.RowDefinitions>

        <StackPanel x:Name="TitlePanel" Grid.Row="0" Margin="24,24,0,12">
            <TextBlock x:Name="ApplicationTitle" Text="MoveBallDemo"
Style="{StaticResource PhoneTextNormalStyle}"/>
        </StackPanel>
        <Button Content="Start" Height="72"
                HorizontalAlignment="Left" x:Name="btnStart"
                VerticalAlignment="Top" Width="160"
                Click="btnStart_Click" Margin="8,537,0,0"
                Grid.Row="1" d:LayoutOverrides="HorizontalAlignment" />
        <Button Content="Stop" Height="72"
                HorizontalAlignment="Left" x:Name="btnStop"
                VerticalAlignment="Top" Width="160"
                Click="btnStop_Click" Margin="168,537,0,0"
```

```
            Grid.Row="1" />

    <Canvas x:Name="ContentGrid" Margin="0,8,8,0"
            Grid.Row="1" HorizontalAlignment="Right"
            Width="472" Height="479" VerticalAlignment="Top">
        <Ellipse x:Name="ball" Canvas.Left="126"
                Fill="#FF963C3C" HorizontalAlignment="Left"
                Height="47" Stroke="Black" StrokeThickness="1"
                VerticalAlignment="Top" Width="46"
                Canvas.Top="222"/>
    </Canvas>
</Grid>

</phone:PhoneApplicationPage>
```

Once you've loaded the XAML code, you should see the layout shown in Figure 6–16. Now it's time to animate the ball and add the sound effect by wiring up some events, which you'll do next.

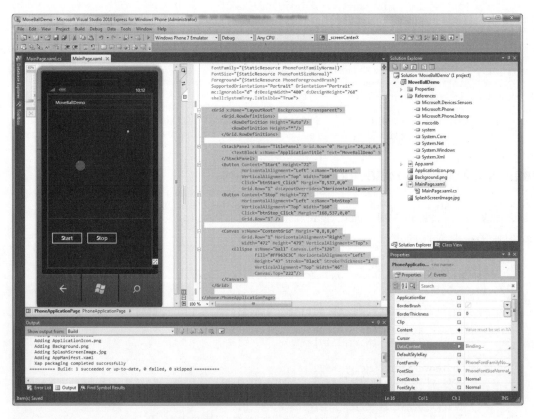

Figure 6–16. MoveBall demo design view

Coding the Application

In Solution Explorer, open `MainPage.xaml.cs` and replace the code there with the following code C# code blocks.

Specifying the Namespaces

Begin by listing the namespaces the application will use. Notice our inclusion of `Microsoft.Devices.Sensors` that will allow us to start and stop Windows Phone's accelerometer.

```csharp
using System;
using System.Windows;
using System.Windows.Controls;
using Microsoft.Phone.Controls;
using Microsoft.Devices.Sensors;

namespace MoveBallDemo
{
    public partial class MainPage : PhoneApplicationPage
    {
```

Initializing Variables

The variable `_ac`, an `Accelerometer` object, will be used to start and stop the sensor, and retrieve x, y, z and time value. Also notice the `ReadingChanged` event, which sends the captured accelerometer data to be displayed in the UI. Also the starting position of the ball is set to the center of the canvas where the ball is placed.

```csharp
        private Accelerometer _ac;

        public MainPage()
        {
            InitializeComponent();

            SupportedOrientations = SupportedPageOrientation.Portrait;

            ball.SetValue(Canvas.LeftProperty, ContentGrid.Width / 2);
            ball.SetValue(Canvas.TopProperty, ContentGrid.Height / 2);

            _ac = new Accelerometer();
            _ac.ReadingChanged += new
EventHandler<AccelerometerReadingEventArgs>(ac_ReadingChanged);
        }
```

Handling Captured Accelerometer Data

Notice that here, as in the previous demo, you cannot directly change the UI elements upon receiving the accelerometer data because the accelerometer data comes from a different thread than the current UI thread. If you try to change the UI elements directly here, you will get an "Invalid cross-thread access" error, as shown in Figure 6–13 In order to overcome this problem, you must use the Dispatcher in the current UI thread, as shown in the following code.

```
private void ac_ReadingChanged(object sender, AccelerometerReadingEventArgs e)
{
    Deployment.Current.Dispatcher.BeginInvoke(() => MyReadingChanged(e));
}
```

Applying Captured Accelerometer Data to the Ball

The following code achieves the behavior where if the phone is tilted in vertically with the display facing toward you, based on the algorithm specified in the method, the ball will fall straight very fast. But if you tilt the phone slightly while the display is facing up, the ball will slowly slide to the direction in which the phone is tilted.

```
private void MyReadingChanged(AccelerometerReadingEventArgs e)
{
    double distanceToTravel = 2;
    double accelerationFactor = Math.Abs(e.Z) == 0 ? 0.1 : Math.Abs(e.Z);
    double ballX = (double)ball.GetValue(Canvas.LeftProperty) +
distanceToTravel * e.X / accelerationFactor;
    double ballY = (double)ball.GetValue(Canvas.TopProperty) -
distanceToTravel * e.Y / accelerationFactor;

    if (ballX < 0)
    {
        ballX = 0;
    }
    else if (ballX > ContentGrid.Width)
    {
        ballX = ContentGrid.Width;
    }

    if (ballY < 0)
    {
        ballY = 0;
    }
    else if (ballY > ContentGrid.Height)
    {
        ballY = ContentGrid.Height;
    }

    ball.SetValue(Canvas.LeftProperty, ballX);
    ball.SetValue(Canvas.TopProperty, ballY);
}
```

Adding Start and Stop Button Events

Implement the button event for stopping and starting the accelerometer.

```
private void btnStart_Click(object sender, RoutedEventArgs e)
{
    if (_ac == null)
    {
        _ac = new Accelerometer();
```

```
            }
            _ac.Start();
        }

        private void btnStop_Click(object sender, RoutedEventArgs e)
        {
            if (_ac == null)
            {
                _ac = new Accelerometer();
            }
            _ac.Stop();
        }
    }
}
```

Testing the Finished Application

To test the finished application, press F5. Remember to choose to run the application on a Windows Phone 7 device, as shown in Figure 6–15 Once the application runs on the Windows Phone, click the Start button. Tilt the phone and watch the ball move in the direction the phone is being tilted.

Summary

In this chapter, you learned about the fundamentals of the accelerometer. In the first demo, you learned to capture the accelerometer data and display it by updating UI elements on the currently executing UI thread. In the second demo, you learned to move a ball on the phone screen by using captured accelerometer data to calculate its speed and position.

In Chapter 7, you will learn to create an application bar to create shortcuts for the most commonly used tasks in the application and how to design it to deliver a compelling application.

CHAPTER 7

■ ■ ■

Application Bar

When you are ready to program your Windows Phone 7 application in Visual Studio, in most cases you will be aware of the general features that your application will provide. Each of the major application features will need to be accessible via a shortcut or some form of a navigation menu. For Windows Phone 7 applications, Microsoft recommends that you use a standard Windows Phone 7 Application Bar to provide shortcuts for most common tasks within the application. We have covered Metro User Interface design concepts for Windows Phone 7 in Part 1 of this book. The use of an Application Bar within the application helps ensure that these guidelines are properly observed.

An Application Bar is essentially a Windows Phone 7 menu system with clickable icons that conform to the general Metro UI guidelines provided by Microsoft. For example, take a look at the Windows Phone 7 version of the popular social networking application Foursquare (one place you can find its screenshots is 4square.codeplex.com). At the bottom of the screen, you will see an Application Bar with shortcuts to most common features of the application. Another example is Graphic.ly (www.pcworld.com/article/191549/graphicly.html), which is an application that uses Deep Zoom capabilities of Silverlight to provide an immersive comic book reading experience. On its Application Bar, Graphic.ly naturally has shortcuts to zoom into and zoom out of the comic book contents, since those features are the most important ones for that application.

Within each application, two types of Application Bars can be present: a global Application Bar and a local one. If a global Application Bar is defined, then it can be added to any .xaml page within the application via a single XAML statement. Alternately, a local Application Bar would be local to a single page and must be defined for each .xaml page separately. You will create both global and local Application Bars in this chapter. The position of the Application Bar on the screen varies with the phone orientation. When the phone is in default portrait orientation, an Application Bar is displayed as a single row of icons at the bottom of the screen. Figure 7–1 shows an example of an Application Bar with three icons for Add, Save, and Delete. The ellipsis to the right of the Delete button signifies the presence of additional shortcuts in the Application Bar (called Menu Items) that will become visible to you when you click that ellipsis button. In this chapter, we'll show you how to create visually appealing application bars that conform to the best practices published by Microsoft.

Figure 7–1. An Application Bar with Add (+ icon), Save (disk icon), and Delete (trash can icon) on Windows Phone 7

Introducing the Application Bar

The contents of an Application Bar are limited to a maximum of four elements. The elements are added and are automatically centered in the Application Bar from left to right. Additional application shortcuts can be added to the Application Bar via text-based menu items and are hidden from view by default. The presence of an ellipsis to the right of the main Application Bar icons hints that, in addition to the main icons, there are text-based menu items in the Application Bar. These items serve as additional shortcuts and slide up as a list when the user clicks the ellipsis or the empty space right underneath the ellipsis. An example of what the phone screen looks like when there are menu items present in the application and the ellipsis is pressed is shown in Figure 7–2.

There is good news and bad news when it comes to working with the Application Bar. The good news is that it's easy to create and comes by default with a lot of built-in functionality that you don't have to code. For example, when the phone changes orientation from portrait to landscape, the Application Bar automatically moves to the left side of the phone screen. In addition, there is a default animation for showing text-based menu items (shown in Figure 7–2) that did not fit in the four main icon slots on the Application Bar. Finally, a minor but handy feature that ensures consistent user experience is the automatic addition of a circle around each Application Bar icon (i.e., you as the developer do not have to draw it) and the conversion of textual menu items to lower-case text.

The bad news is that there is little flexibility for creating icons and menus for the Application Bar. The height of the Application Bar is fixed and cannot be changed. The size of the icons in the Application Bar is 48 pixels wide and 48 pixels high (generally expressed as 48x48); icons of other sizes will be scaled to fit that size, which usually means distortion and is not recommended. The actual graphic within the icon has to be 26x26 pixels to properly fit within the circle that the Application Bar automatically draws for each icon. Microsoft also recommends that you always try to use default system theme colors for the Application Bar because the use of custom colors can lead to unpredictable and potentially unfavorable effects on display quality, menu animations, and power consumption.

In the following section, you will learn how to create an Application Bar that looks like Figure 7–2. Later on in this chapter, we will write code to react to Application Bar events and access features of our application.

Adding an Application Bar to a Windows Phone 7 Application

Windows Phone 7 provides two types of Application Bar for use with phones apps: a global bar and a local bar. The global Application Bar must be defined in `App.xaml`, and it can be added to any page within the Windows Phone 7 application with a single line of XAML code. There are two ways to define a local Application Bar and add it to a particular application page:

1. Using XAML

2. Using Managed Code (i.e., C#)

You'll get to try both methods in this chapter, where you'll learn to build an Application Bar that provides simple functionality and asks for a person's name, then acts like that name has been saved to the database or the cloud storage. Regardless of the approach you choose and regardless of whether you are building a local or a global Application Bar, there is a preparatory step you should take before you can properly display and use it. That step involves adding images for your Application Bar buttons to project resources.

Figure 7–2. Application Bar with menu items shown. Note how menu items appear in lower-case, regardless of the letter casing when they were created.

Adding Images for Use with Application Bar Buttons

Because the maximum size of each Application Bar icon is 48x48 pixels, the size of each icon you add is limited to 26x26 pixels so that a circle can be properly drawn around it. Since Windows Phone 7 supports the concept of themes, the background of an icon has to match the rest of the theme, and therefore should be made transparent. On this transparent background, the actual graphic should have white foreground color using an alpha channel. Fortunately, in many cases, you won't have to create icons yourself, since Microsoft has released a set of commonly used images for Windows Phone 7, all properly sized and formatted in Microsoft's approved style. You can grab a copy of those icons here: www.microsoft.com/downloads/details.aspx?FamilyID=369b20f7-9d30-4cff-8a1b-f80901b2da93&displaylang=en.

■ **Tip** Like everything else on the Internet, the aforementioned URL is subject to change. If, for some reason, you are not able to download icons by using that link, simply go to bing.com and search for "Application Bar Icons for Windows Phone 7 Series."

---

1. Once you've downloaded the small 260KB ZIP file containing the images, unzip them to an easy-to-access location on your computer. Follow the next steps to properly include those images into the project. Start off by creating a new Visual Studio Project and naming it ApplicationBarSample.

2. Next, let's organize the project for easier readability by creating a folder for the icon images you'll use in the ApplicationBarSample project. Right-click the project name in the Solution Explorer, select Add➤New Folder. Name the folder "Images."

3. Next, copy the downloaded icon images to the newly created folder within your project. Using Windows Explorer, go to the folder to which you downloaded the zipped icons file and copy the image files you need from there to the Images folder of your project. In the example that follows, you will be using the images located in the WP7AppBarIcons_basic_shellcommon\dark subfolder of the downloaded archive. Make sure to copy the *.png files only, without any folder structure.

4. Now the images are copied, but the Visual Studio still needs to make them a part of the project. Right-click Solution Explorer, then select Add➤Existing Item. Select all images by clicking each one while holding the Ctrl key down, or (quicker) by clicking the first image, holding down the Shift key, and then clicking the last image in the set.

5. Finally, you need to instruct Visual Studio to include new images in every build. For each image, right-click the image in the Solution Explorer and choose Properties (you can also press F4 to bring up the Properties dialog). In the Properties dialog box, set the Build action to "Content" and set the Copy to Output property to "Copy Always," as shown in Figure 7–3.

Figure 7–3. For each image, make sure to set Build Action to "Content" and Copy to Output Directory to "Copy Always".

Now that the project knows where to find the icon images for an Application Bar, it's time to create a project to showcase the Application Bar's features.

Adding a Global Application Bar Using XAML

A global Application Bar is created as an application resource in the app.xaml section. Follow these steps to create and add a global Application Bar.

1. In Solution Explorer, right-click the App.xaml file for the ApplicationBarSample project and select Open. This action causes Visual Studio to display the XAML code for the application's resource and configuration page.

2. Next, you need to paste the complete XAML definition of the Application Bar with three icons and two menu items in the Application Resources section. Locate the <Application.Resources> section of the App.xaml and paste the following code within that section. Note that setting the Text property for each control is required:

```
<shell:ApplicationBar x:Key="GlobalAppMenuBar" Opacity="1" IsVisible="True"
IsMenuEnabled="True">
        <shell:ApplicationBar.Buttons>
            <shell:ApplicationBarIconButton IconUri="/Images/appbar.add.rest.png"
Text="add">
            </shell:ApplicationBarIconButton>
            <shell:ApplicationBarIconButton IconUri="/Images/appbar.save.rest.png"
Text="save">
            </shell:ApplicationBarIconButton>
            <shell:ApplicationBarIconButton IconUri="/Images/appbar.delete.rest.png"
Text="delete">
            </shell:ApplicationBarIconButton>
        </shell:ApplicationBar.Buttons>
        <shell:ApplicationBar.MenuItems>
            <shell:ApplicationBarMenuItem Text="Menu Item 1" IsEnabled="True">
            </shell:ApplicationBarMenuItem>
            <shell:ApplicationBarMenuItem Text="Menu Item 2" IsEnabled="True">
            </shell:ApplicationBarMenuItem>
        </shell:ApplicationBar.MenuItems>
    </shell:ApplicationBar>
```

3. With the global Application Bar defined, you are ready to add it to the pages within our application. Open MainPage.xaml and add the following attribute within the <phone:PhoneApplicationPage> node:

```
ApplicationBar="{StaticResource GlobalAppMenuBar}"
```

4. Press F5 to run the application. You should see an Application Bar identical to the one shown in Figure 7–2.

Before moving onto the next section and taking a look at a local Application Bar, let's clean up the MainPage.xaml code by removing the ApplicationBar="{StaticResource GlobalAppMenuBar}" XAML. If we don't do that, we will get an application exception after we add a local Application Bar.

Adding a Local Application Bar Using XAML

One of the two ways to add a local Application Bar to a Windows Phone 7 application is to use XAML markup. Using XAML markup wherever possible is considered best practice since it allows for the separation of design (XAML) and logic (C#) of an application. The following steps show the XAML you need to add to ApplicationBarSample to construct a local Application Bar for the app.

1. In Solution Explorer, right-click the `MainPage.xaml` and select Open. This action causes Visual Studio to display the XAML code for the application's main page.

2. You must define a PhoneNavigation element within XAML before adding an Application Bar. To accomplish that, inside the `phone:PhoneApplicationPage`, add a `phone:PhoneApplicationPage.ApplicationBar` element, as shown here. Notice how this element is automatically available for selection via Visual Studio IntelliSense once you start typing the first few characters—an excellent way to ensure that there are no spelling errors.

```
<phone:PhoneApplicationPage.ApplicationBar>
</phone:PhoneApplicationPage.ApplicationBar>
```

3. It is now time to add the Application Bar XAML to the page. Inside the `phone:PhoneApplicationPage.ApplicationBar` element, add a `shell:ApplicationBar` element. Set the `IsVisible` and the `IsMenuEnabled` properties to `True`, and set the `Opacity` property to 1, as illustrated here.

```
<shell:ApplicationBar Opacity="1" IsVisible="True" IsMenuEnabled="True">
    </shell:ApplicationBar>
```

4. Now that you have created an Application Bar in XAML, you are ready to create buttons for it. The buttons you add are a part of the `shell:ApplicationBar.Buttons` element, so let's go ahead and add that element now inside the `shell:ApplicationBar` element:

```
<shell:ApplicationBar.Buttons>
</shell:ApplicationBar.Buttons>
```

5. Inside the `shell:ApplicationBar` element, you will create three `shell:ApplicationBarIconButton` XAML elements to add three button definitions: one for Add, one for Save, and one for Delete. If we had any text-based menu items to add, the ellipsis in the right corner of the Application Bar would be created automatically for us by Windows Phone 7. The ellipsis is not counted as one of the buttons on the Application Bar; therefore we could have a maximum of four buttons plus an ellipsis. The XAML markup to add three buttons is shown here:

```
<shell:ApplicationBarIconButton IconUri="/Images/appbar.add.rest.png" Text="add">
</shell:ApplicationBarIconButton>
        <shell:ApplicationBarIconButton IconUri="/Images/appbar.save.rest.png" Text="save">
        </shell:ApplicationBarIconButton>
        <shell:ApplicationBarIconButton IconUri="/Images/appbar.delete.rest.png"
Text="delete">
        </shell:ApplicationBarIconButton>
```

6.   Note that the `IconUri` properties in this code snippet refer to the default names of the images that come as part of the download from Microsoft. If you have changed default names of those images, make sure to properly edit the reference used in `IconUri` as well. Also note the Text element—it is a required element and it cannot be an empty string. This text will be visible if you click the ellipsis in the right corner of the Application Bar, as shown in Figure 7–2.

7.   At this point, you are done creating Icon Buttons and should make sure that the `shell:ApplicationBar.Buttons` element is properly closed. You can go ahead and press F5 to view the results of your work—the Application Bar containing three items should be shown at the bottom of the phone screen.

Now it's time to add some menu items to the Application Bar. Since menu items are text-based, they are useful in cases where text conveys a better meaning of the shortcut than an icon in the Application Bar. Of course, if we need more than four items to be present in the Application Bar, our only choice is to resort to menu items. In the next section, we'll add menu items to our Application Bar.

Adding Menu Items

Let's add two menu items, "Menu Item 1" and "Menu Item 2," to the `ApplicationBarSample` app.

1.   All menu items are a part of `shell:ApplicationBar.MenuItems` element, so go ahead and add that element now inside the `shell:ApplicationBar` element:

```
<shell:ApplicationBar.MenuItems>
</shell:ApplicationBar.MenuItems>
```

2.   Finally, we will define MenuItems themselves by adding `shell:ApplicationBarMenuItems` inside the `shell:ApplicationBar.MenuItems` element:

```
    <shell:ApplicationBarMenuItem Text="Menu Item 1" IsEnabled="True">
    </shell:ApplicationBarMenuItem>
<shell:ApplicationBarMenuItem Text="Menu Item 2" IsEnabled="True">
    </shell:ApplicationBarMenuItem>
```

If you run the application, you will now see an Application Bar displayed by the Windows Phone emulator that is identical to the one shown in Figure 7–1. If you click the ellipsis to the right of the icons, the application bar slides up, revealing the two menu items, identical to Figure 7–2. Try it by pressing F5.

Let's talk briefly about the **Opacity** property of an Application Bar we used in this example. Even though its values can range from 0 to 1, Microsoft recommends that developers use only three values for this property: 0, 0.5, and 1. If the Opacity is set to anything less than 1, the Application Bar will overlay the displayed page of an application. If Opacity is set to 1, however, the Application Bar will have a dedicated region at the bottom of the screen and will not be overlaying any portion of an application.

The full XAML markup for creating an Application Bar with three main icons and two menu items is shown here.

Listing 7–1. *XAML Code to Implement an Application Bar*

```
<phone:PhoneApplicationPage.ApplicationBar>
<shell:ApplicationBar Opacity="1" IsVisible="True" IsMenuEnabled="True">
        <shell:ApplicationBar.Buttons>
            <shell:ApplicationBarIconButton IconUri="/Images/appbar.add.rest.png"
Text="add">
            </shell:ApplicationBarIconButton>
```

```
                    <shell:ApplicationBarIconButton IconUri="/Images/appbar.save.rest.png"
Text="save">
                    </shell:ApplicationBarIconButton>
                    <shell:ApplicationBarIconButton IconUri="/Images/appbar.delete.rest.png"
Text="delete">
                    </shell:ApplicationBarIconButton>
                </shell:ApplicationBar.Buttons>
                <shell:ApplicationBar.MenuItems>
                    <shell:ApplicationBarMenuItem Text="Menu Item 1" IsEnabled="True">
                    </shell:ApplicationBarMenuItem>
                    <shell:ApplicationBarMenuItem Text="Menu Item 2" IsEnabled="True">
                    </shell:ApplicationBarMenuItem>
                </shell:ApplicationBar.MenuItems>
            </shell:ApplicationBar>
</phone:PhoneApplicationPage.ApplicationBar>
```

Adding an Application Bar via XAML is pretty straightforward thanks to all the powerful and easy-to-use tooling provided by Visual Studio 2010. Using XAML allows you to separate presentation from logic, which is a very good practice. We recommend you use XAML wherever possible. Sometimes, however, XAML alone is not sufficient for the task. Luckily, it is perhaps even easier to work with the Application Bar from managed code, especially if you have a little bit of programming experience. In the next section, we will show you how to do that.

Adding an Application Bar Using Managed Code

The second way to create an Application Bar for a Windows Phone 7 application is to use one of the .NET languages. At the time of this writing, only C# is supported, but plans to support other .Net languages are certainly in the works. Perhaps when you read this, it may even be possible to write applications for Windows Phone 7 with F#!

The steps necessary to create an Application Bar using C# are described here. But first, be sure to remove all of the Application Bar XAML code you wrote for the previous walkthroughs.

1. You will be editing the MainPage code of your application. To accomplish that, locate the MainPage.xaml.cs file by expanding the MainPage.xaml file in the Solution Explorer. Right-click MainPage.xaml.cs and select View Code.

2. For easier reference to an Application Bar component inside the Microsoft.Phone assembly (i.e., to avoid typing Microsoft.Phone.Shell.ApplicationBar before each component name), add the following using directive to the top of the MainPage.xaml.cs file:

```
using Microsoft.Phone.Shell;
```

3. Inside the constructor for the page (i.e., inside the public MainPage() code block), right after InitializeComponent(), initialize the Application Bar and set its IsVisible and IsMenuEnabled properties, as shown in the following code:

```
ApplicationBar = new ApplicationBar();
ApplicationBar.IsVisible = true;
ApplicationBar.IsMenuEnabled = true;
```

4. Initialize Application Bar buttons, providing the relative URI to the image that will be used for each button. Note that you must set the Text property of each button—otherwise you will cause an exception.

```
ApplicationBarIconButton btnAdd = new ApplicationBarIconButton(new
Uri("/Images/appbar.add.rest.png", UriKind.Relative));
btnAdd.Text = "add";
ApplicationBarIconButton btnSave = new ApplicationBarIconButton(new
Uri("/Images/appbar.save.rest.png", UriKind.Relative));
btnSave.Text = "save";
ApplicationBarIconButton btnDelete = new ApplicationBarIconButton(new
Uri("/Images/appbar.delete.rest.png", UriKind.Relative));
btnDelete.Text = "delete";
```

   5.   Add the buttons to the Application Bar via the following code:

```
ApplicationBar.Buttons.Add(btnAdd);
ApplicationBar.Buttons.Add(btnSave);
ApplicationBar.Buttons.Add(btnDelete);
```

   6.   Next, we will create two menu items that will appear as text when the ellipsis
        button is clicked next to the icons on the Application Bar. Very similar to adding
        icons, there are initialization and addition steps for each menu item. The
        initialization code for the menu items looks like this:

```
ApplicationBarMenuItem menuItem1 = new ApplicationBarMenuItem("Menu Item 1");
ApplicationBarMenuItem menuItem2 = new ApplicationBarMenuItem("Menu Item 2");
```

The strings "Menu Item 1" and "Menu Item 2" are the text for the two menu items; in your
application, you will certainly change that text to something much more meaningful and fun.

   7.   Add menu items to the Application Bar.

```
ApplicationBar.MenuItems.Add(menuItem1);
ApplicationBar.MenuItems.Add(menuItem2);
```

   8.   Finally, you are ready to test the Application Bar. Save your work and press F5
        to start debugging the application using Windows Phone 7 emulator. You
        should see an Application Bar identical to the one shown in Figure 7–1. If you
        click the ellipsis to the right of the icons, the Application Bar slides up, revealing
        two menu items, identical to Figure 7–2.

The full code listing for adding the Application Bar using managed C# code appears here. The full
MainPage() constructor listing is included for readability purposes.

Listing 7–2. C# Code to Implement an Application Bar

```
public MainPage()
{
InitializeComponent();
SupportedOrientations = SupportedPageOrientation.Portrait |
SupportedPageOrientation.Landscape;

        ApplicationBar = new ApplicationBar();
        ApplicationBar.IsVisible = true;
        ApplicationBar.IsMenuEnabled = true;

ApplicationBarIconButton btnAdd = new ApplicationBarIconButton(new
Uri("/Images/appbar.add.rest.png", UriKind.Relative));
btnAdd.Text = "add";
ApplicationBarIconButton btnSave = new ApplicationBarIconButton(new
```

```
Uri("/Images/appbar.save.rest.png", UriKind.Relative));
btnSave.Text = "save";
ApplicationBarIconButton btnDelete = new ApplicationBarIconButton(new
Uri("/Images/appbar.delete.rest.png", UriKind.Relative));
btnDelete.Text = "delete";

        ApplicationBarMenuItem menuItem1 = new ApplicationBarMenuItem("Menu Item 1");
        ApplicationBarMenuItem menuItem2 = new ApplicationBarMenuItem("Menu Item 2");

        ApplicationBar.Buttons.Add(btnAdd);
        ApplicationBar.Buttons.Add(btnSave);
        ApplicationBar.Buttons.Add(btnDelete);

        ApplicationBar.MenuItems.Add(menuItem1);
        ApplicationBar.MenuItems.Add(menuItem2);

}
```

While adding the Application Bar to Windows Phone 7 is cool in itself, we cannot do much with that Application Bar right now. We can push buttons a few hundred times, but nothing changes on the phone screen or inside the application. To react to button press events, we need to write some managed (C# in our case) code, also called the event handler code. In the next section, you'll learn how to write code that processes and reacts to the button press events.

Wiring Up Events to an Application Bar

There are two parts to writing code that reacts to Application Bar events:

1. Writing a small snippet of "glue code" that links Application Bar button or menu item click to the function that does all the processing (the "worker" function).

2. Writing a "worker" function that performs all the heavy lifting—i.e., rearranging UI elements on the screen, saving data, prompting the user for input or anything else that the developer decides to do in response to the button or the menu item click event.

Let's start with the Add button, which you'll wire up in the next section.

Adding "Glue" Code and a "Worker Function" to the Add Button

Visual Studio has made adding both "glue code" and a "worker" function virtually a two-keystroke procedure. Let's see how easy it is to create an event handler for the "Add" button on our Application Bar using a couple of Visual Studio shortcuts. The walkthrough assumes that you have already created the Application Bar via managed code (not XAML, which we will talk about shortly) by following the steps in previous sections.

1. Once again, we will be editing the code of the MainPage of our application. To accomplish that, locate the MainPage.xaml.cs file by expanding the MainPage.xaml file in the Solution Explorer. Right-click MainPage.xaml.cs and select View Code.

2. At the very end of the MainPage() constructor, type the following code:

171

```
btnAdd.Click+=
```

3. Notice the appearance of a small pop-up window to the right of the "=" sign as you type it. You should sew the following message with the message

```
new EventHandler(btnAdd_Click); (Press TAB to insert)
```

4. Go ahead and press the Tab key, and notice how a line of code is automatically added after the "=" sign. This one line of code is the "glue code" you need to tie together user interaction with the Add button.

```
btnAdd.Click+=new EventHandler(btnAdd_Click);
```

5. Now press the Tab key again, and Visual Studio automatically creates a skeleton for the "worker" function for you. This may not seem like a big deal at first, but it's usually a challenge to remember exactly what parameter types this "worker" function must have. This shortcut is just one example of how Visual Studio really enhances developer productivity.

6. The "worker" code that Visual Studio adds to your application looks like this:

```
void btnAdd_Click(object sender, EventArgs e)
{
            throw new NotImplementedException();
}
```

Now you're ready to add a bit of interactivity to your Application Bar, which you'll do in the next section.

■ **Tip** You are certainly not required to use the shortcut just described to generate event handler code for the Application Bar or for any other event for that matter. You can write all of the foregoing code by hand, but be very careful to pass the proper parameter types and the proper number of parameters to the event handler.

Reacting to Add Button Events

With a "worker" function in place for the Add button, let's expand it to accommodate a simplified real-world scenario: when a user clicks the Add button (the button with a "+" icon) on the Application Bar), we will show a text box on the screen that is ready and waiting for user input. We will also add functionality to the Save button (the button with a floppy disk icon) that will display the thank-you message and hide the text box. Of course, in the real world, you would want to store the values entered by the user and react on the user input in some fashion, but that is slightly beyond the scope of the current chapter.

Follow these steps to add interactivity to the Application Bar events.

1. Locate MainPage.xaml in the Solution Explorer and double-click that file to bring up XAML designer. Click the View menu➤Other Windows➤Toolbox. You should see XAML designer and a toolbox side-by-side, as shown in Figure 7–4. If you see the toolbox, Windows Phone 7 design surface, and XAML code on the screen side-by-side as in Figure 7–5, click the Collapse Pane (>> icon) in the area between the design surface and XAML to hide the XAML code, as illustrated in Figure 7–5.

■ **Tip** If you do not see the XAML view, click the Expand Pane (<< icon) to bring that view back, as shown in Figure 7–6.

2. In the Toolbox, click and drag the text box to the Windows Phone 7 design surface, as shown in Figure 7–4. Right-click the text box, and select Properties to show the Properties window in the right corner of the screen.

3. Set the Text property to blank and set the Visibility property to Collapsed.

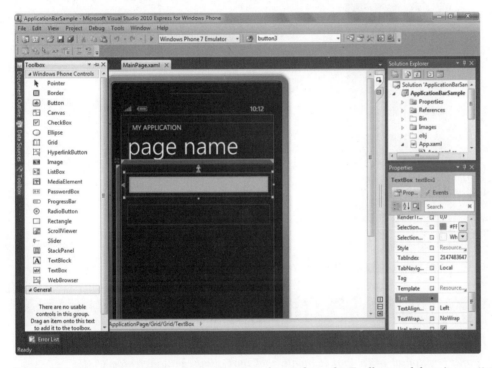

Figure 7–4. To add a text box to the application, drag it from the Toolbox and drop it onto MainPage.xaml on the Windows Phone 7 design surface. Set the Visibility property to Collapsed, and delete all contents from the Text property.

4. In the Toolbox, click and drag the TextBlock to the Windows Phone 7 design surface and place it right underneath the text box. Right-click the TextBlock and select Properties to show the Properties window in the right corner of the screen.

5. Set the Text property to "Please enter your name" and set the Visibility property to Collapsed.

6. Now edit the worker function that was created for you by Visual Studio 2010 in the previous section. Right-click the `MainPage.xaml.cs` file and select View Code. Remove the following line from the `btnAdd_Click` function.

```
throw new NotImplementedException();
```

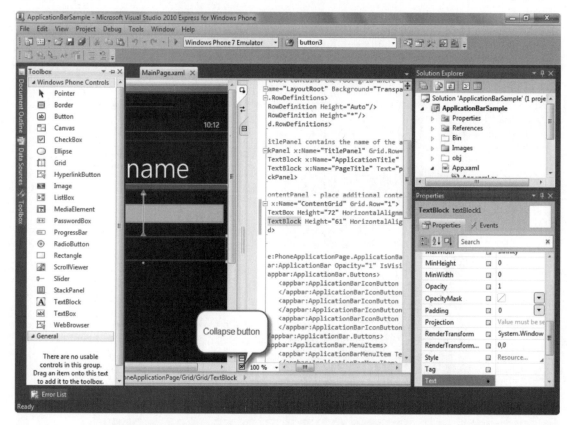

Figure 7–5. *If the toolbox, Windows Phone 7 design surface, and XAML are present on one screen and that interferes with proper positioning of Toolbox elements, click the Collapse button to hide XAML.*

7. Edit the `btnAdd_Click` function to match the following code:

```
void btnAdd_Click (object sender, EventArgs e)
{
        textBox1.Visibility = Visibility.Visible;
        textBlock1.Visibility = Visibility.Visible;
}
```

8. Press F5 to view the results of your work.

Now, when you click the "+" icon on the Application Bar, the text box is ready to accept user input.

Reacting to Save Button Events

Continuing the walkthrough, let's now add an event handler to the Save button of the Application Bar. You'll write code so that the user clicks the Save button, and the application will hide the text box and change the text of the textblock to thank the user for entering a name.

1. Locate `MainPage.xaml` in the Solution Explorer, and right-click and select View Code. Add the following line of code to the `MainPage()` constructor code. Don't forget to use the "Tab+Tab" trick to let Visual Studio automatically generate skeleton code for you (described in the previous section):

```
btnSave.Click += new EventHandler(btnSave_Click);
```

2. Add the following code to the `btnSave_Click` function:

```
void btnSave_Click(object sender, EventArgs e)
{
textBlock1.Text = "Thank you, "+ textBox1.Text;

textBox1.Visibility = Visibility.Collapsed;
}
```

3. Press F5 to see the results of your work. When you click the "+" icon, you will be prompted to enter your name. Once you enter your name and press the Save button on the Application Bar, the application displays a simple thank-you message. If, for some reason, the full text of the message does not fit within the textblock we created, you can increase both the width and the height of the textblock by setting the `TextWrapping` property of the textblock to "Wrap."

Now you're ready to enhance the Application Bar even further by writing code for your menu items to do some meaningful work.

Reacting to Menu Events

The code you write to react to menu click events is almost identical to code for Application Bar button events, with the "glue code" attached to the menu item instead of the Application Bar button. The block of code shown here displays a simple text message when the user clicks on the first menu item in the Application Bar that you created previously. Note that only a portion of the `MainPage()` constructor is shown, since the rest of it remains unchanged from the prior walkthrough.

```
menuItem1.Click+=new EventHandler(menuItem1_Click);
}

void menuItem1_Click(object sender, EventArgs e)
{
textBlock1.Visibility = Visibility.Visible;
textBlock1.Text = "You just clicked on Menu Item 1";
}
```

Press F5 to run the application now. You should see an Application Bar appear with an ellipsis in the right corner. If you press the ellipsis, two menu items become visible. Once clicked, the text on the phone screen changes to reflect the name of the menu item clicked.

In the real application, you will certainly want to do something more meaningful than what we have done. For instance, you may have menu items for "Help" and "About." If the user clicks Help, a Web Browser control (discussed in the next section) could be programmed to display a set of application Help files. If the "About" menu item is clicked, you can use the Web Browser control again to show your company's web page, or to simply display basic contact information.

One final thing we need to look at before leaving this chapter is using XAML to link event handling code to XAML elements.

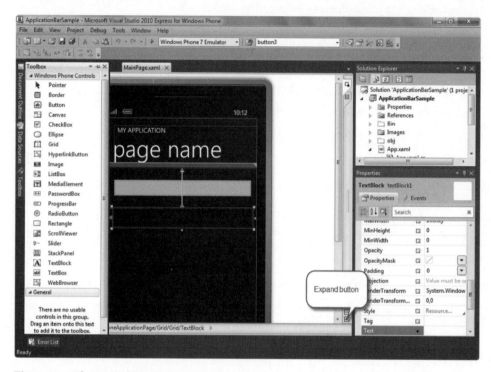

Figure 7–6. *If you need to edit XAML code but it's not visible on the screen, click the Expand button to show XAML for the current page.*

Adding Event Handlers with XAML

It is also possible to write the necessary code that attaches (or "glues") a certain event to a managed code in XAML. For code readability and understandability purposes, this approach may be preferable to the managed code approach that we have already discussed. Imagine that you are trying to maintain an application that someone else wrote—it would be easier for you to understand and trace application behavior by starting with the XAML design elements and following their "glue code" into the event handlers. The steps you follow to wire up events in XAML are pretty straightforward, as illustrated here.

1. Locate MainPage.xaml in the Solution Explorer and double-click that file to bring up XAML designer.

2. If only Windows Phone 7 design surface is shown and no XAML code is visible, click the Expand Pane (<<) button in the lower right portion of the screen, as shown in Figure 7–6.

3. Paste the following XAML in MainPage.xaml (it is identical to XAML from the "Adding a Local Application Bar Using XAML" section of this chapter):

```
<phone:PhoneApplicationPage.ApplicationBar>
    <shell:ApplicationBar IsVisible="True" IsMenuEnabled="True">
        <shell:ApplicationBar.Buttons>
            <shell:ApplicationBarIconButton IconUri="/Images/appbar.add.rest.png"
Text="add">
            </shell:ApplicationBarIconButton>
            <shell:ApplicationBarIconButton IconUri="/Images/appbar.save.rest.png"
Text="save">
            </shell:ApplicationBarIconButton>
            <shell:ApplicationBarIconButton IconUri="/Images/appbar.delete.rest.png"
Text="delete">
            </shell:ApplicationBarIconButton>
        </shell:ApplicationBar.Buttons>
        <shell:ApplicationBar.MenuItems>
            <shell:ApplicationBarMenuItem Text="Menu Item 1" IsEnabled="True">
            </shell:ApplicationBarMenuItem>
            <shell:ApplicationBarMenuItem Text="Menu Item 2" IsEnabled="True">
            </shell:ApplicationBarMenuItem>
        </shell:ApplicationBar.MenuItems>
    </shell:ApplicationBar>
</phone:PhoneApplicationPage.ApplicationBar>
```

4. Locate the <shell:ApplicationBarIconButton IconUri="/Images/appbar.add.rest.png" Text="add"> statement in XAML and add "Click" to the end of that statement, so that it resembles the code here:

```
<shell:ApplicationBarIconButton IconUri="/Images/appbar.add.rest.png" Text="add"  Click=">
```

Note how Visual Studio automatically shows a choice of "New Event Handler" right after the double quotes. If you press the Tab key now, the skeleton code for the "worker function" will be automatically inserted in the MainPage.xaml.cs file and it will have a default name of ApplicationBarMenuItem_Click. To add functionality to the Application Bar button click event, open MainPage.xaml.cs (by right-clicking the MainPage.xaml file and selecting View Code) and edit that function in a way similar to the preceding button click event function.

Summary

In this chapter, you learned how to add an Application Bar with buttons and menu items to your Windows Phone 7 application using either XAML or managed (C#) code. You also learned basic guidelines for Application Bar development and wrote code to react to Application Bar button and menu item events. The presence of an Application Bar is certainly an expected behavior for any mobile application today, and Visual Studio has made the process of adding on easy and straightforward.

In the next chapter, we will talk about the Web Browser control on Windows Phone 7. The Web Browser control helps us provide professional-looking application Help files as well as easily navigate the billions of web pages. We will also take a look at dynamically generating HTML content and showing it in the Web browser.

CHAPTER 8

WebBrowser Control

It felt like false advertising when, at the end of last century, cellular phone companies began to promote Internet access as a feature of their devices. As customers quickly learned when they tried to get online, their phones could only access web pages written in Wireless Markup Language (WML), and not the traditional HyperText Markup Language (HTML) used by the vast majority of the web sites. Very few sites could afford to build and maintain code in two separate languages—HTML for desktop and WML for mobile phones—and, as a result, web browsing on mobile phones never took off.

But we live in much more progressive times. Windows Phone 7 devices ship with Internet Explorer 7 installed, which means that any content that can be viewed in the desktop version of Internet Explorer 7 can be viewed on the phone as well. Even better, the Windows Phone 7 SDK includes a WebBrowser control that you can use to embed one or more instances of a small but fully capable browser inside your applications. In this chapter, you'll learn how and when to use it. But first, let's look at three common scenarios.

■ **Note** The WebBrowser control on Windows Phone 7 is very similar to the Silverlight WebBrowser control, with few notable differences. Certain features, such as the ability to download and install ActiveX controls, have been designed to prevent security risks originating from such components. Other differences, such as the ability to access local storage and the absence of cross-domain restrictions in the Windows Phone 7 WebBrowser control, allow for a more flexible behavior of the browser on Windows Phone 7 as compared to Silverlight.

Introducing the WebBrowser Control

The most obvious reason to use the WebBrowser control is to display web content within the page of a Windows Phone 7 application. For instance, you may be developing an application that shows Twitter feeds in a portion of the screen. The easiest way to do this would be to create a WebBrowser control in the application and navigate to a given Twitter page from within that control.

Another reason to use the WebBrowser control may be to show HTML-formatted content that resides locally on Windows Phone 7. For example, if you decide to include help files with your application, the easiest way to create those files would be in the form of HTML web pages. Then, you can load those web pages in Windows Phone 7 and display them in the WebBrowser control.

Finally, you can use WebBrowser content that Windows Phone 7 application generates on the fly. That means that you can compose an HTML page dynamically in code and, without first writing that web page out to disk, display it. This is certainly a handy feature that avoids the intermediate steps of first writing an HTML file to local storage and then reading it. This feature is important when the HTML pages you want to show the user are context-sensitive: for instance, if you are developing an application that tracks basketball teams and you want to provide links to information about each individual player on the team, you will want to build your list of players based on the name of the team the user selects. Dynamic content generation allows you to do just that.

In this chapter, you'll learn how to use these capabilities in an application by building a simple car browser application that can search the web for photos of popular car models and display them. To get started, you first must create a main page and add some UI, including a WebBrowser control to display web and HTML content.

Adding a WebBrowser Control

Before you can use the WebBrowser control to browse for the images of cars online, you need to first add the control to your application. Follow these steps to place the WebBrowser control inside your application.

1. Create a new Windows Phone 7 Application project. Launch Visual Studio 2010 Express and select the Windows Phone Application template, then change the Project name to "WebBrowserSample," select OK, and Visual Studio will set up a new project.

2. Click the View menu➤Other Windows➤Toolbox (alternately, you can also click the Toolbox icon in the Visual Studio application bar).

3. From the Toolbox window on the left, select the WebBrowser control, click it, and drag it onto the Windows Phone 7 design surface, as shown in Figure 8–1.

4. Position and resize the control as needed. In Figure 8–1, the WebBrowser control is positioned to take the upper third of the phone screen.

5. Finally, change the name of the application from "My Application" to "My Car Browser" and change the name of the page to "Car Explorer." You can do that by double-clicking MainPage.xaml and editing the ApplicationTitle and PageTitle elements accordingly.

■ **Note** You can set the Height and the Width properties to Auto (this is the default when the control is first dropped on the Windows Phone design surface and is not resized). You can also set the Horizontal Alignment and Vertical Alignment properties to Stretch, which will allow the browser window to expand as much as possible on the phone without covering other visible elements present on the phone screen.

With the WebBrowser control in place, you are now ready to look at how to use this control for each of the scenarios previously described.

Figure 8–1. *To add the WebBrowser control to the application, drag it from the Toolbox and drop it onto* `MainPage.xaml` *on the Windows Phone 7 design surface.*

Using a WebBrowser Control to Display Web Content

In the first of our WebBrowser walkthroughs, we will use this control to display the contents of the web site—we will show a list of photos of the best car in the world, the Lamborghini Gallardo.

1. With the WebBrowser control in place, it's time to add some code to initialize its content when it loads work. First, right-click `MainPage.xaml` in Solution Explorer and select View Code (or go directly to the `MainPage.xaml.cs` file).

2. Whenever the My Car Browser application loads the WebBrowser control, it fires off a `Loaded` event. By creating a `Loaded` event handler, you can write code to display a web page with car photos. Add the following code to the `MainPage()` constructor to create the handler:

```
webBrowser1.Loaded += new RoutedEventHandler(webBrowser1_Loaded);
```

Notice how the same Visual Studio shortcuts we used for the Application Bar code apply here as well: namely, right after typing "+=" Visual Studio hints that if you press the Tab key twice, it will create all of the necessary code stubs you need for a handler.

3. Next, let's code the event handler. To the `webBrowser1_Loaded()` function, add the following code, which will navigate to Microsoft Bing's image search page and pass the phrase "cars Lamborghini Gallardo" to it:

```
webBrowser1.Navigate(new Uri("http://www.bing.com/images/search?q=cars+Lamborghini+Gallardo"",
UriKind.Absolute));
```

4. This code creates a new Uri object and specifies that the Uri is not local to our application (that would be `UriKind.Relative`), but rather a location on the Internet (`UriKind.Absolute`).

Press F5 to debug your application and see the results so far. You should see photos of the most beautiful car in the world, courtesy of the Microsoft Bing engine. You can easily extend this example to respond to user input. For example, you could use the Bing image search to show photos of any car whose name a user enters. Here's how.

5. Now let's add a text box to the page so the user can change the name of the car for which Bing searches. To do that, go to `MainPage.xaml` and display the page in the Designer (either by double-clicking `MainPage.xaml` or by right-clicking `MainPage.xaml` and selecting View Designer). If the Toolbox is not visible, go to View menu➤Other Windows➤Toolbox or click the Toolbox icon in the Visual Studio application bar. Click and drag the text box from the Toolbox, and position it below the WebBrowser control. Next, click and drag the Button, and position it next to the text box.

6. Right-click the text box and select Properties. Delete everything from the Text property. Next, right-click the button and change the value of its Content property to "`Show It!`" (without the double quotes). The end result should resemble Figure 8–2.

7. It's time to add some interactivity to our application. With `MainPage.xaml` still open in Designer view, double-click the button. Notice how the method `button1_Click` opens by default when you do that, ready for your code. Place the following code in the body of that method:

```
webBrowser1.Navigate(new Uri
("http://www.bing.com/images/search?q=cars " + textBox1.Text,
UriKind.Absolute));
```

8. Press F5 to run the application. Initially, you should see the photos of the Lamborghini Gallardo added in the first part of this walkthrough. Go ahead and type "Ford Mustang" in the text box, and press the "Show It!" button. In the WebBrowser control, you should now see a set of photos of this great American muscle car.

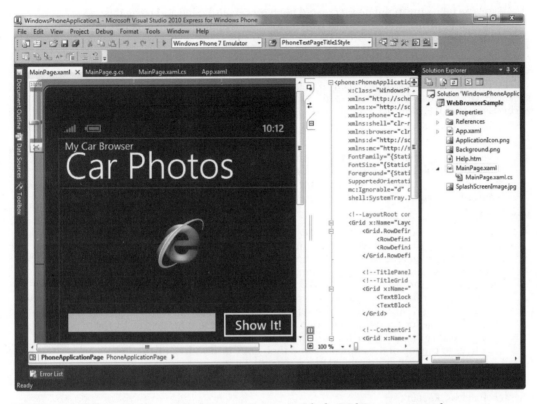

Figure 8–2. Adding a text box and a button to interact with the WebBrowser control

But there's more. You can also use a WebBrowser control to display HTML files—and even strings—that have been stored locally. We'll use that capability to add some Help to the Car Browser application in the next section.

Using a WebBrowser Control to Display Local HTML Content

Frequently, you will want to include documentation with your application to advertise its features to users and answer their most common questions. Because of its simplicity and ubiquity, HTML, the same language used to create web pages, has become the default format for such documentation. In this section, you'll create a simple HTML page describing how to work with the car photo application that you created in the previous section. Follow these steps to create and show HTML content on Windows Phone 7.

1. Because adding an HTML file is not an option on Windows Phone 7, you will need to add a new XML file to the project. XML files support automated syntax verification features, making it harder for you to make accidental mistakes. Right-click the WebBrowserSample project in the Solution Explorer and select Add ➤ New Item. Then, select XML File from the list of available item types.

2. Type the following in the newly created file (you can also copy and paste this code from the files available for download for this book).

```html
<html>
<title>Web Browser Help File</title>
<body>
        <h1>Welcome to the Windows Phone 7 Car Browser Application!
  To view the car photos, type the name of the car in the textbox and press "Show It!"
  <br/><br/>For example, "Ford Mustang"</h1>
</body>
</html>
```

3. Save the file by pressing the Save button in Visual Studio. Next, right-click XMLFile1.xml in the Solution Explorer and click Rename. Change the name of that file to Help.htm and make sure that the Build action for that file is set to "Content" (by right-clicking and selecting Properties to bring up the Properties window).

4. Now you will need to jump slightly ahead to the material covered in Chapter 13 (Isolated Storage). Here's why: while you would expect the Help.htm file to be automatically available to the application running on Windows Phone 7, it isn't. Before it is available to your application, the Help.htm file created in the previous step needs to be available to your application in the Isolated Storage, which you can think of as disk space reserved for use by your application on Windows Phone 7. As your application loads, you'll need to copy Help.htm to an Isolated Storage location first, and then retrieve it from there for display by the WebBrowser control. For the time being, simply add the following using directives to the top of the code page and then copy into your code the SaveHelpFileToIsoStore method shown in Listing 8–1.

```csharp
using System.IO.IsolatedStorage;
using System.Windows.Resources;
using System.IO;
```

Listing 8–1. *SaveHelpFiletoIsoStore Method*

```csharp
private void SaveHelpFileToIsoStore()
        {
                string strFileName = "Help.htm";
                IsolatedStorageFile isoStore = IsolatedStorageFile.GetUserStoreForApplication();

                //remove the file if exists to allow each run to independently write to
                // the Isolated Storage
                if (isoStore.FileExists(strFileName) == true)
                {
                    isoStore.DeleteFile(strFileName);
                }
                StreamResourceInfo sr = Application.GetResourceStream(new Uri(strFileName,
UriKind.Relative));
                using (BinaryReader br = new BinaryReader(sr.Stream))
                {
                    byte[] data = br.ReadBytes((int)sr.Stream.Length);
                    //save file to Isolated Storage
                    using (BinaryWriter bw = new BinaryWriter(isoStore.CreateFile(strFileName)))
                    {
```

184

```
            bw.Write(data);
            bw.Close();
        }
    }
}
```

5. Finally, you will invoke the SaveHelpFileToIsoStore method you wrote earlier
    to display the contents of Help.htm in the web browser when the browser first
    loads. Add the call to SaveHelpFileToIsoStore in the webBrowser1_Loaded
    method and set the webBrowser URL to navigate to the Help.htm file, as shown
    here:

```
void webBrowser1_Loaded(object sender, RoutedEventArgs e)
{
    SaveHelpFileToIsoStore();
    webBrowser1.Navigate(new Uri("Help.htm", UriKind.Relative));
}
```

6. Press F5 to run the application. You should see the simple HTML Help page
    displayed in the WebBrowser control.

In the next section, you will learn how to bypass Isolated Storage and show HTML generated directly
by code.

Using a WebBrowser Control to Display Dynamic Content

Suppose now that the user enters "Ford" in the text box of the photo browsing application developed in
the previous section. Unless you query the user, you won't know whether the user meant "Ford
Mustang" or "Ford F-150." One way to find out would be to create a page with HTML markup and
display it to the user, asking for more information. You could then save the generated file to Isolated
Storage, and load it using the technique described in the previous section (Using a WebBrowser Control
to Display Local HTML Content). But that would certainly be a cumbersome approach for such a simple
task. Luckily, there's a much easier way to show a dynamically generated HTML page: using the
NavigateToString() method of the WebBrowser control. This method takes a single argument—a
string—that contains all of the HTML needed to display the page you have in mind in the WebBrowser
control.

The next walkthrough shows just how easy it is to use this method.

1. Bring up the MainPage.xaml.cs file in the code editor (either by double-clicking
    it or clicking the MainPage.xaml file in the Solution Explorer and choosing View
    Code).

2. Next, you will construct the HTML code to display to the user. Make the
    button1_Click method look identical to the following code—notice how
    NavigateToString loads up what amounts to a basic HTML page directly into
    the WebBrowser control, without your having to save this HTML to the Isolated
    Storage. Also note that building an HTML string in code becomes a bit ugly very
    quickly, so NavigateToString should not be abused for large HTML
    messages/files.

```
webBrowser1.NavigateToString(@"<html>
```

```
<body><center><div style='font: Arial 12px;'>
Which Ford
        model would you like to see?<br><br>
                <a href='http://www.bing.com/images/search?q=cars+Ford+Mustang'>Ford
Mustang</a> or <a href='http://www.bing.com/images/search?q=cars+Ford+F150'>Ford F-
150</a></div></center></body></html>");
```

3. Press F5 to run the application. Now if you type "Ford" in the text box and press the "Show It!" button, you should see a dynamically generated HTML message with hyperlinks asking you to clarify which Ford model you would like to see, just like Figure 8–3.

■ **Note** Of course, users will get this response no matter *what* they type, but delving into more complex search logic is not the purpose of this chapter.

Figure 8–3. Showing dynamically generated HMTL content

Many web-based applications have been built, from translators to elaborate e-commerce systems, and all of them are easily accessible and could even be potentially enhanced with the use of the WebBrowser control on Windows Phone 7. But the WebBrowser control can do even more: in the next section, we will learn how to save the web pages locally, so that we can potentially parse certain information or search within them.

Saving Web Pages Locally

You can also save the contents of web sites and web pages to a Windows Phone 7 as strings of HTML commands, using isolated storage and the SaveToString method of the WebBrowser control. This approach saves only the HTML on a page (of course, you probably already guessed that from the name of the method!) and ignores its images and CSS files. After saving HTML to Isolated Storage, you can load it on demand, but before doing that, make sure to read the security considerations at the end of this chapter.

The next walkthrough will show you how to save an HTML web page locally and then load it at a later time.

1. Open the WebBrowserSample project and bring up MainPage.xaml in the design window.

2. Add two buttons to the Windows Phone 7 design surface, as shown in Figure 8–4. Change the Content property of the top button to "save to local storage." Change the Content property of the bottom button to "load saved content."

3. Make sure to change the names of both buttons, as shown in Figure 8–4. You can change the name in the Properties window by clicking next to the "Button" text. Name the top button "btnSave" and name the bottom button "btnLoad".

4. Next, let's write the event handler code for the Save button click. Double-click the top button to bring up MainPage.xaml.cs in the code view. Change the btnSave_Click method to be identical to the following:

```
private void btnSave_Click(object sender, RoutedEventArgs e)
{
        string strWebContent = webBrowser1.SaveToString();
        SaveStringToIsoStore(strWebContent);
}
```

5. Next comes event handler code to load the previously saved web page. Double-click the bottom button and make the btnLoad_Click method look like the code block here.

```
private void btnLoad_Click(object sender, RoutedEventArgs e)
{
    webBrowser1.Navigate(new Uri("web.htm", UriKind.Relative));
}
```

6. Jumping ahead to what will be covered in Chapter 13 again, we need to add the implementation of the SaveStringToIsoStore method that will perform the actual save of the HTML string to a file in the local storage.

```
private void SaveStringToIsoStore(string strWebContent)
{
    IsolatedStorageFile isoStore = IsolatedStorageFile.GetUserStoreForApplication();

    //remove the file if exists to allow each run to independently write to
    // the Isolated Storage
    if (isoStore.FileExists("web.htm") == true)
    {
        isoStore.DeleteFile("web.htm");
    }
```

```
            StreamResourceInfo sr = new StreamResourceInfo(new
MemoryStream(System.Text.Encoding.UTF8.GetBytes(strWebContent)), "html/text");
            using (BinaryReader br = new BinaryReader(sr.Stream))
            {
                byte[] data = br.ReadBytes((int)sr.Stream.Length);
                //save file to Isolated Storage
                using (BinaryWriter bw = new BinaryWriter(isoStore.CreateFile("web.htm")))
                {
                    bw.Write(data);
                    bw.Close();
                }
            }
        }
    }
```

7. Make sure the button1_Click event looks identical to the one here:

```
private void button1_Click(object sender, RoutedEventArgs e)
{
    webBrowser1.Navigate(new Uri
    ("http://www.bing.com/images/search?q=cars " + textBox1.Text,
    UriKind.Absolute));
}
```

8. You are now ready to test the application. Press F5 to run it, type "Ford Mustang" in the text box, and press the "Show It!" button. Photos of the Ford Mustang should appear in the browser window. Next, press "Save Content to Isolated Storage" button. Then, erase the word "Mustang" from the text box, leaving only "Ford" and pressing "Show It!" Our friendly reminder that we need to provide more information pops up. Finally, press "Load Saved Content" to show the (distorted) thumbnails of the Ford Mustang.

Notice that the content is distorted since only HTML of the web page is saved. Many CSS stylesheets that control positioning of the elements and their look are not persisted as part of the SaveToString method.

Choosing Display and Security Settings

Usually, you can safely assume that web sites and web pages will look the same in both the desktop version of Internet Explorer 7 and the Windows Phone 7 Internet Explorer Mobile browser, on which the WebBrowser control is based. There are a few cases, however, where special considerations apply to the WebBrowser control running on Windows Phone 7. In the next few sections, we will go over those special cases.

Viewport

In Internet Explorer Mobile (which is the version of Internet Explorer 7 running on Windows Phone 7), the viewport is a rectangular region that controls where text will wrap on the page. At the time of this writing, only three properties are supported for the viewport: height, width, and user-scalable. Height and width properties control the height and the width of the viewport accordingly, with values ranging between 480 and 10,000 for the height and between 320 and 10,000 for the width. The user-scalable property controls whether a user can zoom in and out of the content of the viewport. This property has two possible values: "yes" and "no." The default (and recommended) setting for this property is yes.

CSS

There is also a CSS property, `-ms-text-size-adjust`, that controls the size of the text displayed on the screen. When Windows Phone 7 renders text in the browser (and the WebBrowser control), it adjusts the size of that text based on this `-ms-text-size-adjust` property. If this CSS property is set to auto for a given element, Windows Phone 7 tries to determine the text size that will be most readable on a given screen. If that property is set to none, Windows Phone 7 does not make any adjustments to text. There is also a third option for this property: a numeric percentage value, which will scale the text from its original size according to the percentage specified. Just as any other CSS property, `-ms-text-size-adjust` can be set for the whole page or any portion of the page. Let's take a look at the example that will help you visualize this property.

1. Refer to the `Help.htm` file we created for showing static HTML content in the WebBrowser control. Edit that file to make it look like the HTML block here—in essence, we are simply adding a CSS DIV element and introducing `-ms-text-size-adjust` around one of the elements:

```
<html>
  <head>
    <title>Web Browser Help File</title>
    <meta id="viewport" name="viewport" content="width=900;" />
  </head>
<body>
        <h1>Welcome to the Windows Phone 7 Car Browser Application!
  To view car photos, type the name of the car in the textbox and press "Show It!"
  <br/><br/>For example, <div style= "-ms-text-size-adjust:250%">"Ford Mustang"</div>
</h1>
</body>
</html>
```

2. Press F5 to run the application. You should see the text "Ford Mustang" two and half times (250%) larger than the rest of the text on this page.

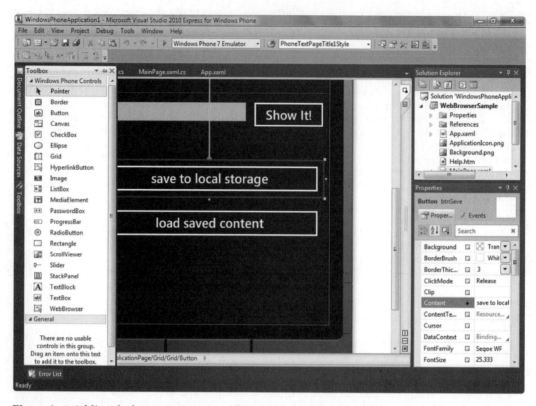

Figure 8–4. *Adding the buttons to persist web content to Isolated Storage*

Early documentation from Microsoft stated that Internet Explorer Mobile also supports the -webkit-text-size-adjust property, used by other mobile browsers to control text size, in place of –ms-text-size-adjust. However, support for the –webkit-text-size-adjust property has been withdrawn since then.

Security

With phones becoming "smarter and smarter," there is always the danger of applications behaving badly, whether intentionally or not. To help protect users from the most common security problems plaguing desktop computers connected to the Internet, Microsoft introduced a set of security rules for loading web content onto the phone. All Windows Phone 7 applications must observe those rules if they are to run on Windows Phone 7 Series.

As Windows Phone 7 developers, we must be aware of those security restrictions to ensure the smoothest possible performance of our applications. This list summarizes items that are either disabled or just different in the Internet Explorer Mobile version compared to its desktop counterpart:

1.   Script is disabled by default in the WebBrowser control. To enable it, the developer must explicitly set the IsScriptEnabled property of the control.

2. Internet Explorer Mobile does not allow users to download and install third-party plug-ins, such as ActiveX controls. That includes Adobe Flash plug-ins. Sites that rely on such plug-ins for their functionality will not work properly on Windows Phone 7.

3. Within the WebBrowser control, users cannot navigate from `https://` (secure) to `http://` (unsecure) Internet locations.

4. Applications cannot share cookies with Internet Explorer Mobile.

In addition to this list, there are special cross-site considerations applicable to the WebBrowser control. When a web page loads into the Windows Phone 7 WebBrowser control from the network location (i.e., the Internet), it is prohibited from making web service calls into the domain other than the one it has been loaded from. This is done to prevent unauthorized access to sensitive information without a user's knowledge. This behavior is identical to the behavior of a Silverlight application restricted to web service calls into its own domain unless a special `crossdomain.xml` file is present at the root of another domain allowing remote calls.

However, on Windows Phone 7, content loaded from the Isolated Storage or via the `NavigateToString` method is not subject to cross-domain restrictions. That also includes content previously loaded from the network location and saved to the Isolated Storage via the `SaveToString` method. It is therefore extremely important to consider the possible cross-domain consequences of saving web pages into the local storage and then re-loading them.

Summary

In this chapter, you learned to use the WebBrowser control for Windows Phone 7 to search for and display web content in an application. You created a simple Car Browser application using the WebBrowser control and displayed local static and dynamically generated HTML pages. You also learned how to store and retrieve web and HTML content from local storage on the phone itself. You'll explore local storage in greater depth in Chapter 13. Finally, you should now have a basic understanding of the viewport and custom Internet Explorer Mobile CSS elements, and an appreciation of the security issues you'll encounter when you use the WebBrowser control.

In the next chapter, you'll explore what is perhaps the most important aspect of any modern application: its styling. We will go over general principles of appealing layouts and themes, as well as delve into the specifics of visually engaging controls within applications.

CHAPTER 9

■ ■ ■

Working with Controls and Themes

Every time you pass through an airport or a train station, you expect to see a myriad of signs directing you to points of interest—connecting gates, luggage pickup, or a taxi line. And while the words on these signs are certainly important, perhaps just as important are the visual symbols drawn on them that are used to better communicate their meaning. Our minds become so accustomed to visual elements that often we don't even need to read the words to understand a sign's meaning, and the presence of visual elements certainly saves us when we're traveling to another country whose language we don't speak.

This universal visual language of signs is the big idea behind the user interface system in Windows Phone 7. Microsoft designers want Windows Phone 7 User Interface (UI) elements to direct users to the content that they want, just as airport signs direct people where they need to go. Within Microsoft, this contemporary UI has been code-named Metro and, per the User Interface Design and Interaction Guide, elements of Metro UI are meant to be visually appealing and to encourage exploration of the applications you build.

In this chapter, you will explore the most important design principles at the heart of Metro UI, and learn how you can ensure that your application conforms to them. You will also gain an understanding of themes on the Windows Phone 7 device and how to ensure that your application is theme-aware. Finally, you will take a look at the controls that are available to you for use in Windows Phone 7 applications, especially the innovative `Panorama` and `Pivot` controls that are unique to Windows Phone 7. You have already used a few in the previous chapters of this book, so here we will recap and introduce you to the controls used not quite as frequently.

Introducing the Metro Design System

The big idea behind the Windows Phone 7 design system (Metro) is to direct users to the content they want using design elements that are both effective in conveying their message and attractive. The UI Design and Interaction Guide for Windows Phone 7 (available as a PDF download from `http://go.microsoft.com/fwlink/?LinkID=183218`) specifically states that visual elements within applications "should encourage playful exploration so that the user feels a sense of wonder and excitement" when using your application. Microsoft strongly encourages all application developers to adopt Metro design principles in their applications. Fortunately, to help those of us who may not be particularly strong in graphic design, Microsoft ensured that all controls available for you to build applications (i.e., text box, button, etc.) are Metro-compliant by default. These controls that ship with Windows Phone 7 development tools already have the look and feel dictated by Metro UI guidelines—it is our job as developers that we preserve that look and feel throughout our applications.

When you first start working with standard controls within Windows Phone 7 applications, you may be surprised by their minimalistic, two-dimensional look. That appearance, however, emphasizes another one of the main principles of Metro UI design: "Delight through content instead of decoration." Microsoft encourages developers to reduce the complexity of visual elements that are not part of content and to communicate with users of their applications as directly as possible. According to the Metro designers, the content and the functionality of the application should be the most engaging factor of the Windows Phone 7 application.

Another pillar of Metro UI is the use of a standard contemporary-looking font. *Segoe WP* is the standard system font on Windows Phone 7 devices and it is a Unicode font. It is available in five styles:

1. Regular

2. Bold

3. Semi-bold

4. Semi-light

5. Black

You can also embed your own fonts in any application you write, but they will be available for use only within your application and not outside of it. To conform with the Metro guidelines, however, it is probably wise to stick with the standard fonts that ship with the tools.

Windows Phone Chrome

The term *Windows Phone Chrome* refers to two areas on the device screen, one at the top and the other at its bottom, as illustrated in Figure 9–1. The *System Tray* is one of two primary components of Windows Phone Chrome; the *Application Bar* is the other.

The System Tray is the top portion of Windows Phone Chrome and contains several indicators that display system-level status information. The System Tray displays the following icons, left to right, in the order listed here.

1. Signal strength

2. Data connection

3. Call forwarding

4. Roaming

5. Wireless network signal strength

6. Bluetooth status

7. Ringer mode

8. Input status

9. Battery power level

10. System clock

■ **Note** The screen shown in Figure 9–1 is the emulator screen, and it does not include all of the items mentioned in the preceding list.

By default, only the system clock is visible at all times. To make other items visible, you need to double-tap (double-click in the emulator) in the System Tray area. These indicators slide into view for approximately eight seconds before sliding out of view. Note that although you can programmatically hide the System Tray, it is not a recommended practice under Metro guidelines.

In Chapter 7, you learned how to work with the Application Bar, the second part of Windows Phone 7 Chrome. To quickly recap, the Application Bar is limited to four icons—if there are more navigational items to display, they should be put inside the menu items. There is a set of default Application Bar icons included with each distribution of Windows Phone 7 tools, and it can be used to build basic Application Bars quickly.

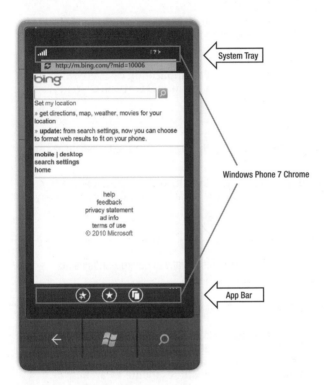

Figure 9–1. *Windows Phone 7 Chrome*

Screen Orientations

Windows Phone 7 supports three screen orientations: *portrait*, *landscape left*, and *landscape right*. In portrait orientation, the page is vertically oriented with hardware buttons appearing at the bottom of the device. Portrait orientation is the default orientation of the device, and the Start screen is always shown in portrait orientation. In Landscape left, the System Tray appears on the left of the device, and in Landscape right, the System Tray appears on the right.

Your application cannot switch the orientation of its screen by itself, since the Orientation property is read-only. You can, however, set a fixed orientation, where you disallow application support for certain screen orientations. Some system components can adjust to changes in orientation. For example, application bar icons automatically rotate when the device changes from portrait to landscape mode. Other components with similar orientation-aware behaviors include the System Tray, Application Bar Menu, Volume/Ring/Vibrate Display, Push Notifications, and Dialogs.

Having discussed major principles and some of the components of Metro UI, it is time to turn our attention to the support for themes on Windows Phone 7 devices. Themes make the phone more personal, which goes hand in hand with the Metro guideline that the experience of using the phone should be an engaging one.

Themes on Windows Phone 7 Devices

A Windows Phone 7 *theme* is a combination of a background and an accent color. Users can select from themes that ship with the phone, developers can access them in their code, and companies can alter them to match their own branding colors. Themes are set in the Settings ➤ Themes portion of the Windows Phone 7 device or the emulator.

Themes can also be applied dynamically during the runtime of an application by overwriting or injecting the custom themes into `Resources.MergedDictionaries` found in `Application.Current,` as shown in the following code snippet:

```
ResourceDictionary res = new ResourceDictionary();
res.Source =
    new Uri("/MyApplication;component/Assets/MyStyles.xaml", UriKind.RelativeOrAbsolute);
Application.Current.Resources.MergedDictionaries.Add(res);
```

Currently, there are two possible background settings—Dark (default) and Light. There are ten accent colors to choose from, starting with a Microsoft-ish blue (the default) and ranging all the way to a decidedly 70s lime green.

■ **Note** Microsoft recommends you use as little white color as possible (especially in backgrounds), since excessive use of white color may have a negative impact on battery life.

The combination of two background colors and ten accent colors provides the user with a total of twenty possible themes, delivering on the engagement and personalization promise of Metro design principles. Applications automatically adjust to the selected theme and ensure that all UI elements appear consistently across the platform. A quick walkthrough demonstrates theme-awareness of Windows Phone 7 controls and UI elements.

Applying a Theme

In this walkthrough, you will add a set of Windows Phone 7 controls to an application, creating some of them with XAML and some through managed code. You will change the theme in the emulator and observe the effect this change has on those controls. Follow these steps to get a better understanding of theming support in Windows Phone 7.

Creating a User Interface

First, you will add a set of standard controls to a Windows Phone 7 application.

1. Launch Visual Studio 2010 Express and select the Windows Phone Application template. Change the Project Name to "Theming," select OK, and Visual Studio will set up a new project.

2. Open MainPage.xaml in design mode and add a text box, textblock, check box, button, and a black rectangular shape to the page. Your end goal is a simple interface that resembles the one in Figure 9–2. Here's the XAML:

```
<!--LayoutRoot is the root grid where all page content is placed-->
<Grid x:Name="LayoutRoot" Background="Transparent">
    <Grid.RowDefinitions>
        <RowDefinition Height="Auto"/>
        <RowDefinition Height="*"/>
    </Grid.RowDefinitions>

    <!--TitlePanel contains the name of the application and page title-->
    <StackPanel x:Name="TitlePanel" Grid.Row="0" Margin="12,17,0,28">
        <TextBlock x:Name="ApplicationTitle" Text="THEMES AND COLORS"
Style="{StaticResource PhoneTextNormalStyle}"/>
        <TextBlock x:Name="PageTitle" Text="THEMES" Margin="9,-7,0,0"
Style="{StaticResource PhoneTextTitle1Style}"/>
    </StackPanel>

    <!--ContentPanel - place additional content here-->
    <Grid x:Name="ContentPanel" Grid.Row="1" Margin="12,0,12,0">
        <TextBox Height="72" HorizontalAlignment="Left" Margin="-4,6,0,0" Name="textBox1"
Text="TextBox" VerticalAlignment="Top" Width="454" />
        <TextBlock Height="30" HorizontalAlignment="Left" Margin="11,80,0,0"
Name="textBlock1" Text="TextBlock" VerticalAlignment="Top" Width="329" />
        <CheckBox Content="CheckBox" Height="72" HorizontalAlignment="Left"
Margin="12,116,0,0" Name="checkBox1" VerticalAlignment="Top" />
        <Button Content="Button" Height="72" HorizontalAlignment="Left" Margin="9,194,0,0"
Name="button1" VerticalAlignment="Top" Width="160" />
        <Rectangle Height="110" HorizontalAlignment="Left" Margin="249,137,0,0"
Name="rectangle1" Stroke="Black" StrokeThickness="1" VerticalAlignment="Top" Width="156" />
    </Grid>
</Grid>
```

Adding Code to Draw an Elliptical Shape

In addition to using the powerful Visual Designer to add controls to Windows Phone 7 pages, as you just did, you can add controls programmatically. The steps here show you how to do that.

1. Go to the Theming project in Solution Explorer and open MainPage.xaml.cs (right-click MainPage.xaml and choose View Code).

2. To add a white ellipse to the page, paste the following code inside the MainPage constructor:

```
Ellipse e = new Ellipse();
e.Width = 100.0;
e.Height = 120.0;
e.StrokeThickness = 2.0;
```

```
e.HorizontalAlignment = HorizontalAlignment.Left;
e.VerticalAlignment = VerticalAlignment.Top;

Color backgroundColor = Color.FromArgb(255, 255, 255, 255);
e.Fill = new SolidColorBrush(backgroundColor);
e.Margin = new Thickness(10, 300, 10, 10);

ContentPanel.Children.Add(e);
```

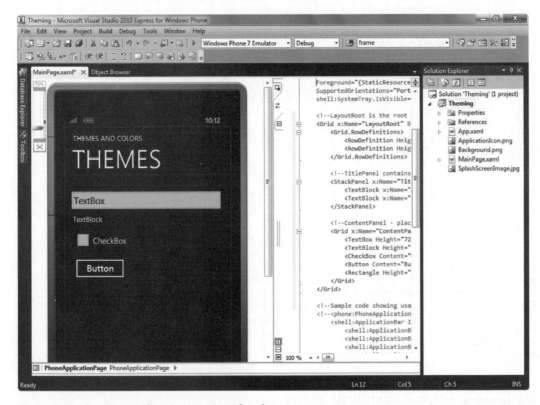

Figure 9–2. Theming application user interface layout

Press F5 to run the application. The application screen should now display all of the controls you've added, including a white ellipse.

Changing the Theme

In this part of the walkthrough, you will change the emulator's theme to observe the effect it has on the Theming application.

1. Press the Windows button on the emulator to bring up the Start screen. Then press the ➤ key and select Settings ➤ Themes to bring up the Themes dialog.

2. Change the background to Light, and change the accent color to Red (note that you may have to scroll to locate the red accent color).

3. Press the Windows button again to go back to the Start screen. Note that your application is no longer running (it stopped when you pressed the Windows button), so go back to Visual Studio 2010 Express and press F5 to re-launch your application.

4. Notice how you can see the same controls as before, except the ellipse that you drew from code is nowhere to be found. Figure 9–3 shows two versions of the same application side by side , each with a different theme:

Figure 9–3. Two themes applied to the same theming application example

By now, you have probably guessed that the reason the ellipse is not visible is that the application paints it white and then displays it on a white background. But how did the other controls manage to show up on the white background, when they originally were white themselves? And how can we make the ellipse behave the same way?

The answer to both of these questions lies in a Windows Phone 7 concept known as theme awareness. By default, Windows Phone 7 controls are theme-aware and adjust their appearance based on the theme selected on the device. Problems arise when the color values are hard-coded in the control, as you have done for the ellipse and the rectangle border. In the next few steps, we correct the issue of hard-coded colors, first with a designer and the second in code:

5. If it's still running, stop the application. Open MainPage.xaml in the design view, and select the rectangular shape. Press F4 to bring up the Properties window, and then click the diamond symbol to the right of the Stroke property.

6. From the pop-up dialog that comes up, click Apply Resource. From the next dialog, double-click the PhoneAccentBrush setting to use the currently selected accent color to draw a rectangle.

7. Now, you will adjust the color of the ellipse to the currently selected accent color. Since you drew the ellipse from code, open the MainPage.xaml.cs file and change the following line of code.

```
Color backgroundColor = Color.FromArgb(255, 255, 255, 255);
```

to

```
Color backgroundColor = (Color)Application.Current.Resources["PhoneAccentColor"];
```

Press F5 to run your application. You should see both the rectangle and ellipse appear in red (or the currently selected accent color).

■ **Note** Avoid using hard-coded values for color if at all possible. It is hard to predict what combination of themes a user will choose, and your visual elements may not show up as desired. Instead, use one of the predefined theme resources (a full list of resources is available at http://msdn.microsoft.com/en-us/library /ff769552(v=VS.92).aspx) to ensure that your application is fully theme-aware, in accordance with Metro design principles.

Now that you know how to ensure your application is theme-aware, in the next section you will learn how approach cases where you absolutely must customize your application based on the currently selected theme.

Detecting the Currently Selected Theme

Sooner or later, you're likely to encounter cases where you'll want to customize your application depending on whether a dark or a light theme is currently active. For example, you may have a beautiful custom graphic within your application that simply does not render well when the background theme colors are changed; instead you would like to show a different graphic depending on the currently active theme. The following walkthrough shows you how to accomplish just that—it detects the currently selected theme and adjusts the message based on whether the current theme has a light or a dark background.

1. Launch Visual Studio 2010 Express and select the Windows Phone Application template. Change the Project Name to "DetectTheme," select OK, and Visual Studio will set up a new project.

2. Open `MainPage.xaml` in design mode, and add a `TextBlock` to the page. For this walkthrough, you will simply modify the message within this `TextBlock`; for real-world applications, you will probably choose to do something a bit more exotic than this, such as showing different images.

3. Open `MainPage.xaml.cs` (right-click `MainPage.xaml` in Solution Explorer and choose View Code) and add the following code to the `MainPage()` constructor, right below the `InitializeComponent()` method:

```
Visibility v = (Visibility)Resources["PhoneLightThemeVisibility"];
if (v == System.Windows.Visibility.Visible)
{
        textBlock1.Text = "Let there be light!";
}
else
{
        textBlock1.Text = "It's dark!";
}
```

Notice how you are using the `Visibility` property to determine whether the light theme is visible, and to then take action accordingly.

Press F5 to run the application. If you still have a light background selected from the previous walkthrough, you will see a "Let there be light!" message. Otherwise, a "It's dark!" message will be displayed.

In the previous sections of this chapter, we touched on the basics of theming and took a look at how to make your application theme-aware and how to customize its behavior based on the theme selected. Now, you will look at the controls provided as part of Windows Phone 7 Developer tools, since it's those controls that really complete the Metro experience.

Panorama and Pivot Controls

In earlier chapters, you made use of several base controls that ship with the Windows Phone 7 development tools, including text boxes, textblocks, and buttons, the kinds of controls you'd expect with any UI framework. But the Windows Phone developer tools include a number of unique controls as well, including a web browser and a Bing maps control, both of which we'll present in later chapters. Two others are the `Panorama` and `Pivot` controls, which are integral to Metro and the Windows Phone user experience.

The `Panorama` and `Pivot` controls offer two ways to develop an application that requires page navigation. With a `Panorama` control, you can present the UI of an application on one horizontal canvas that extends beyond the left and right boundaries of the device screen and can be flicked to the left and right with touch gestures. With a `Pivot`, you can present the UI of an application as a series of pages—much like tabbed pages—by touching its header or flicking through the pages. A `Panorama` is like a scroll; a `Pivot` is more like a series of cards laid down from left to right.

In the following section, you'll learn how to use a `Panorama` control to create some engaging UI for an airport application that displays arrivals and departures. You'll also take a brief look at the `Pivot` control, whose outfitting and use is nearly identical to the `Panorama` control, though its effects are quite different.

Using the Panorama Control

In every video ad for a Windows Phone 7 device, the scrollable UI of the Panorama control is usually the first thing that people notice. The People hub on the Start screen of Windows Phone 7 is implemented using this control. These interactions essentially involve the ability to keep scrolling horizontally far past the end of the screen. The Panorama control allows for a unique experience that is associated with the native Windows Phone 7 look and feel.

A Panorama control is essentially a long, horizontal canvas. A secondary control called a PanoramaItem serves as a container that hosts other content and controls such as TextBlocks, Buttons, and Links. There are three ways to incorporate Panorama behavior into your application:

1. Create a new Windows Phone project and choose Windows Phone Panorama Application as the template to use for the application. While this is an extremely powerful approach, this type of template creates a Model-View-ViewModel (MVVM)–based project, which has a significant learning curve and is quite different from the way we have developed Windows Phone 7 applications so far in this book (for an example of an MVVM application, however, see Chapter 3).

2. Add the Panorama control to the Visual Studio Toolbox (via right-clicking the Toolbox and navigating to the assembly containing this control) and then drag and drop it to your application.

3. Add a new page to your application that contains a Panorama control. This is perhaps the easiest way to quickly incorporate the Panorama control inside our application; this is the approach we will pursue in our walkthrough for this section.

In the following walkthrough, you will create an application to display the arrival and departures of flights at a fictional airport. In addition, you will add a search capability (or just the user interface elements of it) to this application. You will use the Panorama control to implement this functionality where the long background gives you the feeling that you are inside the airport as you navigate left or right to the pages.

Your application will not contain any code, since your primary goal in this chapter is to explore the Windows Phone 7 Panorama control. You will use Option 3 from the list in the previous section, and use XAML to build a new page with a Panorama control:

1. Launch Visual Studio 2010 Express and select the Windows Phone Application template. Change the Project Name to "Panorama," select OK, and Visual Studio will set up a new project.

2. Right-click the project name in Solution Explorer and select Add➤New Item➤Windows Phone Panorama Page. Accept the default name of PanoramaPage1.xaml for the file, and press the OK button.

3. You now have a page with the Panorama control in it within the application, but there is no way to get to it. You could either add navigation from MainPage.xaml, or simply make PanoramaPage1.xaml the main page within the application. To implement the second choice, rename the current MainPage.xaml to MainPage1.xaml and then rename PanoramaPage1.xaml to MainPage.xaml. Now the Panorama page should be the default page that comes up when the application is launched.

4. It is time to customize and add content to the Panorama control. Go ahead and change the <controls:Panorama... element to the following.

```
<controls:Panorama Title="airport" Foreground="Red">
```

5. To add new "tabs" or containers to the Panorama control, you would use the `<controls:PanoramaItem...` XAML element. Go ahead and add a third `PanoramaItem` that will contain a text box and a button to search for departures to a specific city right above the closing tag for the Panorama control `</controls:Panorama>`. Notice that as you add `PanoramaItem`, your designed view reflects the changes.

```
<!--Panorama item three-->
<controls:PanoramaItem Header="search" Foreground="{StaticResource
PhoneAccentBrush}">
        <Grid>
            <TextBox Height="72" HorizontalAlignment="Left" Margin="-12,-2,0,0"
Name="textBox1" Text="TextBox" VerticalAlignment="Top" Width="271" />
            <Button Content="Search" Height="72" HorizontalAlignment="Left"
Margin="242,-4,0,0" Name="button1" VerticalAlignment="Top" Width="160" />
        </Grid>
</controls:PanoramaItem>
```

■ **Note** Notice the use of `Foreground="{StaticResource PhoneAccentBrush}"` binding. It allows the foreground color of the text to be the current theme's accent color.

---

6. Make some minor adjustments to the first two Panorama items to bring them in line with the rest of the UI layout. Replace the top two `<controls:PanoramaItem...` elements with the following XAML:

```
<!--Panorama item one-->
<controls:PanoramaItem Header="arrivals" Foreground="{StaticResource
PhoneAccentBrush}">
        <Grid>
        </Grid>
</controls:PanoramaItem>

<!--Panorama item two-->
<controls:PanoramaItem Header="departures" Foreground="{StaticResource
PhoneAccentBrush}">
        <Grid/>
</controls:PanoramaItem>
```

7. Finally, add a background image to the Panorama control. The recommended size for the background image is 800 pixels high (of course, that's the standard resolution of Windows Phone 7 devices) and 2,000 or fewer pixels wide. To specify the background image, add the following XAML tag right below the `<controls:Panorama …` tag:

```
<controls:Panorama.Background>
    <ImageBrush ImageSource="PanoramaBackground.jpg"></ImageBrush>
</controls:Panorama.Background>
```

Press F5 to run the application. You should see a screen that looks very similar to Figure 9–4 (minus the background image, perhaps). Flicking the `Panorama` control from right to left should allow you to see Arrivals and Departures plus a separate tab designated for searching airport schedules.

Figure 9–4. Panorama control example

As you can see, it is pretty easy to use a `Panorama` control, and you can place different contents within the `PanoramaItem` tag. Using the `Panorama` control, together with the `Pivot` control that we will discuss next, provides a very easy way to impress your users with cool designs, layouts, and coding techniques. Considering you didn't have to hire a graphics designer to get there, that is a very powerful weapon in the Windows Phone 7 developer arsenal. In the next section, we will take a look at another powerful control—the `Pivot` control for Windows Phone 7.

■ **Note** Microsoft recommends limiting the number of `PanoramaItems` to a maximum of four to ensure smooth application performance. In addition, it is considered best practice to hide `PanoramaItem` until it has content to display.

Using the Pivot Control

The Pivot control is a close cousin of the Panorama control: the basic premise of having multiple pages easily accessible is preserved; however, the ability to click the header to show the contents of a new page is not possible with a Panorama control. A screenshot of a simple Pivot control is shown in Figure 9–6. There, a user could tap (or click in the emulator) the word "departures" and be immediately presented with the portion of the application dealing with airport departures.

Creating a Pivot control is very much like creating a Panorama control; there are still three possible ways of adding it to your application (except you would add a Windows Phone Pivot Page, of course). Within the control itself, you would work with PivotItems, not PanoramaItems, but the rest of the design approaches are almost identical. If you feel uncertain about how to work with Pivot controls on Windows Phone 7, you can always visit MSDN instructions on working with the Pivot control at http://msdn.microsoft.com/en-us/library/ff941123(v=VS.92).aspx for a quick reference.

Understanding Frame and Page Navigation

To navigate from screen to screen in a Windows Phone 7 application, an understanding of the PhoneApplicationFrame and PhoneApplicationPage controls is important. There is only one PhoneApplicationFrame available to a Windows Phone 7 application; this frame reserves space for the System Tray and the Application Bar, as well as the content area where PhoneApplicationPage controls live. You can create as many different pages as needed and then navigate to those pages from the frame. See Figure 9–5 to see how the controls are placed in the phone.

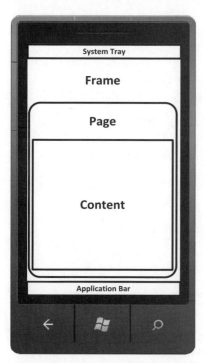

Figure 9–5. PhoneApplicationFrame and PhoneApplicationPage

To navigate from page to page within your application, use the NavigationService class. This class exposes methods to navigate to pages given a URI, as well as to go back to the previous page. The following walkthrough illustrates the use of the NavigationService class.

Creating a User Interface for NavigationTest Project

The NavigationTest project will contain two XAML pages (MainPage.xaml and Page1.xaml) and will navigate between the two.

1. Launch Visual Studio 2010 Express and select the Windows Phone Application template. Change the Project Name to "NavigationTest," select OK, and Visual Studio will set up a new project.

2. Right-click the project name in Solution Explorer and select Add ➤ New Item ➤ Windows Phone Portrait Page. Accept the default name of Page1.xaml and press OK.

3. Open MainPage.xaml in Design View. From the toolbox, drag and drop the HyperlinkButton control. With that control selected, press F4 to display its properties and change the Contents to be "Go to Page1."

4. Open Page1.xaml in the design view, and add a button to that page from the toolbox. Edit the Contents of the button to say "Go Back to MainPage."

5. Add a TextBlock underneath the button on Page1.xaml. This TextBlock will be used to show the parameters passed in to this page.

In the next section, we will use NavigationService to navigate between pages.

Adding Navigation Code

When the user clicks the "Go to Page 1" hyperlink, you will be using NavigationService to move to Page1.

1. Open MainPage.xaml and double-click the hyperlink on that page. Implement the hyperlinkButton1_Click event handler with the following code:

```
private void hyperlinkButton1_Click(object sender, RoutedEventArgs e)
{
    NavigationService.Navigate(new Uri("/Page1.xaml", UriKind.Relative));

}
```

2. Open Page1.xaml and double-click the button on that page. Implement the button1_Click event handler with the following code:

```
private void button1_Click(object sender, RoutedEventArgs e)
{
    NavigationService.GoBack();
}
```

3. Press F5 to run the application. Now when you click the hyperlink on MainPage.xaml, you are taken to Page1.xaml. When you click the button on Page1.xaml, you are taken back to MainPage.xaml. In the next section, we will enhance this application slightly to pass parameters between the pages.

Adding Code to Pass Parameters Between Pages

In the previous section, you learned how to successfully navigate from page to page. In this section, you will see how you can pass parameters from one page to another.

1. Open `MainPage.xaml.cs` and change the `hyperlinkButton1_Click` event handler to the following:

```
private void hyperlinkButton1_Click(object sender, RoutedEventArgs e)
{
    NavigationService.Navigate(new Uri("/Page1.xaml?message=Hello,World",
UriKind.Relative));
}
```

Here, you are passing the hard-coded string "Hello, world" to `Page1.xaml` for processing.

2. In `Page1.xaml`, you will try to read the query string passed from the prior pages to see if there are non-empty values. Open `Page1.xaml.cs` and add the following code to that file:

```
protected override void OnNavigatedTo(System.Windows.Navigation.NavigationEventArgs
e)
{
    base.OnNavigatedTo(e);
    string msg = "";
    if (NavigationContext.QueryString.TryGetValue("message", out msg))
        textBlock1.Text = msg;
}
```

3. Press F5 to run the application. Now, if you press the hyperlink from `MainPage.xaml`, you should see the "Hello, world" message displayed on `Page1`.

Having talked about controls, we will close out this chapter with a neat effect you can add to your application to increase the buzz about it.

Adding Transition Effects

To spice up your application, you can add what is called a "tilt" effect to the visual elements. The tilt effect provides visual feedback to the user of the Windows Phone 7 application during manipulation of visual elements within the application. So, instead of just "pressed" and "unpressed" states, elements can also have "being pressed" and "being unpressed" states. The integration of tilt is pretty straightforward, and in the end it will certainly be completely up to you whether you would like to use it within your application. But if you do decide to give this effect a try, follow this walkthrough.

Creating a User Interface

The user interface for the test application will be composed of four controls within the page: `ListBox`, `Button`, `Hyperlink`, and a `Checkbox`.

1. Launch Visual Studio 2010 Express and select the Windows Phone Application template. Change the Project Name to "TiltableTest," select OK, and Visual Studio will set up a new project.

2. Open `MainPage.xaml` in design mode, and add a `ListBox` with four items, a `Button`, a `Hyperlink`, and a `Checkbox` to the page, with the end goal of creating a user interface like the one shown in Figure 9–6.

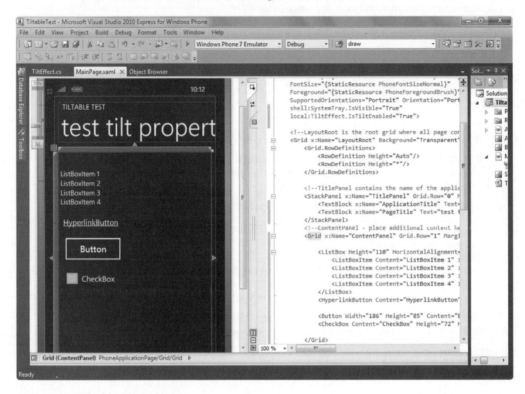

Figure 9–6. *TiltableTest UI layout*

3. You can also paste the following XAML code to get the same interface depicted in Figure 9–7:

```xml
<!--ContentPanel - place additional content here-->
<Grid x:Name="ContentPanel" Grid.Row="1" Margin="12,0,12,0">

        <ListBox Height="110" HorizontalAlignment="Left" Margin="6,47,0,0" Name="listBox1"
VerticalAlignment="Top" Width="460" ItemsSource="{Binding}" >
                <ListBoxItem Content="ListBoxItem 1" ></ListBoxItem>
                <ListBoxItem Content="ListBoxItem 2" ></ListBoxItem>
                <ListBoxItem Content="ListBoxItem 3" ></ListBoxItem>
                <ListBoxItem Content="ListBoxItem 4" ></ListBoxItem>
        </ListBox>
        <HyperlinkButton Content="HyperlinkButton" Height="30" HorizontalAlignment="Left"
Margin="-109,185,0,0" Name="hyperlinkButton1" VerticalAlignment="Top" Width="409" />

        <Button Width="186" Height="85" Content="Button" HorizontalAlignment="Left"
VerticalAlignment="Top" Margin="9,234,0,0" />
```

```
        <CheckBox Content="CheckBox" Height="72" HorizontalAlignment="Left"
Margin="12,325,0,0" Name="checkBox1" VerticalAlignment="Top" />

    </Grid>
```

Now that you've added controls to the MainPage, in the next section, you will be adding Tilt effects to the controls you added.

Downloading TiltEffect.cs and Applying Dependency Properties

To integrate the Tilt effect into your application, you will need to download TiltEffect.cs and properly integrate it into your project.

1. Download the Tilt Effect Control Sample from http://go.microsoft.com/fwlink/?LinkId=200720, and extract the contents of the zip file to a known location.

2. From within the TiltableTest project you created previously, right-click the Add ➤ Existing Item, navigate to the location from Step 1, and find the TiltEffect.cs file.

3. With TitlEffect.cs now a part of your project, double-click that file to open it. Change the following statement as shown here.

```
namespace ControlTiltEffect
```

to

```
namespace TiltableTest
```

Essentially, you just changed the namespace of this file so that it now belongs to your application.

4. Now you need to add the IsTiltEnabled dependency property to the MainPage.xaml page. Open MainPage.xaml in a XAML view and, at the very top of the page, right below the xmlnss:mc=… add the following statement:

```
xmlns:local="clr-namespace:TiltableTest"
```

5. You are almost done—at the top of the page, beneath the statement

```
shell:System Tray.IsVisible="True"
```

add

```
local:TiltEffect.IsTiltEnabled="True">
```

6. Right-click the project and select Build. After the project builds, you are ready to run the application.

Press F5 to run the application. Now when you click the button or the items in the ListBox, you should see an animation in which these items first contract and then expand. That's another element of interactivity that you can add to your application if you desire.

■ **Note** You can suppress the Tilt effect on any control by adding the `local:TiltEffect.SuppressTilt="True"` attribute to that control.

Summary

In this chapter, you have learned the basic concepts of Metro Design System, as well as theme support on Windows Phone 7 devices. You have learned how to detect which theme is being used, as well as how to create theme-aware applications. After that, you learned to work with `Panorama` and `Pivot` controls and got familiar with the `PhoneApplicationFrame` and `PhoneApplicationPage` controls. Finally, you learned how to further enhance user interaction via the introduction of tiltable effects in your applications. In the next chapter, you will learn about tightly integrating your applications with Windows Phone OS 7.0.

■■■

CHAPTER 10

Integrating Applications with the Windows Phone OS

When a third-party application runs on a Windows Phone, it runs in an execution environment that is highly restricted. The Windows Phone OS must be restrictive in order to protect unsuspecting users of mobile devices from potential malicious application behavior, which may include stealing personal data stored on the phone, dialing phone numbers without users' knowledge, or corrupting other applications' data stores. One of the major restrictions that Windows Phone OS places on mobile applications is limiting them to their own execution environment, or **sandbox**, and not allowing them access to other applications' space or internals of the operating system. Sandboxing and other Windows Phone security features are covered in great detail in the last chapter of this book, Chapter 19.

Yet many applications need to access the system features of the phone, to play a music file in the media library, for example, or to take a photo, or to send a text message or an e-mail. Windows Phone 7 OS enables such application interactions with the device via a set of Application Programming Interface (API) tasks referred to as **launchers** and **choosers**. It is relatively easy to use launchers and choosers from within your application, but when one is invoked or when a user presses hardware buttons on the phone, managing application state does get a little tricky.

In this chapter, you will learn about the several launchers and choosers available on the Windows Phone 7 platform, as well as various states an application can enter when you invoke them. You'll conclude this chapter with a quick look at Windows Phone 7 hubs, which bring many applications found on desktop devices and in the cloud to the palm of your hand.

Introducing Windows Phone 7 Launchers and Choosers

When an application executes, the Windows Phone 7 OS confines it to its own space, or sandbox. Both memory and file storage are isolated within that sandbox—one application cannot access or alter another's memory or file storage. Neither can one application directly call another or access a shared data store—such as a list of contacts, for example. There are obvious reasons for this behavior; Microsoft must ensure that the Windows Phone 7 platform is as secure and stable as possible, and isolating applications is one giant step toward getting there.

There is a set of built-in APIs that provide access to the most common features of Windows Phone 7. These APIs help us perform tasks, such as saving a contact's e-mail address or phone number, or placing a phone call (with the mandatory prior user authorization, of course), that require access to shared resources on the phone.

Launchers and choosers, which can be thought of as system functions provided by the Windows Phone OS, provide you with the means to call into these applications. The difference between a launcher and a chooser is small but important: choosers provide a return value into the calling application, whereas launchers do not. If you think about a task of composing an e-mail message, for example, then it is sufficient to "fire and forget" an e-mail application, allowing users to create and send an e-mail. A launcher is an ideal solution for this task. On the other hand, an application allowing us to select a photo from the photo library on the phone needs to pass the selected photo to our application. Windows Phone 7 provides a chooser to perform such a task.

An important concept to remember is that launchers and choosers are separate applications. Since one of the core design principles behind Windows Phone 7 is to maximize battery life, only one application is allowed to execute on the phone at any time. Therefore, if you invoke a launcher or chooser from within your application, that launcher or chooser will replace your application and become the running application. Depending on the circumstances, your application may enter one of several states when that happens. We will cover the possibilities when we cover the application life cycle in depth later in this chapter, but in the meantime, Tables 10–1 and 10–2 list the launchers and choosers available on the Windows Phone 7 platform today. You'll find all of them in the `Microsoft.Phone.Tasks` namespace; therefore, to use any of them, be sure to import that namespace into your application.

Launchers

Table 10–1 lists launchers offered on the Windows Phone 7 platform, together with a brief description of functionality offered by each one of those launchers.

Table 10–1. *Windows Phone 7 Launchers and Their Functions*

Launcher	Function
`EmailComposeTask`	Launch the e-mail application with a new message displayed.
`MarketplaceDetailTask`	Launch the Windows Phone Marketplace client application and display the details page for the specified product.
`MarketplaceHubTask`	Launch the Windows Phone Marketplace client application.
`MarketplaceReviewTask`	Launch the Windows Phone Marketplace client application and display the review page for the specified product.
`MarketplaceSearchTask`	Launch the Windows Phone Marketplace client application and display the search results from the specified search terms.
`MediaPlayerLauncher`	Launch the media player.
`PhoneCallTask`	Launch the Phone application; use this to allow users to make a phone call from your application.
`SaveEmailAddressTask`	Launch the Contacts application; use this to allow users to save an e-mail address from your application to a new or existing contact.
`SavePhoneNumberTask`	Launch the Contacts application; use this to allow users to save a phone number from your application to a new or existing contact.

Launcher	Function
SearchTask	Launch the Web Search application.
SmsComposeTask	Launch the SMS application.
WebBrowserTask	Launch the Web Browser application.

Choosers

Table 10–2 lists and describes the choosers available on the Windows Phone 7 platform.

Table 10–2. Windows Phone Choosers and Their Functions

Chooser	Function
EmailAddressChooserTask	Launch the Contacts application and obtain the e-mail address of a contact selected by the user.
CameraCaptureTask	Launch the Camera application and allow users to take a photo from your application (for more information and in-depth examples, please refer to Chapter 16).
PhoneNumberChooserTask	Launch the Contacts application and obtain the phone number of a contact selected by the user.
PhotoChooserTask	Launch the Photo Chooser application and select a photo (refer to Chapter 16 for more information).

Working with Launchers and Choosers

In this section, you will explore how to work with launchers and choosers from within your application. You will use PhoneNumberChooserTask and SmsComposeTask to create an application that selects a contact from the shared list of contacts on the phone and then composes a text message to that contact's phone.

Creating the User Interface

The user interface for this sample consists of a single button; when the user clicks this button, a list of contacts will be displayed, allowing the user to pick one.

1. Launch Visual Studio 2010 Express, and select the Windows Phone Application template. Change the project name to "Tasks," select OK, and Visual Studio will set up a new project.

2. Open MainPage.xaml in design mode, and add a button to the page. Change the button's caption to be "Send SMS."

Coding Application Logic

When the user clicks the "Send SMS" button of your application, she should be presented with a list of contacts available on your device. Conveniently for us, even on the emulator, Microsoft has included a sample list of contacts for us to test an application with.

1. Open `MainPage.xaml.cs` (right-click `MainPage.xaml` and select View Code). At the top of the page, add the following using statement:

```
using Microsoft.Phone.Tasks;
```

2. Declare the following module-level variable for the `PhoneNumberChooserTask` chooser (insert it right above the `MainPage()` constructor):

```
private PhoneNumberChooserTask _choosePhoneNumberTask;
```

3. Instantiate a new `PhoneNumberChooserTask` object within the `MainPage()` constructor, and associate a method to invoke when the user selects a contact from the list. The method to call upon the chooser's return will accept the phone number selected as one of the parameters. Use the following two lines of code to accomplish that:

```
_choosePhoneNumberTask = new PhoneNumberChooserTask();
_choosePhoneNumberTask.Completed += new
EventHandler<PhoneNumberResult>(ChoosePhoneNumberTaskCompleted);
```

4. Code the `ChoosePhoneNumberTaskCompleted` method that will be invoked upon selection of a contact from the list. Note the use of an `SmsComposeTask` launcher to create a new text message to the person you have selected from the contact list:

```
private void ChoosePhoneNumberTaskCompleted(object sender, PhoneNumberResult e)
{
    new SmsComposeTask() { Body = "SMS using Windows Phone 7 Chooser", To =
e.PhoneNumber }.Show();
}
```

5. Finally, add code to react to the button-click event by opening the `PhoneNumberChooser` launcher. The easiest way to accomplish this is to double-click the button with `MainPage.xaml` open in design view and make the button-click event look like the following:

```
private void button1_Click(object sender, RoutedEventArgs e)
{
    _choosePhoneNumberTask.Show();
}
```

6. Press F5 to run your application. Click the Send SMS button, and select Andrew R. (Andy) Hill from the list of contacts that comes up on the emulator. Immediately after selecting Andy, you should see a screen similar to Figure 10–1, where the SMS message has been composed and is ready to be sent to Andrew.

To summarize what you have learned so far, your application integrates with the Windows Phone OS via a set of API methods referred to as launchers and choosers. Working with launchers and choosers is fairly straightforward, as illustrated by the foregoing example. If that was all there was to application integration, it would have made for a very brief chapter. But there's more.

One major limitation of mobile platforms is their inherently short battery life. This limitation causes OS designers and phone manufacturers to come up with various techniques to balance short battery life with positive user experience. One such technique is to allow only one application to run on the phone at any given time. You may be wondering then, what happens when your application yields execution to the built-in Windows Phone OS application invoked with the launcher? That brings us to the important Windows Phone concept of application **tombstoning**, a subject you'll explore along with the Windows Phone application life cycle in the next section.

Figure 10–1. SMS is composed and ready to go to Andrew.

Working with the Windows Phone 7 Application Life Cycle

To program responsive applications on a Windows Phone 7 device, you must be familiar with the concept of tombstoning on that platform. The simplest way to explain tombstoning is to describe it as an event that happens when your application loses focus on the Windows Phone 7 device, such as when a user invokes a launcher or a chooser, or presses the hardware Start button. When your application loses focus, the Windows Phone OS realizes that there is a good chance that the user will want to come back, or reactivate your application shortly, and he or she will expect to find it in its previous state. Therefore, instead of simply terminating your application as soon as it loses focus, the Windows Phone OS remembers its state and provides developers with a means to save session-related information to a custom State dictionary object. However, with tombstoning, there is always a chance that your application may never be reactivated. So, if there is data that needs to be permanently preserved within your application, you should save it to the isolated storage instead of the transient State object.

You will get to observe tombstoning at work shortly, but before that, you need to walk through a typical life cycle of a Windows Phone 7 application. Table 10–3 summarizes the application events that can occur during the execution of a typical Windows Phone 7 application. The table also describes the actions you as a developer should take when each of those events occurs.

Table 10–3. Applications Events, Triggers, and Actions

Application Event	Occurs When	Your Actions
Application_Launching	The user taps the entry for an application on the installed applications screen, and a new instance of an application is created.	Do not read application settings from the isolated storage as that will slow down the loading process; do not attempt to restore transient state. When an application launches, it should always appear as a new instance.
Application_Activated	For this event to occur, two conditions must be met: (1) the user navigates away from your application, either by using a launcher or a chooser, or by starting another application and (2) the user then comes back to your application by either completing the launcher or chooser or using the hardware Back button. This event is *not* raised when an application is first launched.	The application should allow the user to continue interaction as if she had never left the application; transient state information should be restored, but the application should not attempt to read the contents of the isolated storage to avoid potential slowdown.
Application_Deactivated	The user navigates away from your application either by invoking a launcher or a chooser, or by launching another application. This event is not raised when your application is closing.	You should save all transient (i.e., related to the current application session) state into the State dictionary. You should save persistent state to an isolated storage. Applications are given ten seconds to complete this event; after ten seconds, if this event is still not completed, an application will be terminated and not tombstoned.
Application_Closing	The user uses the Back key to navigate past the first page of your application.	Save all of the persistent state into the isolated storage.

In the next section, you will code and observe the conditions under which each of the events in the application life cycle is triggered.

Observing Application Life Cycle Events

To help you better understand the conditions under which tombstoning occurs and the events that are fired, let's enhance the application built previously in this chapter to trace the events raised within the application.

Enhancing the User Interface

You will enhance the application user interface by adding a text box and a button control to the design surface of MainPage.xaml to make it look similar to Figure 10–2.

1. Launch Visual Studio 2010 Express, and open the previously created Tasks project.

2. Double-click MainPage.xaml in Solution Explorer, and add a text box and a button to the design surface, as shown in Figure 10–2. Clear the Text property of the text box, and set the button's caption to "Launch Browser."

Adding Application Logic to Invoke WebBrowserTask Launcher and Log Events

Now, you will add logic to invoke a WebBrowserTask launcher and navigate to www.windowsphone.com, as well as add messages to print in the Debug window when various application life cycle events occur.

1. Add the following using directive to the top of MainPage.xaml:

```
using System.Diagnostics;
```

2. You will launch the web browser when the user clicks the Launch Browser button. Double-click the Launch Browser button on MainPage.xaml, and make that button's Click event handler look like the following:

```
private void button2_Click(object sender, RoutedEventArgs e)
{
    WebBrowserTask webTask = new WebBrowserTask();
    webTask.Show();
    webTask.URL = "http://www.windowsphone.com";
}
```

3. Application life cycle events that we have discussed in the previous section are all automatically stubbed out (in other words, they contain basic method signatures without any implementation logic) in the App.xaml.cs file. Open that file (one way to do it is to right-click App.xaml and select View Code) so that you can modify those events by adding tracing logic to them.

4. Within the Application_Launching event, add the following line of code:

```
Debug.WriteLine("Application Launching");
```

5. Within the Application_Activated event, add the following line of code:

```
Debug.WriteLine("Application Activated");
```

6. Within the Application_Deactivated event, add the following line of code:

```
Debug.WriteLine("Application Deactivated");
```

7. Within the Application_Closing event, add the following line of code:

```
Debug.WriteLine("Application Closing");
```

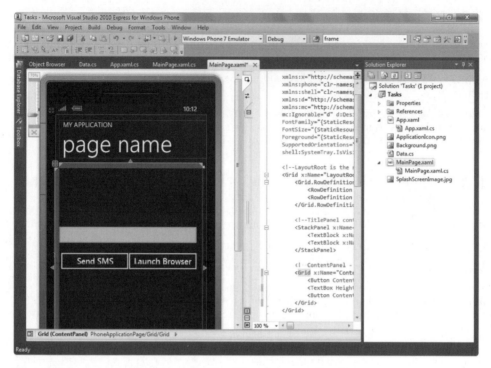

Figure 10–2. User interface for application lifecycle test application

Running the Application

Before running the application, make sure to bring the Visual Studio Output window to the forefront—in Visual Studio, select Debug ➤ Windows ➤ Output on the menu bar. Press F5 to run the application that you have built in the previous steps and observe the messages displayed in the Output window.

1. When the application first comes up, observe how an "Application Launching" message is printed in the Output window, indicating that the `Application_Launching` event has fired, but the `Application_Activated` event has not fired upon the initial launch of an application.

2. Click the Launch Browser button to bring up Internet Explorer with the Windows Phone web site open. In the Visual Studio Output window, notice how the `Application_Deactivated` event fired as soon as the web browser was launched (see Figure 10–3), indicating possible tombstoning of your application.

3. Click the Back button on the emulator screen. Notice how the `Application_Activated` event fires and prints a message in the Output window.

4. Click the Start button, and observe how `Application_Deactivated` is fired again. If you click the Back button now, the `Application_Activated` event is triggered.

5. Finally, click the Back button again. Since you have navigated past the first page of the application, the application is terminated, triggering the `Application_Closing` event and printing the corresponding message in the Output window.

To summarize the foregoing experiments, any time your application lost focus, an `Application_Deactivated` event was triggered. Any time an application gained focus (except for the initial launch), an `Application_Activated` event was triggered. These concepts are important to keep in mind as we discuss saving and retrieving state information in Windows Phone 7 applications in the next section.

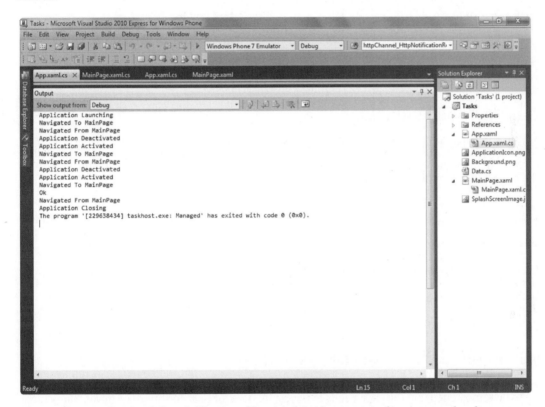

Figure 10–3. Application life cycle illustrated by switching between applications on the phone

Table 10–4 summarizes the actions you took and the corresponding events raised within your application. You can reference Table 10–3 for actions to take to persist state when a given event is raised within your application.

Table 10–4. Summary of Your Actions and Resulting Application Events

Your Action	Application Event
Pressed F5 to start the application	`Application_Launching`
Pressed Launch Browser button to launch IE on the phone	`Application_Deactivated`
Clicked the Back button to go back to your application	`Application_Activated`
Clicked the Start button	`Application_Deactivated`
Clicked the Back button to return to your application	`Application_Activated`
Clicked the Back button to go past the first page of your application	`Application_Closing`

Managing Application State

Let's try the following experiment: open the Tasks project if it's not already open within Visual Studio 2010 Express for Windows Phone, and press F5 to run it. In the text box field that comes up, type "Hello, world" (you can press the Page Up key to allow you to type from the keyboard in the emulator). Next, click the Launch Browser button, and then press the Back button to return to your application.

Notice how the text box is blank (the "Hello, world" text is gone) once you come back to the main application screen. Now imagine if your application were a real-world application capturing many different pieces of data and it provided a WebBrowserTask to allow quick lookup of data on the Internet. It would certainly not be acceptable to the end user to have to retype all the information once the WebBrowserTask completes. Hence, you must devise a mechanism to preserve such data when the application is being tombstoned. Enterstate management.

If you have done any sort of web development, the concept of state management will already be very familiar to you. And if you haven't been exposed to state management before, it's a fairly easy concept to grasp. Per Microsoft's documentation, when an application like the Tasks application of the previous example is tombstoned, it should save state information in case it is reactivated. In the sections that follow, we will show you how to save and retrieve state information within your application.

Managing State at the PhoneApplicationPage Level

The concept of state management at the page level applies not only to those times when an application is about to be tombstoned and the page needs to persist its state for possible future retrieval. Many times, individual pages within a Windows Phone 7 application must save their session data to allow navigation to other pages within that same application; and if the user comes back to the original page, it should be smart enough to retrieve data previously entered by the user.

To accomplish session persistence for both tombstoning and page navigation scenarios, each page relies on the following three methods within the PhoneApplicationPage class:

- OnNavigatedFrom(), which is called when the page is no longer an active page in a frame

- OnNavigatedTo(), which is called when the page becomes the active page in a frame

- OnBackKeyPress(), which is called when the hardware Back key is pressed

In the following code walkthrough, you will use each one of these methods, as well as the State dictionary object, to persist data from the text box in the Tasks application that you have built in this chapter. Follow these steps to accomplish this task.

You will not be making any changes to the user interface of the Tasks application—it will stay very basic, as shown in Figure 10–2. You will, however, add code to the Tasks application to persist the information that has been entered inside the single text box in that application.

1. Launch Visual Studio 2010 Express, and open the previously created Tasks project, if it's not already open.

2. Open MainPage.xaml.cs (one way is to right-click MainPage.xaml and select View Code). You will add code to save text entered in the text box on MainPage.xaml into the session objects if the page becomes no longer active in a frame—i.e., in that page's OnNavigatedFrom event. Add the following code to the MainPage.xaml.cs file:

```
protected override void
OnNavigatedFrom(System.Windows.Navigation.NavigationEventArgs e)
    {
        Debug.WriteLine("Navigated From MainPage");

        if (State.ContainsKey("TextboxText"))
            State.Remove("TextboxText");

        State.Add("TextboxText", textBox1.Text);

        base.OnNavigatedFrom(e);
    }
```

Notice the use of the State dictionary object—it is indeed very similar to the Session variable of ASP.NET web-based applications, and in the foregoing method we add the value from the text box into the State dictionary object.

3. Next, you will add code to retrieve values from the State dictionary object when the user navigates to the current page; you will do that inside the OnNavigatedTo method:

```
protected override void OnNavigatedTo(System.Windows.Navigation.NavigationEventArgs
e)
    {
        Debug.WriteLine("Navigated To MainPage");

        if (State.ContainsKey("TextboxText"))
        {
            string strTextboxText = State["TextboxText"] as string;

            if (null != strTextboxText)
                textBox1.Text = strTextboxText;
        }

        base.OnNavigatedTo(e);
    }
```

The code you have written thus far is sufficient to save the text from the text box for the duration of the application session; even if an application is tombstoned, and the user later returns to the currentx page, the text will be properly preserved. Let's test this out really quickly: press F5 to run this application, enter "Hello, world" in the text box, and press the Launch Browser button. Once the browser comes up, press the Back button—you should see "Hello, world" still displayed in the text box, unlike the behavior we saw previously in this chapter, where we did not handle any state information at all.

While saving information for the duration of the session is extremely important, there are many occasions when you would like to save information permanently, so that even if you turn your phone off (or the battery dies), you will still have access to that information. Let's expand our walkthrough to accommodate saving text into the isolated storage on the Windows Phone 7, so that text is available for use as long as the application's isolated storage is intact (and as long as we don't remove this information from the isolated storage, of course). Follow these steps to accomplish this task.

4. Add the following two using directives to the top of the MainPage.xaml.cs file:

```
using System.IO.IsolatedStorage;
using System.IO;
```

5. You will add code to save text into the isolated storage area of your application if the user presses the Back button. If you would like to get more familiar with isolated storage, we cover it in Chapter 13 of this book. Add the following method to the MainPage.xaml.cs file:

```
protected override void OnBackKeyPress(System.ComponentModel.CancelEventArgs e)
{
    base.OnBackKeyPress(e);
    MessageBoxResult res = MessageBox.Show("Do you want to save your work before
leaving?", "You are exiting the application", MessageBoxButton.OKCancel);

    if (res == MessageBoxResult.OK)
    {
        Debug.WriteLine("Ok");
        SaveString(textBox1.Text, "TextboxText.dat");
    }
    else
    {
        Debug.WriteLine("Cancel");
    }
}
```

Notice how the message box is used to ask the user whether to save information to the file inside isolated storage; if the user chooses Yes, the SaveString method is called, passing the value to save and the file to save it to.

6. Finally, you need to code the SaveString method that performs all the heavy lifting within the isolated storage. This method accepts the name of the file as one of the parameters, and then it creates a file with that name within the isolated storage. After the file is created, the method saves the data string passed to it inside that file. While persisting string values inside the file is perfectly acceptable for the small application that you are building in this walkthrough, you might consider a different data structure for bigger production applications with lots of data to persist. Serializing data to XML would be a better alternative for such applications, as would be saving data inside a dictionary or key-value collection objects. Here is the full listing of that method; make sure it is also present in your code.

```
private void SaveString(string strTextToSave, string fileName)
{
    using (IsolatedStorageFile isf =
```

```
IsolatedStorageFile.GetUserStoreForApplication())
        {
            //If user choose to save, create a new file
            using (IsolatedStorageFileStream fs = isf.CreateFile(fileName))
            {
                using (StreamWriter write = new StreamWriter(fs))
                {
                    write.WriteLine(strTextToSave);
                }
            }
        }
    }
}
```

You are now ready to run your application. Press F5 to launch it, type "Hello, world" in the text box shown, and press the Back button. Remember, pressing the Back button past the first page of an application results in termination of that application. Click "Yes" on the message box prompting you to save your work before leaving. Next, re-launch your application. You should see "Hello, world" displayed in the text box—but you don't. What happened? If you guessed that we still have to retrieve the values previously stored inside the isolated storage, you are correct. We will retrieve those values in the next section, together with looking at the best practices for retrieving this information.

Retrieving Application Initial State

Microsoft guidelines state that within the Application_Launching event there should not be any isolated storage access or web service calls, so that the application comes up and is available for use as quickly as possible. Instead, Microsoft recommends *asynchronously* loading values from the isolated storage of an application once the application is fully loaded. This set of restrictions forces us as developers to code the initialization routines using the following two guidelines:

1. Invoke data initialization and retrieval on a separate thread so as to maximize the responsiveness of an application.

2. Perform application initialization inside the OnNavigatedTo method of the PhoneApplicationPage class.

In the next walkthrough, you will add the necessary methods to properly load application data from the isolated storage.

3. You will continue modifying the Tasks project that you have worked with throughout this chapter. At the top of MainPage.xaml.cs, add the following using directive:

```
using System.Threading;
```

4. Open MainPage.xaml.cs and go to the OnNavigatedTo method within that code. You will make adjustments to that method to load data asynchronously (on a separate thread) from the isolated storage, if there is no data in the State dictionary. Make the OnNavigatedTo method look like the following:

```
protected override void OnNavigatedTo(System.Windows.Navigation.NavigationEventArgs
e)
    {
        Debug.WriteLine("Navigated To MainPage");

        if (State.ContainsKey("TextboxText"))
```

```
{
    string strTextboxText = State["TextboxText"] as string;

    if (null != strTextboxText)
        textBox1.Text = strTextboxText;
}
else
{
    LoadAppStateDataAsync();
}

base.OnNavigatedTo(e);
}
```

5. The GetDataAsync method is responsible for invoking a method that accesses isolated storage data on a separate thread. The full method is shown here:

```
public void LoadAppStateDataAsync
{
    Thread t = new Thread(new ThreadStart(LoadAppStateData));
    t.Start();
}
```

6. Finally, the GetData method accesses isolated storage data looking for a particular file (hard-coded to be "TextboxText.dat" at the moment) and the settings within that file:

```
public void LoadAppStateData()
{

string strData = String.Empty;

    //Try to load previously saved data from IsolatedStorage
    using (IsolatedStorageFile isf =
IsolatedStorageFile.GetUserStoreForApplication())
    {
        //Check if file exits
        if (isf.FileExists("TextboxText.dat"))
        {
            using (IsolatedStorageFileStream fs = isf.OpenFile("TextboxText.dat",
System.IO.FileMode.Open))
            {
                using (StreamReader reader = new StreamReader(fs))
                {
                    strData = reader.ReadToEnd();
                }
            }
        }
    }

    Dispatcher.BeginInvoke(() => { textBox1.Text = strData; });

}
```

7. Your application is now complete, and it should handle both transient and persistent states. To test it, press F5 and enter "Hello, world" in the text box presented. Next, press the Back button and answer "Yes" to save work before leaving. The application is now terminated; if you press F5 again to re-launch the application, the screen should come with "Hello, world" already populated within it.

Best Practices for Managing the Application Life Cycle on the Windows Phone 7 OS

Microsoft provides an important set of guidelines to follow to ensure a consistent and positive user experience on a Windows Phone 7 platform. Some of the highlights of those best practices are as follows.

1. Ensuring that when the user launches a new instance of an application, it is clear that it's a new instance (in other words, our last example of automatically retrieving settings from the isolated storage may not be ideal). At the same time, if an application is being reactivated, the user should feel that the reactivated application has returned in its previous state.

2. Since the user may never return to the application once it becomestombstoned, any data that needs to be saved to a persistent data store should be saved with either the Closing or Deactivated event fires.

3. Invoking a launcher or a chooser will always deactivate an application and *may* cause it to become tombstoned. An application may not be tombstoned if it launches an experience that feels like it's a part of the original application. Microsoft currently lists the following launchers and choosers as not automatically tombstoning the calling application (it clarifies, however, that an OS *may* still choose to tombstone the calling application if the resources are needed elsewhere):

- PhotoChooserTask

- CameraCaptureTask

- MediaPlayerLauncher

- EmailAddressChooserTask

- PhoneNumberChooserTask

- MultiplayerGameInvite [games]

- GamerYouCard [games]

You can take a look at the full list of best practices for managing the application life cycle (most of which we have already covered throughout the chapter) at http://msdn.microsoft.com/en-us/library/ff817009(v=VS.92).aspx.

Windows Phone 7 Hubs

Among the many strengths of the Windows Phone 7 platform is the extent of its integration into the rest of the .NET ecosystem developed by Microsoft over the years, which remains one of its biggest advantages over competing phone platforms. The integrated experience comes in the form of hubs on the phone Start screen, which are essentially menu areas that collect data based on functions. The following hubs are available and are tightly integrated into the Windows Phone 7 OS:

- The **People Hub** integrates feeds from Windows Live and Facebook, and, if you connect other services to Windows Live like LinkedIn, YouTube, Flickr, WordPress, and over 70 more, you and your friends will also see these in the People Hub experience on Windows Phone 7.

- The **Pictures Hub** makes it easy to share pictures and video with your friends via social networks.

- The **Games Hub** with its first and only Xbox Live app, which allows for game, avatar, achievements, and profile integration.

- The **Music and Video Hub** makes the full collection of music and videos available to Zune devices also integrated with Windows Phone 7.

- The **Marketplace Hub** allows users to find and install certified applications and games on the phone.

- The **Office Hub** with its support of Exchange and Exchange ActiveSync, Outlook (with e-mail, calendar, and contacts all available), PowerPoint, SharePoint, Word, and Excel. You can edit Office documents on your mobile device and have your changes available in real time (i.e., as you change them) to others.

The marketing campaign for Windows Phone 7 is about allowing users to "glance and go," or to get the information or the functionality they need from the phone very quickly (quicker than competing platforms, that is). Hubs play a critical role in providing this "glance and go" experience, and your application can raise that role even further by integrating with hubs directly. When you integrate with one of the hubs, your application becomes visible and available through that hub, and not just through the standard list of applications installed on the device. Of course, the functionality provided by your application must jive with the functionality a user might expect from the hub; for example, a music discovery service that allows you to search and find new music based on what you currently like and own should certainly fit within the Music and Video Hub.

We provide detailed instructions that show you how to integrate with the Pictures Hub in Chapter 16 (Photos) by using the Extras... feature of that hub. Here, we will talk briefly about the Music and Video Hub, giving you a general idea of what it would take for your application to appear there, giving users more of the "glance and go" experience.

Integrating with Music and Video Hub is simple: once you ensure that your application makes use of the MediaHistory and MediaHistoryItem classes and provide images to display in the Music and Video Hub tile, the Windows Phone application certification process (discussed in detail in Chapter 5) will take care of the rest. Once the certification process detects that your application uses the MediaHistory and MediaHistoryItem classes, your application's hub will be set to Music and Video, and your application will show up on the list titled "Marquee" within that hub.

Once your application is inside the Music and Video Hub, it can manipulate the tile for that hub, and it can also update the history list of media items played or the list of newly available media items. To update the history and new media items lists, your application will instantiate a new MediaHistoryItem object, set its properties, and call WriteRecentPlay and WriteAcquiredItem correspondingly. To update the "Now Playing" tile on the phone, you would once again create a new MediaHistoryItem object, set its properties, and then assign it to the MediaHistory.Instance.NowPlaying property.

It is certainly inconvenient enough that the emulator does not provide any of the hubs to test integration against and you have to deploy your application to a real device to test that integration. What could be even more frustrating is the fact that you may need to wait for your application to be certified before it is available for testing as part of the Music and Video Hub. To help prevent potentially lengthy application development procedures for hub integration, Microsoft has come up with a workaround for testing Music and Video Hub integration. Inside the `WMAppManifest.xml` file, located within the Properties folder in your Solution Explorer, make sure to set the `HubType` value to 1, as illustrated here:

```
<App xmlns="" ProductID="{c98b0a70-e0c1-462f-a756-5d0aff98e066}" Title="Tasks"
RuntimeType="Silverlight" Version="1.0.0.0" Genre="apps.normal"  Author="Tasks author"
Description="Sample description" Publisher="Tasks" HubType="1">
```

We will conclude this chapter with a set of guidelines for images that you must submit during the certification step, should you choose to integrate with the Music and Video Hub:

1. Tile images must be of type JPEG.

2. You must include your application title or logo on each tile image.

3. The "Now Playing" tile must be 358 pixels x 358 pixels in size.

4. Other tiles must be 173 pixels x 173 pixels in size.

Summary

In this chapter, you have learned how applications integrate with the Windows Phone OS. You have learned how to use launchers and choosers to accomplish common tasks on the platform. You have learned what effects launchers and choosers have on the state of the application that uses them, and you have also reviewed the application life cycle and managing state within this life cycle. Finally, you got a brief overview of all the major applications already tightly integrated within Windows Phone 7. In the next chapter, you will learn about Trial API and build sample trial applications for submission to the Marketplace.

■ ■ ■

CHAPTER 11

Creating Trial Applications

Today, most mobile software vendors maintain two versions of their application code, one for the trial version and another for purchase. The code base for the trial version typically includes some—but not all—of the functionality of the full version, as well as code that urges users to upgrade to the full version of the product. The Windows Phone 7 platform, however, eliminates the need for this practice thanks to the handy IsTrial method. The IsTrial method of the Microsoft.Phone.Marketplace.LicenseInformation class provides the functionality you need to create a trial version. Microsoft.Phone.Marketplace.LicenseInformation is a sealed class that contains the methods you'll use to test your applications. You have already learned how to deploy applications to the Windows Phone Marketplace in Chapter 5; in this chapter, you will learn how to add a trial option to applications you deploy so that your potential customers have a chance to try your applications before they buy them. The IsTrial method determines whether an application is running under a trial or a full license, allowing you to limit your application based on the result that IsTrial returns.

Understanding Trial and Full Modes

If you wish to let potential buyers try your application first, you must let Microsoft know that that trial functionality is "allowed"—i.e., available—when you submit it to the Windows Phone Marketplace. If you specify that trials are allowed, then, in the Marketplace, Microsoft will automatically include a Free Trial button, as shown in Figure 11–1. An important consideration for application developers is that, at present, trials do not expire—they can be replaced by full application versions only if customers decide to purchase applications.

The implementation of trial functionality is entirely up to the application developer; the developer may choose to limit the functionality of the application and prompt the user to purchase the full version of an application to access all application features. Alternately, the developer may choose to prevent the trial application from running after a certain time period. The way to accomplish these time-limited trials would be to either store the date the application was run for the first time and stop after a certain time period, or to store the number of times the application has been run and disallow its execution after a certain number of runs.

Microsoft recommends that application providers prompt users of their trial software during the trial period to purchase a full version. If a user selects the purchase option, control of the application should be programmatically transferred to Windows Phone Marketplace and the application details page should be displayed. Within the Windows.Phone.Tasks namespace, there is a set of methods that make it quick and easy to complete Marketplace tasks, including searching within the application or music categories and showing the application details page. You have already seen some of those methods in the previous chapter (Chapter 10) when you read about Launchers and Choosers. If, after reviewing application details, the user decides to purchase your application, the trial license is replaced with the full license, and the execution of the IsTrial method should indicate that the application is no longer running in the trial mode.

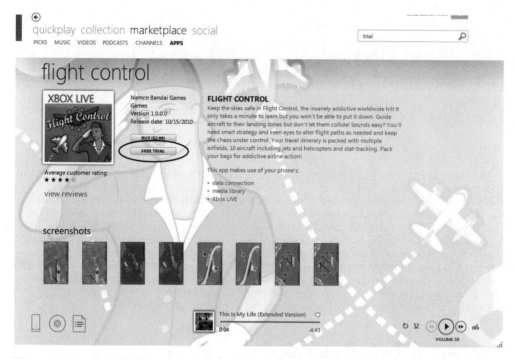

Figure 11–1. A Free Trial button is available for the applications that support Trial mode.

We will now explore in detail both the IsTrial method and the Windows Phone Marketplace API classes that are used to do this work.

Using the IsTrial Method

Using the IsTrial method is straightforward: this method is part of the Microsoft.Phone.Marketplace.LicenseInformation class, and it returns true if an application is being used on a trial basis (i.e., when the user clicks the Free Trial button in the Windows Phone Marketplace instead of Buy) and false if an application is running with a full license. Windows Phone Marketplace handles installation of trial and full licenses and determines when each is appropriate. However, when you execute the IsTrial method while you're developing an application, or before the application user has acquired a trial or a full application license, its behavior is unpredictable. Microsoft documentation currently says that IsTrial would return true, while our tests show the opposite. Regardless of the outcome during the development stage, we should assume that the IsTrial method will work as designed while an application is in development and make provisions for the application to execute properly when it is running under either a trial license or a full license.

The short walkthrough that follows demonstrates the use of the IsTrial method and prints a message onto the screen regardless of whether the current application is running under a trial or a full license.

First, let's create a new application and name it "TrialSample."

1. Launch Visual Studio 2010 Express for Windows Phone and create a new Windows Phone Application project. Name it "TrialSample."

Now add some user interface elements.

2. From the Toolbox, drag and drop a textblock onto the application design surface. Since you are only getting familiar with the IsTrial method, leave the name of the textblock unchanged (textBlock1) and adjust its width to occupy the entire width of the screen.

Next, let's code the demo.

3. Open MainPage.xaml.cs (right-click MainPage.xaml and select View Code), and add the following statement to the top of the page:

    ```
    using Microsoft.Phone.Marketplace;
    ```

4. In the MainPage() constructor, add the following code right after InitializeComponent().

    ```
    LicenseInformation lic = new LicenseInformation();

    if (lic.IsTrial())
    {
        textBlock1.Text = "You are running a trial version of our software!";

    }
    else
    {
        textBlock1.Text = "Thank you for using the full version of our software!";
    }
    ```

5. Press F5 to run the application to see the results of the IsTrial method execution. When the application comes up, you should see a message stating whether you are running a trial version of your application (i.e., the IsTrial method returned true) or the full version.

In the next section, you get to explore options that go beyond simply displaying a text message when the user is executing the trial version of our software. Namely, Windows Phone Marketplace exposes a set of classes to help the user review the details and pay for the full license of our application.

Using the Marketplace APIs

Now that you know how to find out whether an application is running in trial mode, let's add the ability to review an application and buy it. To do that, you'll need two new classes found in the Microsoft.Phone.Tasks namespace: MarketplaceDetailTask and MarketplaceReviewTask. These classes, known as application launchers on the Windows Phone 7 platform and described in the previous chapter (Chapter 10), contain all the necessary functionality for your application to switch from trial to full mode.

Both MarketplaceDetailTask and MarketplaceReviewTask classes implement a Show method that launches the Windows Phone Marketplace application and navigates to the specified application page. For the purposes of allowing users to switch from trial license to full license, there is little difference between these two classes. However, for reference purposes, note that MarketplaceDetailTask allows an application developer to specify an ID of the application (in the ContentIdentifier property) to show the Windows Phone Marketplace page for. This application ID is optional—if it's not supplied to the MarketplaceDetailTask class, the details for the current application are shown in the Marketplace. The MarketplaceReviewTask class, on the other hand, does not expose any public properties, and its Show method displays the review page with an option to buy for the current application only.

Let's enhance the TrialSample application created in the previous walkthrough with an option to review and buy the application from the Windows Phone Marketplace. We will enhance the code so that if an application is executing in the trial mode, it will show two buttons—one with an option to "Upgrade to Full Version" and another with an option to "Cancel" and return to the main screen.

Follow these steps to complete these enhancements. First, you'll add the new namespace reference that contains the APIs you need, and then add the two new buttons:

1. Launch Visual Studio 2010 Express for Windows Phone if it is not already open, and open the Windows Phone Application project called "TrialSample" created during the previous walkthrough.

2. Add the following statement to the top of the page:

using Microsoft.Phone.Tasks;

3. From the Toolbox, drag and drop a button onto the design surface directly beneath the textBlock1 control, as shown in Figure 11–2. With that button selected, press F4 to bring up the button properties window, change the button's Content property to "Upgrade to Full Version," and set the button's Visibility property to "Collapsed." Change the button's name to "btnUpgrade."

4. From the Toolbox, drag another button onto the design surface and drop it next to btnUpgrade, as shown in Figure 11–2. With that button selected, press F4 to bring up the button properties window and change the button's Content property to "Cancel." Change the button's Visibility property to "Collapsed." Change the button's name to "btnCancel." You should now end up with a design surface resembling Figure 11–2.

Next, you need to add code that responds to the new buttons.

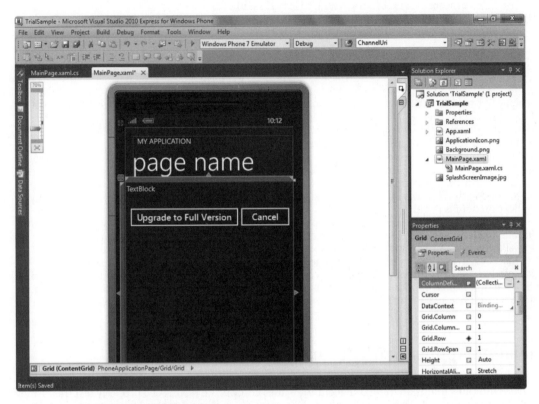

Figure 11–2. TrialSample application layout

5.   Double-click the Upgrade to Full Version button and change the
     btnUpgrade_Click method to the following:

```
private void btnUpgrade_Click(object sender, RoutedEventArgs e)
{
    MarketplaceReviewTask marketplaceReviewTask = new MarketplaceReviewTask();
    marketplaceReviewTask.Show();
}
```

6.   In MainPage.xaml.cs, change the MainPage() constructor to the following:

```
public MainPage()
{
    InitializeComponent();

    LicenseInformation lic = new LicenseInformation();

    if (lic.IsTrial() == true)
    {
        textBlock1.Text = "You are running a trial version of our software!";
        btnUpgrade.Visibility = Visibility.Visible;
```

```
            btnCancel.Visibility = Visibility.Visible;
        }
        else
        {
            textBlock1.Text = "Thank you for using the full version of our software!";
        }
    }
```

When you press F5 to run the application now, there are two issues that immediately jump out at you. First, the IsTrial method, in its current implementation within Windows Phone 7 Framework, always returns false to the emulator. Because of this, given the logic of the application's current implementation, you will not see the buttons with options to upgrade to the full version of an application. If you try to force those buttons to appear, by incorrectly changing the if (lic.IsTrial() == true) statement to if (lic.IsTrial() == false), for example, then when you click the Upgrade to Full Version button, a second issue surfaces. Since the application has not been approved and is not even registered with Windows Phone Marketplace, you will get an error (as expected) trying to display the application details page.

For details on the Windows Phone Marketplace registration and application approval process, you should refer to Chapter 5. Here, let's assume that once the proper application registration is in place, Windows Phone Marketplace will properly display the application details page using the MarketplaceReviewTask class and then swap the trial license and a full application license if the user decides to purchase the program. That still leaves us with the need to properly test the application using both trial and full license modes before submitting the application to the Marketplace to ensure that all functionality that belongs to the full mode only is not available to trial users. The process of simulating trial application mode is the subject of the next section.

Simulating Application Trial and Full Modes

While the ability to create both trial and full application versions in the same code base is a boon to the developers who must maintain them, the technique does complicate testing. To properly test the functionality of your application, you must be able to simulate trial and full application modes before you submit it to the Marketplace. There are certainly many ways to do this, from conditional compilation to use of the SimulateTrialMode property within the Microsoft.Xna.Framework.GamerServices namespace. Each approach has its merits; however, the best approach is often the one that requires the least amount of change to your code.

One way to test an application with virtually no change to its code is to implement your own fake version of the LicenseInformation class. As you've seen, the LicenseInformation class can implement the single IsTrial method discussed earlier in this chapter. By implementing this class, you can fully control the value returned by the IsTrial method and thus the behavior of the application. Then, before going to production, you can swap your implementation of the LicenseInformation class for the sealed class provided by Microsoft within the Microsoft.Phone.Marketplace namespace.

In this section, you'll create such a class. In the next section, you will build an application that uses this class to test features available to trial and full versions of an application to ensure none of the premium content or features of the applications are leaked to trial users.

To help you create your own implementation of the LicenseInformation class, you can (but certainly don't have to) use Reflector.NET, a free tool available for download from Red Gate's web site, at www.red-gate.com/products/reflector/. Reflector is a great tool and becomes very handy when you would like to peek at the implementation details of common libraries. You can certainly gather a wealth of information not just about the LicenseInformation file, but also about the Microsoft.Phone assembly in general. Here's how to set up Reflector.NET to help you implement the example that follows:

1. Download and run Reflector.NET, select File ➤ Open, and navigate to the
   `Microsoft.Phone.dll` file located by default at `C:\Program Files`
   `(x86)\Reference`
   `Assemblies\Microsoft\Framework\Silverlight\v4.0\Profile\WindowsPhone`.

2. Drill down into `Microsoft.Phone.dll` ➤ `Microsoft.Phone.Marketplace` ➤
   `LicenseInformation`, right-click the `LicenseInformation` class, and click
   Disassemble. Be sure to also click the Expand Methods link on the right.

You will see a screen similar to the one shown in Figure 11–3, which you will use to speed up your
own implementation of the `LicenseInformation` class.

Now follow these steps to implement a version of the `LicenseInformation` class:

1. Launch Visual Studio 2010 Express for Windows Phone if it is not already open,
   and open the Windows Phone Application project called "TrialSample," created
   during the previous walkthroughs.

2. Right-click the project name in Solution Explorer, select Add ➤ New Item, and
   then select Class from the list of available items. Name the new class
   "LicenseInformation" and click OK.

3. Now, you can copy the `LicenseInformation` class definition and
   implementation from Reflector.NET and paste it into your application. Here's a
   copy of what you'll see.

```
public sealed class LicenseInformation
{
    // Fields
    private bool m_fIsTrial = true;

    // For testing purpose only!
    public bool IsTrial()
    {
        return m_fIsTrial;
    }
    // Nested Types
    internal static class NativeMethods
    {
        // Fields
        internal const int S_FALSE = 1;
        internal const int S_OK = 0;
    }
}
```

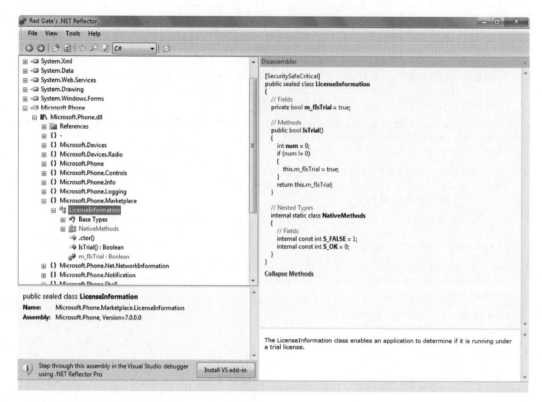

***Figure 11–3.** Using Reflector.NET to peek into the* `LicenseInformation` *class*

■ **Note** There's no reason not to simplify your own version of the class definition by implementing only the `IsTrial` method. There is no LicenseClass interface for you to follow.

---

4. To eliminate any potential confusion between the fake version of the `LicenseInformation` class you use for testing your application and the real one provided by Microsoft, you will use the var keyword to create an instance of the `LicenseInformation` class and then use the fully qualified name to help you visually distinguish between your own implementation of `LicenseInformation` and the implementation provided by Microsoft. Open `MainPage.xaml.cs` and change the following line of code at the top of the page from

```
LicenseInformation lic = new LicenseInformation();
```

to

```
var lic = new TrialSample.LicenseInformation();
```

Now, we can fully control return values of the IsTrial method by changing the value of the m_fIsTrial variable.

5. Set the m_fIsTrial variable to true and press F5 to run the application.

With these modifications, your TrialSample application will now prompt the user to upgrade to the full version. Changing the value of the m_fIsTrial variable to false and re-running the application results in a message that thanks the user for running an application with the full license.

Once you've verified that the application will behave correctly when you deploy it to the Marketplace, it's time to restore the official version of the LicenseInformation class. Here's how:

1. To switch back to the LicenseInformation class within the Windows Phone 7 Framework, right-click LicenseInformation.cs in Solution Explorer and select "Exclude from Project." This action effectively excludes the file from the solution, but does not delete it from the computer system.

2. Finally, we need to change the instance of LicenseInformation to be the instance of the LicenseInformation class provided by Microsoft. Open MainPage.xaml.cs and change the following line of code from

```
var lic = new TrialSample.LicenseInformation();
```

to

```
var lic = new LicenseInformation();
```

Creating trial Windows Phone 7 applications is a relatively straightforward process, as you have seen so far. The biggest challenge is probably testing these applications to ensure that they behave as expected with both trial and full licenses. Luckily, you have several approaches at your disposal, which we've summarized and one of which we have described in detail.

In the next section, you will create trial and full versions of a more complete application and employ several other Windows Phone 7 development techniques that we cover elsewhere in this book. We hope that this short review will help you further solidify your knowledge of the Windows Phone 7 programming.

Building a Trial Application

The trial software application that you will build in this section is a currency converter. It calls a web service to obtain the current exchange rate for the currencies a user specifies, and then tells users how much of the desired currency they will receive in exchange for the currency they wish to exchange. If the application is running with a trial license, users will be able to convert currencies for free.

However, as we all know, consumers never get the official market exchange rates. Various middlemen take a decent-size cut of foreign exchange transactions, so to calculate the actual amount of foreign currency you can expect to receive, the full application provides another screen, called the "More Stuff" screen. With "More Stuff," users can enter the actual exchange rate quoted by an exchange broker and see how much foreign currency they will receive after they have paid a commission. This "More Stuff" screen will be available only to those who have paid you $.99 and acquired the full version of the application. Future enhancements to this application could include maps, shared between all users of this application, that show the best places to exchange currency around town, with the commission rates as a percentage of the transaction charged by those places. Power to the consumers at last!

To create this application, you will employ several Windows Phone 7 techniques that we cover in this book. As we introduce such features, we will point to the location in the book that you can refer to for more in-depth coverage of the material. We will also emphasize the functionality that is available and disabled with an application running with a trial license, and we will utilize the approach that we have covered in this book to simulate both trial and full license modes and to ensure that our application functions correctly under both.

Now let's build and test the application.

Building the User Interface

The Currency Converter application includes three pages: one for the main application screen that performs currency conversions; one to prompt the user to upgrade to the full application license the application is running under a trial license; and one for additional options, such as determining how much money you actually lose on a conversion. In this section, you will create each of these pages. Follow these steps to create a Currency Converter project and add application pages:

1. Launch Visual Studio 2010 Express for Windows Phone, and create a new Windows Phone Application project. Name it "CurrencyConversion."

2. Make sure `MainPage.xaml` is open in Design view. For `MainPage.xaml`, the end goal is to have a screen with a layout similar to the one shown in Figure 11–4. The screen looks a little busy, so we will go over each screen element, one by one, to understand the type of the element and element's name. Element names and types will be referred to from code and, hence, are important to get right. Table 11–1 summarizes field names and types. A portion of the XAML code that creates the "Amount to Convert" text box, two list boxes, and the corresponding captions is shown here:

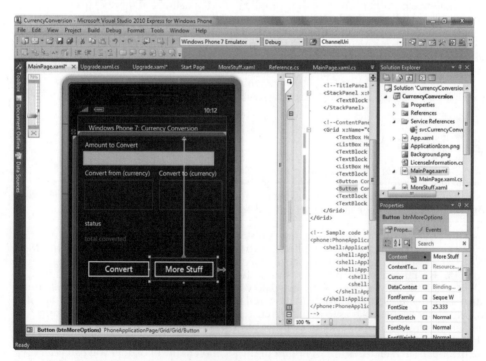

Figure 11–4. Currency Converter `MainPage.xaml` page layout

```
        <TextBlock Height="30" HorizontalAlignment="Left" Margin="24,14,0,0"
Name="textBlock1" Text="Amount to Convert" VerticalAlignment="Top" />
        <TextBox Height="68" HorizontalAlignment="Left" Margin="6,36,0,0"
Name="txtAmountToConvert" Text="" VerticalAlignment="Top" Width="446" />
        <ListBox Height="93" HorizontalAlignment="Left" Margin="24,137,0,0"
Name="lstConvertFrom" VerticalAlignment="Top" Width="220" />
        <TextBlock Height="30" HorizontalAlignment="Left" Margin="24,101,0,0"
Name="textBlock2" Text="Convert from (currency)" VerticalAlignment="Top" Width="220" />
        <TextBlock Height="28" HorizontalAlignment="Left" Margin="262,101,0,0"
Name="textBlock3" Text="Convert to (currency)" VerticalAlignment="Top" Width="190" />
        <ListBox Height="93" HorizontalAlignment="Left" Margin="263,137,0,0"
Name="lstConvertTo" VerticalAlignment="Top" Width="205" />
```

Table 11–1. User Controls for MainPage.xaml

Application Field	Field Name	Field Type
Amount to Convert	txtAmountToConvert	TextBox
Convert from (currency)	lstConvertFrom	ListBox
Convert to (currency)	lstConvertTo	ListBox
Status	txtStatus	TextBlock
Total Converted	txtTotalConverted	TextBlock
Convert Button	btnConvert	Button
More Stuff Button	btnMoreOptions	Button

Next, add the "nag" page, or the page that will try to get users to purchase the full version of our application if the user is executing our application under a trial license.

3. To do that, right-click the project name in Solution Explorer and select Add ➤ New Item ➤ Windows Phone Portrait Page. Name the page Upgrade.xaml and select OK.

4. Bring up the design surface of the Upgrade.xaml page, and make it look like Figure 11–5.

The page consists of a message and two buttons. The message prompts the user to upgrade. One of the buttons enables the user to purchase a full license, and the other one simply returns the user to the main application screen. Ensure that the buttons are properly named by verifying their names with Table 11–2:

Table 11–2: User Controls for Upgrade.xaml

Application Field	Field Name	Field Type
Yes, upgrade	btnUpgrade	Button
No, take me back	btnGoBack	Button

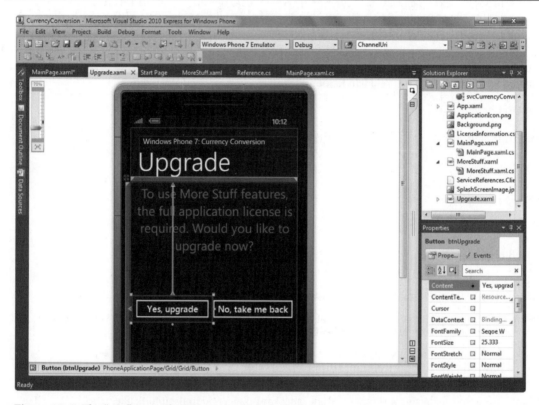

***Figure 11–5.** The "nag" screen layout*

Finally, add the "More Stuff" page, or the page that will display features available only to paid users. Sadly, the users of our application will most likely feel cheated at the moment: our only feature available to them will be the calculation of the money they do not get as a result of using the currency conversion services.

5. To add the "More Stuff" page, right-click the project name in Solution Explorer and select Add ➤ New Item ➤ Windows Phone Portrait Page. Name the page MoreStuff.xaml and select OK.

6. Bring up the design surface of the MoreStuff.xaml page, and make it look like Figure 11–6. Refer to Table 11–3 field names and types:

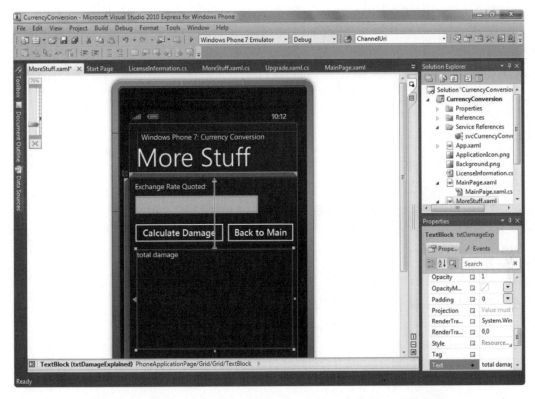

Figure 11–6. The "More Stuff" screen layout with functionality available to full-license users only

Table 11–3. User Controls for `MoreStuff.xaml`

Application Field	Field Name	Field Type
Exchange Rate Quoted	txtExchangeRateQuoted	TextBox
Calculate Damage	btnCalculateDamage	Button
Back to Main	btnBackToMain	Button
Total damage	txtDamageExplained	TextBlock

With design layout complete, you are now ready to add code to the application. In the next section, you will add code feature-by-feature, starting with a reference to the web service that supplies current exchange rates.

Connecting to a Web Service

To retrieve current currency exchange rates, you will be using a web service located at
www.webservicex.net/CurrencyConvertor.asmx. While there are several ways to connect to a web service
and retrieve data, we will be using the approach discussed Chapter 18, which draws on the new
Microsoft Reactive Extensions, or Rx.NET. Using Rx.NET makes it easier to follow the flow of execution
by the program, since it abstracts—behind a solid Observer pattern—the complexities of invoking of a
web service asynchronously. Follow these steps to add a reference to the Currency Conversion service
and to wrap the results returned by that service within Rx.NET.

1. With the CurrencyConversion project open, right-click Solution Explorer and
    select Add Service Reference. Paste the following URL into the Address field, as
    shown in Figure 11–7:

http://www.webservicex.net/CurrencyConvertor.asmx

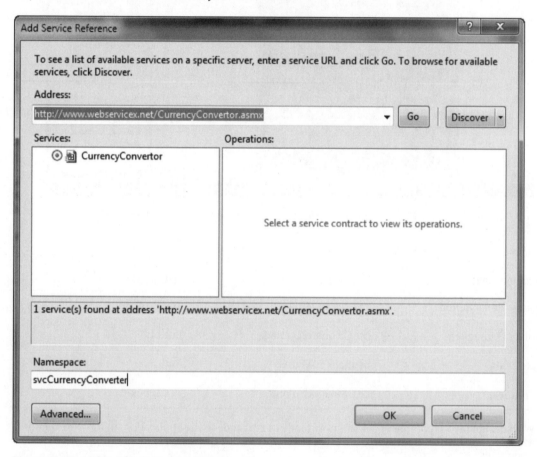

Figure 11–7. Add Service Reference dialog

Once you click the Go button, Visual Studio should be able to locate the CurrencyConverter service.

2. Change the namespace in the Add Service Reference Page to svcCurrencyConverter and click OK.

Next, you will need to add reference to the assemblies that contain the Rx.NET modules.

3. To accomplish that, right-click the project name in Solution Explorer, select Add Reference, and add references to Microsoft.Phone.Reactive and System.Observable assemblies.

4. Switch to the code view for MainPage.xaml (right-click MainPage.xaml and select View Code) and add the following using directive to the top of the page:

```
using Microsoft.Phone.Reactive;
```

5. Create a module-level variable referencing the currency converter web service (this would be a local MainPage class variable that should be initialized just above the constructor). Also, declare and initialize a module-level rate variable :

```
svcCurrencyConverter.CurrencyConvertorSoapClient currencyClient = new
svcCurrencyConverter.CurrencyConvertorSoapClient();
        Double dblRate = 0.0;
```

6. Within the MainPage()constructor, create an Rx.NET subscription to the CurrencyConverter web service by pasting the following code.

```
        //create subscription to the web service
        var currency =
Observable.FromEvent<svcCurrencyConverter.ConversionRateCompletedEventArgs>(currencyClient,
"ConversionRateCompleted");

        currency.ObserveOn(Deployment.Current.Dispatcher).Subscribe(evt =>
        {
dblRate = evt.EventArgs.Result;
            txtStatus.Text = "The current rate is 1 " +
lstConvertFrom.SelectedItem.ToString()  + " to " + evt.EventArgs.Result.ToString() + " " +
lstConvertTo.SelectedItem.ToString();

            if (txtAmountToConvert.Text.Length>0)
            {
                Double decTotal = evt.EventArgs.Result *
Convert.ToDouble(txtAmountToConvert.Text);
                txtTotalConverted.Text = txtAmountToConvert.Text + " " +
lstConvertFrom.SelectedItem.ToString() + " = " + decTotal.ToString() + " " +
lstConvertTo.SelectedItem.ToString();
            }
        },
            ex => { txtStatus.Text = "Sorry, we encountered a problem: " + ex.Message; }
        );
```

This code creates a subscription to all of the results returned by the currency converter service. It processes the results and shows the conversion rates requested on the screen, including multiplying the total amount to be converted by the conversion rate.

If you would like to understand more about Rx.NET, skip to Chapter 18. Since the second part of this book is organized as a set of independent tutorials, the chapters in the second part do not have to be read sequentially, but should instead be referred to when needed.

You are almost done establishing a connection and retrieving data from the Currency Converter web service. The one piece that remains to be written is the invocation of this web service, which, in our example, is done via the Convert button.

7. In the design view of `MainPage.xaml`, double-click the Convert button and change the `btnConvert_Click` method to look like the following:

```
private void btnConvert_Click(object sender, RoutedEventArgs e)
{
currencyClient.ConversionRateAsync((svcCurrencyConverter.Currency)
 lstConvertFrom.SelectedItem, (svcCurrencyConverter.Currency)
 lstConvertTo.SelectedItem);
}
```

This code invokes the web service asynchronously and passes it the parameters selected by the user (currency names only, in our case). Note how we have to properly cast the parameters to the type expected by the web service (`svcCurrencyConverter.Currency` type in our case). The results of this asynchronous invocation are returned to the application and are processed within the subscription code just created within the `MainPage()` constructor code.

With the web service wired up and the data coming back through the Rx.NET subscription to the application, the backbone of our application is complete. Now, we have to introduce navigation between different pages of the application.

Adding Page-to-Page Navigation

In the "Building the User Interface" section, you created three separate pages that make up the application. However, in the application's present state, only a single (`MainPage.xaml`) page is available during runtime. In this section, you will review navigation between pages in the Windows Phone 7 application. For more in-depth coverage of this material, please refer to Chapter 2 of this book.

The envisioned flow of the application is that a separate "More Stuff" page is available to users with full licenses; users with trial licenses should see an "Upgrade" page that prompts them to upgrade. Navigating between pages in Windows Phone 7 is similar to navigating between web pages: you can use the same `NavigationService.Navigate` method and pass it the name of the XAML page within the application to navigate to. This is exactly what you'll do in the Currency Converter application.

1. With the Currency Converter application open, double-click the More Stuff button and make the `btnMoreOptions_Click` method look like the one here:

```
private void btnMoreOptions_Click(object sender, RoutedEventArgs e)
{
    //use Microsoft implementation of LicenseInformation class
    var lic = new LicenseInformation();

    if (lic.IsTrial() == true)
    {
        NavigationService.Navigate(new Uri("/Upgrade.xaml",
UriKind.RelativeOrAbsolute));
    }
    else
    {
        NavigationService.Navigate(new Uri("/MoreStuff.xaml?rate=" +
dblRate.ToString() + "&total=" + txtAmountToConvert.Text,
UriKind.RelativeOrAbsolute));
    }
}
```

Notice how this method uses the IsTrial method to check whether an application is executing under a trial or full license, and then it uses the NavigationService.Navigate method to display the Upgrade.xaml page if IsTrial returns true, and it displays the MoreStuff.xaml page if IsTrial returns false. Note that when you navigate to the MoreStuff.xaml page, you also pass two parameters to that page. One way of passing parameters on Windows Phone 7 is identical to parameter passing on the Web—here, you included our parameters for currency rate and amount as part of the URL. Parameters start after the name of the page, MoreStuff.xaml, are prefixed by the "?" symbol, and are separated from each other by the "&" symbol.

Passing parameters is not enough in itself; an application must know how to properly process those parameters.

2. Open MoreStuff.xaml in the code view and add the following method to receive parameters and assign them to global variables:

```
protected override void OnNavigatedTo(System.Windows.Navigation.NavigationEventArgs e)
{
    base.OnNavigatedTo(e);
    string strExchgRate = "";
    string strTotalToConvert = "";

    if (NavigationContext.QueryString.TryGetValue("rate", out strExchgRate))
        dblExchgRate = Convert.ToDouble(strExchgRate);

    if (NavigationContext.QueryString.TryGetValue("total", out strTotalToConvert))
        decTotalToConvert = Convert.ToDecimal(strTotalToConvert);

}
```

To make the foregoing code work, we must add the following two module-level variables to the MoreStuff.xaml.cs file:

```
Double dblExchgRate;
Decimal decTotalToConvert;
```

What's left is to add navigation to the other pages within the application.

3. Open MoreStuff.xaml in design view, double-click the Back to Main button, and make that button click event handler look like the following:

```
private void btnBackToMain_Click(object sender, RoutedEventArgs e)
{
    NavigationService.Navigate(new Uri("/MainPage.xaml",
UriKind.RelativeOrAbsolute));
}
```

4. Open Upgrade.xaml in Design view, double-click the Back to Main button, and make that button click event handler look like this:

```
private void btnGoBack_Click(object sender, RoutedEventArgs e)
{
    NavigationService.GoBack();
}
```

Note the different navigation implementation in this case: you are simply using the code to go to the previous page within the application instead of navigating to the specific page.

At this point, application navigation is complete. You are ready to make sure that the trial version of the application does not allow access to the "More Stuff" page.

Verifying Trial and Full Mode

Creating trial applications is the central theme of this chapter and we have spent the first part of it looking at various issues that may arise as part of trialing an application. When you allow application trials, one of your most important tasks is to ensure that certain application features are accessible to full license holders only; otherwise, there would be no reason to buy an application.

For the Currency Converter application, you must ensure that that the MoreStuff.xaml page is visible only when the application runs with a full license. You have already seen the code that performs that check; in this section, you must verify that the trial mode indeed behaves as expected. You will learn the technique of writing your own version of the LicenseInformation class just discussed to validate the trial mode of an application.

1. With the Currency Converter application open, right-click the project name in Solution Explorer, select Add ➤ New Item, and then select Class from the list of available items. Name the new class "LicenseInformation" and click OK.

2. Make the LicenseInformation class look like the one here (as we have seen earlier in this chapter, this class definition has been copied from the information generated by Reflector.NET for the LicenseInformation class of the Windows Phone 7 Framework):

```
public sealed class LicenseInformation
{
    // Fields
    private bool m_fIsTrial = true;

    // Methods
    public bool IsTrial()
    {
        int num = 0;
        if (num != 0)
        {
            this.m_fIsTrial = true;
        }
        return this.m_fIsTrial;
    }

    // Nested Types
    internal static class NativeMethods
    {
        // Fields
        internal const int S_FALSE = 1;
        internal const int S_OK = 0;
    }
}
```

You will test the trial mode shortly, right after we put finishing touches on our Currency Converter application.

Adding Finishing Touches

You are nearly ready to test the Currency Converter application—just a few items remain. In this section, we will complete the application and take it for a test drive. Follow these steps to get there.

Before an application is functional, it needs to know what currency to convert to what. We have created two list boxes inside the MainPage.xaml file to allow the user to make her selection. To keep things simple in the first version, you include only three currencies: the US dollar, the euro, and the Russian ruble. When an application loads, you need to load list boxes with those currencies.

1. Open MainPage.xaml.cs and paste the following LoadCurrencies method inside the MainPage() constructor.

```
private void LoadCurrencies()
{
    lstConvertFrom.Items.Add(svcCurrencyConverter.Currency.USD);
lstConvertFrom.Items.Add(svcCurrencyConverter.Currency.EUR);
    lstConvertFrom.Items.Add(svcCurrencyConverter.Currency.RUB);

    lstConvertTo.Items.Add(svcCurrencyConverter.Currency.USD);
    lstConvertTo.Items.Add(svcCurrencyConverter.Currency.EUR);
    lstConvertTo.Items.Add(svcCurrencyConverter.Currency.RUB);
}
```

MoreStuff.xaml needs code to perform calculations on the currency rates passed in and entered into the application. This code belongs inside the btnCalculateDamage_Click event.

2. In Design view, double-click the Calculate Damage button and replace the btnCalculateDamage_Click event code with the following:

```
private void btnCalculateDamage_Click(object sender, RoutedEventArgs e)
{
    decimal decTotalToReceive;
    decimal decTotalAccordingToConversionRate;

    decTotalToReceive = Convert.ToDecimal(txtExchangeRateQuoted.Text) *
decTotalToConvert;
    decTotalAccordingToConversionRate = Convert.ToDecimal(dblExchgRate) *
decTotalToConvert;

    txtDamageExplained.Text = "With exchange rate quoted, you will receive " +
decTotalToReceive.ToString() + "\r\n";
  txtDamageExplained.Text = txtDamageExplained.Text +  "Given market exchange
rate, you should receive " + decTotalAccordingToConversionRate.ToString() + "\r\n";

    txtDamageExplained.Text = txtDamageExplained.Text + "You lose " +
(decTotalAccordingToConversionRate - decTotalToReceive).ToString();
    }
```

Finally, Upgrade.xaml needs code to bring up the Windows Phone Marketplace and load the application review page, which will enable the user to purchase a full version of the application if the user elects to do so. As discussed earlier in this chapter, this is the job for one of the classes within the

Microsoft.Phone.Tasks namespace. The Microsoft.Phone.Tasks namespace is covered in much greater detail in the "Launchers and Choosers" section of Chapter 10.

3. Add the following using directive to the top of the Upgrade.xaml.cs file:

    ```
    using Microsoft.Phone.Tasks;
    ```

4. Next, bring up the Upgade.xaml page in design mode and double-click the "Yes, Upgrade" button. Make that button's click event look like the following:

    ```
    private void btnUpgrade_Click(object sender, RoutedEventArgs e)
    {
        MarketplaceReviewTask marketplaceReviewTask = new MarketplaceReviewTask();
        marketplaceReviewTask.Show();
    }
    ```

You're now done writing code for the Currency Converter application. The application should compile and run if you press F5 now. If, for some reason, there are errors preventing an application from launching, it's best to compare your code to code available for download for this chapter.

Assuming the code runs, the current value of the IsTrial method returned by our own implementation of the LicenseInformation class is true. Therefore, if we run the application and click the More Stuff button, we should see a message prompting us to upgrade to the full version of an application. That is the expected behavior. Let's go ahead and change the value of m_fIsTrial to false. We should now see the "More Stuff" screen, just as we expected the application with full license to behave.

We can also verify that the program works as expected by entering values and asking it to convert those from one currency to another. For instance, today, as shown in Figure 11–8, $345 is only 267.86 euros. To get that output, type "345" in the "Amount to Convert" text box, select "USD" from the "Convert From" list box and select "EUR" from the "Convert To" list box. Then, press the Convert button. Assuming that the connection to the Internet is available, you should get results that are similar.

While the Currency Converter application is functional, it can stand many improvements, particularly in the area of validating user input. For instance, an application throws an error if the user tries to go to the "More Stuff" screen without entering a value in the "Amount to Convert" text box. Addressing this and other issues is left as an exercise for the reader.

Figure 11–8. Currency Converter application converting $345 to euros

Summary

In this chapter, you learned about Windows Phone 7 trial modes. You learned that there is a single code base for both trial and production versions of an application, and that application developers control which functionality to disable for trial modes using the IsTrial method. You have also learned about simulating trial mode, an important technique when creating trial applications. Finally, in this chapter, you have also walked through creating a Currency Converter application that utilized several techniques discussed in this book and perhaps solidified your understanding of several key concepts of Windows Phone 7 development.

In the next chapter, you will learn about internationalizing applications to make them available to many markets whose language and date/time constructs are quite different from those of the American market.

CHAPTER 12

■ ■ ■

Internationalization

Strong growth in mobile computing propelled by increasingly capable mobile devices is not just a North American phenomenon—people all over the world are increasingly relying on their phones both for business and leisure. This, of course, is wonderful news for Windows Phone 7 developers—the greater the customer base, the more potential revenue or exposure the application gets. There is just one small gotcha when taking mobile application development to the world—the vast majority of customers outside North America speak very little to no English.

That means that if your goal is to create an application that succeeds globally, you must ensure that it can "speak" many languages. Certainly, one way to make that happen is to create many versions of an application, one for each language market you target. Unfortunately, that approach quickly becomes a nightmare to maintain. Imagine making a small code change to an application, such as rearranging UI controls on its main page—that code change would have to be made to each language version of the application! Fortunately, .NET Framework provides a set of culture-aware classes and a general approach to implementing multilingual applications via a set of resource files.

In this chapter, you'll learn some simple steps that you can take to prepare an app for distribution in more than one language, ones that will save you time later. This topic deserves a book of its own, and a few have actually been written already (www.amazon.com/s/ref=nb_sb_ss_i_0_17?url=search-alias%3Daps&field-keywords=.net+internationalization). But we hope that our advice in this chapter will help you avoid extra work when your brilliant application becomes a worldwide phenomenon and you're ready to roll it out to the world. Let's begin, however, with a closer look at the topic and the support that the Windows Phone SDK provides.

Understanding Internationalization

Translating your application's interface or its documentation into other languages may be the most important task you'll face when you target your application for a global audience, but it's not the only one. Cultures differ in the ways they display dates, numbers, currencies, and even text. For instance, in the United States, the month is always the first part of the numeric representation of a date. In England, on the other hand, the month comes after the day. This could potentially create confusion—imagine the payment due dates being missed because the date was not formatted according to a culture's standards. One way to avoid misinterpretation of numeric dates is to adopt an international standard, such as ISO 8601, that specifies that all dates are to be represented, from the most significant to the least significant element: year, month, day, hour, and so on.

Similarly, disagreements over cultural representations of decimal separators have the power to almost stall the development of the programming language (http://en.wikipedia.org/wiki/Decimal_separator). To illustrate how such heated debates can originate, consider the following example: the number "one thousand one and one tenth" would be written in the United States as "1,001.1", with the comma symbol used as the separator for the thousands and the period symbol used for separating the decimals. The same number would be written in Europe as "1.001,1", with the dot used for separating thousands and the comma used to separate the decimals. The Windows Phone 7 operating system, fortunately, automatically makes these locale-aware changes for us. As developers, however, we must help the framework out a little and ensure that we use appropriate data types and appropriate formatting options for the operations we perform in our applications. For example, we should never represent dates or numbers as strings and hard-code the formatting of those strings in our application.

In addition to these variations in the way different cultures handle numbers and dates, languages also differ in the number of words they require to express an idea, with some more verbose than others. For instance, it is estimated that an average sentence in the German language is 44 percent longer than the same sentence in English. That means that a Windows Phone 7 user interface written in English—its labels, textblocks, text boxes, and so on—may need to reserve additional available white space when designed in the English language and later translated (dynamically, as we will see shortly) into German or other languages.

Also, if you are targeting international markets, the design of an application should be flexible enough to allow it to "speak" different languages without your having to make extensive changes to the source code. That means that all strings, images, and audio and video content must be placed in separate resource-only files—one for each target culture and language to make it easy to package the application for a new locale. By sticking with Unicode characters to encode your strings content, with its over 95,000 characters, you'll be able to display virtually any language in the world.

Another important consideration in deciding how to prepare to support your application in multiple languages is the amount of material that will need to be translated. Later in this chapter, we recommend you use resource-only files inside Visual Studio. This technique is perfectly acceptable for smaller applications, when there are only a handful of items to translate. However, if the translation requires the use of third-party translation services, you will be better served by looking at more specialized localization tools, such as Alchemy Catalyst, Globalizer.Net, Lingobit Localizer, or Radialix. While the use of such tools is beyond the scope of the current chapter, if you ever find that editing resource files in Visual Studio becomes hard to manage, you can refer to the foregoing list to determine whether any of these products makes the task easier.

In MSDN documentation, there are usually two separate sections on internationalizing applications—globalization and localization. Roughly, *globalization* refers to ensuring that all commonly used application concepts, such as dates and currency, are properly represented and used in the system regardless of the locale of the user. *Localization*, on the other hand, refers to translating application resources, such as text of the user interface, into local representation. What is a bit more confusing, in the non-Microsoft world, is that the term internationalization is used to represent globalization. Since this is already confusing, for the purposes of this chapter, we won't make such a distinction; when we talk about "internationalizing" an application, we refer to ensuring that the application will work without problems in all countries and regions it was intended to work in—i.e., the Microsoft concepts of globalization and localization are blurred.

.NET and the Windows Phone 7 SDK include a number of tools to help you ready an app for international distribution. These tools include the `CultureInfo` class to properly determine the culture that an application is running in, as well as easy management of resource files that were custom developed for each culture. You will explore these tools in the remaining portion of this chapter.

Using Culture Settings with ToString to Display Dates, Times, and Text

To see how you can go about preparing an application for the world, you'll build a simple application that announces a new product, in this case a Windows Phone. But first, you will learn how to use the `CultureInfo` class to ensure dates, numbers, and text appear in the right form regardless of the culture in which the announcement is made. Then you'll see how, by using resource (.resx) files, you can easily add translated content to your app to reach new markets. Figure 12–8 shows how the finished application will look.

Let's jump into code that will set the stage for our discussion of internationalization of Windows Phone 7 applications.

1. Let's start by creating a new project inside Visual Studio and naming it InternationalizationSample.

By default, the MainPage.xaml file is created in the application, with the designer and XAML windows open and ready to program.

2. Double-click MainPage.xaml to bring up the XAML designer window. For convenience and simplicity, we will alter the content of textblocks in the TitleGrid block. Make the XAML of the TitleGrid look identical to the XAML here.

```
<StackPanel x:Name="TitlePanel" Grid.Row="0" Margin="24,24,0,12">
        <TextBlock x:Name="ApplicationTitle" Text="Current Culture Setting"
Style="{StaticResource PhoneTextNormalStyle}"/>
        <TextBlock x:Name="PageTitle" Text="culture" Margin="-3,-8,0,0"
Style="{StaticResource PhoneTextTitle1Style}"/>
    </StackPanel>
```

Your project should now look like Figure 12–1. So far you've simply changed the text of the default title textblock in the Windows Phone 7 application.

1. Now double-click MainPage.xaml.cs to bring up the code view. Alternately, you can right-click the MainPage.xaml file and select "View Code."

2. Add the following statement to the top of the MainPage.xaml.cs file:

```
using System.Globalization;
```

3. Paste the following code in the MainPage() constructor:

```
PageTitle.Text = CultureInfo.CurrentCulture.ToString();
```

4. Press F5 to run the application. You should see a phone emulator screen that looks like the one in Figure 12–2.

Notice how the caption in Figure 12–2 reads "en-US." This caption represents two parts of the current Culture setting on Windows Phone 7. The first part—"en"—states that the English language is the current language on this Windows Phone 7 device (or device emulator in our case) and it is a part of an ISO standard to represent culture code associated with the language. The second part—"US"—represents that the current locale is the United States, and indicates that dates, currency, and other region-specific items should be shown in the format that is native to people in the United States. That part is an ISO standard as well, to represent a subculture code associated with a country or region.

A concept of culture in .Net Framework refers to a set of user preferences specific to the user, such as dates, currency, and calendar format. Besides CurrentCulture, the CultureInfo class contains many properties that may be of interest to you as you internationalize your applications; you can find the full list here: http://msdn.microsoft.com/en-us/library/system.globalization.cultureinfo_properties.aspx. For instance, we could have used the DisplayName property to show a friendlier description of the current culture (in our case, we would get "English (United States)." As has already been mentioned, there is a lot of material to cover when it comes to internationalization—a good place to refer to for more information is MSDN documentation of the System.Global namespace, which can be found here: http://msdn.microsoft.com/en-us/library/abeh092z.aspx.

You might think that the locale setting is of minor importance, yet it is extremely important to properly localize your application: in England, for instance, people speak English (certainly!), but the numeric date format is "dd/mm/yyyy," where the "dd" is the numeric representation of the day, "mm" is the numeric representation of the month, and "yyyy" is the numeric representation of the year. Compare this to the United States, where people speak English as well, but for numerical date representations, the month comes first! It would be very time-consuming to keep track of all possible localization issues that may arise. In the end, we are also very likely to make mistakes. It is much easier to stand on the shoulders of giants who have thought through many internationalization issues and have made standard libraries and functions available for our use. Our main task is to make sure to use those libraries.

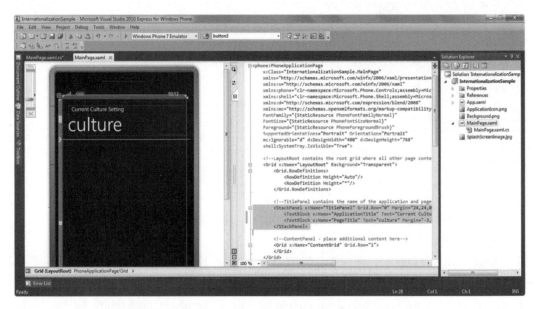

Figure 12–1. Preparing the phone design surface for the internationalization demo

Using the .NET Culture Hierarchy to Ensure Culture Neutrality

Suppose that you have built international support for only a portion of an application. What would happen when a user from a different country accesses features of an application that have not been internationalized? Will the application stop working, display a blank screen, etc.? The answer to this question lies in the concept of the .NET framework called "culture hierarchy."

There are three types of cultures that we as developers must be aware of: invariant, neutral, and specific. These cultures are arranged in a hierarchical manner, with invariant culture being at the top of the hierarchy, neutral in the middle, and specific culture at the bottom, as illustrated in Figure 12–3. When international users access Windows Phone 7 applications, the operating system starts at the bottom of this hierarchy and checks whether an application implements the specific culture of a given user. This check includes whether an application has the resources, such as text for menus and labels, which have been localized for the user's location. If such localized resources are not available, the system then moves up the culture hierarchy and checks whether there are provisions in the application for neutral cultures. Finally, if that check fails, the application defaults to the invariant culture, which is the same as English (US) culture.

Figure 12–2. Running the internationalization demo

For example, if a French-speaking user from Canada accesses Windows Phone 7 applications, the first thing the system checks is whether there are application resources implementing specific "fr-CA" culture. If that specific culture is not supported by an application, the system then performs a check of whether the neutral "fr" culture is supported. If the neutral culture is not supported, then the system defaults to the invariant culture, where none of the resources are localized.

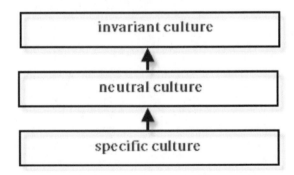

Figure 12–3. Culture hierarchy in Windows Phone 7

Storing and Retrieving Current Culture Settings

On Windows Phone 7, the System.Globalization.CultureInfo class contains all of the necessary information about the phone's current culture settings. In this section, we will write code to retrieve basic properties of the CultureInfo class, as well as code to change the current culture of the phone and to react to those changes. In real-world applications, we are not likely to adjust the current culture in code, since the culture setting should be fully controlled by the user.

In the following walkthrough, you will create a simple announcement of an upcoming event, and then, with a click of a button, adjust culture settings to properly display the date, time, and the cost of the event in a different region of the world—Spain. To accomplish that, you will instantiate a new CultureInfo class and set the current thread's CurrentCulture property to this new class. Later on in this chapter, we will expand upon this walkthrough and make our event advertisement speak different languages without having to change the source code.

■ **Note** You are probably wondering by now where and how the Windows Phone 7 culture is set. On both the phone and the emulator, the culture is adjusted in **Settings ➤ Region and Language**. Region and Language Settings can be accessed by clicking the small arrow to the right of the tiles on the phone screen (it is right next to the Internet Explorer tile in the emulator). Click on Region Format, and select an international format from the list that you'd like. Notice how both Short and Long Date properties, as well as the First Day of the Week property, adjust to the new format specific to the locale selected. Figure 12–4 illustrates how you can adjust Regional Settings on your phone.

Figure 12–4. Changing the phone's regional settings

1.   Start by creating a Visual Studio project and naming it "WP7LaunchParty."

2.   Double-click `MainPage.xaml` in Solution Explorer to bring up the XAML designer window.

For this first walkthrough, you will display the contents of just two fields on the screen: the name of the event as well as the event's date and time.

3.   Let's go ahead and remove one of two default textblocks automatically added to the design surface by Visual Studio. Highlight the textblock with "MY APPLICATION" text in it (either in XAML or on the design surface) and hit the Delete key.

4.   Now let's add the additional six text box controls that you need. If the toolbox is not visible, either click the Toolbox button on the Visual Studio Application Bar or select View ➤ Other Windows ➤ Toolbox. Drag six textblocks to the design surface and position them two per row, one underneath each other, as shown in Figure 12–5.

5.   Change the text of the three textblocks on the left to the following: "Event Date," "Event Time," and "Event Cost," as shown in Figure 12–5.

6.   Click on each textblock in the right column, press F4, and change the textblock names to "txtEventDate," "txtEventTime," and "txtEventCost" correspondingly.

7.   Finally, add a button to the design surface and change its content to "Español."

You should now end up with XAML code that matches the XAML shown in Listing 12–1 (you can simply copy and paste XAML code from the source code downloads for this chapter instead of adding elements to the design surface one-by-one, as we've done in the previous steps).

Listing 12–1. WP7 Launch Party UI Code (XAML)

```
<Grid x:Name="LayoutRoot" Background="{StaticResource PhoneBackgroundBrush}">
<Grid.RowDefinitions>
    <RowDefinition Height="Auto"/>
    <RowDefinition Height="*"/>
</Grid.RowDefinitions>

<!--TitleGrid is the name of the application and page title-->
<Grid x:Name="TitleGrid" Grid.Row="0">
    <TextBlock Text="WP7 Launch" x:Name="textBlockListTitle" Style="{StaticResource
PhoneTextTitle1Style}"/>
</Grid>

<!--ContentGrid is empty. Place new content here-->
<Grid x:Name="ContentGrid" Grid.Row="1">
    <TextBlock Height="44" HorizontalAlignment="Left" Margin="204,48,0,0"
Name="txtEventDate" Text="TextBlock" VerticalAlignment="Top" Width="276" />
    <TextBlock Height="43" HorizontalAlignment="Left" Margin="5,49,0,0"
Name="textBlock1" Text="Event Date:" VerticalAlignment="Top" Width="193" />
    <TextBlock Height="44" HorizontalAlignment="Left" Margin="204,98,0,0"
Name="txtEventTime" Text="TextBlock" VerticalAlignment="Top" Width="276" />
    <TextBlock Height="43" HorizontalAlignment="Left" Margin="5,99,0,0"
Name="textBlock3" Text="Event Time:" VerticalAlignment="Top" Width="193" />
```

```
            <TextBlock Height="44" HorizontalAlignment="Left" Margin="205,146,0,0"
Name="txtEventCost" Text="TextBlock" VerticalAlignment="Top" Width="276" />
            <TextBlock Height="43" HorizontalAlignment="Left" Margin="6,147,0,0"
Name="textBlock4" Text="Event Cost:" VerticalAlignment="Top" Width="193" />
        <Button Content="Español" Height="70" HorizontalAlignment="Left" Margin="6,233,0,0"
Name="button1" VerticalAlignment="Top" Width="160" Click="button1_Click" />
        </Grid>
    </Grid>
```

8. Double-click MainPage.xaml.cs to bring up the code view. Alternately, you can right-click the MainPage.xaml file and select "View Code."

9. Add the following statements to the very top of the page (right below the last using statement):

```
using System.Globalization;
using System.Threading;
```

10. Next, we will code the function that will populate event details and the function that toggles event locale. Add the code shown in Listing 12–2.

Listing 12–2. ShowEventDetails and ToggleEventLocale functions (C#)

```csharp
private void ShowEventDetails()
{
    textBlockListTitle.Text = "WP7 Launch";
    //create the date of November 6, 2010 at 9:00 PM
    DateTime dtLaunchDate = new DateTime(2010, 11, 6, 21, 0, 0);
    //make the cost equal to $5
    decimal decEventCost = 5.0M;

    //ToString() can also return values in specified culture
    //txtEventDate.Text = dtLaunchDate.ToString("D");
    txtEventDate.Text = dtLaunchDate.ToString("D",
Thread.CurrentThread.CurrentCulture);
    txtEventTime.Text = dtLaunchDate.ToString("T");

    txtEventCost.Text = decEventCost.ToString("C");
}

private void ToggleEventLocale()
{
    //default to English-US culture
    String cul = "en-US";

    if (button1.Content.ToString() == "Español")
    {
        //change the culture to Spanish
        cul = "es-ES";
    }
    else
    {
        cul = "en-US";
    }
```

```
CultureInfo newCulture = new CultureInfo(cul);
Thread.CurrentThread.CurrentCulture = newCulture;

ShowEventDetails();
}
```

Now you will call a function to show event details right after the application loads.

1. Paste the call to the ShowEventDetails() function in the MainPage() constructor to show event details in English when the application is launched:

```
ShowEventDetails();
```

Finally, you need to add an event handler to handle the button click, which will toggle the current culture between English and Spanish. The best way to add it is to bring up MainPage.xaml in design view and double-click the button.

11. Add the following code:

```
private void button1_Click(object sender, RoutedEventArgs e)
{
    ToggleEventLocale();
}
```

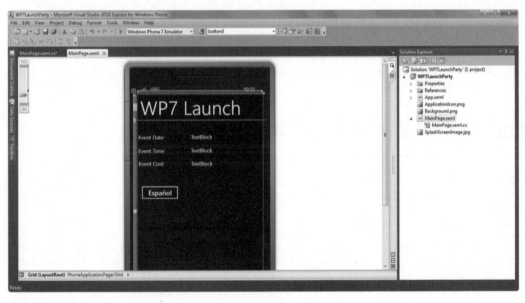

Figure 12–5. Design surface of the WP7LaunchSample application

12. Press F5 to run the application. Notice how the date, time, and cost are all shown in the familiar American format. If you press the "Español" button, you will see the date in Spanish, time in the 24-hour format, and the cost in euros. The labels with "Date," "Time," and "Cost" did not change, however, since we have not provided any localization provisions in our code for those. We will localize those resources shortly, as that will be the subject of the next section of this chapter.

In the preceding walkthrough, there are a couple of interesting points that are worth discussing in a bit more detail. The first one is how we switched from one culture to another in code. To accomplish that, we instantiated a new CultureInfo class and set the current thread's CurrentCulture property to this new class. During the instantiation of the CultureInfo class, we passed a string to its constructor representing a specific culture ("es-ES" for Spanish and "en-US" for American English). The second important point is the illustration of the use of standard formatting constructs in our code to make internationalizing our application easier. For example, let's put the following line of code at the end of the ShowEventDetails() function:

```
txtEventDate.Text = dtLaunchDate.ToString("MM/dd/yyyy");
```

Now when you run the application, notice how the date will be displayed as "11/06/2010" for both Spanish and English versions of our event. This certainly is confusing for residents of Spain, who would think that the Windows Phone 7 launch date is actually on June 11, 2010. Remember to use standard formatting options for all UI elements—in the case of the date, the standard formatting we have used with the following line of code to show the "long date representation" is certainly more appropriate:

```
txtEventDate.Text = dtLaunchDate.ToString("D");
```

The third and final important point in the foregoing walkthrough is the ease of switching specific cultures on Windows Phone 7. If we pass "es-MX" instead of "es-ES" into the CultureInfo() constructor in the ToggleEventLocale() function, we can still see the date translated into the Spanish language, but thecurrency and time are formatted according to the Mexican standard and not the standard of Spain.

Using Resource Files to Localize Content

Assume now that we have been diligent designing our application for international markets: we have allowed enough space on the user interface for more verbose languages, and we have used only standard formatting options for date, time, and currency values. We still have to perform translation of the application interface and resources to other languages. This could be, certainly, the most labor-intensive part of internationalizing our application.

As has been mentioned already, the application should be flexible enough to function in different locales without the need for code change and recompilation. That means that all resources required for proper functioning of the application need to be located outside the source code of an application and loaded on demand in response to request for culture-specific elements. The location of those resources are the resource-only files, or *.resx files. In this section's walkthrough, we will enhance the WP7 Launch announcement application we built in the previous walkthrough with the use of .resx files.

■ **Note** Large resource files may take some time to load on the Windows Phone 7 device. However, according to the Windows Phone 7 Application Certification Requirements document, a Windows Phone 7 application must render its first screen within five seconds of launch. Make sure to always include a splash screen image within the root of your package submitted to the Marketplace (see Chapter 19 for more details about the Marketplace). This splash screen image can be any .jpg file of your choosing named SplashScreenImage.jpg. Even with the splash screen image, however, be aware that the Microsoft Certification Requirements document further states that an application must be responsive to user input within 20 seconds after its launch—make sure to use resource files diligently where they don't unnecessarily slow down your application.

One benefit of using .resx files is that Windows Phone 7 will automatically find and use the resource file appropriate for the user's locale based on the current user's culture settings. Another benefit of resource files comes from the concept of culture hierarchy mentioned previously—.NET Framework provides a default fallback mechanism (i.e., going one level up in the culture hierarchy) for those resources that have not been localized. Also, .resx files are easily parseable by external tools, since they are simply XML files. This allows easy editing of those files by third-parties (such as translation services).

■ **Note** Throughout this book, you will see references to .NET Framework on Windows Phone 7. To be completely accurate, however, it is the compact version of .NET Framework (.NETCF) that powers Windows Phone 7. Compact .NET Framework is a portable version of the full .NET Framework, and it has a much smaller size and footprint to accommodate smaller devices. Windows Phone 7 runs .NETCF version 3.7. So whenever you encounter a reference to .NET Framework in this book, remember that the reference is really to the .NETCF 3.7.

1. Unless it's already open, open the WP7LaunchParty solution.

2. Right-click the WP7LaunchParty project and select Add ➤ New Item ➤ Resources File.

3. This resource file will contain the values for English-US culture. Name the resource file AppResources.resx and click Add.

Remember our discussion of culture hierarchies earlier in this chapter? The fact that our resource file does not contain any locale information in the file name (unlike the Spanish one that we will be creating shortly) makes this an invariant culture resource file, or the file that will be shown if no locale-specific resource files are found on the device.

4. Double-click the AppResources.resx file to bring up an empty table. Next, add four entries to that table for Event Title, Event Date, Event Time, and Cost, all in English, as shown in Figure 12–6.

Note that the contents of the first and second columns are extremely important: the first one contains the key that the code will use to reference the element, and it must be unique in this resource file.

The second column contains the value, or the actual content that will be displayed on the UI at runtime. The third column is useful, but not essential: you can provide descriptive comments about each value in this column.

We will now add a resource file for Spanish translation of the user interface elements.

5. Right-click the WP7LaunchParty project and select Add ➤ New Item ➤ Resources File.

6. Name the resource file `AppResources.es-ES.resx` and click Add.

Note the "es-ES" portion of the file name—it is extremely important to name resource files in accordance with the specific cultures they represent. In our case, we will provide Spanish (Spain) translation of the user interface only, hence the "es-ES" in the resources file name. If we wanted to add German (Germany) translation as well, our resource file would have the name `AppResource.de-DE.resx`.

7. Add four entries for `Event Title`, `Event Date`, `Event Time,` and `Cost` in Spanish, as shown in Figure 12–7.

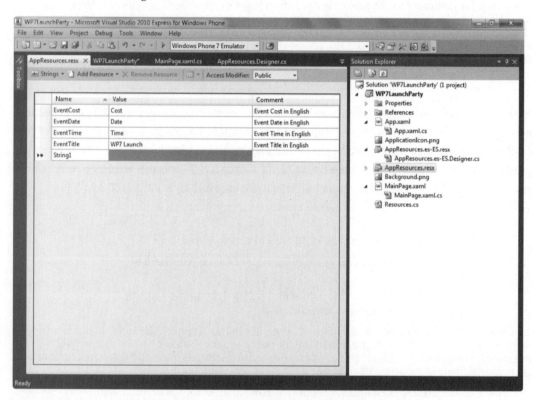

Figure 12–6. Resource file for English -US translation of WP7LaunchParty application

---

■ **Note** The translations are approximate and are used for demonstrative purposes only—please forgive the authors if we are not 100 percent accurate.

---

8. We need to rename the textblocks used for captions in our application so that we can easily refer to them in code. Bring up `MainPage.xaml` and change `textBlock1` to `txtEventDateCaption`, `textBlock3` to `txtEventTimeCaption`, and `textBlock4` to `txtEventCostCaption`. You should end up with XAML that matches the following markup:

```
<Grid x:Name="ContentGrid" Grid.Row="1">
        <TextBlock Height="44" HorizontalAlignment="Left" Margin="204,48,0,0"
Name="txtEventDate" Text="TextBlock" VerticalAlignment="Top" Width="276" />
        <TextBlock Height="43" HorizontalAlignment="Left" Margin="5,49,0,0"
Name="txtEventDateCaption" Text="Date:" VerticalAlignment="Top" Width="193" />
        <TextBlock Height="44" HorizontalAlignment="Left" Margin="204,98,0,0"
Name="txtEventTime" Text="TextBlock" VerticalAlignment="Top" Width="276" />
        <TextBlock Height="43" HorizontalAlignment="Left" Margin="5,99,0,0"
Name="txtEventTimeCaption" Text="Time:" VerticalAlignment="Top" Width="193" />
        <TextBlock Height="44" HorizontalAlignment="Left" Margin="205,146,0,0"
Name="txtEventCost" Text="TextBlock" VerticalAlignment="Top" Width="276" />
        <TextBlock Height="43" HorizontalAlignment="Left" Margin="6,147,0,0"
Name="txtEventCostCaption" Text="Cost:" VerticalAlignment="Top" Width="193" />
        <Button Content="Español" Height="70" HorizontalAlignment="Left"
Margin="6,233,0,0" Name="button1" VerticalAlignment="Top" Width="160" Click="button1_Click" />
    </Grid>
```

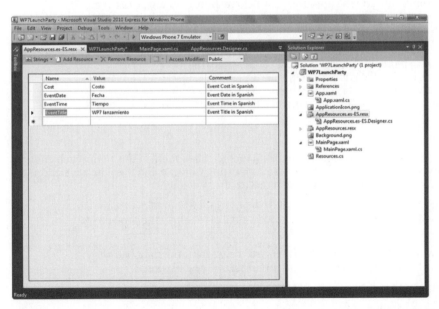

Figure 12–7. Resource file for Spanish-Spain translation of WP7LaunchParty application

9. To the top of the page, add the following two statements:

```
using System.Resources;
using System.Reflection;
```

10. In `MainPage.xaml.cs`, change the `ShowEventDetails()` function to match the code chunk shown here. Notice how we commented out the setting of default (English) caption from code.

```
private void ShowEventDetails()
{
    //textBlockListTitle.Text = "WP7 Launch";
    ResourceManager rm = new ResourceManager("WP7LaunchParty.AppResources",
Assembly.GetExecutingAssembly());
    textBlockListTitle.Text = rm.GetString("EventTitle");
    txtEventCostCaption.Text = rm.GetString("EventCost");
    txtEventDateCaption.Text = rm.GetString("EventDate");
    txtEventTimeCaption.Text = rm.GetString("EventTime");

    //create the date of November 6, 2010 at 9:00 PM
    DateTime dtLaunchDate = new DateTime(2010, 11, 6, 21, 0, 0);
    //make the cost equal to $5
    decimal decEventCost = 5.0M;

    txtEventDate.Text = dtLaunchDate.ToString("D");
    txtEventTime.Text = dtLaunchDate.ToString("T");

    txtEventCost.Text = decEventCost.ToString("C");
}
```

11. Press F5 to compile and run the application. Click the button to toggle between Spanish and English. Do you see all captions and the event title being properly translated? Probably not, since we have not indicated that our project must support different locales and which locales it must support.

12. Open Windows Explorer and navigate to the folder where the `WP7LaunchParty.csproj` file is located. Open `WP7LaunchParty.csproj` in any text editor (Notepad is good) and find the `<SupportedCultures>` node. More than likely, that node will not contain any elements. Edit that node to look like text here:

```
<SupportedCultures>es-ES;
</SupportedCultures>
```

Were we supporting more than one culture, we would include all of them in this node, each culture code separated by a semicolon. For example, if we were supporting German and Russian translations as well, we would put "es-ES;de-DE;ru-RU;" in the `<SuportedCultures>` element.

13. Save `WP7LaunchParty.csproj` in the text editor. Visual Studio should detect an external change to this file and ask you if you would like to reload the project. Click Yes.

14. Add the following line of code to the `ToggleEventLocale` method, right below the statement `Thread.CurrentThread.CurrentCulture = newCulture;`:

```
Thread.CurrentThread.CurrentUICulture = newCulture;
```

15. Press F5 to run the application.

You have provided a non-locale specific (invariant) file, AppResources.resx, with English (US) captions for the invitation text in it. That's why you see an English interface upon launching the application. Once you click the button to toggle the application into Spanish, you should see the event title and captions translated into the Spanish language, as shown in Figure 12–8.

If you examine Figure 12–8 carefully, you will notice a couple of things. First, the title of the application ran off the screen in Spanish—a clear mistake on our part for making the font too large and not allowing an extra 40 percent of space inside that title for languages that are more verbose than English. Second, the caption for Cost did not translate into Spanish—it should be "Costo" in Spanish, not "Cost." What's going on here?

The reason for this is that in AppResources.es-ES.resx, there is not entry named "EventCost." There is an entry with the name "Cost," but that is not the name we are referring to from code. This mistake is a good demonstration of the application's cultural fallback: there was no entry in the Spanish version for "EventCost," so the application "fell back" to the default language (English-US) to represent a given caption—the raison d'être of the resource files!

Let's go ahead and correct this typo: double-click the AppResources.es-ES.resx file, change the name of the "Cost" entry to "EventCost," and re-run the application. You should see the proper caption, "Costo," for the Spanish version of our announcement.

■ **Note** The MSDN documentation for internationalizing Windows Phone 7 applications proposes an entirely different approach than the one we've advocated in our walkthrough in this section. MSDN walkthroughs encourage you to add a separate class to return resources. In our walkthrough, however, we have simplified things a bit and used the ResourceManager class to locate resources within our resource files.

The main reason our walkthrough differs from the approach advocated by the MSDN documentation is that we are dynamically (i.e., in code) changing the culture of an application. We needed to do this for demonstration purposes, since changing local culture is a bit cumbersome. Dynamic rebinding of elements (to toggle captions between English and Spanish) would be a bit more involved. The addition of a separate class and references to that class, as illustrated in the MSDN documentation, could have also taken away from the main points illustrated during the walkthrough. But we could certainly have used an approach other than the ResourceManager class to accomplish the localization of our application.

Summary

In this chapter, you learned how to prepare an application to work in parts of the world other than the United States, including the use of stored culture information and the ToString function to determine how to display data, how to use ISO culture codes to reset an app's CulturalInfo object to the user's preferred language and country environment, and finally how to use resource files to provide translated versions of field names, documentation, and even media. We have discussed specific issues to consider when developing applications for international markets, such as dates, numbers, and currency translations between locales, as well as demonstrated approaches to translate application resources via Visual Studio resource files.

In the next chapter, we will take a look at how to persist files and settings on Windows Phone 7 via the use of local storage. We will save images and application settings and show how to load them on demand.

Figure 12–8. *Spanish application interface*

CHAPTER 13

■ ■ ■

Isolated Storage

In Chapter 3 you learned that Microsoft Azure provides a reliable place to store and access data, but that using it requires Internet access. Sometimes it is more efficient to cache frequently accessed data on the Windows Phone device itself.

Isolated storage is a place on a Windows Phone 7 device where an application can save files, configuration information, and other data. Each application is allocated its own portion of the available space, but cannot access file systems used by the operating system itself, a limitation that prevents a rogue application from accessing system data and possibly corrupting it. The amount of storage that can be assigned to any single application depends on the phone's available space, which, unlike iPhones and Android devices, cannot be increased by the use of removable SD cards.

With isolated storage, a Windows Phone application can create and maintain a virtual file storage system that can contain virtual folders and files; you will not have direct access to the underlying Windows Phone file system and the isolated storage will provide you with API to work with the file system. All input and output operations can be performed only on the application's isolated storage level.

Support for isolated storage on a Windows Phone is provided by the following two namespaces, whose features are depicted by Figure 13–1.

- *Isolated File Storage*: `System.IO.IsolatedStorage.IsolatedStorageFile` allows you to create, use, and remove directories and files in the virtual isolated storage. The files can be added and retrieved through file stream using `System.IO.IsolatedStorage.IsolatedFileStream`. Isolated file stream can be used to cache images, sounds, and files that are dynamically loaded from the Web. In the first demo, you will learn how use isolated storage to cache an image loaded from the Web.

- *Isolated Local Settings*: `System.IO.IsolatedStorage.IsolatedStorageSettings` provides APIs for storing and working with key-value pairs cached in isolated storage. Use this to store application settings and user specific settings.

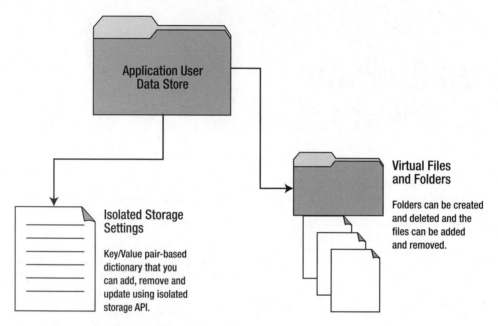

Figure 13–1. Using isolated storage API

In this chapter, you will learn how to work with a phone's isolated storage. The first example will show you a technique to cache an image downloaded from the Web into the isolated storage file. The second demo will show you how to save and retrieve name and value pairs using isolated storage settings.

Working with Isolated Directory Storage

We'll begin by building an application to work with the local storage on a phone. The application, IsolatedStorageStoreImageDemo, whose UI is shown in Figure 13–2, demonstrates the basic functions available through the isolated storage APIs, including the following:

- Retrieve application-specific isolated storage
- Get isolated storage quota
- Save and retrieve isolated storage files

In this demo, when the "Get Image" button is clicked for the first time, the application checks to see whether there is enough space available in isolated storage. If there is, the image will be downloaded from the web site and then saved to isolated storage via isolated storage file stream. If the button is clicked again, the image will be loaded into an isolated storage file.

Figure 13–2. IsolatedStorageStoreImageDemo

You'll build the demo in three steps. First, you need to create a new Visual Studio project. Next you'll build the project's user interface and finish up by adding code to respond to commands from the user.

Creating the IsolatedStorageStoreImageDemo Project

To set up the IsolatedStorageStoreImageDemo project, follow the steps you've used for previous examples in this book:

1. Open Microsoft Visual Studio 2010 Express for Windows Phone on your workstation.

2. Create a new Windows Phone Application by selecting File ➤ New Project on the Visual Studio command menu. Select the Windows Phone Application template, name the application "IsolatedStorageStoreImageDemo," and click OK, as shown in Figure 13–3.

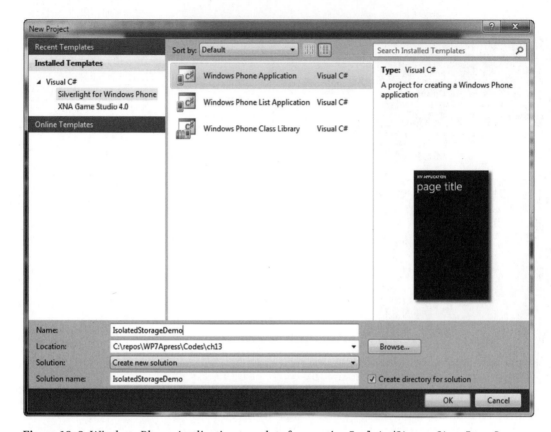

Figure 13–3. Windows Phone Application template for creating IsolatedStorageStoreImageDemo

Coding the User Interface

You'll first code the user interface, which we've chosen to implement in XAML. Sometimes it is faster to work with XAML than with managed code, especially when you're working with a simple example, like this one, which requires only a few controls. Go to the Solution Explorer, open `MainPage.xaml`, and replace the XAML you find there with the code that appears in the following sections.

Selecting the UI Resources

Begin by adding the following XAML markup to `MainPage.xaml` to identify where the resource to build the application's main page will be found.

```
<phone:PhoneApplicationPage

    x:Class="IsolatedStorageStoreImageDemo.MainPage"
    xmlns="http://schemas.microsoft.com/winfx/2006/xaml/presentation"
    xmlns:x="http://schemas.microsoft.com/winfx/2006/xaml"
    xmlns:phone="clr-namespace:Microsoft.Phone.Controls;assembly=Microsoft.Phone"
```

```
xmlns:shell="clr-namespace:Microsoft.Phone.Shell;assembly=Microsoft.Phone"
xmlns:d="http://schemas.microsoft.com/expression/blend/2008"
xmlns:mc="http://schemas.openxmlformats.org/markup-compatibility/2006"
mc:Ignorable="d" d:DesignWidth="480" d:DesignHeight="768"
FontFamily="{StaticResource PhoneFontFamilyNormal}"
FontSize="{StaticResource PhoneFontSizeNormal}"
Foreground="{StaticResource PhoneForegroundBrush}"
SupportedOrientations="Portrait" Orientation="Portrait"
shell:SystemTray.IsVisible="True">
```

Referencing the namespace as xmlns="http://schemas.microsoft.com/winfx/2006/xaml/presentation"
allows you to use common Windows Phone controls such as text boxes, buttons, and list boxes to create
the main page. The code snippet also includes a reference to a code-behind class
(x:Class="IsolatedStorageStoreImageDemo.MainPage") that will handle the main page controls' events.

Building the Main Page and Adding Components

Next, to create the main application page and populate it with controls, add the following XAML markup
to the preceding block of code, also in MainPage.xaml.

```
<Grid x:Name="LayoutRoot" Background="{StaticResource PhoneBackgroundBrush}">
    <Grid.RowDefinitions>
        <RowDefinition Height="Auto"/>
        <RowDefinition Height="*"/>
    </Grid.RowDefinitions>

    <!--TitleGrid is the name of the application and page title-->
    <Grid x:Name="TitleGrid" Grid.Row="0">
        <TextBlock Text="IsolatedStorageStoreImageDemo"
                   x:Name="textBlockPageTitle"
                   Style="{StaticResource PhoneTextTitle1Style}"
                   FontSize="28" />
    </Grid>

    <!--ContentGrid is empty. Place new content here-->
    <Grid x:Name="ContentGrid" Grid.Row="1">

<Image Height="458" HorizontalAlignment="Left"
               Margin="20,134,0,0" Name="image1" Stretch="Uniform"
               VerticalAlignment="Top" Width="423" />
        <Button Content="Get Image" Height="70"
                HorizontalAlignment="Left" Margin="0,598,0,0"
                Name="btnGetImage" VerticalAlignment="Top"
                Width="443" Click="btnGetImage_Click" />
        <TextBox Height="72" HorizontalAlignment="Left"
                 Margin="12,29,0,0" Name="txtImageUrl"
                 Text="http://res1.newagesolution.net/Portals/0/twitter2_icon.jpg"
                 VerticalAlignment="Top" Width="460" />
    </Grid>
</Grid>

</phoneNavigation:PhoneApplicationPage>
```

Once you've loaded the XAML code for the main page, you should see the layout shown in Figure 13–4. Now it's time to use the Isolated Storage APIs to add behavior to the application, as you'll learn in the next section.

Figure 13–4. IsolatedStorageStoreImageDemo design view

Coding the Application

In Solution Explorer, open `MainPage.xaml.cs` and replace the code there with the following C# code blocks, in precisely the order in which they are presented.

Specifying the Namespaces

Begin by specifying the namespaces the application will use. `System.IO.IsolatedStorage` and `System.IO` contain the APIs needed to work with the isolated file storage.

```
using System;

using System.Net;
using System.Windows;
using Microsoft.Phone.Controls;
```

```
using System.Windows.Media.Imaging;
using System.IO.IsolatedStorage;
using System.IO;

namespace IsolatedStorageStoreImageDemo
{
```

Initializing Variables

Now add the following block of code to MainPage.xaml.cs to initialize the application's variables.

```
public partial class MainPage : PhoneApplicationPage
{
    private string ImageFileName = null;


    WebClient _webClient; // Used for downloading the image first time from the web site
...
```

Initializing the Application

Now add the application's constructor, which uses the WebClient.OpenReadCompleted event to download its target image. The code contains logic to check whether enough space is available in the phone's isolated storage to save the downloaded image. If space is available, the image gets saved; otherwise it's loaded directly into the image control.

```
public MainPage()
{
    InitializeComponent();

    SupportedOrientations = SupportedPageOrientation.Portrait |
SupportedPageOrientation.Landscape;

    _webClient = new WebClient();
    // Handles when the image download is completed
    _webClient.OpenReadCompleted += (s1, e1) =>
        {
            if (e1.Error == null)
            {
                try
                {
                    bool isSpaceAvailable =
IsSpaceIsAvailable(e1.Result.Length);

                    if (isSpaceAvailable)
                    {
                        // Save Image file to Isolated Storage
                        using (IsolatedStorageFileStream isfs =
new IsolatedStorageFileStream(ImageFileName,
                            FileMode.Create,
                            IsolatedStorageFile.GetUserStoreForApplication())))
```

```
                          {
                              long imgLen = e1.Result.Length;
                              byte[] b = new byte[imgLen];
                              e1.Result.Read(b, 0, b.Length);
                              isfs.Write(b, 0, b.Length);
                              isfs.Flush();
                          }

                          LoadImageFromIsolatedStorage(ImageFileName);
                      }
                      else
                      {
                          BitmapImage bmpImg = new BitmapImage();
                          bmpImg.SetSource(e1.Result);
                          image1.Source = bmpImg;
                      }
                  }
                  catch (Exception ex)
                  {
                      MessageBox.Show(ex.Message);
                  }
              }
          };
      }
```

■ **Note** In order to create a sub-directory, you must create a directory path string, such as
"MyDirectory1\SubDirectory1" and pass it to the CreateDirectory method. To add a file to SubDirectory1,
you must create a string that combines the file name with its path, such as
"MyDirectory1\SubDirectory1\MyFileInSubDirectory1.txt", and then use IsolatedStorageFileStream to
create a file. In order to add contents to the file, use StreamWriter.

When you use the Remove method in IsolatedStorageFile, use it with caution as it will delete all directories and
files. To avoid accidently deleting everything in the isolated storage, create a warning prompt window to confirm
with the user that it will be OK to delete everything in the isolated storage. Another possibility is to use
IsolatedStorage.DeleteFile or IsolatedStorage.DeleteDirectory to delete a specific file or directory to
avoid removing all files or directories. Please refer to MSDN documentation for more information at
http://msdn.microsoft.com/en-us/library/kx3852wf(VS.85).aspx.

■ **Tip** System.IO.Path.Combine provides a great way to combine directory paths and files without worrying if
the backslashes "\" are properly added. Also, when searching files or directories, you can use a wild card "*"
when building a directory or file path.

Checking Availability of Isolated Storage Space

Now add code for the isSpaceAvailable helper method that the application uses to determine whether there is enough space available in isolated storage to store the image.

```
// Check to make sure there are enough space available on the phone
        // in order to save the image that we are downloading on to the phone
        private bool IsSpaceIsAvailable(long spaceReq)
        {
            using (IsolatedStorageFile store =
IsolatedStorageFile.GetUserStoreForApplication())
    {
                long spaceAvail = store.AvailableFreeSpace;
                if (spaceReq > spaceAvail)
                {
                    return false;
                }
                return true;
            }
        }
```

Adding a Button Event to Retrieve the Image from Isolated Storage

When the "Get Image" button is clicked, we check to see if the image exists in the isolated storage. If the image exists, the image is loaded from the isolated storage, otherwise the image is downloaded from the web site.

```
        private void btnGetImage_Click(object sender, RoutedEventArgs e)
        {
            using (IsolatedStorageFile isf =
IsolatedStorageFile.GetUserStoreForApplication())
          {
                bool fileExist = isf.FileExists(ImageFileName);

                if (fileExist)
                {
                    LoadImageFromIsolatedStorage(ImageFileName);
                }
                else
                {
                        if (!string.IsNullOrEmpty(txtImageUrl.Text))
                  {
                        // Use Uri as image file name
                        Uri uri = new Uri(txtImageUrl.Text);
                        ImageFileName = uri.AbsolutePath;
                        _webClient.OpenReadAsync(new Uri(txtImageUrl.Text));
                  }

                }

            }

        }
```

Adding a Method to Retrieve the Image from Isolated Storage

The image is streamed directly from the isolated storage into the image control.

```
private void LoadImageFromIsolatedStorage(string imageFileName)
{
    // Load Image from Isolated storage
    using (IsolatedStorageFile isf =
IsolatedStorageFile.GetUserStoreForApplication())
    {
        using (IsolatedStorageFileStream isoStream =
isf.OpenFile(imageFileName, FileMode.Open))
        {
            BitmapImage bmpImg = new BitmapImage();
            bmpImg.SetSource(isoStream);
            image1.Source = bmpImg;
        }
    }
}
```

Testing the Finished Application

To test the completed application, press F5 on your keyboard and run it.

In this brief demo, you've learned to work with isolated storage files by storing a downloaded image into the isolated storage and then retrieving the image from the isolated storage. In the next demo, you will learn to interact with the name and value dictionary of the isolated storage settings.

Working with Isolated Storage Settings

In this section, you'll build an application that demonstrates CRUD operation (create, read, update, and delete) of System.IO.IsolatedStorage.IsolatedStorageSettings. We've named it IsolatedStorageSettingsDemo. Figure 13–5 shows how its UI will look on a Windows Phone.

Figure 13–5. IsolatedStorageSettingsDemo

In the IsolatedStorageSettingsDemo application, as shown in Figure 13–5, when the Save button is clicked, the value in the "Value" text box will be added to the isolated storage settings using the key in the "Key" text box. Whenever new key-value pair data is added to the isolated storage settings, the key will be added to the list box of keys. When any of the keys in the list box of keys is selected, the "Key" text box and the "Value" text box will be populated with the data retrieved from the isolated storage settings. The Delete button will delete the selected key from the isolated storage settings.

To build the demo, you'll first create a new project, then add XAML markup to create a new main page and its controls. Finally, you'll add behavior to the application with C# code that makes use of isolated storage APIs to save and retrieve key-value pairs.

Creating a New Project

To create the new IsolatedStorageSettingsDemo project, open Microsoft Visual Studio 2010 Express for Windows Phone. Select File ➤ New Project on the Visual Studio menu, select the Windows Phone Application template on the New Project dialogue, name the application "IsolatedStorageSettingsDemo," and click OK, as shown in Figure 13–6.

Now you'll build the application main page.

Figure 13–6. Windows Phone Application template for creating IsolatedStorageSettingsDemo

Building the Application UI (XAML)

To create the UI for IsolatedStorageSettingsDemo, go to Solution Explorer, open MainPage.xaml, and replace XAML with the following chunks of XAML markup in the sequence shown.

Selecting the UI Resources

The following code identifies where to find the UI controls that will be used to build this main page for this application. Using the namespace
xmlns="http://schemas.microsoft.com/winfx/2006/xaml/presentation" will allow you to add common Windows Phone controls like text boxes, buttons, and list boxes, which will be used to create the main page. Also we are adding a reference to a code-behind class
(x:Class="IsolatedStorageSettingsDemo.MainPage") that will handle the main page controls' events.

```
<phone:PhoneApplicationPage
    x:Class="IsolatedStorageSettingsDemo.MainPage"
    xmlns="http://schemas.microsoft.com/winfx/2006/xaml/presentation"
```

```xml
    xmlns:x="http://schemas.microsoft.com/winfx/2006/xaml"
    xmlns:phone="clr-namespace:Microsoft.Phone.Controls;assembly=Microsoft.Phone"
    xmlns:shell="clr-namespace:Microsoft.Phone.Shell;assembly=Microsoft.Phone"
    xmlns:d="http://schemas.microsoft.com/expression/blend/2008"
    xmlns:mc="http://schemas.openxmlformats.org/markup-compatibility/2006"
    FontFamily="{StaticResource PhoneFontFamilyNormal}"
    FontSize="{StaticResource PhoneFontSizeNormal}"
    Foreground="{StaticResource PhoneForegroundBrush}"
    SupportedOrientations="Portrait" Orientation="Portrait"
    mc:Ignorable="d" d:DesignWidth="480" d:DesignHeight="768"
    shell:SystemTray.IsVisible="True">
```

Building the Main Page and Adding Controls

Now add the various controls and layouts you need to create the UI shown in Figure 13–5.

```xml
<Grid x:Name="LayoutRoot" Background="{StaticResource PhoneBackgroundBrush}">
    <Grid.RowDefinitions>
        <RowDefinition Height="Auto"/>
        <RowDefinition Height="*"/>
    </Grid.RowDefinitions>

    <!--TitleGrid is the name of the application and page title-->
    <Grid x:Name="TitleGrid" Grid.Row="0">
        <TextBlock Text="Isolated Storage Settings Demo"
                   x:Name="textBlockListTitle"
                   Style="{StaticResource PhoneTextTitle1Style}"
                   FontSize="30" />
    </Grid>

    <!--ContentGrid is empty. Place new content here-->
    <Grid x:Name="ContentGrid" Grid.Row="1">
        <TextBox Height="72" HorizontalAlignment="Left"
                 Margin="172,46,0,0" Name="txtKey" Text=""
                 VerticalAlignment="Top" Width="212" />
        <Button Content="Save" Height="70"
                HorizontalAlignment="Left" Margin="78,228,0,0"
                Name="btnSave" VerticalAlignment="Top" Width="160"
                Click="btnSave_Click" />
        <ListBox Height="168" HorizontalAlignment="Left" Margin="94,392,0,0"
                 Name="lstKeys" VerticalAlignment="Top" Width="274"
                 BorderThickness="1" SelectionChanged="lstKeys_SelectionChanged" />
        <TextBlock Height="39" HorizontalAlignment="Left" Margin="94,62,0,0"
                   Name="textBlock1" Text="Key" VerticalAlignment="Top" />
        <TextBox Height="74" HorizontalAlignment="Left" Margin="172,124,0,0"
                 Name="txtValue" Text="" VerticalAlignment="Top" Width="212" />
        <TextBlock Height="39" HorizontalAlignment="Left" Margin="94,140,0,0"
                   Name="textBlock2" Text="Value" VerticalAlignment="Top" />
        <Button Content="Delete" Height="70" HorizontalAlignment="Left"
                Margin="224,228,0,0" Name="btnDelete" VerticalAlignment="Top"
                Width="160" Click="btnDelete_Click" />
        <TextBlock Height="39" HorizontalAlignment="Left" Margin="94,347,0,0"
                   Name="textBlock3" Text="List of Keys" VerticalAlignment="Top" />
```

```
        </Grid>
    </Grid>

</phoneNavigation:PhoneApplicationPage>
```

Once you've added the XAML markup blocks displayed in this section to `MainPage.xaml`, you should see the UI shown on the Visual Studio Design View tab in Figure 13–7.

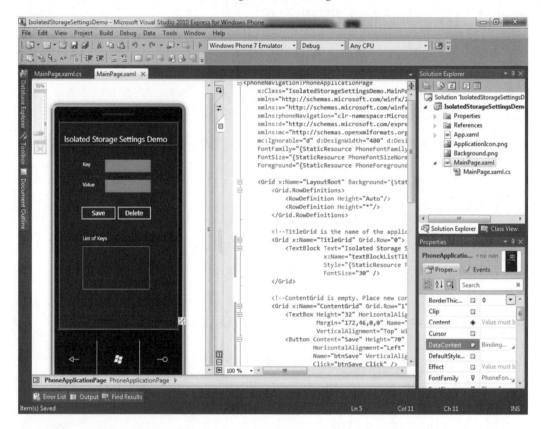

Figure 13–7. IsolatedStorageSettingsDemo design view

Now it's time to add behavior to the application.

Coding Application Behavior (C#)

From Solution Explorer, open MainPage.xaml.cs and replace the code you find there with the following blocks of C# code.

Specifying the Namespaces

Begin by listing the namespaces the application will use. Notice our inclusion of System.IO.IsolatedStorage in order to work with the isolated storage settings.

```
using System;
using System.Windows;
using System.Windows.Controls;
using Microsoft.Phone.Controls;
using System.IO.IsolatedStorage;
namespace IsolatedStorageSettingsDemo
{
    public partial class MainPage : PhoneApplicationPage
    {
        private IsolatedStorageSettings _appSettings;
```

Initializing the Application

Now add the next code block to the MainPage class. Notice the use of the BindKeyList() method, which will retrieve all keys from the isolated storage settings and bind them to the list box created in the previous section.

```
        public MainPage()
        {
            InitializeComponent();
            SupportedOrientations = SupportedPageOrientation.Portrait;
            _appSettings = IsolatedStorageSettings.ApplicationSettings;
BindKeyList();
        }
```

Adding the Save Button Event Handler

Now add an event handler for the Save button. When the Save button is clicked, the application reads the key and the value from user-inputted text boxes into the isolated storage settings.

```
        // Handles Create and Update
// If the key does not exist key-value pair will be added
// ElseIf the key exists the value will be updated
        private void btnSave_Click(object sender, RoutedEventArgs e)
        {
            if (!String.IsNullOrEmpty(txtKey.Text))
            {
                if (_appSettings.Contains(txtKey.Text))
                {
```

```
                    _appSettings[txtKey.Text] = txtValue.Text;
            }
            else
            {
                    _appSettings.Add(txtKey.Text, txtValue.Text);
            }
_appSettings.Save();
            BindKeyList();
        }
    }
```

■ **Note** An isolated storage file will perform much better than isolated storage settings because a file can be streamed in and out of the isolated storage file as raw data by using `StreamWriter` and `StreamReader`, whereas the storage and retrieval of data in an isolated storage settings key-value pair dictionary require serialization. However, there is complexity in using isolated storage files, where you need to use the file stream to save and retrieve the data and must be careful to dispose the stream after each use, whereas in the isolated storage settings, there is inherent simplicity in using the key to save and retrieve the data.

Adding the Delete Button Event Handler

Next, add an event handler for the Delete button. When the Delete button is clicked, we remove the selected key from the isolated storage settings and rebind the list box.

```
        private void btnDelete_Click(object sender, RoutedEventArgs e)
        {
            if (lstKeys.SelectedIndex > -1)
            {
                    _appSettings.Remove(lstKeys.SelectedItem.ToString());
_appSettings.Save();
                BindKeyList();
            }
        }
```

Adding the Listbox Changed Event

Finally, you'll use the Listbox changed event to update the Key and Value text boxes of the application interface. When the user selects a key from the list box, the application will load the key and its associated value from the isolated storage settings using the selected key and then populate the key and value text boxes.

```
// When key is selected value is retrieved from the storage settings
        private void lstKeys_SelectionChanged(object sender, SelectionChangedEventArgs e)
        {
            if (e.AddedItems.Count > 0)
            {
                string key = e.AddedItems[0].ToString();
```

```
            if (_appSettings.Contains(key))
            {
                txtKey.Text = key;
                txtValue.Text = _appSettings[key].ToString();
            }
        }
    }

    private void BindKeyList()
    {
        lstKeys.Items.Clear();
        foreach (string key in _appSettings.Keys)
        {
            lstKeys.Items.Add(key);
        }
        txtKey.Text = "";
        txtValue.Text = "";
    }

  }
}
```

Testing the Finished Application

To test the finished application, press F5. The result should resemble the screenshot shown in Figure 13–5.

Summary

In this chapter, you learned how to save application data on a Windows Phone device using either an isolated storage file or isolated storage settings. From the demo applications, you learned to create, read, update, and delete isolated storage data.

In Chapter 14, you will learn to pinpoint the location of the phone by working with the Windows Phone's global positioning system (GPS), connected networks, and cellular telephone networks. And then you will learn to interact with Microsoft Bing map.

■ ■ ■

Using Location Services

All Windows Phone devices are required to ship with a GPS receiver and, thus equipped, allow you to develop applications that are *location aware*. The GPS receiver in the Windows Phone will allow you to receive the data in the form of longitude and latitude. The longitude and latitude represent the mapping coordinates that are needed to plot the location on the Bing Maps Silverlight control. Also, in order to plot an address, you would need to convert the address into longitude and latitude using the Bing Maps service.

There are many popular applications available for phones these days that use location data, like restaurant finder applications, and navigation applications that give driving directions and plot the street address on a map using the services like Yahoo, Google, and Microsoft Bing Maps. With Microsoft Bing Maps service, you can convert the address into a GPS coordinate system and be able to plot using the Bing Maps Silverlight control of the Windows Phone.

Even search engines take advantage of the phone's GPS by providing relevant search results based on the location of the phone. There is an application that tracks your location while you are running, and based on the distance travelled, the application gives you total calories burned.

Social networking applications like Twitter and Facebook also take advantage of the GPS tracking system on your phone by tagging your tweets or uploaded photos with the location information. There are applications that even allow you to share your current location with your friends and family. There was a big news headline about a lost sea kayaker who was found out in the ocean because he had a phone in his possession and the Coast Guard was able to locate him by his GPS location.

Understanding Windows Phone Location Services Architecture

A Windows Phone device can determine its current position on the surface of the earth in one of three ways. The first approach is to use the built-in GPS receiver, which uses satellites and is the most accurate, but which also consumes the most power. The second and third approaches are to use Wi-Fi and the triangulation of the cell phone towers, which are much less accurate then GPS receiver but consume less power. Fortunately, the Windows Phone Location Service automatically decides which option is best for the location of a device and presents its best guess of longitude and latitude through the Bing Maps location service. With a longitude and latitude reading in hand, an application can plot it on a Bing Maps Silverlight control map. Or you can use a street or *civic* address returned by the on-board location service to query the Bing Maps web service for its corresponding GPS coordinates (longitude and latitude) and plot them on a Bing Maps map.

In upcoming sections, you will learn to take advantage of the Windows Phone's GPS receiver to track your movements and also learn to plot an address on the Bing Maps Silverlight control using the Microsoft Bing Maps service.

Introducing the Windows Phone Location Service and Mapping APIs

In order to use the location service on a device, you need to reference the System.Device assembly and declare System.Device.Location in your code. And before you can take advantage of the location service, you must enable the location service on the phone by going to Settings ➤ Location ➤ turn on Location Services option. You can detect whether the phone's location service is enabled using the StatusChanged event of GeoCoordinateWatcher, as seen in the following code.

```
GeoCoordinateWatcher geoCoordinateWatcher;
geoCoordinateWatcher = new GeoCoordinateWatcher(GeoPositionAccuracy.High);
geoCoordinateWatcher.MovementThreshold = 100; // in Meters
geoCoordinateWatcher.StatusChanged += (s, e) =>
    {
        if (e.Status == GeoPositionStatus.Disabled)
        {
            MessageBox.Show("Please enable your location service by going to Settings ->
Location -> Turn on Location Services option.");
        }
    };
```

Another way to check if the location service is enabled is to use TryStart to see if the GeoCoordinateWatcher can be started.

```
if (!_geoCoordinateWatcher.TryStart(true, TimeSpan.FromSeconds(5)))
{
        MessageBox.Show("Please enable Location Service on the Phone.",
"Warning", MessageBoxButton.OK);
}
```

Next you have to set DesiredAccuracy and provide MovementThreshold in GeoCoordinateWatcher as seen in the foregoing code.

GeoPositionAccuracy.Default will use Wi-Fi or the cell phone towers and depends on the availability of the sources. Windows Phone will automatically choose one to use, and GeoPositionAccuracy.High will use the GPS receiver built into the phone device. MovementThreshold is a very important property to set because MovementThreshold specifies the change in distance in meters before the PositionChanged event notifies the application that new coordinates are available; the lower the value of MovementThreshold, the more accurately the position will be tracked, but you will pay a price in higher power consumption. Microsoft recommends that you set MovementThreshold to at least 20 meters to filter out this noise.

In the following sections, you will learn how to use the Windows Phone Location Service by simulating the behavior of the GPS receiver. This simulation allows you to test location-aware applications, like the ones you'll build in this chapter, in the emulator, which lacks a real GPS receiver.

Simulating the Location Service

In order to simulate use of the location service, you will be intercepting the GeoCoordinateWatcher's PositionChanged event using an Observable object. With an Observable object, you can subscribe to an event and then stream the data received to the subscribed event delegates. For the examples in this chapter, you will subscribe to the PositionChanged event to feed GPS data to the parts of your application that consume it. The use of Observable objects is covered in more detail in Chapter 18, "Reactive Extensions."

Creating the GeoCoordinateWatcherDemo Project

To set up the GeoCoordinateDemo project, follow the steps you've used for previous examples in this book. In order to use the .NET Reactive Extension, you will need to add a reference to Microsoft.Phone.Reactive. You'll also need to reference System.Device in order to use the location service and, most importantly, System.Observable, in order to feed GPS data to the location service.

1. Open Microsoft Visual Studio 2010 Express for Windows Phone on your workstation.

2. Create a new Windows Phone Application by selecting File ➤ New Project on the Visual Studio command menu. Select the Windows Phone Application template, and name the application "GeoCoodinateWatcherDemo."

3. Add a reference to Microsoft.Phone.Reactive in order to use Reactive Extension. Also add a reference to System.Device in order to use the location service. In Solution Explorer, you should be able to see the added reference as shown in Figure 14–1.

Figure 14–1. Project references to use the Reactive Extension and the location service

Coding the User Interface

You will be building the user interface using the XAML in the Visual Studio. For building simple controls, it is faster to work with the XAML code. Go to the solution, open `MainPage.xaml`, and replace the XAML you find there with the following codes.

Declaring the UI Resources

The namespaces you see in the following code snippet are typically declared by default when you first create a Windows Phone project. In particular, namespaces `xmlns:phone="clr-namespace:Microsoft.Phone.Controls;assembly=Microsoft.Phone"` allow you to add common Windows Phone controls to the application main page.

```
<phone:PhoneApplicationPage
    x:Class="GeoCoordinateWatcherDemo.MainPage"
    xmlns="http://schemas.microsoft.com/winfx/2006/xaml/presentation"
    xmlns:x="http://schemas.microsoft.com/winfx/2006/xaml"
    xmlns:phone="clr-namespace:Microsoft.Phone.Controls;assembly=Microsoft.Phone"
    xmlns:shell="clr-namespace:Microsoft.Phone.Shell;assembly=Microsoft.Phone"
    xmlns:d="http://schemas.microsoft.com/expression/blend/2008"
    xmlns:mc="http://schemas.openxmlformats.org/markup-compatibility/2006"
    mc:Ignorable="d" d:DesignWidth="480" d:DesignHeight="768"
    FontFamily="{StaticResource PhoneFontFamilyNormal}"
    FontSize="{StaticResource PhoneFontSizeNormal}"
    Foreground="{StaticResource PhoneForegroundBrush}"
    SupportedOrientations="Portrait" Orientation="Portrait"
    shell:SystemTray.IsVisible="True">
```

Building the Main Page and Adding Components

Now add two textblocks, `txtLatitude` and `txtLongitude`, to display the longitude and latitude that the phone location service provides.

```
<Grid x:Name="LayoutRoot" Background="Transparent">
    <Grid.RowDefinitions>
        <RowDefinition Height="Auto"/>
        <RowDefinition Height="*"/>
    </Grid.RowDefinitions>

    <StackPanel x:Name="TitlePanel" Grid.Row="0" Margin="12,17,0,28">
        <TextBlock x:Name="ApplicationTitle" Text="GeoCoordinateWatcherDemo"
Style="{StaticResource PhoneTextNormalStyle}"/>
    </StackPanel>

    <Grid x:Name="ContentPanel" Grid.Row="1" Margin="12,0,12,0">
        <TextBox Height="72" Name="txtLongitude" Text=""
                Margin="193,142,41,393" />
        <TextBox Height="72" Name="txtLatitude" Text=""
                Margin="193,236,41,299" />
        <TextBlock Height="30" HorizontalAlignment="Left"
                Margin="78,202,0,0" Name="textBlock1"
                Text="Longitude" VerticalAlignment="Top" />
```

```
<TextBlock Height="30" HorizontalAlignment="Left"
           Margin="78,306,0,0" Name="textBlock2"
           Text="Latitude" VerticalAlignment="Top" />
    </Grid>
  </Grid>
</phone:PhoneApplicationPage>
```

Once you have loaded the XAML code, you should see the layout shown in Figure 14–2. In the next section, you will be adding events to handle updating the UI with the received GPS data from the location service.

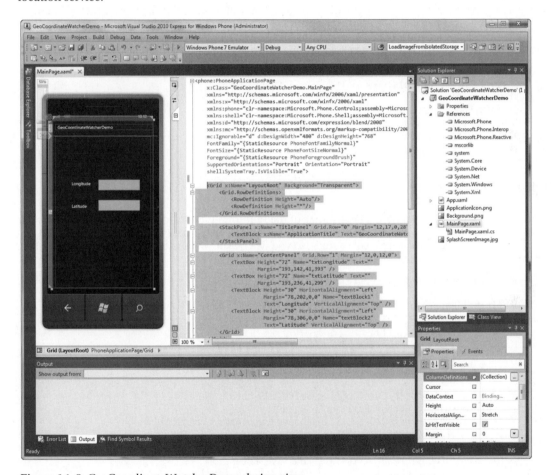

Figure 14–2. GeoCoordinateWatcherDemo design view

Coding the Application

In Solution Explorer, open `MainPage.xaml.cs` and replace the code there with the following C# code blocks, which will implement the UI updates using the location service with the data received from Reactive Extension.

Specifying the Namespaces

Begin by listing the namespaces the application will use. You will need `System.Device.Location` in order to use the location service. Declare `Microsoft.Phone.Reactive` in order to use the Reactive Extension's Observable. Also note that you will need `System.Threading` in order to feed the GPS data into the location service; you can think of Reactive Extension's Observable as if it were the satellite, Wi-Fi, or communication tower sending the GPS data.

```
using Microsoft.Phone.Controls;
using System.Threading;
using Microsoft.Phone.Reactive;
using System.Device.Location;
using System.Collections.Generic;
using System;
```

Initializing Variables

The variable `_geoCoordinateWatcher` is an instance of the Windows Phone location class that you'll use to access and retrieve location data. Notice in the constructor we declared the `PositionChanged` event in order to receive the location service's GPS data. Also you will be starting the thread that will simulate the GPS data that is sent to the `PositionChanged` event delegate.

```
GeoCoordinateWatcher _geoCoordinateWatcher;

public MainPage()
{
    InitializeComponent();

    // initialize GeoCoordinateWatcher
    _geoCoordinateWatcher = new GeoCoordinateWatcher();

    // PositionChanged event will receive GPS data
    _geoCoordinateWatcher.PositionChanged +=
        new EventHandler<GeoPositionChangedEventArgs<GeoCoordinate>>
            (_geoCoordinateWatcher_PositionChanged);

    // simulateGpsThread will start Reactive Extension
    // where EmulatePositionChangedEvents will be feeding
    // the data to PositionChanged event
    Thread simulateGpsThread = new Thread(SimulateGPS);
    simulateGpsThread.Start();
}
```

Simulating GPS Data Using Reactive Extension's Observable

In the foregoing constructor, you initiated a thread that executes the SimulateGPS method. In the SimulateGPS method, the Reactive Extension's Observable subscribes to the PositionChanged event in order to feed the GPS data. Notice that GPSPositionChangedEvents constantly sends GeoPositionChangedEventArgs every two seconds, which then gets received by GeoCoordinateWatcher's PositionChanged event and the GPS data.

```
// Reactive Extension that intercepts the _geoCoordinateWatcher_PositionChanged
// in order to feed the GPS data.
private void SimulateGPS()
{
    var position = GPSPositionChangedEvents().ToObservable();
    position.Subscribe(evt => _geoCoordinateWatcher_PositionChanged(null, evt));
}

private static IEnumerable<GeoPositionChangedEventArgs<GeoCoordinate>>
GPSPositionChangedEvents()
{
    Random random = new Random();

    // feed the GPS data
    while (true)
    {
        Thread.Sleep(TimeSpan.FromSeconds(2));

        // randomly generate GPS data, latitude and longitude.
// latitude is between -90 and 90
double latitude = (random.NextDouble() * 180.0) - 90.0;
// longitude is between -180 and 180
double longitude = (random.NextDouble() * 360.0) - 180.0;
        yield return new GeoPositionChangedEventArgs<GeoCoordinate>(
                new GeoPosition<GeoCoordinate>(DateTimeOffset.Now, new
GeoCoordinate(latitude, longitude)));
    }
}
```

Displaying GPS Data

In this demo, the received GPS data is displayed directly to the user. Notice here that you are using Dispatcher.BeginInvoke to execute the lamda expression of an anonymous method. Using Dispatcher.BeginInvoke to update the UI with the GPS data is absolutely necessary because the PositionChanged event is executed in a different thread than the UI, and thus you must explicitly use Dispatcher.Invoke to run UI specific codes.

```
private void _geoCoordinateWatcher_PositionChanged(object sender
    , GeoPositionChangedEventArgs<GeoCoordinate> e)
{
    this.Dispatcher.BeginInvoke(() =>
    {
        txtLatitude.Text = e.Position.Location.Latitude.ToString();
        txtLongitude.Text = e.Position.Location.Longitude.ToString();
    });
}
```

Testing the Finished Application

To test the application, press F5. The result should resemble the screenshot in Figure 14–3, and you will see constantly changing longitude and latitude in the textblocks.

Figure 14–3. GeoCoordinateWatcherDemo

Using GeoCoordinateWatcher and the Bing Maps Control to Track Your Movements

We will begin by building an application to work with the phone's location service, GeoCoordinateWatcher. The application, Bing Map Demo, is shown in Figure 14–4 and demonstrates the basic functions available through GeoCoordinateWatcher, the location service that we introduced in the previous section. The application will display your location with a blinking icon on a map and continuously update your position as you move.

In this demo, when you click the Start button, it will start the location service that will send notification when the position is changed, and upon the changed position event, the Bing Maps map will be updated with the new position. You can actually start the application while you are walking and watch the position of the locator (red dot) on the map change as you move.

Figure 14–4. Bing Maps Demo using GeoCoordinateWatcher

You'll build the demo in four steps. First, you need to register with the Bing Maps service portal and then create a new Visual Studio project. Next you'll build the project's user interface and finish up by adding code to respond to commands from the user.

Registering with the Bing Maps Service Portal and Installing the Bing Maps SDK

Before you can use the Bing Maps Silverlight control and its service offerings, you must register with Bing Maps at www.bingmapsportal.com/.

Go to www.bingmapsportal.com/ and you should see something similar to Figure 14–5.

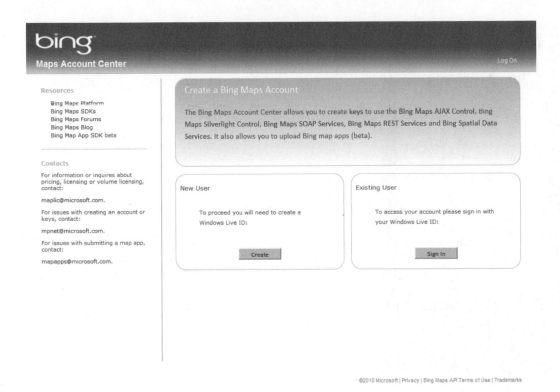

Figure 14–5. Bing Maps portal to create new user

1. Click the Create button and follow the instructions provided by Microsoft.

2. Once you create a Bing Maps service user, you must create an application key so that you can use the Bing Maps control and the Bing Maps service from Windows Phone. Sign in to the Bing Maps portal, and once you are logged in, click the "Create or view keys" hyperlink as shown in Figure 14–6.

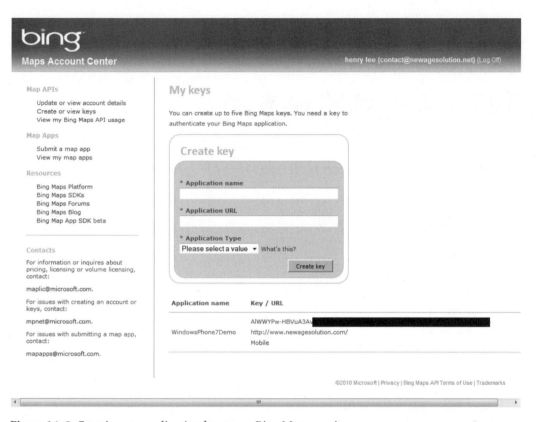

Figure 14–6. Creating an application key to use Bing Maps service

Once you've created the Bing Maps application key, you must install the Windows Phone SDK found at `http://developer.windowsphone.com/windows-phone-7/`.

If you successfully installed the Windows Phone SDK, the binaries (`Microsoft.Phone.Controls.Maps`) can be referenced from the project in order to use the Bing Maps Silverlight control.

Creating the BingMapDemo Project

To set up the BingMapDemo project, follow the steps you've used for previous examples in this book:

1. Open Microsoft Visual Studio 2010 Express for Windows Phone on your workstation.

2. Create a new Windows Phone Application by selecting File ➤ New Project on the Visual Studio command menu. Select the Windows Phone Application template, and name the application "BingMapDemo."

295

3. In order to use Bing Maps control in Windows Phone, you must reference `Microsoft.Phone.Controls.Maps`, and in order to track your movement, you need to add reference to `System.Device` to use the location service. Open Solution Explorer and add those references now. Check to ensure that your list of references matches the list shown in Figure 14–7.

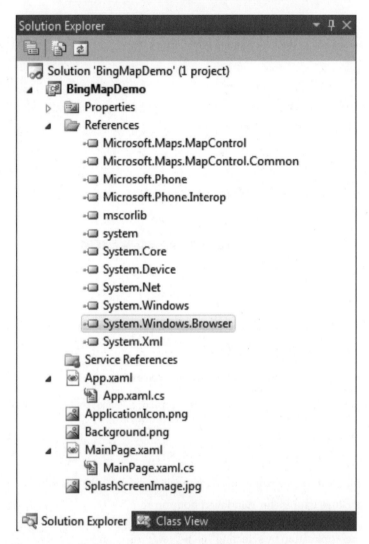

Figure 14–7. Referenced assemblies needed for Bing Maps control

Coding the User Interface

Now it's time to code the user interface, which we've chosen to implement in XAML. Sometimes it is faster to work with XAML when working with a simple example that requires only a few controls. Go to Solution Explorer, open MainPage.xaml, and replace the XAML you find there with the following two blocks of code.

Declaring the UI Resources

Most of the namespaces you see in this snippet are typically declared by default when you first create a Windows Phone project. The following namespace is unique to this application and allows you to add the Bing Maps control you will use to plot your location: xmlns:BingMap="clr-namespace:Microsoft.Phone.Controls.Maps;assembly=Microsoft.Phone.Controls.Maps".

```
<phone:PhoneApplicationPage
    x:Class="BingMapDemo.MainPage"
    xmlns="http://schemas.microsoft.com/winfx/2006/xaml/presentation"
    xmlns:x="http://schemas.microsoft.com/winfx/2006/xaml"
    xmlns:phone="clr-namespace:Microsoft.Phone.Controls;assembly=Microsoft.Phone"
    xmlns:shell="clr-namespace:Microsoft.Phone.Shell;assembly=Microsoft.Phone"
    xmlns:d="http://schemas.microsoft.com/expression/blend/2008"
    xmlns:mc="http://schemas.openxmlformats.org/markup-compatibility/2006"
    xmlns:BingMap=
"clr-namespace:Microsoft.Phone.Controls.Maps;assembly=Microsoft.Phone.Controls.Maps
"
    FontFamily="{StaticResource PhoneFontFamilyNormal}"
    FontSize="{StaticResource PhoneFontSizeNormal}"
    Foreground="{StaticResource PhoneForegroundBrush}"
    SupportedOrientations="Portrait" Orientation="Portrait"
    mc:Ignorable="d" d:DesignWidth="480" d:DesignHeight="768"
    shell:SystemTray.IsVisible="True">
```

Building the Main Page and Adding a Bing Maps Control

To the main page, you will be adding a Bing Maps control to display your position and a button to start the location service. You'll also add an animation storyboard named BlinkLocator to cause the locator icon to blink by changing its color. Notice that inside bingMap control there is a BingMap:Pushpin named bingMapLocator. The map layer bingMapLocator contains an Ellipse control named locator, whose initial map position in latitude and longitude is (0, 0). In this application, the location service will provide changing positions in the latitude and longitude so that the locator position can be properly updated. This is a very simple but very powerful demonstration of using the location service and Bing Maps control. You can use the same technique for Yahoo or Google Maps, as their API is very similar to Bing Maps.

```
<phone:PhoneApplicationPage.Resources>
    <Storyboard x:Name="BlinkLocator" AutoReverse="True" RepeatBehavior="Forever">
        <ColorAnimationUsingKeyFrames
Storyboard.TargetProperty="(Shape.Fill).(SolidColorBrush.Color)"
Storyboard.TargetName="locator">
            <EasingColorKeyFrame KeyTime="0" Value="Red"/>
            <EasingColorKeyFrame KeyTime="0:0:1" Value="#FFCEFF00"/>
        </ColorAnimationUsingKeyFrames>
```

```
            </Storyboard>
        </phone:PhoneApplicationPage.Resources>

        <Grid x:Name="LayoutRoot" Background="Transparent">
            <Grid.RowDefinitions>
                <RowDefinition Height="Auto"/>
                <RowDefinition Height="*"/>
            </Grid.RowDefinitions>

            <StackPanel x:Name="TitlePanel" Grid.Row="0" Margin="24,24,0,12">
                <TextBlock x:Name="ApplicationTitle" Text="Bing Map Demo"
                            Style="{StaticResource PhoneTextNormalStyle}"/>
            </StackPanel>

            <Grid x:Name="ContentGrid" Grid.Row="1">
                <BingMap:Map Name="bingMap" NavigationVisibility="Collapsed"
                            Margin="0,0,0,72">
                    <BingMap:Pushpin Name="bingMapLocator">
                        <BingMap:Pushpin.Content>
                            <Ellipse Fill="Red" Width="20" Height="20"
                                    BingMap:MapLayer.Position="0,0"
                                    Name="locator" />
    <BingMap:Pushpin.Content>
            </BingMap: Pushpin>
            </BingMap:Map>
                <Button Content="Start" Height="72" HorizontalAlignment="Right"
Margin="0,633,0,0" Name="btnStart" VerticalAlignment="Top" Width="160"
Click="btnStart_Click" />
                <TextBlock Height="30" HorizontalAlignment="Left" Margin="6,657,0,0"
Name="txtStatus" Text="Status" VerticalAlignment="Top" Width="308" />
            </Grid>
        </Grid>

    </phone:PhoneApplicationPage>
```

■ **Tip** Notice here that we changed the content of the Pushpin, which is the locator that specifies where you are. You can add any type of control and change the appearance of the Pushpin. You can even put a placeholder and dynamically change the content of the Pushpin.

Once you have loaded the XAML code, you should see the layout shown in Figure 14–8. In the next section, you will be adding an event to consume the GPS data and then to plot the data onto the map layer of the Bing Maps Silverlight control.

Figure 14–8. BingMapDemo design view

Coding the Application

In Solution Explorer, open `MainPage.xaml.cs` and replace the code there with the following C# code blocks, which will implement the media player's functionalities.

Specifying the Namespaces

Begin by listing the namespaces the application will use. Notice the inclusion of `Microsoft.Maps.Control`, which will allow you to manipulate Bing Maps control, and `System.Device`, which will allow you to work with `geoCoordinateWatcher`, which will retrieve the location data from GPS, Wi-Fi, or cellular towers.

```
using System;
using System.Windows;
using Microsoft.Phone.Controls;
using Microsoft.Maps.MapControl;
using System.Device.Location;
```

```
namespace BingMapDemo
{
    public partial class MainPage : PhoneApplicationPage
    {
```

Initializing Variables

The variable _geoCoordinateWatcher is an instance of the location service class that you'll use to access and retrieve location data. Notice that you will be using GeoPositionAccuracy.High, which will use the phone device's GPS, and for this to work you must use the real Windows Phone device. If you need to simulate the location service, you can refer to the previous section in this chapter or Chapter 18 ("Reactive Extensions") to simulate fake GeoCoordinateWatcher service. Also here you will be setting MovementThreshold to 100 meters so that the PositionChanged event fires every 100 meters, and you will be plotting your current location on the Bing Maps map.

GeoCoordinateWatcher has StatusChanged and PositionChanged events that notify the application whenever the new updated position is received from the GPS.

As for bingMap, you will hide the Microsoft Bing Maps logo and copyright in order to make things cleaner and make more space for other controls for the application. Finally, in order to use the map control at all, you must set ClientTokenCredentialsProvider to the value of the application key you obtained when you registered at the Bing Maps site.

```
        GeoCoordinateWatcher _geoCoordinateWatcher;


        public MainPage()
        {
            InitializeComponent();
            // Add your own BingMap Key
            bingMap.CredentialsProvider =
new ApplicationIdCredentialsProvider("ADD-YOUR-OWN-KEY");

            // Remove Bing Maps logo and copyrights in order to gain
            // extra space at the bottom of the map
            bingMap.LogoVisibility = Visibility.Collapsed;
            bingMap.CopyrightVisibility = Visibility.Collapsed;

            // Delcare GeoCoordinateWatcher with high accuracy
            // in order to use the device's GPS
            _geoCoordinateWatcher = new GeoCoordinateWatcher(GeoPositionAccuracy.High);
            _geoCoordinateWatcher.MovementThreshold = 100;

            // Subscribe to the device's status changed event
            _geoCoordinateWatcher.StatusChanged +=
                new  EventHandler<GeoPositionStatusChangedEventArgs>(
_geoCoordinateWatcher_StatusChanged);

            // Subscribe to the device's position changed event
            // to receive GPS coordinates (longitude and latitude)
            _geoCoordinateWatcher.PositionChanged +=
                New EventHandler<GeoPositionChangedEventArgs<GeoCoordinate>>(
_geoCoordinateWatcher_PositionChanged);
        }
```

Responding to StatusChanged and PositionChanged GeoCoordinateWatcher Events

In GeoCoordinateWatcher, StatusChanged fires when the GPS status changes and PositionChanged fires when the GPS receives new a position. In StatusChanged, if the received status is Disabled, you must notify the user that the device's location service is disabled and must be turned on. You can enable the location service on the device by going to Settings ➤ Location ➤ Turn on the location service.

Note here that the PositionChanged event will not fire until the position of the phone has changed by at least 100 meters as specified by MovementThreshold. When the StatusChanged event fires, txtStatus will be updated, and when the PositionChanged event fires, the locator icon you have added to the Bing Maps layer will be moved accordingly.

```
        private void _geoCoordinateWatcher_PositionChanged(object sender,
GeoPositionChangedEventArgs<GeoCoordinate> e)
        {
            Deployment.Current.Dispatcher.BeginInvoke(() => ChangePosition(e));
        }

        private void ChangePosition(GeoPositionChangedEventArgs<GeoCoordinate> e)
        {
            SetLocation(e.Position.Location.Latitude,
e.Position.Location.Longitude, 10, true);
        }

        private void _geoCoordinateWatcher_StatusChanged(object sender,
GeoPositionStatusChangedEventArgs e)
        {
            Deployment.Current.Dispatcher.BeginInvoke(() => StatusChanged(e));
        }

private void StatusChanged(GeoPositionStatusChangedEventArgs e)
        {
            switch (e.Status)
            {
                case GeoPositionStatus.Disabled:
                    txtStatus.Text = "Location Service is disabled!";
                    break;
                case GeoPositionStatus.Initializing:
                    txtStatus.Text = "Initializing Location Service...";
                    break;
                case GeoPositionStatus.NoData:
                    txtStatus.Text = "Your position could not be located.";
                    break;
                case GeoPositionStatus.Ready:
                    break;
            }
        }
```

Starting the Location Service: GeoCoordinateWatcher

When the user clicks the Start button, the location service will be started. TryStart will return false if the phone's location service is disabled. If the location service is disabled, a message box is displayed to the user, instructing the user to enable the location service on the phone.

```
private void btnStart_Click(object sender, RoutedEventArgs e)
{
    if (!_geoCoordinateWatcher.TryStart(true, TimeSpan.FromSeconds(5)))
    {
        MessageBox.Show("Please enable Location Service on the Phone.",
"Warning", MessageBoxButton.OK);

    }
}
```

Plotting the Location on the Bing Maps MapLayer

BingMap has a SetView method that allows you to set the current view on the screen using the location data, latitude and longitude, received from GeoCoordinateWatcher. The zoomLevel property indicates how far into the location the map will be zoomed. BingMap also has MapLayer, which can set the position of the map layer with respect to the received location. To make things interesting, we animated bingMapLocator with simple color blinks.

```
private void SetLocation(double latitude, double longitude,
double zoomLevel, bool showLocator)
    {
        Location location = new Location(latitude, latitude);
        bingMap.SetView(location, zoomLevel);
        MapLayer.SetPosition(locator, location);
        if (showLocator)
        {
            locator.Visibility = Visibility.Visible;
            BlinkLocator.Begin();
        }
        else
        {
            locator.Visibility = Visibility.Collapsed;
            BlinkLocator.Stop();
        }
    }
}
}
```

Testing the Finished Application

To test the application, press F5. The result should resemble Figure 14–4 on the phone device. Remember that you must have a real phone device to be able to use real GPS. In the following section, we will utilize Bing Maps geocoding service to convert the address into geocode of longitude and latitude in order to plot the address on the Bing Maps Silverlight control.

Plotting an Address on a Bing Maps Map and Working with the Bing Maps Service

Microsoft provides three main services hosted on the cloud to be used by any clients, including Windows Phone devices, as shown in the following:

- *GeoCodeService*: Allows an address to be converted to longitude and latitude or convert geocode into the address. Web service can be consumed by accessing the URL at `http://dev.virtualearth.net/webservices/v1/geocodeservice/geocodeservice.svc`.

- *RouteService*: Includes services such as calculating the distance between two addresses, providing driving and walking directions from address to address, and provides step-by-step navigational service. Web service can be consumed by accessing the URL at `http://dev.virtualearth.net/webservices/v1/routeservice/routeservice.svc`.

- *Searchservice*: Provides location-based search results. For example, based on the submitted address, it will find restaurants in a 5-mile radius. Web service can be consumed by accessing the URL at `http://dev.virtualearth.net/webservices/v1/searchservice/searchservice.svc`.

In the following section, you will be using GeoCodeService to convert any address into geocode (longitude and latitude) and plot the address on the Bing Maps Silverlight Control. Through the demo, you will learn to access the Bing Maps service using the credential that you received when you registered.

The following demo interface will contain a text box where you can enter an address to be plotted on the map and a button to invoke a method to convert the address, using the Bing Maps geocode service. It then plots the geocode onto the Bing Maps Silverlight control, as shown in Figure 14–9.

Figure 14–9. AddressPlottingDemo application

Creating the AddressPlottingDemo Application

To set up the BingMapDemo project, follow the steps you've used for previous examples in this book:

1. Open Microsoft Visual Studio 2010 Express for Windows Phone on your workstation.

2. Create a new Windows Phone Application by selecting File ➤ New Project on the Visual Studio command menu. Select the Windows Phone Application template, and name the application "AddressPlottingDemo."

3. In order to use Bing Maps control in Windows Phone, you must reference `Microsoft.Phone.Controls.Maps` and `System.Device`.

Adding a Service Reference to the Bing Maps GeoCodeService

In order to use the Bing Maps `GeoCodeService`, you need to add a service reference to your project.

1. In Solution Explorer, right-click the `References` folder and choose Add Service Reference.

2. When the Add Service Reference window pops up, enter
   `http://dev.virtualearth.net/webservices/v1/geocodeservice/geocodeservice`
   `.svc` into the Address field and press Go.

3. You see a list of services. In the Namespace text box, enter
   "BingMapGeoCodeService" and you should see a result similar to Figure 14–10.

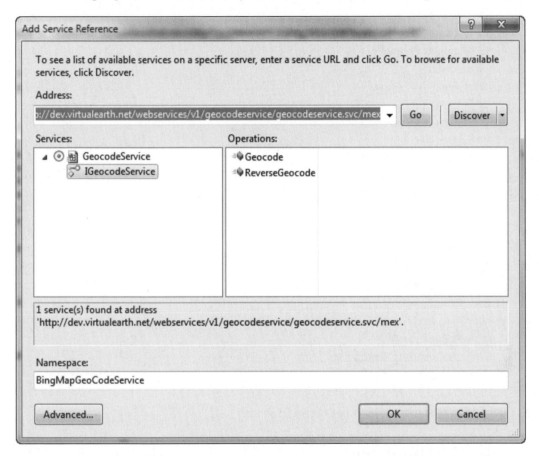

Figure 14–10. Adding a service reference

4. Click OK and you should see `BingMapGeoCodeService` in Solution Explorer, as shown
   in Figure 14–11.

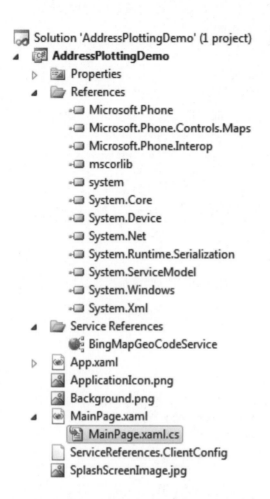

Figure 14–11. Service reference to Bing Maps GeoCodeService

Coding the User Interface

AddressPlottingDemo has a very simple UI, consisting of the textblock for capturing the address, the button to invoke a method for plotting the address onto the map, and the Bing Maps Silverlight control.

Declaring the UI Resources

The namespaces you see in the following code snippet are typically declared by default when you first create a Windows Phone project. In particular, namespaces `xmlns:phone="clr-namespace:Microsoft.Phone.Controls;assembly=Microsoft.Phone"` allow you to add common Windows Phone controls to the application main page.

```
<phone:PhoneApplicationPage
    x:Class="AddressPlottingDemo.MainPage"
    xmlns="http://schemas.microsoft.com/winfx/2006/xaml/presentation"
    xmlns:x="http://schemas.microsoft.com/winfx/2006/xaml"
    xmlns:phone="clr-namespace:Microsoft.Phone.Controls;assembly=Microsoft.Phone"
    xmlns:shell="clr-namespace:Microsoft.Phone.Shell;assembly=Microsoft.Phone"
    xmlns:d="http://schemas.microsoft.com/expression/blend/2008"
    xmlns:mc="http://schemas.openxmlformats.org/markup-compatibility/2006"
    xmlns:BingMap="clr-
namespace:Microsoft.Phone.Controls.Maps;assembly=Microsoft.Phone.Controls.Maps"
    mc:Ignorable="d" d:DesignWidth="480" d:DesignHeight="768"
    FontFamily="{StaticResource PhoneFontFamilyNormal}"
    FontSize="{StaticResource PhoneFontSizeNormal}"
    Foreground="{StaticResource PhoneForegroundBrush}"
    SupportedOrientations="Portrait" Orientation="Portrait"
    shell:SystemTray.IsVisible="True">
```

Creating the Main Page

The main page consists of the Bing Maps Silverlight control, button, and address textblock to capture the user address input. Notice on the bingMap control that CopyrightVisibility and LogoVisibity are set to Collapsed, giving you much more needed real estate on the screen.

```
<Grid x:Name="LayoutRoot" Background="Transparent">
    <Grid.RowDefinitions>
        <RowDefinition Height="Auto"/>
        <RowDefinition Height="*"/>
    </Grid.RowDefinitions>

    <StackPanel x:Name="TitlePanel" Grid.Row="0"
                Margin="12,17,0,28">
        <TextBlock x:Name="ApplicationTitle"
                Text="AddressPlottingDemo"
                Style="{StaticResource PhoneTextNormalStyle}"/>
    </StackPanel>

    <Grid x:Name="ContentPanel" Grid.Row="1" Margin="12,0,12,0">

        <BingMap:Map Name="bingMap"
                    Width="425" Height="513"
                    Margin="0,0,19,25"
                    CopyrightVisibility="Collapsed"
                    LogoVisibility="Collapsed"
                    VerticalAlignment="Bottom" HorizontalAlignment="Right">
            <BingMap:Pushpin Name="bingMapLocator"
                        Background="Transparent">
                <BingMap:Pushpin.Content>
                    <Ellipse Fill="Red" Width="20" Height="20"
                        Name="locator" />
                </BingMap:Pushpin.Content>
            </BingMap:Pushpin>
        </BingMap:Map>
        <TextBox Height="72" Margin="110,10,6,0" Name="txtAddress"
```

```
                    Text="4237 Salisbury Rd, Suite 114 Jacksonville FL, 32216"
                    VerticalAlignment="Top" />
          <TextBlock Height="30" HorizontalAlignment="Left"
                    Margin="33,32,0,0" Name="textBlock1"
                    Text="Address" VerticalAlignment="Top" />
          <Button Content="Show on map" Height="72"
                    Name="btnPlot" Margin="17,68,192,556"
                    Click="btnPlot_Click" />
      </Grid>
   </Grid>
</phone:PhoneApplicationPage>
```

Coding the Application

One of most important things to notice in this demo application is its use of the Bing Maps geocode service to convert a street address to longitude and latitude measures, so that it can be plotted on the map. Also, in order to use the Bing Maps geocode service, you must provide the Bing Maps credential that you created during the registration.

Specifying the Namespaces

Once the service is referenced, you will be able to declare the namespace of the Bing Maps geocode service, AddressPlottingDemo.BingMapGeoCodeService. Notice also that you are including System.Linq because you will be using Linq to query returned GeoCodeResults with the highest confidence.

```
using System.Windows;
using Microsoft.Phone.Controls;
using AddressPlottingDemo.BingMapGeoCodeService;
using Microsoft.Phone.Controls.Maps;
using System.Collections.ObjectModel;
using System.Linq;
```

Initializing Variables

The GeocodeServiceClient variable _svc is a proxy class that lets you connect to the Bing Maps geocode service to geocode the address in order to plot on the map. Notice that you would need to subscribe to GeocodeCompleted event in order to receive result that contains longitude and latitude.

```
        GeocodeServiceClient _svc;
        public MainPage()
        {
            InitializeComponent();

            // instantiate Bing Maps GeocodeService
            _svc = new GeocodeServiceClient();
            _svc.GeocodeCompleted += (s, e) =>
                {
                    // sort the returned record by ascending confidence in order for
                    // highest confidence to be on the top.
    // Based on the numeration High value is
                    // at 0, Medium value at 1 and Low volue at 2
```

```
                    var geoResult = (from r in e.Result.Results
                                     orderby (int)r.Confidence ascending
                                     select r).FirstOrDefault();
                    if (geoResult != null)
                    {
                        this.SetLocation(geoResult.Locations[0].Latitude,
                            geoResult.Locations[0].Longitude,
                            10,
                            true);
                    }
                };
            }
```

Handling the Button Event That Plots Address Data onto the Bing Maps Map

When btnPlot is clicked, you will be making a web service request to the Bing Maps geocode service to convert txtAddress.Text to return geocoordinates in longitude and latitude. When the event, GeoCodeCompleted, is raised you will receive multiple results that contain only the highest confidence level. Using GeoCodeResult you will be making a call to SetLocation that will plot the location on the Bing Maps Silverlight control.

```
private void SetLocation(double latitude, double longitude,
double zoomLevel, bool showLocator)
        {
            // Move the pushpin to geo coordinate
            Microsoft.Phone.Controls.Maps.Platform.Location location =
new Microsoft.Phone.Controls.Maps.Platform.Location();
            location.Latitude = latitude;
            location.Longitude = longitude;
            bingMap.SetView(location, zoomLevel);
            bingMapLocator.Location = location;
            if (showLocator)
            {
                locator.Visibility = Visibility.Visible;
            }
            else
            {
                locator.Visibility = Visibility.Collapsed;
            }
        }

        private void btnPlot_Click(object sender, RoutedEventArgs e)
        {
            BingMapGeoCodeService.GeocodeRequest request =
new BingMapGeoCodeService.GeocodeRequest();

            // Only accept results with high confidence.
            request.Options = new GeocodeOptions()
            {
                Filters = new ObservableCollection<FilterBase>
                {
                    new ConfidenceFilter()
                    {
```

```
                    MinimumConfidence = Confidence.High
                }
            }
        };


        request.Credentials = new Credentials()
        {
            ApplicationId = "Put-Your-BingMap-Credential-Id"
        };

        request.Query = txtAddress.Text;

        // Make asynchronous call to fetch the geo coordinate data.
        _svc.GeocodeAsync(request);
    }
```

Testing the Finished Application

To test the application, press F5. The result should resemble the display shown in Figure 14–9. Enter an address into Address text box and press the "Show on map" button. You should see the pushpin move from its current position to the coordinates provided by the Bing Maps geocode service.

Summary

In this chapter, you learned to start the location service to receive the position in latitude and longitude. Upon receiving the position, you learned to pass the location data into the Bing Maps control and use the Bing Maps map layer to indicate your current GPS position. This is a very simple but powerful concept for you to begin creating your own location-aware application. Also you learned to utilize the Bing Maps geocode service, which converts the address to geocoordinates so you can plot the address location on the map.

In Chapter 15, you will learn to use the media elements of the phone to play video and audio. You will be able to stream movies and sounds from external sites, and you will also learn how media elements play a significant role in making sound effects in a game.

CHAPTER 15

■ ■ ■

Media

In today's smartphone era, content is everything. Think of YouTube, which provides fun videos to the masses through browsers. Now smartphones, too, have the ability to play high-quality movies, music, and more, anywhere. What was once possible only on desktop computers can now be done with the smartphone you carry all the time, regardless of whether you are near a cell tower or Wi-Fi connection.

Windows Phones will come equipped with powerful media features for developers and designers to use to create compelling applications that can play back music, audio, and video in a host of formats. A good example of the kind of media player such functionality supports can be found at the NBC Olympics web site, where the Olympic games were streamed live, and then archived, and can now be viewed again in high definition (www.nbcolympics.com/video/index.html). Also, pay-per-view fighting matches from the Ultimate Fighting Championship (UFC) are streamed live (http://modules.ufc.com/live/). The NBC Olympic video player includes a "BOSS" button, which, when clicked, pauses the video player and pops up a full-screen display that resembles Microsoft Excel, creating the impression for you-know-who that you are working really hard. MediaElement provides incredible building flexibility that is more than just a simple video player. Windows Phone provides the ability to play videos and sounds, listen to FM radio, interact with the music and video hub, and launch Windows Marketplace to allow the user to buy songs.

In this chapter, you will learn to embed in your application and customize a media player control that can play videos and sounds using MediaElement. You'll also learn to use MediaPlayerLauncher, which activates the stand-alone media player application that ships with Windows Phone. Please refer to Chapter 5 for more information on how to interact with Windows Marketplace by directing the user to buy songs and your application. As for FMRadio API, this chapter will not be covering the topic—instead, you can find more information at http://msdn.microsoft.com/en-us/library/ff769541(VS.92).aspx.

Introducing MediaElement

MediaElement is a Windows Phone control that you can add to an application to play video and sound. It's a control that appeared first with .NET and was later ported to Silverlight and then to Windows Phone. When the MediaElement control is placed on the Visual Studio or Blend design view, you will see only a rectangle, which is not what you would expect of a video or audio player. This is because the MediaElement control is left in somewhat of a blank slate to leave designers full control over its look, and its play, stop, pause, mute, and seek buttons. For developers, MediaElement exposes APIs for full control of a player's play, stop, pause, mute, and seek behavior, as well as stream buffering, the progress of downloads, and volume control.

You'll want to use MediaElement when you are creating an application that requires more than a simple media player, and you want a player to be a part of your application, not something you have to exit the application to access. Also MediaElement gives flexibility to customize the look and add more functionality, like being able to share videos via Twitter, Facebook, SMS, or e-mail. Another thing you can do is to allow the user to provide ratings and comments, or play the video player that has the chapters to skip to with the thumbnails of each chapter. MediaPlayerLauncher is more useful if you simply want to play video or audio using the default media player of the Windows Phone. The default media player that comes with Windows Phone supports basic functions such as play, pause, move forward, move backward, and play time elapsed. MediaElement will support a variety of video and audio formats. See Table 15–1 for the most commonly used formats that are supported by Windows Phone. A complete list can be found at http://msdn.microsoft.com/en-us/library/ff462087(VS.92).aspx.

Table 15–1. Media Formats Supported on Windows Phone

Media Type	Supported Formats
Audio	WAV, MP3, WMA, MP4
Video	WMV, MP4, AVI
Images	JPEG, PNG, GIF, BMP, TIF

The first example will show you a technique to stream the video file from the Internet or play the video file that is part of the application content using MediaElement, and then you will learn to play the same video content using MediaPlayerLauncher.

Working with Video

In this first demo, you will build a media player (plays video and audio) that can play, stop, pause, mute, and seek (which is a video player function that lets you move the video forward or backward to any position), whose UI is shown in Figure 15–1. You will learn to stream video content from the Internet as well as play content that is part of the application. Just remember that you wouldn't want to package the video as part of the phone application because video or audio files can get very big; so in the real world, you must think about the strategy of deploying media content to the Web and allowing the phone application to simply play the URL. In Chapter 13, you learned about caching the image download into the isolated storage. The same exact technique can be used to download video or music content the first time and then save it into isolated storage.

Also, you can store video content on a Windows IIS media server and take advantage of the smooth streaming technology for HD-quality content and Microsoft DRM protection the server provides. Netflix, for example, uses DRM technology to secure the content of its streaming videos. Microsoft DRM provides a platform to protect digital materials and deliver the contents that can be played on any devices. Also IIS media server can effectively distribute the HD video content to low-bandwidth and low-performing computers (smooth streaming technology). If you would like to learn more about DRM using IIS media streaming server, please refer to http://msdn.microsoft.com/en-us/library/cc838192(VS.95).aspx, as you will not be learning about this advanced topic in this chapter. Another way to store video content is in the cloud using Microsoft Azure (please refer to Chapter 3 for Windows Azure data store).

Figure 15–1. Media Player Demo application

You will build the demo application in three major steps. First you will create a Windows Phone project. Next you will build the user interface of the media player and finish up by wiring up the commands in the code that respond to the user.

Creating the MediaPlayerDemo Project

To create the Video Demo project, follow the steps you have used in previous examples in this book.

1. Open Microsoft Visual Studio 2010 Express for Windows Phone on your workstation.

2. Create a new Windows Phone Application by selecting File ➤ New Project on the Visual Studio command menu. Select the Windows Phone Application template, name the application "MediaPlayerDemo," and click OK.

Building the User Interface

You will build the user interface in Visual Studio with XAML. For building simple controls, it is faster to work with the XAML code. Go to Solution Explorer, open `MainPage.xaml`, and replace the XAML you find there with the following code snippets.

Declaring the UI Resources

The namespaces you see in the following code snippets are typically declared by default when you first create the Windows Phone project. The namespace `xmlns:phone="clr-namespace:Microsoft.Phone.Controls;assembly=Microsoft.Phone"` will allow you to add common Windows Phone controls required to build this demo: buttons, textblocks, text boxes, list boxes, sliders, and media elements.

```
<phone:PhoneApplicationPage
    x:Class="MediaPlayerDemo.MainPage"
    xmlns="http://schemas.microsoft.com/winfx/2006/xaml/presentation"
    xmlns:x="http://schemas.microsoft.com/winfx/2006/xaml"
    xmlns:phone="clr-namespace:Microsoft.Phone.Controls;assembly=Microsoft.Phone"
    xmlns:shell="clr-namespace:Microsoft.Phone.Shell;assembly=Microsoft.Phone"
    xmlns:d="http://schemas.microsoft.com/expression/blend/2008"
    xmlns:mc="http://schemas.openxmlformats.org/markup-compatibility/2006"
    FontFamily="{StaticResource PhoneFontFamilyNormal}"
    FontSize="{StaticResource PhoneFontSizeNormal}"
    Foreground="{StaticResource PhoneForegroundBrush}"
    SupportedOrientations="Portrait" Orientation="Portrait"
    mc:Ignorable="d" d:DesignWidth="480" d:DesignHeight="768"
    shell:SystemTray.IsVisible="True">
```

Building the Main Page and Adding Media Player Components

Next, add the code shown in Listing 15–1, which creates the common media controls the application will use, like play, pause, stop, mute, and seek. You will be using the `Slider` control to implement the function that will allow the user to see how much time is elapsed in playing the media content. Also, by clicking the `Slider`, the user can skip backward and forward. Also you will be adding labels to track video buffering and video downloading status using the textblocks. Lastly, there is a button called "btnMediaPlayerLauncher" that will launch the default Windows Phone's media player to play the media content.

Listing 15–1. Custom Media Player Main Page and UI (XAML)

```
<phone:PhoneApplicationPage
    x:Class="MediaPlayerDemo.MainPage"
    xmlns="http://schemas.microsoft.com/winfx/2006/xaml/presentation"
    xmlns:x="http://schemas.microsoft.com/winfx/2006/xaml"
    xmlns:phone="clr-namespace:Microsoft.Phone.Controls;assembly=Microsoft.Phone"
    xmlns:shell="clr-namespace:Microsoft.Phone.Shell;assembly=Microsoft.Phone"
    xmlns:d="http://schemas.microsoft.com/expression/blend/2008"
    xmlns:mc="http://schemas.openxmlformats.org/markup-compatibility/2006"
    FontFamily="{StaticResource PhoneFontFamilyNormal}"
    FontSize="{StaticResource PhoneFontSizeNormal}"
```

```
        Foreground="{StaticResource PhoneForegroundBrush}"
        SupportedOrientations="Portrait" Orientation="Portrait"
        mc:Ignorable="d" d:DesignWidth="480" d:DesignHeight="768"
        shell:SystemTray.IsVisible="True">

        <Grid x:Name="LayoutRoot" Background="Transparent">
            <Grid.RowDefinitions>
                <RowDefinition Height="Auto"/>
                <RowDefinition Height="*"/>
            </Grid.RowDefinitions>

            <StackPanel x:Name="TitlePanel" Grid.Row="0" Margin="24,24,0,12">
                <TextBlock x:Name="PageTitle" Text="MediaPlayerDemo" Margin="-3,-8,0,0"
                            Style="{StaticResource PhoneTextTitle1Style}" FontSize="48" />
            </StackPanel>

            <Grid x:Name="ContentGrid" Grid.Row="1">
                <MediaElement Height="289" HorizontalAlignment="Left"
                            Margin="26,148,0,0" x:Name="mediaPlayer"
                            VerticalAlignment="Top" Width="417"
                            AutoPlay="False"/>
                <Button Content="&gt;" Height="72"
                        HorizontalAlignment="Left" Margin="13,527,0,0"
                        x:Name="btnPlay" VerticalAlignment="Top" Width="87"
                        Click="btnPlay_Click" />
                <Button Content="O" Height="72"
                        HorizontalAlignment="Right" Margin="0,527,243,0"
                        x:Name="btnStop" VerticalAlignment="Top" Width="87"
                        Click="btnStop_Click" />
                <Button Content="||" Height="72" Margin="0,527,313,0"
                        x:Name="btnPause" VerticalAlignment="Top"
                        Click="btnPause_Click" HorizontalAlignment="Right" Width="87" />
                <Slider Height="84" HorizontalAlignment="Left"
                        Margin="13,423,0,0" Name="mediaTimeline"
                        VerticalAlignment="Top" Width="443"
                        ValueChanged="mediaTimeline_ValueChanged"
                        Maximum="1" LargeChange="0.1" />
                <TextBlock Height="30" HorizontalAlignment="Left"
                            Margin="26,472,0,0" Name="lblStatus"
                            Text="00:00" VerticalAlignment="Top" Width="88" FontSize="16" />
                <TextBlock Height="30"
                        Margin="118,472,222,0" x:Name="lblBuffering"
                        Text="Buffering" VerticalAlignment="Top" FontSize="16" />
                <TextBlock Height="30"
                        Margin="0,472,82,0" x:Name="lblDownload"
                        Text="Download" VerticalAlignment="Top" FontSize="16"
HorizontalAlignment="Right" Width="140" />
                <Button Content="Mute" Height="72"
                        HorizontalAlignment="Left" Margin="217,527,0,0"
                        Name="btnMute" VerticalAlignment="Top" Width="89"
                        FontSize="16" Click="btnMute_Click" />
                <TextBlock Height="30" HorizontalAlignment="Left"
                            Margin="315,551,0,0" Name="lblSoundStatus"
                            Text="Sound On" VerticalAlignment="Top" Width="128" />
```

```
        <Button Content="Use MediaPlayerLauncher" FontSize="24" Height="72"
                HorizontalAlignment="Left" Margin="13,591,0,0"
                Name="btnMediaPlayerLauncher" VerticalAlignment="Top"
                Width="411" Click="btnMediaPlayerLauncher_Click" />
        <TextBox x:Name="txtUrl" Height="57" Margin="91,33,8,0"
                TextWrapping="Wrap" VerticalAlignment="Top" FontSize="16"

Text="http://ecn.channel9.msdn.com/o9/ch9/7/8/2/9/1/5/ARCastMDISilverlightGridComputing_ch9.wm
v"/>
        <TextBlock x:Name="lblUrl" HorizontalAlignment="Left" Height="25"
                Margin="8,48,0,0" TextWrapping="Wrap" Text="Video URL:"
                VerticalAlignment="Top" Width="83" FontSize="16"/>
        <TextBox x:Name="txtBufferingTime" Height="57" Margin="151,78,0,0"
                TextWrapping="Wrap" VerticalAlignment="Top" FontSize="16"
HorizontalAlignment="Left" Width="86" Text="20"/>
        <TextBlock x:Name="lblBufferingTime" HorizontalAlignment="Left"
                Height="25" Margin="8,93,0,0" TextWrapping="Wrap"
                Text="Buffering Time (s):" VerticalAlignment="Top"
                Width="139" FontSize="16"/>
    </Grid>
  </Grid>

</phone:PhoneApplicationPage>
```

Once you have loaded the XAML code, you should see the layout shown in Figure 15–2. In the next section, you will add code to respond to UI events and implement MediaElement's behaviors.

Figure 15–2. MediaPlayerDemo design view

Coding the Application

In Solution Explorer, open MainPage.xaml.cs and replace the code you find there with the following C#
code blocks that will implement the media player's functions.

Specifying the Namespaces

Begin by listing the namespaces the application will use. Notice the inclusion of Microsoft.Phone.Tasks
that will allow us to launch Windows Phone's default media player. As for the MediaElement, it is declared
in the XAML page, which you will simply reference here by the control's name.

```
using System;
using System.Windows;
using System.Windows.Media;
using Microsoft.Phone.Controls;
using Microsoft.Phone.Tasks;

namespace MediaPlayerDemo
{
    public partial class MainPage : PhoneApplicationPage
```

Initializing Variables

The variable _updatingMediaTimeline is an extremely important variable that stops the infinite loop in
this demo. By setting _updatingMediaTimeline to true while the media timeline (Slider control) is being
updated during the CompositionTarget.Rendering event, the media's backward and forward event will
wait to be processed until the timeline update is completed. Another way to look at this complexity is to
see the purpose of the Slider control that is responsible for displaying the timeline of the media being
played. But the Slider control is also responsible for allowing the user to interact to drag the slider
forward or backward in order to move the media position. _updatingMediaTimeline will allow only one
specific behavior to happen in the Slider control, thereby avoiding unwanted application behavior.

```
        private bool _updatingMediaTimeline;

        public MainPage()
        {
            InitializeComponent();

            _updatingMediaTimeline = false;

            // rewinds the media player to the beginning
            mediaPlayer.Position = System.TimeSpan.FromSeconds(0);
```

Handling Video Download Progress

As the video file download progresses, you will be receiving the percentage of the file got downloaded and you will be displaying the progress updates back to the user by updating the lblDownload.

```
// Download indicator
mediaPlayer.DownloadProgressChanged += (s, e) =>
    {
        lblDownload.Text = string.Format("Downloading {0:0.0%}",
mediaPlayer.DownloadProgress);
    };
```

Handling Video Buffering

You will be setting video BufferingTime property and as the video buffering time progresses you will receive a callback where you will update lblBuffering.

```
// Handle media buffering
mediaPlayer.BufferingTime =
                TimeSpan.FromSeconds(Convert.ToDouble(txtBufferingTime.Text));
mediaPlayer.BufferingProgressChanged += (s, e) =>
    {
        lblBuffering.Text = string.Format("Buffering {0:0.0%}",
mediaPlayer.BufferingProgress);
    };
```

Showing Time Elapsed in the Media Player

CompositionTarget.Rendering is a frame-based event that will fire once per frame, allowing you to update the media timeline (Slider control) that reflects how much of the media is played. By default the event will fire 60 times in one second. You can check this by checking the value of Application.Current.Host.Settings.MaxFrameRate. By using the CompositionTarget.Rendering event, you will be able to see the smooth media player timeline filling up as the media plays.

```
// Updates the media time line (slider control) with total time played
// and updates the status with the time played
CompositionTarget.Rendering += (s, e) =>
    {
        _updatingMediaTimeline = true;
        TimeSpan duration = mediaPlayer.NaturalDuration.TimeSpan;
        if (duration.TotalSeconds != 0)
        {
            double percentComplete =
mediaPlayer.Position.TotalSeconds / duration.TotalSeconds;
            mediaTimeline.Value = percentComplete;
            TimeSpan mediaTime = mediaPlayer.Position;
            string text = string.Format("{0:00}:{1:00}",
                (mediaTime.Hours * 60) + mediaTime.Minutes, mediaTime.Seconds);

            if (lblStatus.Text != text)
```

```
                    lblStatus.Text = text;

                _updatingMediaTimeline = false;
            }
        };
    }
```

■ **Tip** When defining the event handler of `CompositionTarget.Rendering`, you can use the lambda expression to create a delegate that contains the programming logic. For example, you can rewrite `CompositionTarget.Rendering += (s, e) => { … }` by first declaring the event handler `CompositionTarget.Rendering += new EventHandler(CompositionTarget_Rendering)` and then creating a method `void CompositionTarget_Rendering(object sender, EventArgs e) { … }`. Using the lambda expression technique makes the code much more readable and in this demo project gives you the ability to group the relevant code together. For more information on the lambda expression, please refer to `http://msdn.microsoft.com/en-us/library/bb397687.aspx`.

Implementing the Pause Button

When the Pause button is clicked, invoke `MediaElement.Pause` to pause the media player. Notice also here that you are updating the Status label, communicating to the user the media is in pause mode. Also notice that for unknown reasons, the media player might not be able to pause. You can use `mediaPlayer.CanPause` to make sure you can pause and otherwise set the Status label to warn the user it could not pause.

```
        private void btnPause_Click(object sender, RoutedEventArgs e)
        {
            if (mediaPlayer.CanPause)
            {
                mediaPlayer.Pause();
                lblStatus.Text = "Paused";
            }
            else
            {
                lblStatus.Text = "Can not be Paused. Please try again!";
            }
        }
```

Implementing the Stop Button

When the stop button is clicked, invoke `MediaElement.Stop` to stop the media player and then rewind the media player back to the beginning and update the Status label as "Stopped."

```
        private void btnStop_Click(object sender, RoutedEventArgs e)
        {
            mediaPlayer.Stop();
```

```
            mediaPlayer.Position = System.TimeSpan.FromSeconds(0);
            lblStatus.Text = "Stopped";
        }
```

Implementing the Play Button

When the play button is clicked, invoke MediaElement.Play to play the media player.

```
        private void btnPlay_Click(object sender, RoutedEventArgs e)
        {
            mediaPlayer.Play();
        }
```

Implementing the Mute Button

When the Mute button is clicked, set MediaElement.IsMuted to true in order to mute the sound or set it to false to turn on the sound.

```
        private void btnMute_Click(object sender, RoutedEventArgs e)
        {
            if (lblSoundStatus.Text.Equals("Sound On",
StringComparison.CurrentCultureIgnoreCase))
            {
                lblSoundStatus.Text = "Sound Off";
                mediaPlayer.IsMuted = true;
            }
            else
            {
                lblSoundStatus.Text = "Sound On";
                mediaPlayer.IsMuted = false;
            }

        }
```

■ **Note** To mute the player, you could have set MediaElement.Volume to zero instead of setting the IsMuted property to true, as we did in our example.

Implementing Seek

When the Slider control that displays the timeline of the media is clicked or dragged, MediaElement.Position moves either forward or backward, depending on the user's input on the Slider control. See Figure 15–3 for dragging the slider to the right in order to move forward in the video timeline.

```
        private void mediaTimeline_ValueChanged(object sender,
                            RoutedPropertyChangedEventArgs<double> e)
```

```
        {
            if (!_updatingMediaTimeline && mediaPlayer.CanSeek)
            {
                TimeSpan duration = mediaPlayer.NaturalDuration.TimeSpan;
                int newPosition = (int)(duration.TotalSeconds * mediaTimeline.Value);
                mediaPlayer.Position = new TimeSpan(0, 0, newPosition);
            }
        }
    }
```

Figure 15–3. Dragging the slider to skip the video

■ **Note** Using MediaElement.Position you can jump to any part of the media. This is very useful when you want to create chapters in a movie similar to those you see in DVD players.

Implementing the MediaPlayerLauncher

When the MediaPlayerLauncher button is clicked, invoke the MediaPlayerLauncher task to launch the default Windows Phone media player.

```
        private void btnMediaPlayerLauncher_Click(object sender, RoutedEventArgs e)
        {
            MediaPlayerLauncher player = new MediaPlayerLauncher();
            player.Media = new
Uri("http://ecn.channel9.msdn.com/o9/ch9/7/8/2/9/1/5/
ARCastMDISilverlightGridComputing_ch9.wmv");
            //player.Media =
//        new Uri("ARCastMDISilverlightGridComputing_ch9.wmv",
//                         UriKind.Relative);
            //player.Location = MediaLocationType.Data;
            player.Show();
        }
```

■ **Note** Notice the commented code where `MediaPlayerLauncher` is going to play the content that is part of the application. `player.Location` is set to `MediaLocationType.Data`, which means that it will look at the isolated storage for the file named `ARCastMDISilverlightGridComputing_ch9.wmv`. Refer to Chapter 13 for the isolated storage demo where the file was downloaded the first time and then saved into the isolated storage for later access. If you set `player.Location` to `MediaLocationType.Install`, the media file must be added to the application as the content and also the media source's `Uri` must have `UriKind.Relative`, which basically means the file is part of the application. The only problem with this is that the size of the application install will get much bigger.

Testing the Finished Application

To test the application, press F5. The result should resemble Figure 15–1. Try clicking each button: Play, Pause, Stop, and Mute. Also, as the movie plays, take note of the buffering and downloading progress status. You can also drag the slider back and forth to skip around the movie scenes. You can also put your own favorite movie link if you know of any.

In this first demo, you learned to create a custom media player and then learned to launch the default Windows Phone media player. Both `MediaElement` and `MediaPlayerLauncher` accessed the video content on the Web because typically video files are very big. But if you are adding simple sound effects to an application, it is not always ideal to download the contents from the Web when you can simply package the sound along with the application. This is especially true if you are planning to create a game where all the graphical and media assets are packaged as the part of the application. In the next demo, you will learn to add sound effects to an application.

Adding Sounds to an Application

Sounds can be used in both applications and games. In the first demo, you played video, but you can also use `MediaElement` to play music files or use it in a game to create sound effects. In the next demo, you will learn to apply a sound effect to an animated object—in this case, a flying robot. Such sound effects are essential to games. Figure 15–4 shows the UI of the demo application. When you press the Play button, the robot flies diagonally toward the bottom right-hand corner of the screen. When it reaches an edge, the robot will bounce several times while making a "swoosh sound" to give the animation that dash of realism it needs to satisfy gamers.

Figure 15–4. Robot sound demo

You will build the RobotSoundDemo in three steps. You will start by creating a Windows Phone project. Next you will build the UI, and then you will add the code to handle control events.

Creating the RobotSoundDemo Project

To create the Video Demo project, follow the steps you have used in previous examples in this book.

1. Open Microsoft Visual Studio 2010 Express for Windows Phone on your workstation.

2. Create a new Windows Phone Application by selecting File ➤ New Project on the Visual Studio command menu. Select the Windows Phone Application template, name the application "RobotSoundDemo," and click OK.

Building the User Interface

Before you can build the user interface, you need to add three files to the project you created in the previous steps:

- Robot.xaml
- Robot.xaml.cs
- sound18.wma

Once you successfully add those files to the project, you should observe the following list of files in the Solution Explorer window, as shown in Figure 15–5.

Figure 15–5. *RobotSoundDemo project after adding the assets*

All three files are included in the source code that is distributed with this book. Located in your unzipped directory of the source codes (c:\[where you unzipped]\Codes\ch15\Assets) are the assets that are needed for this demo. Robot.xaml and Robot.xaml.cs are the vector graphic versions of the robot that you will be using and sound18.wma is the sound effect file that you will be playing when the robot moves.

Selecting the UI Resources

Here you will be adding the namespace of the robot asset you just added to the project using xmlns:uc="clr-namespace:RobotSoundDemo". This namespace will allow you to add the robot user control using the XAML code that looks like <uc:Robot x:Name="ucRobot" …>.

```
<phone:PhoneApplicationPage
    x:Class="RobotSoundDemo.MainPage"
    xmlns="http://schemas.microsoft.com/winfx/2006/xaml/presentation"
    xmlns:x="http://schemas.microsoft.com/winfx/2006/xaml"
    xmlns:phone="clr-namespace:Microsoft.Phone.Controls;assembly=Microsoft.Phone"
```

```
xmlns:shell="clr-namespace:Microsoft.Phone.Shell;assembly=Microsoft.Phone"
xmlns:d="http://schemas.microsoft.com/expression/blend/2008"
xmlns:mc="http://schemas.openxmlformats.org/markup-compatibility/2006"
xmlns:uc="clr-namespace:RobotSoundDemo"
FontFamily="{StaticResource PhoneFontFamilyNormal}"
FontSize="{StaticResource PhoneFontSizeNormal}"
Foreground="{StaticResource PhoneForegroundBrush}"
SupportedOrientations="Portrait" Orientation="Portrait"
mc:Ignorable="d" d:DesignWidth="480" d:DesignHeight="768"
shell:SystemTray.IsVisible="True">
```

Adding Robot Animation to the Main Page Resource Section

You will be adding to the Main page resource section the robot storyboard animation of moving from top left corner to bottom right. Notice in this robot animation the bouncing EasingFunction is added to the robot's movement, which will cause the robot to bounce toward the end of the movement.

```
<phone:PhoneApplicationPage.Resources>
        <Storyboard x:Name="MoveRobot">
                <DoubleAnimationUsingKeyFrames
Storyboard.TargetProperty="(UIElement.RenderTransform).(CompositeTransform.TranslateX)"
Storyboard.TargetName="ucRobot">
                        <EasingDoubleKeyFrame KeyTime="0" Value="0"/>
                        <EasingDoubleKeyFrame KeyTime="0:0:0.6" Value="244">
                            <EasingDoubleKeyFrame.EasingFunction>
                                    <BounceEase EasingMode="EaseOut"/>
                            </EasingDoubleKeyFrame.EasingFunction>
                        </EasingDoubleKeyFrame>
                </DoubleAnimationUsingKeyFrames>
                <DoubleAnimationUsingKeyFrames
Storyboard.TargetProperty="(UIElement.RenderTransform).(CompositeTransform.TranslateY)"
Storyboard.TargetName="ucRobot">
                        <EasingDoubleKeyFrame KeyTime="0" Value="0"/>
                        <EasingDoubleKeyFrame KeyTime="0:0:0.6" Value="421">
                            <EasingDoubleKeyFrame.EasingFunction>
                                    <BounceEase EasingMode="EaseOut"/>
                            </EasingDoubleKeyFrame.EasingFunction>
                        </EasingDoubleKeyFrame>
                </DoubleAnimationUsingKeyFrames>
        </Storyboard>
    </phone:PhoneApplicationPage.Resources>
```

Building the Main Page and Adding Components

This demo has a very simple UI that contains a Play button to animate the robot, and a MediaElement to play the sound effect. Notice here that MediaElement.Source is set to sound18.wma, whereas in a previous demo you set the source to the URL. This is because sound18.wma is a type of Content. You can verify this by right-clicking the sound18.wma file found in Solution Explorer to observe its properties, as shown in Figure 15–6.

Figure 15–6. Sound18.wma file is a type of Content

```xml
<Grid x:Name="LayoutRoot" Background="Transparent">
    <Grid.RowDefinitions>
        <RowDefinition Height="Auto"/>
        <RowDefinition Height="*"/>
    </Grid.RowDefinitions>

    <StackPanel x:Name="TitlePanel" Grid.Row="0" Margin="24,24,0,12">

        <TextBlock x:Name="PageTitle" Text="RobotSoundDemo" Margin="-3,-8,0,0"
Style="{StaticResource PhoneTextTitle1Style}" FontSize="56" />
    </StackPanel>

    <Grid x:Name="ContentGrid" Grid.Row="1">
        <uc:Robot x:Name="ucRobot" Margin="24,27,264,442" RenderTransformOrigin="0.5,0.5"
>

            <uc:Robot.RenderTransform>
                    <CompositeTransform/>
            </uc:Robot.RenderTransform>
        </uc:Robot>
        <Button Content="Play" Height="72" HorizontalAlignment="Left"
                Margin="6,333,0,0" Name="btnPlay"
                VerticalAlignment="Top" Width="160"
                Click="btnPlay_Click" />
        <MediaElement x:Name="robotSound" Height="100"
                    VerticalAlignment="Bottom" Margin="176,0,204,69"
                    Source="sound18.wma" AutoPlay="False"/>
    </Grid>
</Grid>

</phone:PhoneApplicationPage>
```

Once you've loaded the XAML code, you should see the layout shown in Figure 15–7. Now it's time to wire up the events to animate the robot and play the sound effect in the next section.

Figure 15–7. RobotSoundDemo in design view

Coding the Application

In Solution Explorer, open `MainPage.xaml.cs` and replace the code there with the following code C# code blocks.

Specifying the Namespaces

There are no special namespaces that you are defining here.

```
using System.Windows;
using Microsoft.Phone.Controls;
```

```
namespace RobotSoundDemo
{
    public partial class MainPage : PhoneApplicationPage
    {
        public MainPage()
        {
            InitializeComponent();
        }
```

Adding an Event to Handle Play Button Click

When the Play button is clicked, the MoveRobot animation will be played, and, at the same time, the sound effect of the robot moving will also be played.

```
        private void btnPlay_Click(object sender, RoutedEventArgs e)
        {
            MoveRobot.Begin();

            robotSound.Stop();
            robotSound.Play();
        }
    }
}
```

Testing the Finished Application

To test the finished application, press F5. The result should resemble the screenshot shown in Figure 15–4. Test your work by clicking the play button, which should cause the robot to fly to the bottom right-hand corner of the screen, making a "swoosh" sound as it goes. When the robot reaches the bottom, watch for it to bounce several times.

Summary

In this chapter, you learned how to stream media content from the Web or from the resource of the application and then learned to play video and audio using MediaElement and MediaPlayerLauncher. You also learned to apply basic sound effects to an animation using MediaElement.

In Chapter 16, you will learn to interact with the Windows Phone's photo application, which will allow you to create your own version of a photo altering application, or interact with the phone's camera to capture an image and manipulate the captured image.

■ ■ ■

Working with the Camera and Photos

Today, consumers assume that any cell phone they purchase will be able to take photos, and that the quality of photos taken will come close to the quality of photos taken with any entry-level digital camera. Furthermore, the latest mobile devices, and especially the Windows Phone 7 device, allow for the integration of their photo capabilities with the various applications that run on them. For instance, taking a picture with the phone, adding a caption to it, and immediately uploading it to a social media web site are common capabilities of all smartphone platforms today.

In this chapter, you will learn how the Windows Phone 7 platform implements yet another level of integrated user experience when it comes to the picture-taking capabilities of the phone and your application. You will learn how to build an application that takes photos, saves them, lets the user open them, and then sends them to Twitpic, a remote cloud service where they can be embedded in Twitter messages.

A lot of the code you will write in this chapter will have to be physically deployed and debugged on a real Windows Phone 7 device—after all, it is not possible to take a real picture with the emulator or test many features of the pictures application (it is, however, possible to take a "dummy" picture of a small square moving around the emulator perimeter, which proves extremely useful for testing). We highly recommend that before you proceed with this chapter, you get your hands on an actual Windows Phone 7 device. You should also install the necessary Zune software that allows debugging on that device, and connect the device to your development machine (for more information on using Zune software to debug a photo application using a physical device, see Chapter 4).

Introducing Windows Phone 7 Photo Features

Before we delve into developing a Windows Phone 7 application that snaps photos and manipulates them, it's important to understand the model for working with photos on this device. As explained in greater detail in Chapter 19 (on security in Windows Phone 7), each application deployed to the device runs in its own sandbox, or execution environment. This execution sandbox prevents third-party applications from directly accessing common data stores on the phone, such as photos or contact lists, and prevents them from directly invoking the applications that ship with a Windows Phone device, such as the camera or a messaging application. So how can you build an application that can take pictures, manipulate them, and save them to the phone? The answer is through **launchers** and **choosers** as shown in Table 16–1 and 16–2.

Table 16–1. Launchers

Launchers	Description
EmailComposeTask	Opens the default device e-mail composer.
MarketPlaceDetailTask	Opens detailed product information.
MarketPlaceDetailTask	Opens to the Marketplace with specified category.
MarketPlaceReviewTask	Opens the product review for the specified product.
MarketPlaceSearchTask	Opens the MarketPlace search result based on the search term specified.
MediaPlayerLauncher	Opens the default device MediaPlayer.
PhoneCallTask	Opens the Phone application with specified number ready to dial.
SearchTask	Opens the default search application.
SmsComposeTask	Opens the messaging application.
WebBrowserTask	Opens the default device web browser to the specified URL.

Table 16–2. Choosers

Choosers	Description
CameraCaptureTask	Opens the Camera application to capture the image.
EmailAddressChooserTask	Opens the Contact application to choose an e-mail.
PhoneNumberChooserTask	Opens the Phone application to choose a phone number.
PhotoChooserTask	Opens the Photo Picker application to choose the image.
SaveEmailAddressTask	Saves the provided e-mail to the Contact list.
SavePhoneNumberTask	Saves the phone number to the Contact list.

The Windows Phone Launchers and Choosers framework is a collection of APIs you can use to indirectly access core Windows Phone applications, like the phone or contact list, to perform a specific task. Launchers can launch a phone application but return no data. A chooser, such as a photo chooser, on the other hand, returns data to the application that calls it. Tables 16–1 and 16–2 list all of the launchers and choosers that ship with the Windows Phone platform today and how each is used. The CameraCaptureTask chooser launches the built-in Windows Phone camera application, allowing a user of a third-party application to snap photos and for the application to retrieve them for its own purposes by handling the chooser's Completed event. You will write code to capture photos shortly, but before you do that, it's important to understand one more basic concept when working with launchers and choosers—the application execution model and application tombstoning (for a look at the Windows Phone application life cycle, see Chapter 10 for more detail).

As you know by now, the first version of the Windows Phone 7 platform does not support multitasking due to the excessive demands it puts on the battery and other resources on the device. Launchers and choosers are, in essence, separate applications that are launched from within your application. Since support for multitasking does not exist, your application effectively terminates when launchers or choosers are used. This termination is known as tombstoning, and it has direct implications on programming Windows Phone 7 devices that use launchers and choosers, such as the photo management applications you will build in this chapter. The difference between application tombstoning and application termination is that when an application is tombstoned, it is fully expected to be resumed upon completion of the launcher or chooser. Upon resuming, the application should continue in the same state that it was left off in, with data specific to the application session before tombstoning properly preserved. It is up to the application programmer to ensure that happens and that data gets properly restored.

Using a Chooser to Take Photos

The very first application that you will write will take photos and bring them inside your application. The first application will also lay the foundation for the rest of this chapter, since you will enhance and add features to this application as you go along. You will, therefore, create a basic navigation system in this first step for your application using an Application Bar and a standard set of icons that ship with Microsoft Expression for Windows Phone, which is one of the Windows Phone tools you installed in Chapter 2. You'll find the icons for a 32-bit system at C:\Program Files\Microsoft SDKs\Windows Phone\v7.0\Icons, or for a 64-bit system at C:\Program Files (x86)\Microsoft SDKs\Windows Phone\v7.0\Icons.

As has already been mentioned, you will use choosers to implement photo manipulation features on Windows Phone 7. To take photos, you will use the CameraCaptureTask chooser to take the photo and bring that photo inside your application. Follow this walkthrough to accomplish these tasks.

Creating a New Project and Building the User Interface

In the first part of the walkthrough, you will create a new project and add necessary user interface elements to allow photo manipulation in the future sections of this chapter.

1. Launch Visual Studio 2010 Express for Windows Phone, and create a new Windows Phone Application project. Name it "PhotoCapture."

You will create an Application Bar with three icons. The first button of the Application Bar will be for taking photos, which is the subject of the current walkthrough. The second button will be for opening previously taken photos. Finally, the third button will be for saving photos to the phone.

2. Create a separate folder within your application to store Application Bar icons. To do that, right-click the name of the project within Solution Explorer, choose Add ➤ New Folder, and name that folder images.

3. You will use the standard Application Bar icons that came pre-installed with Microsoft Expression Blend for Windows Phone. By default, the icons are installed in the `C:\Program Files\Microsoft SDKs\Windows phone\v7.0\Icons` folder. Within that folder, go to the subfolder called dark, and, using Windows Explorer, copy the following icons into the images folder within your application: `appbar.feature.camera.rest.png`, `appbar.folder.rest.png`, and `appbar.save.rest.png`.

4. Now you need to make the icons part of your solution. Highlight all three icons, and press F4 to bring up the Properties dialog. For the `Build Action` property, specify `Content`. Then, select `Copy Always` for the `Copy to Output Directory` property.

5. With icons ready for use in the Application Bar, you are ready to add an Application Bar to `MainPage.xaml` (for an in-depth explanation of how to add and use an Application Bar within your application, please refer to Chapter 7). Open `MainPage.xaml`, and paste the following code at the end of the XAML file just before the `</phone:PhoneApplicationPage>` closing tag. This XAML replaces the auto-generated template for the Application Bar:

```
<phone:PhoneApplicationPage.ApplicationBar>
    <shell:ApplicationBar IsVisible="True">
        <shell:ApplicationBar.Buttons>
            <shell:ApplicationBarIconButton x:Name="btnCamera" Text="Take Photo"
IconUri="images/appbar.feature.camera.rest.png" Click="btnCamera_Click"/>
            <shell:ApplicationBarIconButton Text="Open Photo"
IconUri="images/appbar.folder.rest.png"/>
            <shell:ApplicationBarIconButton Text="Save Photo"
IconUri="images/appbar.save.rest.png"/>
        </shell:ApplicationBar.Buttons>
    </shell:ApplicationBar>
</phone:PhoneApplicationPage.ApplicationBar>
```

■ **Note** The `btnCamera_Click` event handler will be called when the user clicks the Take Photo button. You will write code for this event handler in the next section.

---

6. Finally, you need to add an `Image` control to show the photos taken within your application. From the Toolbox, drag and drop an `Image` control onto the `MainPage.xaml` design surface, place it in the middle, and size it to be about half of the available screen space. Name it `imgPhoto`.

Writing Code to Take Photos with CameraCaptureTask

Although we may lose a bit of flexibility when programming with launchers and choosers, it is hard to dispute how easy they have made working with common phone tasks, such as taking pictures. In the following steps, you will launch a PhotoCapture application and wire up a callback event to invoke when that application completes.

1. Open MainPage.xaml.cs (right-click MainPage.xaml and select View Code). Add the following using statements to the very top of the code page:

```
using Microsoft.Phone.Tasks;
using Microsoft.Phone;
```

2. Add the following class-level variables within the MainPage class (right above the MainPage constructor):

```
private CameraCaptureTask cameraCaptureTask;
byte[] imageBits;
```

3. Add the following code for the btnCamera_Click method. This will invoke the PhotoCapture application when the user clicks the first button in the Application Bar:

```
private void btnCamera_Click(object sender, EventArgs e)
{
        cameraCaptureTask.Show();
}
```

You are now ready to write event handler code that will be invoked when the CameraCaptureTask chooser completes its work (the user has taken a picture) and control returns to your application. When control returns to your application, the photo taken by the user is passed in as one of the arguments to the callback function; you will take that photo and show it in the imgPhoto image control that you have added previously. Add the following method, which will be executed when the chooser completes, to MainPage.xaml.cs.

```
private void PhotoChooserTaskCompleted(object sender, PhotoResult e)
{
    if (e.ChosenPhoto != null)
    {
        imageBits = new byte[(int)e.ChosenPhoto.Length];
        e.ChosenPhoto.Read(imageBits, 0, imageBits.Length);
        e.ChosenPhoto.Seek(0, System.IO.SeekOrigin.Begin);

        var bitmapImage = PictureDecoder.DecodeJpeg(e.ChosenPhoto);
        this.imgPhoto.Source = bitmapImage;
    }
}
```

4. You need to tell your application's instance of CameraCaptureTask that the PhotoChooserTaskCompleted method must be invoked upon its completion. You will do this within the MainPage() constructor using the following two lines of code:

```
cameraCaptureTask = new CameraCaptureTask();
cameraCaptureTask.Completed += PhotoChooserTaskCompleted;
```

You are now ready to run the application. Note that for this walkthrough, it is not completely necessary to deploy your application to the physical device, since the emulator provides limited simulated photo-taking capabilities.

5. Press F5 to run the application on the emulator, and then press the camera button in the Application Bar to be presented with the Windows Phone 7 PhotoCapture application. Press the button in the upper right-hand corner to simulate photo-taking within the emulator (notice how this simulation consists of a black rectangle moving around the screen's perimeter), and then press the Accept button to accept the photo—you should see a phone screen similar to the one shown in Figure 16–1, with your application displaying the captured image. Of course, if you deploy this application to the actual Windows Phone 7 device, the photos look a bit more exciting.

Throughout the rest of this chapter, you will continue enhancing this application by wiring the rest of the Application Bar icons, getting familiar with the Model-View-ViewModel pattern (covered in Chapter 3), as well as integrating your application within the Windows Phone 7 experience, including handy image uploads to Twitter.

Figure 16–1. Results of PhotoCapture on Windows Phone 7 emulator

Using a Chooser to Open Photos

In the previous section, you learned how to use the CameraCaptureTask chooser to take photos with your phone. In this section, you will learn how to open previously taken photos on your phone using the PhotoChooserTask chooser. As you have already seen and will still see more of, launchers and choosers do make the lives of developers a lot easier by simplifying and abstracting the most common tasks within the Windows Phone 7 Application platform.

In this section, you will enhance the application you have built in the previous one by adding functionality to the second button of the Application Bar—Opening Photos. Windows Phone 7 has several locations, or "folders" so to speak, where the photos are located. Those "folders" are Camera Roll, Saved Pictures, and Pictures Library. Inside Pictures Library, there are general-purpose photos provided by Microsoft that help us in our programming efforts. Since you have already created a user interface for the application in the previous section, in this section you will add code implementing the photo browsing and retrieving functionality.

1. Launch Visual Studio 2010 Express for Windows Phone, and open the "PhotoCapture" project that you created in the previous section.

2. Open `MainPage.xaml.cs`, and paste the following class-level variable declaration right above the `MainPage()` constructor:

   ```
   private PhotoChooserTask photoChooserTask;
   ```

3. You now need to let the `PhotoChooserTask` chooser know that `PhotoChooserTaskCompleted` will be the callback function that this chooser should call upon completion. You do this via the following two lines of code inside the `MainPage()` constructor:

```
photoChooserTask = new PhotoChooserTask();
photoChooserTask.Completed +=
new EventHandler<PhotoResult>(PhotoChooserTaskCompleted);
```

4. As the final step of this walkthrough, you will need to add logic to launch the chooser when the user clicks the second button in the Application Bar. To accomplish this, open the `MainPage.xaml` file, locate the line of XAML code that starts with `<shell:ApplicationBarIconButton Text="Open Photo"`, and indicate that `btnOpenPhoto_Click` must be called when that button is clicked:

```
<shell:ApplicationBarIconButton Text="Open Photo" IconUri="images/appbar.folder.rest.png"
Click="btnOpenPhoto_Click"/>
```

5. Now, switch back to `MainPage.xaml.cs` and paste the `btnOpenPhoto_Click` function:

```
private void btnOpenPhoto_Click(object sender, EventArgs e)
{
        photoChooserTask.Show();
}
```

Press F5 to run application. Now, if you click the Open Photo button in the Application Bar, you should be able to browse through photos on the emulator or (better) on the phone, select a photo, and have it presented to you in the application window.

Being able to navigate to a photo on the phone and display it within an application is certainly important, but hardly a useful feature by itself. However, as we will see shortly, we can use the `PhotoChooserTask` chooser to select photos to upload to a cloud service, such as TwitPic, as well as for loading images inside the application in order to manipulate them (by cropping, adding shapes to them, altering their color composition) and then resaving them back onto the phone or uploading them to a social media cloud service. Although altering photos within an application is slightly beyond the scope of this chapter, we will walk through saving photos onto the phone in the next section. Saving photos could also be used together with `CameraCaptureTask` to save photos taken using that chooser.

Saving Photos to the Phone

In the prior sections, you have seen how choosers can be used to make the taking and opening of photos a breeze on a Windows Phone 7 device. Unfortunately, things become a bit more complicated when it comes to saving photos onto the device, since there are no choosers available to aid us with this task. In fact, the Windows Phone 7 platform does not provide any mechanism you can use to get the job done. How can you do it then? Enter the Windows Phone XNA library.

In this book, we have not covered the XNA Framework on Windows Phone 7 for a reason. The XNA Framework is a very powerful mechanism for programming graphics-intensive interfaces and, as such, is used primarily for game development, whereas Silverlight is used for the vast majority of line-of-business applications. This book is about learning to build line-of-business applications. At times, however, there are situations where you have to resort to using a mix of technologies to get things done, and saving photos onto the Windows Phone 7 device is one example of such a situation. The `Microsoft.Xna.Framework.Media` library provides the `SavePicture` method, which saves a given array of bytes to the Saved Pictures location on the phone. The following walkthrough demonstrates how to add save capabilities to the PhotoCapture application you have built so far.

Adding a Status Message

The user interface built as part of the very first walkthrough of this chapter has an Application Bar button already defined for saving images. Therefore, you need to make only a small enhancement to the user interface to allow the user to see whether the status of the save was successful or not.

Open `MainPage.xaml` and add a `TextBlock` right below the image control. Name this `TextBlock` `txtStatus` and clear its `Text` property.

With user interface enhancements complete, you are ready to add code that saves photos to the Media Library.

Writing Code to Save Photos with the XNA Framework

Before you can use a method from the XNA Framework, you must first add a reference to the `Xna.Framework.Media` library. To accomplish this, right-click the name of the project in Solution Explorer, select Add Reference, and then double-click the `Microsoft.Xna.Framework` assembly. Notice how a warning dialog comes up, telling us that there's a possibility of unexpected behavior—click Yes to complete adding a reference. Follow the rest of the steps to implement photo-saving functionality within your application.

1. Open `MainPage.xaml.cs` and add the following using statement to the top of that page:

```
using Microsoft.Xna.Framework.Media;
```

2. The following method does all the work of saving a photo into the Media Library. Note specifically the `SavePicture` method, which saves the array of bytes passed into the Media Library.

```
private void btnSave_Click(object sender, EventArgs e)
{
    try
    {
        var library = new MediaLibrary();
        library.SavePicture("PhotoCapture Photo", imageBits);
```

```
            txtStatus.Text = "Successfully saved photo.";
        }
        catch (Exception ex)
        {
            txtStatus.Text = "Failed to save photo. Exception: " + ex.Message;
        }
    }
```

3. What remains is to tie the btnSave_Click method with the click event of the Save button on the Application Bar. You will do it by editing the XAML of the MainPage.xaml file. Locate the line that starts with <shell:ApplicationBarIconButton Text="Save Photo" and change it to look like the following:

```
<shell:ApplicationBarIconButton Text="Save Photo"
IconUri="images/appbar.save.rest.png" Click="btnSave_Click"/>
```

You are now ready to run the application on the Windows Phone 7 emulator. Press F5 to start the application, and then press the Camera button on the Application Bar (first button) to take a picture and have it loaded inside your application. Then, press the Save button on the Application Bar—you should get a status message that the image was successfully saved. Now, if you use the middle button of the Application Bar to see photos available, you should see a screen like the one shown in Figure 16–2, with three separate photo "folders," each displayed in a separate tile available to choose photos from.

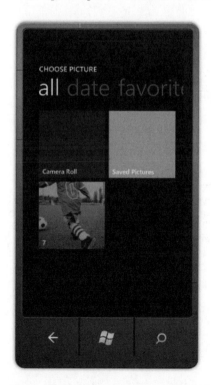

Figure 16–2. The Saved Photos "folder" is available once at least one photo has been saved there.

Integrating Your Application with Windows Phone 7

So far in this chapter, you have built a stand-alone application that uses choosers and parts of the XNA Framework to manage photos snapped with a Windows Phone camera. What's unique about the Windows Phone 7 Framework, however, is that it encourages you to have your application make use of built-in phone applications to perform certain tasks. The Photo application, for example, provides you with hooks you can use to make the functionality of an application like PhotoCapture available to users without having to find it and explicitly launch it. Those hooks are the Extras and the Share commands, which are found on the context menus of each photo where the context menu is displayed when you press the photo for a few seconds.

Both features are best explained by actually observing them at work. With the real Windows Phone 7 in hand, click the Pictures hub, select the "folder" to view the photos from (Camera Roll, for example), and then select a specific photo from the list. Click the ellipsis (…) at the bottom of the screen. When the context menu appears, you'll see an Extras option displayed at the very bottom. This Extras option is available for you to integrate or tie into. What you will do in the next walkthrough is use it to launch the PhotoCapture application so that you can choose a picture, save it to your TwitPic, and share it with your Twitter friends.

The context menu that pops up when you press the picture includes a Share command. The Share option is available when photos are being viewed as a list rather than one at a time. If you click the Share command, you will notice that it offers several ways to share the photo with the world. In the following section, you will learn to build an application that will use TwitPic as a cloud store for the photos on the phone.

■ **Note** Up to this point in the chapter, it has been possible (although a bit quirky) to run code against the Windows Phone 7 emulator. The features discussed in the next two sections are not available on the emulator; to see them in action, you must deploy applications onto the real Windows Phone 7 device.

Using Extras to Launch an Application

The Windows Phone 7 platform is all about providing the best possible phone usage experience to consumers. When consumers look at a photo on the phone, they are using an application known as a Single Photo Viewer (SPV) that provides applications to extend the viewer's functionality via the Extras command of the context menu. In this section, you will further enhance the PhotoCapture application to take advantage of the Extras feature within the Photos application. The PhotoCapture application will be using PhotoChooserTask or CameraCaptureTask to allow the user to select or take a picture once it has been invoked via the Extras feature.

To integrate with SPV, an application needs the following:

1. An Extras.xml file in its root directory with markup to the Extras feature

2. Code to properly read and load or manipulate the photo selected in the Extras dialog

You will implement both of those steps in the next section.

Adding an Extras.xml File to the Project

Adding an `Extras.xml` file is very straightforward; the only potential difficulty may be in the fact that the content of that file has to be precise. Make sure you either copy and paste this content from the source code available with this book, or type it in very carefully.

1. Right-click the project name, select Add ➤ New Item, and then select XML file. Make sure (this is important!) you name it `Extras.xml`.

2. Double-click the `Extras.xml` file to open it. Paste the following contents inside that file, which will enable the Windows Phone 7 framework to locate those applications ready to implement the Extras functionality.

```
<Extras>
  <PhotosExtrasApplication>
    <Enabled>true</Enabled>
  </PhotosExtrasApplication>
</Extras>
```

3. The contents of the file are not very important; however, in the Properties window, make sure to set the `Build Action` property to `Content` and the `Copy To Output` property to `Copy Always` for the this file (click the file and press F4 to bring up the Properties dialog).

Make sure you save `Extras.xml`, but otherwise you are ready to move on to the next step.

Adding Code to Navigate to a Photo

To properly retrieve the photo that the user selected through the Extras feature, the application must override the `OnNavigatedTo` event in `MainPage.xaml.cs`. The steps here show you how to do that:

1. Open `MainPage.xaml.cs` and add the following using statement to the top of the page:

```
using System.Windows.Navigation;
```

2. The reference to the `Microsoft.Xna.Framework` assembly should still be in the project from the prior walkthroughs; however, if you start a new project that implements the Extras functionality, make sure to add a reference to that assembly and the following using statement to properly refer to the Media Library. You will also need `System.Windows.Medi.Imaging` to work with the image source.

```
using Microsoft.Xna.Framework.Media;
using System.Windows.Media.Imaging;
```

3. Paste the following `OnNavigatedTo` method. Note how the basic operation is that of reading a `QueryString` passed in, determining if we have a value for the parameter token, and then trying to retrieve the photo from the Media Library by that token ID.

```
protected override void OnNavigatedTo(NavigationEventArgs e)
{
    try
    {
```

```
                IDictionary<string, string> queryStrings =
this.NavigationContext.QueryString;
                if (queryStrings.ContainsKey("token"))
                {
                    MediaLibrary library = new MediaLibrary();
                    Picture picture = library.GetPictureFromToken(queryStrings["token"]);

                    BitmapImage bitmap = new BitmapImage();
                    bitmap.SetSource(picture.GetImage());
                    WriteableBitmap picLibraryImage = new WriteableBitmap(bitmap);
                    imgPhoto.Source = picLibraryImage;
                }

            }
            catch (Exception ex)
            {
                Dispatcher.BeginInvoke(() => txtStatus.Text = ex.Message);
            }
        }
```

4. Deploy the application to the phone. Then, from the phone's Start screen, select the Pictures hub, pick any picture collection, and select an individual picture of your choice. Click the ellipsis at the bottom of the screen, and select Extras. You should see the PhotoCapture application listed on the next screen that comes up. Clicking the PhotoCapture application should start the application and load the selected photo into the Image control—exactly the expected behavior.

In the next section, you will walk through the steps needed to extend the Share dialog for the photos. The concepts you use to extend the Extras and Share features are very similar; the differences, as you will see shortly, are in the details of the file name and the query string key.

Using Share to Upload PhotoCapture Snapshots to TwitPic

In this walkthrough, you will make more changes to the PhotoCapture application to take advantage of the Share extensibility feature within the Photos application. For simplicity, the PhotoCapture application will load the selected image onto its main screen. In the next section, you will complete the circle and write code to send the image to the TwitPic cloud service for easy reference from the Twitter messages.

As with your implementation of Extras, to extend the Share option to include it, an application needs the following:

1. An EOFOE49A-3EB1-4970-B780-45DA41EC7C28.xml file in its root directory enabling the application's integration with the Share feature (this is not a typo—the XML file must be named exactly like that for the application to belong to the Share feature)

2. Code to properly read and/or share the photo selected in the Share dialog

You will implement both steps in the next section.

Adding an E0F0E49A-3EB1-4970-B780-45DA41EC7C28.xml File to the Project

Adding this strangely named XML file is very straightforward; the only potential difficulty may be the fact that the name is completely unreadable, so it would be best if you could copy and paste it from the source code available for download with this book.

1. Right-click the project name, select Add ➤ New Item, and then select "XML file." Make sure (this is important!) you name it E0F0E49A-3EB1-4970-B780-45DA41EC7C28.xml.

2. While the contents of the file may not be very important, be sure to go to the Properties window and set the Build Action property to Content and the Copy To Output property to Copy Always for the this file (click the file and press F4 to bring up the Properties dialog).

Make sure you save this XML file before moving onto the next step.

Adding Code to Navigate to the Selected Photo

To properly retrieve the photo that the user selected through the Extras feature, the application must override the OnNavigatedTo event in MainPage.xaml.cs. The steps here show you how to do that:

1. If you are continuing from the Extras walkthrough, you already have all the necessary references and using statements in place. However, if you were to start a new project, make sure that you have a reference added to Microsoft.Xna.Framework and the following using statements are in place:

```
using System.Windows.Navigation;
using Microsoft.Xna.Framework.Media;
```

2. Paste the following OnNavigatedTo method (or add to that method if you are continuing from the Extras walkthrough). Note how the basic operation is that of reading a query string passed in, determining whether there is a value for the FileId parameter, and then trying to retrieve the photo from the Media Library by that token ID.

```
        try
        {
            IDictionary<string, string> queryStrings =
this.NavigationContext.QueryString;

                if (queryStrings.ContainsKey("FileId"))
                {
                    MediaLibrary library = new MediaLibrary();
                    Picture picture = library.GetPictureFromToken(queryStrings["FileId"]);

                    BitmapImage bitmap = new BitmapImage();
                    bitmap.SetSource(picture.GetImage());
                    WriteableBitmap picLibraryImage = new WriteableBitmap(bitmap);
                    imgPhoto.Source = picLibraryImage;
                }
        }
        catch (Exception ex)
        {
```

```
        Dispatcher.BeginInvoke(() => txtStatus.Text = ex.Message);
    }
```

3. Deploy the application to the phone.

Now you're ready to test your implementation so far. Just as you did for your Extras integration, from the phone's Start screen, select the Pictures hub on your phone, pick any picture collection, and select an individual picture of your choice. Click the ellipsis (…) at the bottom of the screen, and select Share. You should see Upload to PhotoCapture as one of the options that come up. Clicking that option should start the application and load the selected photo into the Image control—the behavior we expect.

Now you're ready to upload the photos to TwitPic, which is the primary hosting service for photos destined for Twitter, the hottest social media network today. Silverlight in general and Silverlight on Windows Phone 7 in particular differ from other applications in the fact that they rigorously enforce a non-blocking user interface principle: everything, including communications over the network, must happen asynchronously. TwitPic cloud service provides a RESTful API that allows programmers to send messages to that service as long as we conform to the expected message format.

Adding an Upload Button to the UI

On the user interface front, you will need to add an additional button that will trigger the upload of the photo to TwitPic. Figure 16–3 illustrates one possible placement of this button. Name the button btnUpload, and set its caption to TwitPic.

Writing Code to Transfer an Image to TwitPic

Because network access on Windows Phone 7 must be performed asynchronously, it takes quite a bit of code to properly construct the RESTful web service request. Most of the code, however, is repetitive, and all of the major points are summarized in these step-by-step instructions.

1. Right-click the project name in Solution Explorer, select Add Reference, and then select System.Xml.Linq.

2. Add the following using statements to the top of the page:

```
using System.IO;
using System.Text;
using System.Xml.Linq;
```

3. Open MainPage.xaml.cs and paste the UploadPhoto function written here. This will be the only function that will be invoked when the photo upload needs to take place. This function sets the URL and the type of the request, and then it invokes the asynchronous BeginGetRequestStream, which packages the photo and the user credentials.

```
public void UploadPhoto()
{
    HttpWebRequest request =
(HttpWebRequest)WebRequest.Create("http://twitpic.com/api/upload");
    request.ContentType = "application/x-www-form-urlencoded";
    request.Method = "POST";
    request.BeginGetRequestStream(new AsyncCallback(GetRequestStreamCallback),
request);
}
```

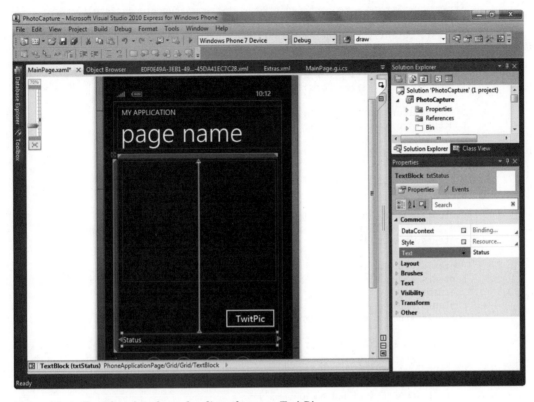

Figure 16–3. User interface for uploading photos to TwitPic

4. Add the following code to define the asynchronous function
   GetRequestStreamCallback that does all of the packaging of proper parameters;
   note that the exact form of the message was dictated by TwitPic, and this
   method simply conforms to it.

■ **Note** The TwitPic API is sensitive to even slightly malformed messages; be sure you copy/paste this method
from the source code that comes with this book instead of manually retyping it and risking making a mistake.

```
private void GetRequestStreamCallback(IAsyncResult asynchronousResult)
{
    try
    {

        HttpWebRequest request = (HttpWebRequest)asynchronousResult.AsyncState;
        string encoding = "iso-8859-1";
        // End the operation
```

```
            Stream postStream = request.EndGetRequestStream(asynchronousResult);
            string boundary = Guid.NewGuid().ToString();
            request.ContentType = string.Format("multipart/form-data; boundary={0}",
boundary);

            string header = string.Format("--{0}", boundary);
            string footer = string.Format("--{0}--", boundary);

            StringBuilder contents = new StringBuilder();
            contents.AppendLine(header);
string fileHeader = String.Format("Content-Disposition: file; name=\"{0}\";
filename=\"{1}\"; ", "media", "testpic.jpg");
            string fileData = Encoding.GetEncoding(encoding).GetString(imageBits, 0,
imageBits.Length);

            contents.AppendLine(fileHeader);
            contents.AppendLine(String.Format("Content-Type: {0};", "image/jpeg"));
            contents.AppendLine();
            contents.AppendLine(fileData);
            contents.AppendLine(header);
            contents.AppendLine(String.Format("Content-Disposition: form-data;
name=\"{0}\"", "username"));
            contents.AppendLine();
            contents.AppendLine("BeginningWP7");

            contents.AppendLine(header);
            contents.AppendLine(String.Format("Content-Disposition: form-data;
name=\"{0}\"", "password"));
            contents.AppendLine();
            contents.AppendLine("windowsphone7");

            contents.AppendLine(footer);

            // Convert the string into a byte array.
            byte[] byteArray =
Encoding.GetEncoding(encoding).GetBytes(contents.ToString());

            // Write to the request stream.
            postStream.Write(byteArray, 0, contents.ToString().Length);
            postStream.Close();

            // Start the asynchronous operation to get the response
            request.BeginGetResponse(new AsyncCallback(GetResponseCallback), request);
        }
        catch (Exception ex)
        {
            Dispatcher.BeginInvoke(() => txtStatus.Text = ex.Message);
        }
    }
```

5. Add the GetResponseCallback function that will asynchronously receive the
   results of the upload (Success or Fail) and parse that result out using LINQ to
   XML.

```
private void GetResponseCallback(IAsyncResult asynchronousResult)
    {
        try
        {
            HttpWebRequest request = (HttpWebRequest)asynchronousResult.AsyncState;
            // End the operation
            HttpWebResponse response =
(HttpWebResponse)request.EndGetResponse(asynchronousResult);
            Stream streamResponse = response.GetResponseStream();
            StreamReader streamRead = new StreamReader(streamResponse);
            string responseString = streamRead.ReadToEnd();

            XDocument doc = XDocument.Parse(responseString);
            XElement rsp = doc.Element("rsp");
            string status = rsp.Attribute(XName.Get("status")) != null ?
rsp.Attribute(XName.Get("status")).Value : rsp.Attribute(XName.Get("stat")).Value;

            // Close the stream object
            streamResponse.Close();
            streamRead.Close();

            // Release the HttpWebResponse
            response.Close();

        }
        catch (Exception ex)
        {
            Dispatcher.BeginInvoke(() => txtStatus.Text = ex.Message);
        }
    }
```

6. Now you need to call the UploadPhoto method when the user clicks the TwitPic button. Open MainPage.xaml in Design view, and double-click the TwitPic button. Inside the btnUpload_Click method, paste the following line of code:

```
UploadPhoto();
```

You are now ready to run the application. Set the Windows Phone 7 emulator as your deployment target, click F5, and when the application comes up, click the camera button (the first button on the Application Bar). Take a picture, accept it, and then click the TwitPic button. If no errors were reported in the status TextBlock, you should see your image on TwitPic's web site, as shown in Figure 16–4.

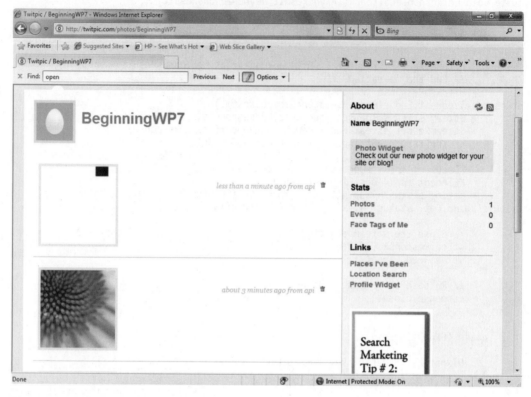

Figure 16–4. Image uploaded to TwitPic

Summary

In this chapter, you worked extensively with photos on a Windows Phone 7 device. You have used choosers to take pictures and load previously saved pictures. You also learned a bit about the XNA Framework and how it helps you work with the Media Library. You then explored the integration between the Windows Phone 7 built-in application for photos and your application. Finally, you uploaded photos that you took with your Windows Phone 7 device to TwitPic, a photo-sharing site used extensively by Twitter.

In the next chapter, you will look into push notifications, a powerful mechanism for mimicking multi-tasking.

CHAPTER 17

■■■

Push Notifications

One day in the somewhat distant future, smartphones and other mobile appliances will ship with batteries that last for weeks without the need to recharge them. But until that day arrives, Windows Phone 7 software developers write applications that use energy sparingly, since a resource-intensive program—such as one that uses the built-in cellular or Wi-Fi radio continuously—can quickly drain a Windows Phone battery. To prevent this from happening, Microsoft has built a number of safeguards into the Windows Phone application platform to ensure that the phone battery lasts as long as possible. One such safeguard prohibits any third-party application from running in the background while another is executing in the foreground, a feature that is also known as multitasking.

Given this limitation, how do you build an application that needs to be—or at least appears to be—always running, providing your users with important alerts and messages, such as when to buy or sell stocks or run from bad weather? In the Windows Phone 7 world, the answer is push notifications, also referred to as Windows Phone Notifications (WPN). In a nutshell, push notifications allow a user of an application to receive notification messages even when it is not running (currently on Windows Phone 7, anytime an application is not in the foreground, it is not running).

In this chapter, you'll learn how notifications work on the Windows Phone, the WPN types that Microsoft provides, and the steps you need to follow to use them in an application. You will build a simple phone application that can receive and process push notifications, and you'll create a simple service that can create and send them. The service will notify the user when the price of Microsoft stock changes (stock symbol MSFT). Without further ado, let's go ahead and start experimenting with this powerful technology available for Windows Phone 7.

Understanding Push Notifications

The Windows Phone 7 platform provides developers with three types of push notifications: *toast* notifications, *tile* notifications, and *raw* notifications. All three types follow the same basic principles of operation and processing, yet differ in the way they display notifications. Toast and tile notification types are used only when the application is not running; raw notifications are used to continuously receive messages while the application is running in the foreground. Let's discuss each notification type in detail.

Toast Notifications

Toast notifications are displayed as overlays at the top of a phone's screen. Only a message title and a line of text can be controlled by the service or an application sending ("pushing") a toast notification; the icon that appears on the left side of a toast notification is the default icon for the application deployed on the Windows Phone 7 device. You can display toast notifications only when an application is not running; if an application is running when a toast notification is sent, it is not displayed on the phone screen.

Toast notifications are used to display information that is timely and urgent. An example of toast notification is shown in Figure 17–1, where it appears as "Time to buy..." text at the top of the phone screen. Here, a notification has been received about Microsoft stock becoming an attractive buy. If the user chooses to tap (or click) the toast notification, an application opens up, allowing users to take additional actions within the application.

Figure 17–1. Sample toast notification

Tile Notifications

Tile notifications can alter the contents of any application tile that is pinned to the Quick Launch area of the phone initial screen (also referred to as Start Experience/Start Screen in Microsoft documentation). Tile notifications are used to communicate information visually, by displaying, say, dark clouds with rain to represent a rapidly approaching storm. Generally, an application tile is a visual representation of an application and its contents or functionality. An application tile typically contains an icon and two strings, and tile notifications can change any of these elements, as well as the background of each tile. To change a tile's background image, a tile notification must include a URI that points to the new image, a URI that can be either local or cloud-based. The string at the bottom of an application tile is referred to as the *tile title*. The string in the middle and slightly to the right is referred to as the *tile counter*.

Figure 17–2 shows the same Windows Phone 7 Start screen as Figure 17–1, but with an update to the PNClient application tile, which has changed the tile's text to "MSFT +2" and set the count property to "2". By continuously updating the tile with new text and images, an application can keep a user informed without the need to launch the application.

Raw Notifications

The third and final type of push notification is the raw notification, which can be used to continuously send messages or updates to a Windows Phone 7 application that is running in the foreground. Contrast this with toast and tile notifications, which are used to send updates to an application when it is not running front and center on the Windows Phone 7 device. Unlike toast and tile notifications, all raw notifications are dropped once an application is no longer running in the foreground on the Windows Phone 7 device. Raw notifications are an energy-friendly alternative to constantly polling web services for data; this type of push notification also eliminates the need to keep connections to web services open for prolonged periods of time.

Each notification type has its "niche," so to speak, or the specific application development scenarios it shines with more than the others. For instance, if an application receives updates only when it's actively used, such as a chat application, then a raw notification is the most appropriate mechanism for transmitting these updates. If an application is ideally suited to communicate updates via the use of visual elements on an ongoing basis, such as weather updates, sports events scores, or stock prices, tile applications are a more appropriate choice. Finally, if text-based messages are the most appropriate form of communication on an around-the-clock basis, such as e-mail receipts, Facebook friend requests, or news alerts, toast notifications would be most suitable.

Having taken a look at three available push notification types, let's turn our attention to the architecture of notification services, since knowing the architecture will help you better understand how to program and troubleshoot push notification services.

Table 17–1. Characteristics of Windows Phone Push Notification Types

PN Type	Must Application Be Running in Foreground?	Must Application Tile be Pinned to Start Screen?	Use
Toast	No	No	Urgent and time-sensitive data (e.g., storm warning)
Tile	No	Yes	Updates (e.g., count of new messages)
Raw	Yes	No	Continuous data (e.g., Twitter client, stock ticker)

Introducing the Push Notifications Architecture

Windows Phone push notifications involve three players, a phone application, a Microsoft service, and a remote web-based service, as illustrated in Figure 17–3. At the heart of push notifications is a service provided by Microsoft called, very appropriately, Microsoft Push Notification Service (MPNS). MPNS "provides a dedicated, resilient, and persistent channel for pushing a notification to a mobile device," according to MSDN documentation. This service is hosted on Microsoft's Azure cloud operating system and is responsible for seamlessly establishing a channel of communication between a Windows Phone 7 device and an application that provides notification data to it. Typically, notifications to Windows Phone 7 devices are provided by a web service (or a "cloud service," as often seen in Microsoft documentation). These cloud services are generally accessible via standard web protocols, such as REST and SOAP, aside from MPNS for data retrieval and updates.

Naturally, you may be wondering what happens when MPNS becomes unavailable for some technical reason. At the moment, the answer is that should that happen, push notifications will not reach their destination, i.e., they will be simply dropped. Hence, push notifications should never be counted on as a reliable form of message delivery.

Figure 17–2. A tile notification

The Life Cycle of a Notification

Let's suppose that you're building a mobile stock trading application that consists of a central web service, which gathers and analyzes trading data, and an application running on Windows Phone 7 devices, which displays data to users. Suppose you want the application to notify users whenever there is a significant jump in the value of Microsoft stock, such as might occur right after the official launch of Windows Phone 7. Architecturally seaking, how would it go about doing that?

First, the application would need to take advantage of Push Notification Services, since this will allow it to keep the user updated on the market conditions even if the user is not constantly running the stock trading app on her Windows Phone 7.

Second, to enable push notifications on Windows Phone 7, a communication channel for notifications must be created between the application and the web service that is collecting stock trading data. In the world of push notifications, a communication channel is represented by a URI that contains all of the information necessary for notifications to reach their destination. A Windows Phone 7 client must request this channel be created, and obtain the URI associated with that communication channel. Third, the URI of this communication channel must be communicated to the web service that will deliver, or "push" notifications about the market conditions to Windows Phone 7 clients. Once this third step is complete, all three types of push notifications are available to the stock trading application.

Figure 17–3 provides detailed visual representation of how a Windows Phone 7 client application would be able to receive stock trading alerts from the server using MPNS. The steps are sequentially numbered and each numbered step is described in detail below:

1. Windows Phone 7 application contacts MPNS and requests for communication channel inside MPNS to be created.

2. MPNS responds with the URI of communication channel, which is unique for a given Windows Phone 7 device and an application on that device.

3. Windows Phone 7 application communicates the URI of the channel created in Step 2 to the service providing stock quotes.

4. The stock quotes service publishes updates to the URI communicated to it in Step 3.

5. MPNS routes the updates to the proper Windows Phone 7 device and application on that device.

When the service needs to send notifications to its clients, it contacts MPNS by making a POST request to the unique URIs created for each client (Step 4 in the outline above). These POST requests have to conform to a predefined XML schema set by Microsoft. The type of notification sent (toast, tile, or raw) is determined by one of the header values inside the POST request—namely, the "X-NotificationClass" header, and you will see how to use this header momentarily.

In the sections that follow, we'll show you how to write code for the steps that have just been described. Using the Windows Phone 7 emulator, you'll implement an application with both toast and tile notifications.

When programming Windows Phone 7 push notifications, perhaps the most common error that occurs is the PayloadFormat error. Generally, that means that the XML or message format received from the MPNS does not conform to the expected format. Things to check in that case would be whether an XML format expected for tile notifications is used for toast notifications or vice versa.

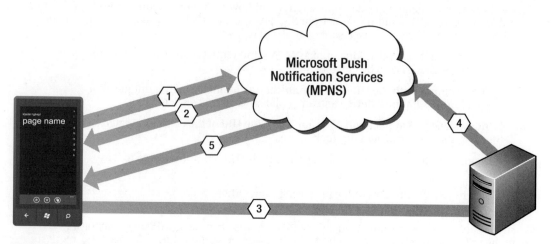

Figure 17–3. Basic push notifications architecture

The Push Notification Framework

The namespace whose APIs do the push notification heavy lifting is Microsoft.Phone.Notification, and the HttpChannelNotification is its workhorse. Before a notification of any type can be sent, a notification channel must be created. The HttpChannelNotification class allows developers to create a new channel or find an existing (previously created) one using its Open and Find methods correspondingly. When programming push notifications, it is a good practice to check whether the channel has been previously created using the Find operation. You will see how this is done shortly in several upcoming walkthroughs. An important note about the Open method: once the channel is open, it is not immediately active. The push notification channel becomes active once it acquires the push notification URI from the MPNS. This URI is acquired in an asynchronous manner, as you will also see in the walkthroughs for this chapter.

Other important methods of the HttpChannelNotification class include BindToShellToast and BindToShellTile. These methods are responsible for associating, or binding, a particular HttpChannelNotification channel instance to toast and tile notifications. These methods have corresponding UnbindToShellToast and UnbindToShellTile methods that disassociate toast and tiles subscriptions correspondingly from a given channel. Finally, the Close method of the HttpChannelNotification class closes the channel and removes all the subscriptions associated with that channel.

Push notifications are most appropriate in situations where Windows Phone 7 applications almost fully depend on the data supplied by the server on the web or somewhere else in the cloud. As such, to demonstrate push notifications in action, you must create two separate projects: one project will be a Windows Phone 7 application, and the other project could be either a web-based application, a web service, or, for the purposes of keeping the current example simple, a Windows Forms application. To create a Windows Forms application that will be used as part of the next walkthrough, you will be using a version of Visual Studio that allows the creation of Windows Forms applications—Visual C# 2010 Express. Alternately, you could use other (paid) editions of Visual Studio 2010 to create Windows Forms applications.

Implementing Toast Notifications

For the toast notifications walkthrough, you will implement a Windows Phone 7 client application that will create a notification channel, and a Windows Forms application that can send the notifications to the Windows Phone 7 application via that channel. The Windows Phone 7 client application will be a single screen application with one button and one text box, as shown in Figure 17–4. The Windows Forms application will consist of the single form shown in Figure 17–5. You will follow this order of program implementation:

1. You will create the Windows Phone 7 Notification client application. This application will establish a notification channel and print the URI of that communication channel into the Output window.

2. Create and execute the Windows Forms application that will send notifications. You will take the URI of the notification channel that you established in Step 1, paste it into the "Push Notifications URL" field of this application, and submit the notification.

3. Verify that you are able to receive toast notifications in the Windows Phone 7 application.

Creating a Client Application

The Windows Phone 7 Notification client application will consist of a command button that will create a push notification channel and print its URI into the Debug window. You will also add a text box to the application to display the URI for visual confirmation. Follow these steps to create the application.

1. Launch Visual Studio 2010 Express for Windows Phone and create a new Windows Phone Application project. Name it "PNClient."

2. From the Toolbox, drag and drop a text box on the design surface. Rename the text box to txtURI, adjust its width to be the full width of the screen, and adjust its height to be about a quarter of the screen's height. Set the text box's TextWrapping property to "Wrap" and clear out its Text property.

3. From the Toolbox, drag and drop a button on the design surface. Rename the button to btnCreateChannel and set the Content property to "Create Channel." Your Windows Phone 7 design surface should now look like Figure 17–6.

4. Add the following using directives to the top of the MainPage.xaml.cs file.

```
using Microsoft.Phone.Notification;
using System.Diagnostics;
```

5. You need to add code that will capture the URI of the notification channel in the Output window. At the top of the code page, right underneath the

```
public partial class MainPage : PhoneApplicationPage
{
```

add the following code:

```
Uri channelUri;
public Uri ChannelUri
{
get { return channelUri; }
```

353

```
set
        {
channelUri = value;
OnChannelUriChanged(value);
}
        }

        private void OnChannelUriChanged(Uri value)
        {
                Dispatcher.BeginInvoke(() =>
                {
                        txtURI.Text = "changing uri to " + value.ToString();
                });

                Debug.WriteLine("changing uri to " + value.ToString());
        }
```

The last bit of code above will print the URI of the push notification channel opened by the application into the Visual Studio Output window, which will allow you to copy and paste that URI into the Windows Forms application that you will be building in the next section. Certainly, in the real-world application, this copy and paste method is not appropriate; a more robust method of exchanging that URI, such as passing it to a web service, would be more appropriate. You will build a more realistic method of exchanging this URI later on in this chapter.

6. Open MainPage.xaml in Design view (right-click MainPage.xaml in Solution Explorer and select View Designer), double-click the "Create Channel" button, and make the btnCreateChannel_Click event handler look like the following:

```
private void btnCreateChannel_Click(object sender, RoutedEventArgs e)
{
        SetupChannel();
}
```

7. Paste the following SetupChannel function into the btnCreate_Click event handler (note that you can always download the code available for this book). Here, you use the HttpNotificationChannel class to try to find an existing push notification channel or open a new channel with a given channel name.

Figure 17–4. *Windows Phone 7 application that will create a push notification URI and receive push notifications*

```
private void SetupChannel()
{
    HttpNotificationChannel httpChannel = null;
    string channelName = "DemoChannel";

    try
    {
        //if channel exists, retrieve existing channel
        httpChannel = HttpNotificationChannel.Find(channelName);
        if (httpChannel != null)
        {
            //If we cannot get Channel URI, then close the channel and reopen it
            if (httpChannel.ChannelUri == null)
            {
                httpChannel.UnbindToShellToast();
                httpChannel.Close();
                SetupChannel();
                return;
            }
            else
```

```
                {
                    ChannelUri = httpChannel.ChannelUri;
                }
            BindToShell(httpChannel);
                }
                else
                {
                httpChannel = new HttpNotificationChannel(channelName);
                httpChannel.ChannelUriUpdated += new
        EventHandler<NotificationChannelUriEventArgs>(httpChannel_ChannelUriUpdated);

                httpChannel.ShellToastNotificationReceived+=new
            EventHandler<NotificationEventArgs>(httpChannel_ShellToastNotificationReceived);

                httpChannel.ErrorOccurred += new
        EventHandler<NotificationChannelErrorEventArgs>(httpChannel_ExceptionOccurred);

                httpChannel.Open();
                BindToShell(httpChannel);
        }

            }
            catch (Exception ex)
            {

                Debug.WriteLine("An exception setting up channel " + ex.ToString());

            }
        }
```

The code in the SetupChannel() function warrants an explanation, since there is quite a bit going on there and this is the nucleus of creating a channel for a Windows Phone 7 Notification client application. In the first few lines, you define a new object of type HttpNotificationChannel, give it a name, and wire up an event to fire when an error occurs. You'll also wire up an event to fire when the URI of the notification channel changes. Next, you'll try to find the channel with a given name for the application and then bind it to receive toast notifications (via the BindToShell function shown here). If the channel is found, you'll use an existing channel to obtain the push notification URI and you will not need to wire various httpChannel event handlers. If the channel is not found, you'll create a new one and wire up appropriate httpChannel events. Notice the ShellToastNotificationReceived event—it occurs if your application is running in the foreground when it receives a toast notification. Normally, push notifications are designed to alert that there is something happening when the application is not running and when application tile needs to be updated. However, occasionally, your application may be running when a toast notification is received—to handle cases like that, ShellToastNotificationReceived event handler is introduced. You will code this event handler in the next step.

8. To handle toast notifications when the application is running in the foreground, add the code below for the ShellToastNotificationReceived event handler. This code will read the notification messages received and print them in the textbox on the screen.

```
void httpChannel_ShellToastNotificationReceived(object sender,
NotificationEventArgs e)
        {
            Dispatcher.BeginInvoke(() =>
            {
                txtURI.Text = "Toast Notification Message Received: ";
```

```
                if (e.Collection != null)
                    {
Dictionary<string, string> collection =
(Dictionary<string, string>)e.Collection;
System.Text.StringBuilder messageBuilder = new System.Text.StringBuilder();
                        foreach (string elementName in collection.Keys)
                        {
                            txtURI.Text+= string.Format("Key: {0}, Value:
{1}\r\n", elementName, collection[elementName]);
                        }
                    }
                });
            }
```

9. To bind a toast notification subscription to a given HttpNotificationChannel instance, you must call the BindToShellToast method of the HttpNotificationChannel class. Underneath the SetupChannel function, paste the following code to accomplish that:

```
private static void BindToShell(HttpNotificationChannel httpChannel)
{
    //This is a toast notification
    try
    {
        httpChannel.BindToShellToast();
    }
    catch (Exception)
    {
        Debug.WriteLine("An exception occurred binding to shell " + ex.ToString());
    }
}
```

10. In the SetupChannel function, you designated the httpChannel_ExceptionOccurred should fire in case of an error. Add this function to your code as defined here:

```
void httpChannel_ExceptionOccurred(object sender, NotificationChannelErrorEventArgs
    e)
    {
        //Display Message on error
        Debug.WriteLine ( e.Message);
    }
```

11. You also need to add code that will fire if the ChannelUri gets updated:

```
void httpChannel_ChannelUriUpdated(object sender, NotificationChannelUriEventArgs e)
{
    //You get the new Uri (or maybe it's updated)
    ChannelUri = e.ChannelUri;
}
```

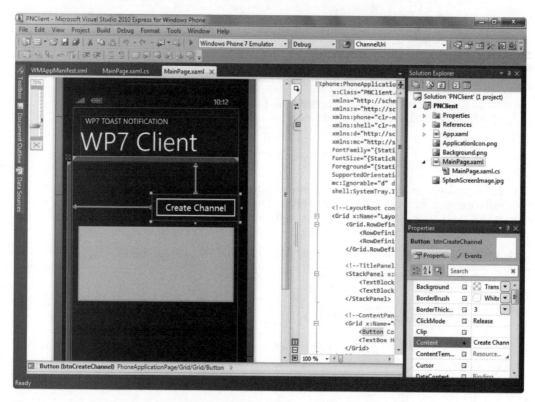

Figure 17–5. *Design surface for Windows Phone 7 Notification client application*

At this point, you have finished building the Windows Phone 7 client application and are ready to implement the Windows Forms application for sending notification messages to the mobile device.

Creating an Application to Send Notifications

In the previous section, you wrote a Windows Phone 7 client application that creates a notification channel to the MPN Service to indicate that it wishes to receive push notification messages. By creating a channel, the application has also created an MPNS endpoint to which the web-based application can send POST requests. The endpoint exists on an MPNS server operated by Microsoft and will forward any requests it receives to the appropriate mobile device and application to which the endpoint points.

You can create POST requests from virtually any application environment, including web sites, web services, and desktop applications, making this type of notification architecture very flexible and easy to use. In this example, you will create a Windows Forms application that packages POST requests to the URI generated in the previous section. This application will create POST requests and send them off to the MPNS in the cloud, which will in turn properly route the requests to the mobile devices and applications.

To ensure proper message routing and successful delivery, there are two key pieces of information that any application sending push notifications to a Windows Phone 7 device must supply. Those key pieces of information are the following:

1. *The URI of the notification channel that the service must use to communicate with a Windows Phone 7 device.* It is up to the Windows Phone 7 client application to request the URI and pass it to the service that will use it.

2. *A proper XML message to POST to the URI.* While the format of the XML message is simple, it has to be followed precisely for the notifications to succeed. To make things slightly more confusing, Microsoft changes schema in its early product releases in an effort to make it more uniform; those changes could break existing functionality and make documentation not relevant.

The latest MPNS XML template for toast notifications looks like the following, where `<Notification Title>` and `<Notification Text>` are the text of the notification title and the text of the toast notification message to be sent to a Windows Phone 7 device:

```xml
<?xml version="1.0" encoding="utf-8"?>
<wp:Notification xmlns:wp="WPNotification">
 <wp:Toast>
  <wp:Text1><Notification Title></wp:Text1>
  <wp:Text2><Notification Text></wp:Text2>
 </wp:Toast>
</wp:Notification>
```

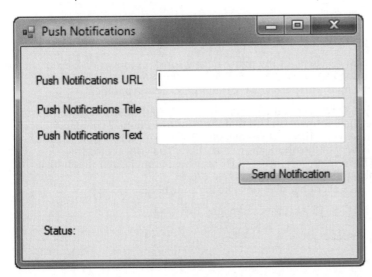

Figure 17–6. Windows Forms application that will send push notifications to WP7 app

Now that you know the XML template format of the expected POST request and, using cut and paste, can quickly obtain the URI of the notification channel, as you'll see shortly, you're ready to create an application to dispatch notifications to the Windows Phone 7 client app. Follow these steps to accomplish that:

3. Launch Visual C# 2010 Express (or another edition of Visual Studio that will allow you to create Windows Forms projects) and create a new Windows Forms project. Name it "PNServer."

4. Form1.cs is added by default. Double-click it to bring up the design view. From the toolbox, drag three labels and three text boxes and make Form1.cs look like Figure 17–5. Name the text boxes txtURL, txtTitle, and txtText accordingly.

5. Add a Button control onto Form1. Change its text property to "Send Notification" and change its name to "btnSendNotification."

6. Finally, add the label control to the bottom of the form and change its name to "lblStatus."

7. Right-click Form1.cs in Solution Explorer and choose View Code (alternately, you can also press F7). Add the following using statements to the top:

```
using System.Net;
using System.IO;
```

8. After the constructor, add the following definition of the XML to be POSTed to MPNS:

```
string ToastPushXML = "<?xml version=\"1.0\" encoding=\"utf-8\"?>" +
    "<wp:Notification xmlns:wp=\"WPNotification\">" +
    "<wp:Toast>" +
    "<wp:Text1>{0}</wp:Text1>" +
    "<wp:Text2>{1}</wp:Text2>" +
    "</wp:Toast>" +
    "</wp:Notification>";
```

9. Switch back to the design view on Form1.cs (by right-clicking Form1.cs in Solution Explorer and choosing View Designer). Double-click the "Send Notification" button to bring up the btnSendNotification_Click event handler.

You'll use the btnSendNotification_Click event handler, with the help of the .NET HttpWebRequest class, to create a POST request, to the push notification URI that the Windows Phone 7 client has obtained. The beauty of communication with MPNS is that once this POST request is composed and sent off, MPNS will take care of the delivery of the notification from there. The critical piece of information is the URI to send the POST request to, since that URI is what uniquely identifies both a Windows Phone 7 device and an application to send push notifications to.

Make the btnSendNotification_Click event handler look like the code here:

```
private void btnSendNotification_Click(object sender, EventArgs e)
{
    if (txtURL.Text == string.Empty)
    {
        MessageBox.Show("Please enter a url");
        return;
    }

    if (txtTitle.Text == string.Empty || txtText.Text == string.Empty)
    {
        MessageBox.Show("Please enter text and title to send");
        return;
    }

    string url = txtURL.Text;

    HttpWebRequest sendNotificationRequest = (HttpWebRequest)WebRequest.Create(url);
```

```
sendNotificationRequest.Method = "POST";
sendNotificationRequest.Headers = new WebHeaderCollection();
sendNotificationRequest.ContentType = "text/xml";

sendNotificationRequest.Headers.Add("X-WindowsPhone-Target", "toast");
sendNotificationRequest.Headers.Add("X-NotificationClass", "2");

string str = string.Format(ToastPushXML, txtTitle.Text, txtText.Text);
byte[] strBytes = new UTF8Encoding().GetBytes(str);
sendNotificationRequest.ContentLength = strBytes.Length;
using (Stream requestStream = sendNotificationRequest.GetRequestStream())
{
    requestStream.Write(strBytes, 0, strBytes.Length);
}

HttpWebResponse response = (HttpWebResponse)sendNotificationRequest.GetResponse();
string notificationStatus = response.Headers["X-NotificationStatus"];
string deviceConnectionStatus = response.Headers["X-DeviceConnectionStatus"];
lblStatus.Text = "Status: " + notificationStatus + " : " + deviceConnectionStatus;
}
```

The POST request includes two headers:

- The X-WindowsPhone-Target header defines the notification type. The possible values for this header are "toast," "token," or not defined. "Toast" defines the notification of toast type, while "token" defines a tile notification. If this header is not defined, then it is a raw notification.

- The X-NotificationClass header defines how soon the MPNS should deliver the notification. The value of "2" specifies that the toast notification is to be delivered immediately. Had you specified the value of "12," for example, the MPNS would have been instructed to wait 450 seconds, or seven and a half minutes before notification delivery.

Now it's time to test the application and its service.

Verifying Delivery of Push Notifications

With the Windows Phone 7 Notification client application ready to receive notification messages and the Windows Forms application ready to send them, you are ready to verify the proper delivery of those notifications. Follow these steps to test push notification delivery:

1. First, you will need to obtain the URI of the notification channel. Open the PNClient project created in the "Creating a Client Application" section. Make sure that you have a connection to the Internet, and press F5 to run the project.

2. Click the Create Channel button and, after a short while, you should see messages (the URI of the notification channel, actually) printed in the text box on the screen—that's a confirmation that the notification URI is available to copy from the Output window.

3. In Visual Studio 2010 Express for Windows Phone, click the Debug ➤ Windows ➤ Output menu option to bring up the Output window. The URI should be printed together with the "changing uri to …" message, as shown in Figure 17–7. Highlight the URI and press Ctrl/C to copy it into the buffer. Make sure to leave the application running in the Windows Phone emulator, since you will be receiving push notifications on this emulator screen.

4. Switch to the PNServer Windows Forms project and press F5 to run it. In the Push Notifications URL text box, paste the URI obtained in Step 1 by pressing Ctrl/V. In the Push Notifications Title and Push Notifications Text text boxes, you can enter any text—for example, "Time to buy!" and "MSFT up $2 after WP7 release." Press the Send Notification button.

Remember that push notifications appear on the phone only when the Windows Phone 7 application associated with these notifications is not running in the foreground on the phone. Therefore, if the PNClient application was running—which is likely—in the foreground when you pressed the Send Notification button, no notifications will have appeared on the phone screen. To enable them, do the following, otherwise skip to the next paragraph:

5. Press the Windows button on the emulator (that's the middle button on the emulator with the Windows logo on it) to switch to the Start screen of the phone, which shuts down PNClient application. In the PNServer app, press the Send Notification button again.

Now, you should see a toast notification like the one shown in the very beginning of this chapter in Figure 17–1.

As you can see, creating and receiving push notifications is a somewhat involved process, with a separate Windows Phone 7 application establishing a notification channel and receiving notifications, and a separate application sending, or "pushing" these notifications to that Windows Phone 7 app. Once you understand how to work with other types of notifications—namely, tile and raw—you will learn how to build a service that will programmatically acquire and keep track of the connected clients. From an application development point of view, the good news is that the process of creating other notification types—tile notifications and raw notifications—is very similar to the process of creating toast notifications that we have described previously. In the next section, you will take a look at how to create tile notifications; but instead of creating everything from scratch, you will concentrate only on the changes needed to the toast notifications already implemented.

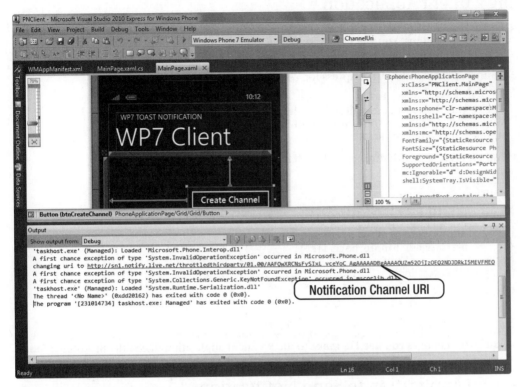

Figure 17–7. Notification channel URI printed in the Output window

Implementing Tile Notifications

Tile notifications can update the images and texts of application tiles, as you saw at the beginning of this chapter in Figure 17–2. Tile notifications are ideal for applications that convey small amounts of information, especially when that information changes frequently. For example, weather reports and compass headings are both good candidates for this category.

You will implement the tile notifications application in the same three steps you followed to implement toast notifications, namely the following:

1. Create a Windows Phone 7 Notification client application. This application will establish a notification channel.

2. Create and execute the Windows Forms client. You will take the URI of the notification channel that you established in Step 1, paste it into the "Push Notifications URL" text box, and submit push notification to the application.

3. Verify that you are able to receive tile notifications in the Windows Phone 7 application.

Creating a Client Application

You will take the PNClient application that you have created and enhance it to accept tile notifications in addition to toast notifications. You will not recreate the application; rather, you will concentrate on the changes needed to enable tile notifications.

1. Launch Visual Studio 2010 Express for Windows Phone and open the PNClient project.

2. Locate the `BindToShell` function inside the `MainPage.xaml.cs` file. Change that function to look like the one here (essentially, you are adding a line to bind this application to tile notifications):

```
private static void BindToShell(HttpNotificationChannel httpChannel)
{
    try
    {
        //toast notification binding
        httpChannel.BindToShellToast();
        //tile notification binding
        httpChannel.BindToShellTile();
    }
    catch (Exception)
    {

    }
}
```

Those are all the changes you need to make to the PNClient application to enable tile notifications.

Creating an Application to Send Notifications

There are a few changes that you need to make to code that sends push notifications to enable tile notifications processing. First, you'll need to use a different XML schema for tile notifications, as shown here:

```
<?xml version=\"1.0\" encoding="utf-8"?>
<wp:Notification xmlns:wp="WPNotification">
 <wp:Tile>
  <wp:BackgroundImage><URI to Image></wp:BackgroundImage>
  <wp:Count><Count Message></wp:Count>
  <wp:Title><Title Message></wp:Title>
 </wp:Tile>
</wp:Notification>
```

The `<URI to Image>` element specifies the location, which is either local or remote, of the background image used to update the application tile. `<Count Message>` is the counter text (the one almost at the center of the tile) to set on the tile and the `<Title Message>` is the message text to set at the bottom of the application tile.

■ **Note** In the current implementation of Push Notifications for Windows Phone 7, to set the background image to an image located on the Internet, you must specify the location of that image when creating a Windows Phone 7 Notification client application. While this is certainly not very flexible (you would have to know beforehand all of the images that you will be using to update tiles with), Microsoft generally does not encourage the use of remote images for tile updates, limiting the maximum allowed size of those images to 80KB and emphasizing in documentation that the use of remote resources leads to excessive battery drain.

Follow these steps to make changes for tile notifications:

1. Open the PNServer project and open code for the `Form1.cs` file (right-click `Form1.cs` in Solution Explorer and select View Code).

2. Now, you will define the XML schema information inside the code. Paste the following string declaration to the top of the file, right underneath the `string ToastPushXML` declaration:

```
string TilePushXML = "<?xml version=\"1.0\" encoding=\"utf-8\"?>" +
        "<wp:Notification xmlns:wp=\"WPNotification\">" +
        "<wp:Tile>" +
        "<wp:Count>{0}</wp:Count>" +
        "<wp:Title>{1}</wp:Title>" +
        "</wp:Tile>" +
        "</wp:Notification>";
```

3. Inside the btnSendNotification_Click event handler, change the following two lines of code:

```
sendNotificationRequest.Headers.Add("X-WindowsPhone-Target", "toast");
sendNotificationRequest.Headers.Add("X-NotificationClass", "2");
```

to

```
sendNotificationRequest.Headers.Add("X-WindowsPhone-Target", "token");
sendNotificationRequest.Headers.Add("X-NotificationClass", "1"); //- tiles
```

4. Finally, you need to change the string that gets sent to the Windows Phone 7 application. To accomplish that, change the following line of code inside the btnSendNotification_Click event handler from:

```
string str = string.Format(ToastPushXML, txtTitle.Text, txtText.Text);
```

to:

```
string str = string.Format(TilePushXML, txtTitle.Text, txtText.Text);
```

Those are all of the changes that you need to make to enable tile notifications on the Windows Phone 7 device. You are now ready to test tile notifications on the Windows Phone 7 emulator.

Verifying Delivery of Push Notifications

Having made changes to both the client and the server portions of the code to enable tile notifications, it's time to take them for a spin.

Just as with toast notifications, you need to obtain the URI of the notification channel.

1. Open PNClient project, make sure that you have a connection to the Internet, and press F5 to run the project.

2. Click the Create Channel button and, after seeing the URI printed on the screen, copy it to the clipboard from the Output window.

Remember that tile notifications appear on the phone only when a Windows Phone 7 application associated with these notifications is not running in the foreground on the phone and (this is important!) only when the application tile is available on the Windows Phone 7 Start screen.

3. To pin the application tile onto the Start screen, with the PNClient application running, click the phone's Windows button, and then click the arrow (➤) to open the Windows Phone 7 Options screen, shown in Figure 17–8.

4. Click and hold the left mouse button down (also referred to as "long click") to bring up the pop-up menu shown in Figure 17–8.

5. Click the Pin to Start option.

Now, the PNClient application tile should be shown on the Start screen, together with the Internet Explorer tile.

6. Switch to the PNServer Windows Forms project, and press F5 to run it.

7. In the Push Notifications URL text box, paste the URI obtained in Step 1. In the Push Notifications Title and Push Notifications Text text boxes, enter text for the counter and tile message accordingly. For example, to get tile notification to appear as in Figure 17–2, enter "2" for Push Notification Title and "MSFT +2" in Push Notification Text field.

Figure 17–8. To receive tile notifications, the application tile must be pinned to the Start screen.

Now you're ready to send and receive tile notifications.

8. Click the Push Notification button in the PNServer application.

You should now see the application tile updated from default to the one containing both the counter text ("2") and the message text ("MSFT +2").

As you can see, processing tile notifications is only slightly different from processing toast applications. Processing raw notifications is also very similar to the foregoing walkthroughs; however, since raw notifications are received when an application is running in the foreground only, you would need to wire up an event inside the Windows Phone 7 application to process messages received, as you will see shortly in the section about implementing raw notifications.

Implementing Raw Notifications

Raw notifications represent the third and final type of push notification available on the Windows Phone 7 platform. Unlike tile and toast notifications, however, raw notifications are available to a Windows Phone 7 application only if that application is running in the foreground. If the application is not running in the foreground, even if the application's icon is pinned to the phone's Start screen, raw notifications are simply dropped.

You will implement raw notifications following the same three general steps as implementing toast and tile notifications, namely the following:

1. Create a Windows Phone 7 Notification client application. This application will establish a notification channel.

2. Create and execute a Windows Forms client. You will take the URI of the notification channel that you established in Step 1, paste it into the "Push Notifications URL" text box, and submit a push notification to the application.

3. Verify that you are able to receive raw notifications in your Windows Phone 7 application.

Creating a Client Application

You will create the RawNotificationPNClient application to accept raw notifications. This application is similar to the PNClient application you have created in the prior sections of this chapter, yet it has subtle differences from that codebase to warrant a separate project.

1. Launch Visual Studio 2010 Express for Windows Phone and create a new Windows Phone Application project. Name it "RawNotificationPNClient."

2. From the Toolbox, drag and drop a text box on the design surface. Rename the text box to txtURI, adjust its width to be the full width of the screen, and adjust its height to be about a quarter of screen's height. Set the text box's TextWrapping property to "Wrap" and clear out its Text property.

3. From the Toolbox, drag and drop a button on the design surface. Rename the button to btnCreateChannel and set the Content property to "Create Channel." Once again, your Windows Phone 7 design surface should now look like Figure 17–6.

4. The `Microsoft.Phone.Notification` namespace contains the functionality necessary to establish a push notification channel and receive push notifications; therefore you need to add the following using directive at the top of the `MainPage.xaml.cs` file:

```
using Microsoft.Phone.Notification;
using System.Diagnostics;
```

5. You will now program the button click event handler to create the push notification URL. In the Windows Phone 7 design surface, double-click the "Create Channel" button and make that button's click event handler look like the following:

```
private void btnCreateChannel_Click(object sender, RoutedEventArgs e)
{
    SetupChannel();
}
```

The `SetupChannel` function, which follows, is responsible for creating a channel within MPNS to receive updates from the server, as well as to wire up event handlers to fire when the error occurs during communication and when the raw notification is received. Remember that raw notifications are available to the application only when it's running; therefore an event handler must be defined in code that processes raw notifications as they come in. The code that binds the raw notification received event to the `httpChannel_HttpNotificationReceived` event handler function lives inside the `SetupChannel` function:

```
httpChannel.HttpNotificationReceived += new
EventHandler<HttpNotificationEventArgs>(httpChannel_HttpNotificationReceived);
```

6. Here's the complete implementation of the SetupChannel function. Add the code to your project:

```
private void SetupChannel()
{
    HttpNotificationChannel httpChannel = null;
    string channelName = "DemoChannel";

    try
    {
        //if channel exists, retrieve existing channel
        httpChannel = HttpNotificationChannel.Find(channelName);
        if (httpChannel != null)
        {
            //If you can't get it, then close and reopen it.
            if (httpChannel.ChannelUri == null)
            {
                httpChannel.UnbindToShellToast();
                httpChannel.Close();
                SetupChannel();
                return;
            }
            else
            {
                ChannelUri = httpChannel.ChannelUri;

                //wiring up the raw notifications event handler
                httpChannel.HttpNotificationReceived += new
EventHandler<HttpNotificationEventArgs>(httpChannel_HttpNotificationReceived);
            }
        }
        else
        {
            httpChannel = new HttpNotificationChannel(channelName);
            httpChannel.ChannelUriUpdated += new
EventHandler<NotificationChannelUriEventArgs>(httpChannel_ChannelUriUpdated);
            httpChannel.ErrorOccurred += new
EventHandler<NotificationChannelErrorEventArgs>(httpChannel_ExceptionOccurred);

            //wiring up the raw notifications event handler
            httpChannel.HttpNotificationReceived += new
EventHandler<HttpNotificationEventArgs>(httpChannel_HttpNotificationReceived);

            httpChannel.Open();
        }
    }
    catch (Exception ex)
    {

    }
}
```

What you do with raw notifications received is totally up to you: raw notifications can be simple status messages to be shown in the Windows Phone 7 client application, or they can be directives to the application to perform a given task. In this application, you will simply print a message into the text box with the text of raw notifications received.

7. To print the raw notification, add the following code:

```
void httpChannel_HttpNotificationReceived(object sender, HttpNotificationEventArgs e)
{
    if (e.Notification.Body != null && e.Notification.Headers != null)
    {
        System.IO.StreamReader reader = new
System.IO.StreamReader(e.Notification.Body);
        Dispatcher.BeginInvoke(() =>
        {
            txtURI.Text = "Raw Notification Message Received: " + reader.ReadToEnd();
        });
    }
}
```

You are very close to completing the client application; what remains is to write an error handling function that will fire off when any errors during communication occur. You will also write a simple event handler that will fire off when the push notification channel URI gets updated.

8. Add the following code to your application:

```
void httpChannel_ExceptionOccurred(object sender, NotificationChannelErrorEventArgs e)
{
//Display Message on error
        Debug.WriteLine ( e.Message);
}

void httpChannel_ChannelUriUpdated(object sender, NotificationChannelUriEventArgs e)
{
//You get the new Uri (or maybe it's updated)
        ChannelUri = e.ChannelUri;
}
```

9. Finally, add the following helper code to the top of the MainPage class. This code will print the push notification channel URI into the Debug window; you will need that URI to test the application shortly:

```
Uri channelUri;

    public Uri ChannelUri
    {
        get { return channelUri; }
        set
        {
            channelUri = value;
            OnChannelUriChanged(value);
        }
    }

    private void OnChannelUriChanged(Uri value)
    {
```

```
Dispatcher.BeginInvoke(() =>
{
    txtURI.Text = "changing uri to " + value.ToString();
});

Debug.WriteLine("changing uri to " + value.ToString());
}
```

With the client application complete, press F5 to make sure that the application compiles and runs. In the next section, you will be building a server piece to send raw notifications to this client application.

Creating an Application to Send Notifications

Sending raw notifications from the server is simpler than sending Tiles or Toasts: there are no XML templates for message formatting for raw notifications. You will reuse the PNServer project created in the prior sections and edit the button click event handler for raw notifications processing. Follow these steps to accomplish that:

1. Open the PNServer project and open code for the Form1.cs file (right-click Form1.cs in Solution Explorer and select View Code).

2. Replace the btnSendNotification_Click event handler with the following code. Note how the X-NotificationClass header value is set to "3" and how the X-WindowsPhone-Targe header value is left blank to indicate that this is a raw notification.

```
private void btnSendNotification_Click(object sender, EventArgs e)
{
    if (txtURL.Text == string.Empty)
    {
        MessageBox.Show("Please enter a url");
        return;
    }

    if (txtTitle.Text == string.Empty || txtText.Text == string.Empty)
    {
        MessageBox.Show("Please enter text and title to send");
        return;
    }

    HttpWebRequest sendNotificationRequest =
(HttpWebRequest)WebRequest.Create(txtURL.Text);

        sendNotificationRequest.Method = "POST";
        sendNotificationRequest.Headers = new WebHeaderCollection();
        sendNotificationRequest.ContentType = "text/xml";

        sendNotificationRequest.Headers.Add("X-WindowsPhone-Target", "");
        sendNotificationRequest.Headers.Add("X-NotificationClass", "3"); //- raw
        string str = string.Format(txtTitle.Text + "\r\n" + txtText.Text);
        byte[] strBytes = new UTF8Encoding().GetBytes(str);
        sendNotificationRequest.ContentLength = strBytes.Length;
```

```
using (Stream requestStream = sendNotificationRequest.GetRequestStream())
{
    requestStream.Write(strBytes, 0, strBytes.Length);
}

HttpWebResponse response = (HttpWebResponse)sendNotificationRequest.GetResponse();
string notificationStatus = response.Headers["X-NotificationStatus"];
string deviceConnectionStatus = response.Headers["X-DeviceConnectionStatus"];
lblStatus.Text = "Status: " + notificationStatus + " : " + deviceConnectionStatus;
}
```

That is all the code necessary to send raw notifications to Windows Phone 7 clients. You are now ready to test raw notifications on the Windows Phone 7 emulator.

Testing Delivery of Raw Notifications

Testing raw notifications is very straightforward: there are no applications to pin to the Start screen—simply start both the client and the server pieces of the application, make sure that the push notification URL is available to both, and fire away! The walkthrough here gives more details on testing raw notifications:

1. Just as with toast and tile notifications, you need to obtain the URI of the notification channel. Open the RawNotificationPNClient project, make sure that you have a connection to the Internet, and press F5 to run the project. Click the Create Channel button and, after seeing the URI printed on the screen, copy it to the clipboard from the Output window.

2. Switch to the PNServer Windows Forms project and press F5 to run it. In the Push Notifications URL text box, paste the URI obtained in Step 1. In the Push Notifications Title and Push Notifications Text text boxes, enter "Hello" and "World" correspondingly. Click the Send Notification button.

3. You should now see the message stating that the raw notification has been received and the "Hello World" message on the Windows Phone 7 emulator screen.

As you can see, implementing raw notifications is very similar to implementing tile and toast notifications, albeit a bit simpler. Each one of the notification types has its purposes; use the most appropriate notification type for your circumstances.

You may be shaking your head by now, thinking that the copy and paste method of communicating the push notification channel URL between the client and the server is completely unrealistic for any commercial application. We agree, and we will show you how to automate that communication piece in the next section.

Implementing Cloud Service to Track Push Notifications

So far in the preceding walkthroughs, you have used a somewhat unrealistic approach to communicating push notification URLs from the Windows Phone 7 client application to the push notification server. You copied that URL from the Debug window of the client application and pasted it into the server application, where it was used to send tiles, toasts, and raw notifications to the Windows Phone 7 applications. To make the stock alerts application a bit more real-world, however, you must automate the URL communication piece. In this section, you will learn how to do that using a cloud service built with the Microsoft Windows Communication Foundation (WCF) stack of technologies.

Creating a WCF Service to Track Notification Recipients

In this section, we will show you how to enhance the PNServer application built previously by adding a WCF service to it. WCF is a very powerful technology with an array of configuration options for creating and hosting cloud services. You will be building what is known as a **self-hosted service**, which means that it will be hosted within the Windows Forms application and you will write code to initialize and start that service. Another important point about this service is that it will be a **RESTful service**, which, for our purposes right now, means that you can access operations of the service over the properly formatted URLs, as you will see shortly.

Before you create a RESTful WCF service, however, you may need to make a small change in the Visual Studio environment to reference assemblies you need to create that service. The reason for this is that, by default, Visual Studio creates a lightweight profile for client applications, such as Windows Forms or Windows Presentation Foundation (WPF) applications. This lightweight profile omits many web-related assemblies by default because the chances of a true client application needing them are slim.

The setting that controls which assemblies are included or left out is the Target Framework setting, and it is located on your project's Properties page. You need to change this setting from ".Net Framework 4 Client Profile" to ".Net Framework 4." To accomplish that, open the PNServer project if it's not already open, right-click the project name, and then select Properties. Locate the Target Framework setting and set it to ".Net Framework 4," as illustrated in Figure 17–9.

Now follow these steps to complete creation of the WCF service. First, before creating the service, you need to include the `System.ServiceModel.Web` assembly to the PNServer project.

1. Right-click the project name and select Add Reference. Locate the `System.ServiceModel.Web` assembly in the list, highlight it, and click OK.

Now, you will add WCF service files to the project. Adding the WCF service files will consist of two parts: creating what is known as a **Service Contract**, which will appear in the form of an Interface file, and defining a class that will physically implement the methods defined within the Service Contract.

2. To create the Service Contract, right-click the project name, choose Add➤New Item, and then scroll almost all the way to the bottom and pick WCF Service. Name the service "Registration Service," and then click OK.

3. Add the following statement to the top of the IRegistrationService.cs file created:

```
using System.ServiceModel.Web;
```

4. Add the following code to the IRegistrationService.cs file:

```
[ServiceContract]
public interface IRegistrationService
{
    [OperationContract, WebGet]
    void Register(string uri);

    [OperationContract, WebGet]
    void Unregister(string uri);
}
```

Note how you defined two operations for the service to perform: Register new Windows Phone 7 clients for push notifications and Unregister them.

Now it's time to add the implementation of the Register and Unregister methods.

5. Double-click the RegistrationService.cs file that Visual Studio added to your project. Make the RegistrationService.cs file look like the code here.

```
public class RegistrationService : IRegistrationService
{
    private static List<Uri> subscribers = new List<Uri>();
    private static object obj = new object();

    public void Register(string uri)
    {
        Uri channelUri = new Uri(uri, UriKind.Absolute);
        Subscribe(channelUri);
    }

    public void Unregister(string uri)
    {
        Uri channelUri = new Uri(uri, UriKind.Absolute);
        Unsubscribe(channelUri);
    }

    private void Subscribe(Uri channelUri)
    {
        lock (obj)
        {
            if (!subscribers.Exists((u) => u == channelUri))
            {
                subscribers.Add(channelUri);
            }
        }
    }

    public static void Unsubscribe(Uri channelUri)
    {
        lock (obj)
        {
            subscribers.Remove(channelUri);
        }
    }

    public static List<Uri> GetSubscribers()
    {
        return subscribers;
    }
}
```

Take a look closer look at the code that you just added to the RegistrationService.cs file. Notice that the RegistrationService class implements the IRegistrationService interface on the very first line—this is important! Aside from that, the code is pretty straightforward: a collection of push notification URIs is maintained in the static subscribers variable, and every client that calls the Register method of the service gets added to that list of subscribers. The lock function is used to prevent multiple clients changing the same data at the same exact moment in time, possibly resulting in incomplete and unpredictable data.

In the beginning of this section, we said that a WCF service hosted by a Windows Forms application needs initialization code to start up. One of the places this initialization code can go is in the load event of Form1.

6. Here's the code you need to start up the service. Copy it to the load event of Form1 here:

```
ServiceHost host;
host = new ServiceHost(typeof(RegistrationService));
host.Open();
```

You are almost done—now you need only to provide some configuration parameters for the WCF service to run.

7. Open the app.config file and add the following configuration parameters to the <system.ServiceModel> element (you should already have configuration settings defined within <system.ServiceModel>, but now you need to make sure those settings match precisely what is pasted here):

```
<system.serviceModel>
    <behaviors>
        <endpointBehaviors>
            <behavior name="EndpointPNServerServiceBehavior">
                <webHttp />
            </behavior>
        </endpointBehaviors>
        <serviceBehaviors>
            <behavior name="">
                <serviceDebug includeExceptionDetailInFaults="true" />
            </behavior>
        </serviceBehaviors>
    </behaviors>
    <services>
        <service name="PNServer.RegistrationService">
            <endpoint address="http://localhost/RegistrationService"
                behaviorConfiguration="EndpointPNServerServiceBehavior"
                binding="webHttpBinding"
                contract="WP7_Push_Notifications.IRegistrationService">
            </endpoint>
        </service>
    </services>
</system.serviceModel>
```

In a nutshell, with these settings you have configured your service to listen at the following address: http://localhost/RegistrationService. You have also specified that the requests to this service will be coming over the http protocol.

Finally, you will modify the main application form (Form1) and add a Broadcast button that will send a push notification to all subscribed clients. Once clicked, the button click handler will get a list of all clients subscribed and send each one of them a push notification (toast notification in the following code). Here's how to do that.

8. Open Form1.cs in Design view and add a button to that form underneath the "Send Notification" button.

a. Change the button's text to "Broadcast," as shown in Figure 17–10.

b. Change the button's name to "btnBroadcast," double-click it, and make sure that the button's Click event contains the following code:

```
private void btnBroadcast_Click(object sender, EventArgs e)
{
    if (txtTitle.Text == string.Empty || txtText.Text == string.Empty)
    {
        MessageBox.Show("Please enter text and title to send");
        return;
    }

    List<Uri> allSubscribersUri = RegistrationService.GetSubscribers();

    foreach (Uri subscriberUri in allSubscribersUri)
    {
        sendPushNotificationToClient(subscriberUri.ToString());
    }
}
```

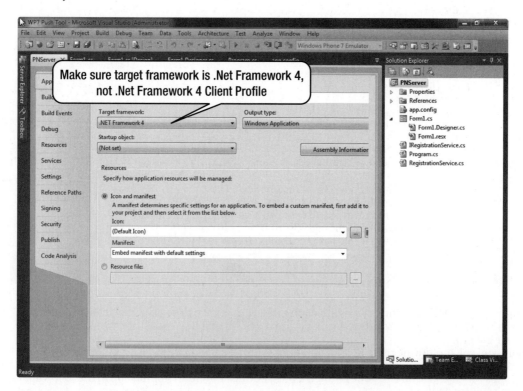

Figure 17–9. To add RESTful WCF service to the Windows Forms application, set the application's target framework to .NET Framework 4.

9. Add the following code to the sendPushNotificationToClient function:

```
private void sendPushNotificationToClient(string url)
{
    HttpWebRequest sendNotificationRequest = (HttpWebRequest)WebRequest.Create(url);

    sendNotificationRequest.Method = "POST";
    sendNotificationRequest.Headers = new WebHeaderCollection();
    sendNotificationRequest.ContentType = "text/xml";

    sendNotificationRequest.Headers.Add("X-WindowsPhone-Target", "toast");
    sendNotificationRequest.Headers.Add("X-NotificationClass", "2");

    string str = string.Format(TilePushXML, txtTitle.Text, txtText.Text);
    byte[] strBytes = new UTF8Encoding().GetBytes(str);
    sendNotificationRequest.ContentLength = strBytes.Length;
    using (Stream requestStream = sendNotificationRequest.GetRequestStream())
    {
        requestStream.Write(strBytes, 0, strBytes.Length);
    }

    try
    {
        HttpWebResponse response =
(HttpWebResponse)sendNotificationRequest.GetResponse();
        string notificationStatus = response.Headers["X-NotificationStatus"];
        string deviceConnectionStatus = response.Headers["X-DeviceConnectionStatus"];
        lblStatus.Text = "Status: " + notificationStatus + " : " +
deviceConnectionStatus;
    }
    catch (Exception ex)
    {
        //handle 404 (URI not found) and other exceptions that may occur
        lblStatus.Text = "Failed to connect, exception detail: " + ex.Message;
    }
```

Note that the TilePushXML variable has been previously defined when we talked about Tile Notifications—specifically, in the Creating an Application to Send Notifications section. With the WCF service tracking subscribed clients and sending push notifications complete, it is now time to enhance the client application to call the web service with its push notification URL.

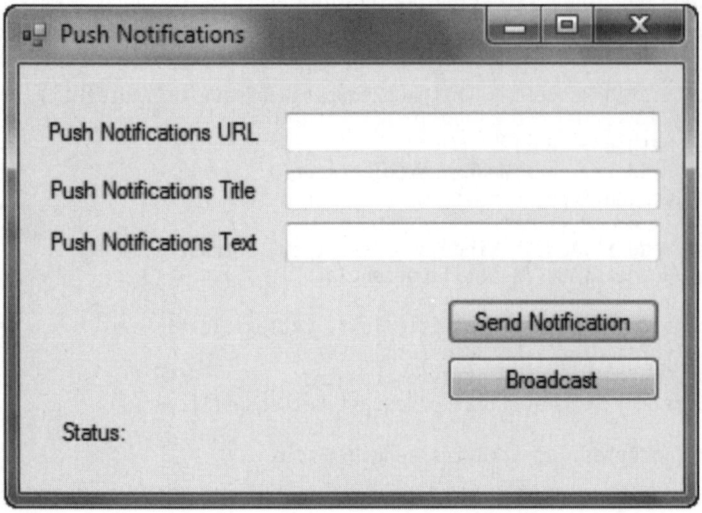

Figure 17–10. *Main application form with Broadcast button*

Modifying the Client to Call the WCF Service

The Windows Phone 7 Push Notification client application needs to be modified to call the newly implemented web service with the push notification URL. Previously, we briefly mentioned that the convenience of creating a RESTful WCF service lies in the fact that the operations of that web service can be accessed as URLs. For instance, the URL http://localhost/RegistrationService/ Register?uri={0} accesses the Register function of the web service created in the previous section; the uri parameter is supplied on the QueryString. With that in mind, you can go ahead and complete the Windows Phone 7 Push Notification client implementation by creating the functions that will register/unregister a Windows Phone 7 client with the server:

1. Launch Visual Studio 2010 Express for Windows Phone and open the PNClient project.

2. Locate the ChannelUri property getter and setter and change them to the following (notice the use of two new functions, RegisterUriWithServer and UnregisterUriFromServer).

```
public Uri ChannelUri
{
    get { return channelUri; }
    set
    {
        //unregister the old URI from the server
        if (channelUri!=null)
            UnregisterUriFromServer(channelUri);

        //register the new URI with the server
        RegisterUriWithServer(value);
```

```
        channelUri = value;
        OnChannelUriChanged(value);
      }
    }
```

3.   Now add the following two functions to invoke the WCF service that you have
      created (note that when it comes time to release your service to production, you
      will be most likely deploying this service somewhere in the cloud).

```
private void RegisterUriWithServer(Uri newChannelUri)
{
    //Hardcode for solution - need to be updated in case the REST WCF service address
```
change
```
    string baseUri = "http://localhost/RegistrationService/Register?uri={0}";
    string theUri = String.Format(baseUri, newChannelUri.ToString());
    WebClient client = new WebClient();
    client.DownloadStringCompleted += (s, e) =>
    {
        if (e.Error == null)
            Dispatcher.BeginInvoke(() => {
                txtURI.Text = "changing uri to " + newChannelUri.ToString();
            });
        else
            Dispatcher.BeginInvoke(() =>
            {
                txtURI.Text = "registration failed " + e.Error.Message;
            });
    };
    client.DownloadStringAsync(new Uri(theUri));

}

private void UnregisterUriFromServer(Uri oldChannelUri)
{
    //Hardcode for solution - need to be updated in case the REST WCF service address
```
change
```
    string baseUri = "http://localhost/RegistrationService/Unregister?uri={0}";
    string theUri = String.Format(baseUri, oldChannelUri.ToString());
    WebClient client = new WebClient();
    client.DownloadStringCompleted += (s, e) =>
    {
        if (e.Error == null)
            Dispatcher.BeginInvoke(() =>
            {
                txtURI.Text = "unregistered uri " + oldChannelUri.ToString();
            });
        else
            Dispatcher.BeginInvoke(() =>
            {
                txtURI.Text = "registration delete failed " + e.Error.Message;
            });
    };
    client.DownloadStringAsync(new Uri(theUri));
}
```

In the preceding code, notice that the URL of the cloud is hard-coded—this URL must match the URL you have specified in the configuration file (app.config) for the WCF service. Notice also how the event handlers (client.DownloadStringCompleted) are wired up—those event handlers provide the status updates on whether the registration/unregistration succeeded or failed.

At this point, you have completed writing both the server and the client piece for automated push notification. It is now time to verify that the server is able to keep track and notify its clients appropriately, without the need to manually copy and paste the push notification URL.

Verifying Automated Push Notification Subscriber Tracking

To test automated push notification tracking, the very first thing you have to do is make sure that the WCF service starts up appropriately and that it is able to process requests coming in. Here's how:

1. WCF Services are designed with security in mind and there are numerous security configuration options for those services. To bypass security configuration options so that you can test the service you built, you will need to run the WCF Service project as Administrator. The quickest way to accomplish that would be to exit Visual Studio, then right-click on the shortcut to Visual Studio and choose "Run as Administrator" option. Once Visual Studio comes up, open the PNServer solution. You are now set to run PNServer as Administrator.

2. To verify that the WCF service is indeed ready to accept client connections, set a breakpoint at the first line of the Register function of the RegistrationService class, and then press F5 to start the PNServer application.

3. If the application is running and the Windows form shown in Figure 17–10 is displayed, then fire up Internet Explorer (or any other browser) and go to the following URL:

http://localhost/RegistrationService/Register?uri=http://www.microsoft.com

If the breakpoint gets hit after you access this URL, this means that the service is running and it is ready for clients to connect.

If the breakpoint does not get hit and you see a message that the page cannot be displayed, verify that the content in the <system.ServiceModel> section of your app.config file in the PNServer project matches the content of that file described in the section on creating a WCF service. Most likely, some sort of configuration issue is preventing you from properly launching the service.

Once you've confirmed that the service is running, you can observe the automated push notification subscriber tracking in action by following these steps:

4. Launch PNClient application and click the Create Channel button. If you still have the breakpoint set in the Register function of the WCF service, that breakpoint should be hit.

5. To be able to see toast notifications on the phone, you need to pin the application icon to the Start screen. To accomplish that, click the phone's Windows button, and then click the arrow (➤) to open the Windows Phone 7 Options screen, as previously shown in Figure 17–8. Click and hold the left mouse button (also referred to as a "long click") to bring up the pop-up menu shown in Figure 17–8, and then click the Pin to Start option.

6. With the application icon pinned onto the Start screen, you are ready to receive notifications on the phone. In the PNServer application window, enter the title and the text of the notification message to send and press the Broadcast button. A second or two later, you should see the push notification coming through to the phone.

With clients and cloud service dynamically exchanging push notification URLs and clients accepting push notifications, this is a good point to conclude push notifications walkthroughs. The next sections will give you a perspective on using push notifications in the real world and summarize what you have learned in this chapter. The solution that you have built in this chapter provides the "full lifecycle" implementation of Push Notifications; however, it has a set of limitations that should be considered before deploying it to production. Windows Phone 7 client applications that go down do not unregister themselves from the server; therefore, the server will try to send notifications to non-existent channels. The server lacks persistency—all of the connected client addresses are kept in-memory, which means that they all will be lost should the service be shut down accidentally or on purpose. Finally, there's no centralized scheduling or event-based mechanism for distributing notifications: you have to push the button on the Windows Forms application to distribute the notifications. In the real world, the notifications will most likely be distributed in response to some external events (such as Microsoft stock rising rapidly), and the service has to be smart about handling those.

Using Push Notifications in the Real World

Push notifications provide a scalable framework for Windows Phone 7 applications that lets them receive important messages without the need to continuously run in the background. This approach preserves device resources (processor, Internet connection) and extends battery life. There are many potential uses for Push notifications: from Twitter updates to severe weather alerts to stock market notifications. This chapter demonstrated how you can send push notifications to Windows Phone 7 devices using a Windows Forms application; just as easily, it could be a web-based or cloud-based application that sends those updates. In this chapter, you built a cloud service to programmatically keep track and send notifications to the connected clients. This same cloud service could be further enhanced to send out push notifications on a schedule.

Currently, there is a limit on how many free push notifications can be sent to a single notification channel URI. That limit is 500 notifications per 24 hours per URI. That means that you can send 500 messages per app per device for free for every 24 hours. This limitation is in place to prevent abuse or malicious attacks and possibly spam through a notification channel. There is a fee to use the Push Notification Service above that limit.

The communication channel between the Windows Phone 7 and the Microsoft Push Notification Service is secure, and customers also have an option (for a fee) to secure the channel between their web service and MPNS.

Summary

This chapter gave the background and provided an introduction to push notification services. You have gained an understanding of various push notification types, as well as the general architecture of push notifications. You have also implemented both toast and tile notifications.

In the next chapter, you will be taking a look at simplifying and abstracting asynchronous and event-based programming with Reactive Extensions for .Net, also referred to as Rx.Net. With Rx.Net, the implementation of concurrent asynchronous and events-based applications becomes easy and manageable.

CHAPTER 18

■ ■ ■

Reactive Extensions for .NET

For developers, the computing world of today is becoming much more concurrent than just a few short years ago. Computer users expect an ever-increasing computational power from their electronic gadgets, including their mobile devices. Unfortunately, it seems that the only way manufacturers will be able to increase computational speed in the near future is through adding additional processors (instead of making a single processor faster, as has been the case over the last few decades). In the case of processors on personal computers, the industry has already hit a proverbial "brick wall" and has pretty much reached the maximum computational capacity available on a single processing unit. An average personal computer today comes with two or more processing units, and the number is certain to increase.

Mobile devices still have some processing speed to grow into before they max out the processing power of a single CPU. However, the average phone will shortly have several processing units as well. In addition to that, uninterrupted Internet access on the phone is assumed—resources needed for proper functioning of an application may be spread around the world (in the "cloud"), but the user is rarely aware of that. A phone application should have the ability to access those resources seamlessly as needed—i.e., it should not stop accepting all input from the user while these resources are accessed. Rather, an application should retrieve the resources without interrupting other functionality of an application—in other words, it should obtain these resources asynchronously. The future for both personal computers and mobile devices is both concurrent and asynchronous.

How do we approach concurrent and asynchronous programming on Windows Phone 7? The answer is, certainly, with great caution, since it is not easy. To help tame that complexity, a powerful framework emerged on the .NET scene at the end of 2009. That framework, called the Reactive Extensions for .NET (also known as Rx.NET), is now available for Windows Phone 7 and provides sophisticated mechanisms to make event processing and asynchronous programming more intuitive. In this chapter, you will learn the concepts behind Reactive Extensions for .NET and build two simple applications using the Rx.NET framework. The first will search and retrieve images on Flickr asynchronously. The second will display the current weather after accepting a zip code as input from the user. As with several other chapters of this volume, a whole book could be written on the subject of Reactive Extensions alone, especially since there is a version of Reactive Extensions for JavaScript available as well.

In this chapter, you will learn the basics of Rx.NET and, we hope, leave with a basic understanding and appreciation of this technology. However, to leverage the power of Rx.NET, you need a good understanding of LINQ. Although the examples in this chapter should be relatively easy for the novice C# programmer even without an in-depth knowledge of LINQ, for expert coverage of the topic we recommend the excellent book *Pro LINQ: Language Integrated Query in C#2008*, by Joseph C. Rattz. Another good resource is "101 LINQ Samples," available for free online at http://msdn.microsoft.com/en-us/vcsharp/aa336746.aspx. Rx.NET also relies heavily on general object-oriented principles; if the concept of interfaces is not familiar to you, it may be a good idea to understand those before reading this chapter. Finally, Rx.NET constructs make extensive use of the newer concepts of the .NET framework, such as lambda expressions and extension methods. While it will be possible to follow examples in this book without in-depth understanding of either of those concepts, to leverage the power of Rx.NET on your own, you will have to understand these features of the .NET framework.

The power of Reactive Framework can be applied to deal with a wide range of computational issues. In this chapter, we will focus on the way that the framework deals with a problem that is probably as old as the personal computer: how do you provide a responsive user interface while utilizing the full computational resources available? And how can you do so in a manner that makes code readable and easy to manage/maintain?

Introducing Reactive Programming

Rx.NET aims to revolutionize reactive programming in the .NET framework. In reactive programming, you register an interest in something and have items of interest handed over, or pushed to the attention of the application, asynchronously, as they become available. A classic example an application that relies heavily on the reactive programming model is the spreadsheet, where an update to a single cell triggers cascading updates to every cell that references it. This concept of having things pushed down as they become available is particularly well suited to applications that use constantly changing data sources, such as the weather application that you will be building later on in this chapter.

Reactive programming is often contrasted with interactive programming, where the user asks for something and then waits for it until it is delivered. To help further differentiate these concepts, let's take a look at a car shopping analogy. Usually, when shopping for a car, you go to a car dealership (or look online) and look at different car makes and models. You pick the ones you like and test-drive them. This arrangement is an example of interactive programming, where you asked for a car and got it in return. In a reactive approach, you would send a note to a dealership expressing interest in a certain make and model and then continue going on with your daily routine. The dealer locates items of interest and notifies you when they become available.

Let's see if we can carry over this analogy to event processing on Windows Phone 7. For the sample application that you will be building later in this chapter, you will want to read the contents of a text box once it can be determined that no keystroke has occurred a half a second since the previous one. In the sample, this will be taken to mean that the user has finished typing and is ready for the application to do something. If you were to use an interactive approach, you would implement this by wiring up the KeyDown event for the text box, and then checking some sort of timer to see whether enough time had elapsed between keystrokes. In a reactive approach, as you will see shortly, things are much simpler: you express interest in being notified of KeyDown events only after a half-second has elapsed between a user's keystrokes. Once notified of such an event, you take action—searching for photos online, in this case. Before you learn how to search for photos in a reactive manner, however, you will walk through several short examples to get a feeling for how Reactive Extensions implement the core Observer pattern, which forms the basis of the Reactive Framework and is described in detail in the following sidebar.

THE OBSERVER PATTERN

The Observer pattern is a commonly used technique (pattern) in the world of object-oriented software development. At its basis, it has a Subject object that keeps track of all the objects (referred to as Observers) that want to be notified about changes to the Subject's state. All Observers are automatically notified of any changes to the Subject. The power of this pattern comes from not having to query the Subject for specific changes to its state—the Subject will promptly let Observers know when it gets modified. For detailed description of the Observer pattern, you can refer to "Design Patterns" by Gamma et al. or you can read about it on Wikipedia at http://en.wikipedia.org/wiki/Observer_pattern.

According to Microsoft DevLabs, where the Reactive Extensions library was developed, the objective of Rx.NET is to enable the composition of asynchronous and event-driven programs. Rx.NET uses **observable collections** to enable such composition. In Rx.NET, Observable collections perform the role of the Subject in the Observer pattern. Observable collections gather data associated with a given event or an asynchronous method call and notify everyone who has subscribed to these collections of the changes as they occur. This might sound a bit confusing, so let's jump into code that will allow you to start using key features of Rx.NET right away to build awesome Windows Phone 7 applications.

Implementing the Observer Pattern with Rx.NET

Before you create an application that asynchronously searches photos on Flickr, we will take a short detour to understand the basics of Rx.NET. In the project that follows, you will generate a simple Observable collection using Reactive Extensions for .NET and read values from this collection as they are pushed down to us. Follow these step-by-step instructions.

Creating a Windows Phone Project

First, you will create a new Windows Phone 7 project and add framework elements necessary to make it work on the mobile platform.

1. Launch Visual Studio 2010 Express for Windows Phone and create a new Windows Phone Application project. Name it "RxSample."

In this project, you will observe the messages generated by the Reactive Extensions framework in the text box on the phone screen.

2. From the Toolbox, select the textblock and drop it on the design surface. Since you are just getting your feet wet with Rx.NET, leave the name of the textblock (textBlock1) unchanged for now and adjust its width and width to occupy the full area of the screen. Highlight the textblock, press F4 to bring up its Properties window, and set the TextWrapping property to "Wrap."

On Windows Phone 7, the Rx.Net implementation is contained within two separate assemblies–Microsoft.Phone.Reactive and System.Observable.

3. Add a Reference to Microsoft.Phone.Reactive and System.Observable assemblies, by right-clicking and selecting Add Reference.

Adding Code to Create and Read Observable Collections

You will now add code to create an Observable collection, subscribe to it, and read values from it.

1. Import the Rx.NET libraries to current code. To do that, open MainPage.xaml.cs (right-click MainPage.xaml and select View Code) and add the following statement to the top of the page:

    ```
    using Microsoft.Phone.Reactive;
    ```

Remember how an Observable collection performs the role of the Subject in the Observer pattern. In Rx.NET, the IObservable<T> interface acts as that Subject. You will now create an Observable collection that will consist of a range of integer values.

2. In the MainPage() constructor, add the following code right after the InitializeComponent() statement:

    ```
    IObservable<int> source = Observable.Range(5, 3);
    ```

Notice the use of the Observable.Range method to create an Observable collection that will consist of a range of integers from 5 to 7 inclusive.

You will now create an Observer for the source Subject created in Step 2. This Observer object will be notified of any changes to the source—in this case, every time a new integer is generated, or "pushed down" to the application.

3. Add the following code to create the Observer:

```
IDisposable subscription = source.Subscribe(x =>
        textBlock1.Text += String.Format(" OnNext: {0}", x),
        ex => textBlock1.Text += String.Format(" OnError: {0}", ex.Message),
        () => textBlock1.Text += " OnCompleted");
```

The Subscribe method of IObservable<T> has several overloads; the one that you just used accepts three **lambda expressions** (see sidebar, "Lambda Expressions") as its parameters: the first lamda expression contains the logic to invoke when another element becomes available to the Observer (OnNext), the second has logic to invoke if there is an exception in the Observer (OnError), and the last one contains logic that gets executed when the Subject completes its useful life (OnComplete). The "completion of useful life" condition varies from Subject to Subject, but generally means that there are no more elements to receive from the Subject. If you are not familiar with lamda expressions, the sidebar contains a brief introduction to this newer feature of the .NET framework.

4. Finally, tell the Observer to discontinue its interest in the Subject's state by issuing a Dispose() method:

```
subscription.Dispose();
```

5. Press F5 to run the application. The Windows Phone 7 emulator screen will appear, showing messages "OnNext: 5," "OnNext: 6," OnNext: 7," and "OnComplete," as shown in Figure 18–1. The Observable object generated three integer values, pushed them down to Observers, and called it quits.

LAMBDA EXPRESSIONS

With the release of C# 3.0, Microsoft borrowed a number of features from the so-called family of functional programming languages. Among these features is the ability to define functions inline known to C# programmers by the intimidating term "lambda expression." At a basic level, lambda expressions are simply functions that differ from "normal" C# functions in their syntax. In our example, x =>textBlock1.Text += String.Format(" OnNext: {0}", x) is a lambda expression that defines a function that accepts x as a parameter and infers its type from context. The textBlock1.Text += String.Format(" OnNext: {0}", x) statement is the body of the function. Note that the ()=> syntax specifies that no parameters are passed in to the lambda expression, as you saw with the last parameter to the Subscribe function.

Figure 18–1. *Reactive Extensions for .NET first steps*

In the foregoing code, notice how subscription does not implement the IObserver<T> interface. That is because the Microsoft.Phone.Reactive assembly contains a set of extension methods that overload the Subscribe() method of IObservable. These overloaded methods accept OnNext, OnError, and OnCompleted handlers defined by the IObserver<T> interface as lambda expressions, just as described in the previous paragraphs. Hence, in our experiments and samples with Rx.NET in this chapter, you will not have to physically implement the IObserver<T> interface.

The output of your first Rx.NET application shown in Figure 18–1 is certainly nothing spectacular. But we are just barely touching the Rx.NET surface there. Imagine subscribing to events, such as keystrokes or data emitted by the location service. Then, imagine having the ability to react to those events only if certain conditions are met. For instance, filter out location values so that only when the location specifies a certain predefined area, the event is raised. In the next section, you will build a small application that uses this approach to make an asynchronous web service call to Flickr once the user has stopped typing text for half a second.

Using Rx.NET Event Handling to Search for Flickr Photographs

In this section, you will build an application that searches Flickr photos asynchronously using Rx.NET. In particular, you will learn how to create Observable data sources from events, as well as how to subscribe to them. The version of Flickr search you'll create is shown in Figure 18–2. The search technique is basic and uses a WebBrowser control to display images; however, this walkthrough will allow you to concentrate on learning the Rx.NET techniques for processing events on the Windows Phone 7. In the next walkthrough, you will build a Weather Service application that will demonstrate asynchronous programming with Rx.NET. Let's get started.

Creating a Windows Phone Project

First, create a new Windows Phone 7 project for the Flickr image search.

1. Launch Visual Studio 2010 Express for Windows Phone and create a new Windows Phone Application project. Name it "FlickrRx."

2. Change the name of the application to "Flickr Search," and change the page title to "Rx at Work" (to accomplish that, highlight the application name, press F4, edit the Text property, and then do the same for the page title).

3. Add a reference (by right-clicking and selecting Add Reference) to `Microsoft.Phone.Reactive` and `System.Observable` assemblies.

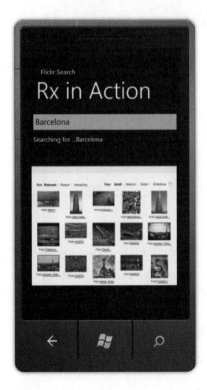

Figure 18–2. Flickr image search with Rx.NET

Adding a User Interface

Now, add some user interface elements to the project. The user interface will consist of a text box, a label, and a WebBrowser control, as shown in Figure 18–3.

1. From the Toolbox, select a text box and drop it on the design surface. Rename the text box to "txtSearchTerms." Make the width of the text box equal the width of the screen and clear the Text property. Next, select a textblock, drop it underneath the text box, rename it "lblSearchingFor," and resize it to be the width of the screen.

2. From the Toolbox, select the WebBrowser control and drop it on the design surface underneath the textblock. Rename the WebBrowser control "webResults" and make it the width of the screen.

You should now have something similar to Figure 18–3.

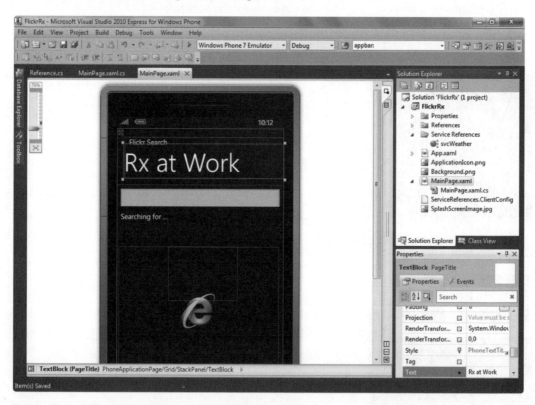

Figure 18–3. Flickr image search using Rx.NET screen layout

Adding Logic to Search Flickr for Images

The next step is to add logic to populate the WebBrowser controls with the results of a Flickr image search.

3. Open `MainPage.xaml.cs` (right-click `MainPage.xaml` and select View Code) and paste the following using statement at the top of the page:

```
using Microsoft.Phone.Reactive;
```

Now, write code to capture the `KeyUp` events of the text box.

4. Paste the following code immediately following the `InitializeComponent()` statement in the `MainPage()` constructor:

```
var keys = Observable.FromEvent<KeyEventArgs>(txtSearchTerms, "KeyUp");

keys.Subscribe(evt =>
{
  lblSearchingFor.Text = "Searching for ..." + txtSearchTerms.Text;
  webResults.Navigate(new Uri("http://www.flickr.com/search/?q="
  + txtSearchTerms.Text));
});
```

The first statement creates an `Observable` data source, keys that will consist of all `KeyUp` events of the `txtSearchTerms` text box. The second statement is a lambda expression that creates an Observer on this collection and attempts to update the `lblSearchingFor` textblock with the text entered into the text box, as well as show the web page representing the results of searching Flickr with the text supplied in the text box. Note the "{" symbol within the lambda expression—that symbol is used to define a lambda expression whose body has more than one statement within it, just as you do in the previous example.

5. Press F5 to run the application. As you type the first character, you should see the WebBrowser control attempting to navigate to the Flickr search page specifying the only character entered as its search criteria. Notice how there is very little visual indication that there's some search or navigation performed behind the scenes. You will improve on that in the sections that follow, where you will create an animation to play while the WebBrowser control is loading with the results of an image search.

Enhancing a Flickr Search with Throttling

At this point, you must certainly be wondering what Rx.NET has added to your toolbox besides the complexities of the Observer pattern. Couldn't you do pretty much everything you have done so far using the standard event handling procedures available to Microsoft developers since the earliest days of Visual Basic (before there ever was VB.NET, that is)? The answer is: Rx.NET has added nothing up until now, and yes, you could have done everything with VB. The power of Reactive Extensions for .NET starts to come through in the next few steps of the walkthrough.

First, modify the application as follows:

1. Change the code line declaring an Observable collection above from

    ```
    var keys = Observable.FromEvent<KeyEventArgs>(txtSearchTerms, "KeyUp");
    ```

    to

    ```
    var keys = Observable.FromEvent<KeyEventArgs>(txtSearchTerms,
                          "KeyUp").Throttle(TimeSpan.FromSeconds(.5));
    ```

2. Change the code block declaring an `Observer` from

    ```
    keys.Subscribe(evt =>
    ```

```
        {
                lblSearchingFor.Text = "Searching for ..." + txtSearchTerms.Text;
webResults.Navigate(new Uri("http://www.flickr.com/search/?q="
+ txtSearchTerms.Text));
        });
```

to

keys.**ObserveOn(Deployment.Current.Dispatcher)**.Subscribe(evt =>

```
        {
                if (txtSearchTerms.Text.Length>0)
                {
                    lblSearchingFor.Text = "Searching for ..." + txtSearchTerms.Text;
                    webResults.Navigate(new Uri("http://www.flickr.com/search/?q=" +
txtSearchTerms.Text));
                }
        });
```

3. Press F5 to run the application. Click the text box and enter the search terms for photo lookup in Flickr, for example, "Barcelona," and watch the WebBrowser control retrieve the images of that beautiful European city from Flickr.

Let's examine the code that you added in the last section. You created an observable collection that consists of all of the KeyUp events generated on txtSearchTerms text box. When you added the Throttle(.5) statement, you effectively told Rx.NET that you wanted to observe only KeyUp events that occur more than half a second apart (0.5 seconds). Let's assume that an average user will be pressing the keys on the keyboard less than half a second apart, and when there is a half-a-second pause between key presses, that should tell the application that the user is ready to "observe" the data source.

In Step 2, you enhanced the application in two ways. First, you added logic not to invoke image search if nothing is entered in the text box (this could happen if the user erased the content with the Backspace key). Second, notice the ObserveOn(Deployment.Current.Dispatcher) construct that was used to help create an Observer. To understand its raison d'être (reason for being) and to allow you to peek under the hood of Rx.NET, let's remove it. As a result, your code for Step 2 will look like the following snippet:

```
keys.Subscribe(evt =>
        {
                if (txtSearchTerms.Text.Length > 0)
                {
                    lblSearchingFor.Text = "Searching for ..." + txtSearchTerms.Text;
                    webResults.Navigate(new Uri("http://www.flickr.com/search/?q=" +
txtSearchTerms.Text));
                }
        });
```

4. Press F5 to run the application now, and you will see the screen shown in Figure 18–4, where Visual Studio displays an "Invalid cross-thread access" message.

What is happening there, as readers familiar with programming User Interface (UI) on the .NET platform know, is that updating UI from a thread other than a UI thread is a tricky undertaking. Under the hood, Reactive Extensions for .NET has created a separate background thread and will be pushing notifications of changes from the Observable data source to the Observers from that thread. This background thread cannot modify the UI thread directly.

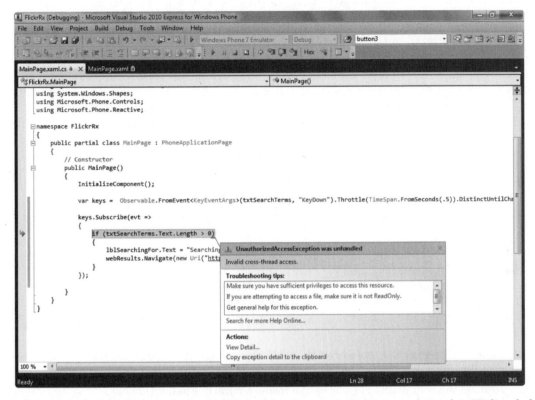

Figure 18–4. *An invalid cross-access thread exception is generated when trying to update UI directly from the background thread.*

Fortunately, the creators of Rx.NET have provided a solution to this problem by providing the `ObserveOn()` extension method in the `Microsoft.Phone.Reactive` assembly. This extension method has several overloads, and one of them accepts a `Dispatcher` object. In the .NET Framework, a `Dispatcher` object maintains a prioritized queue of work items on a specific thread, and here it provides a way for you to observe an `Observable` data source on the UI thread. In the preceding example, you pass the `Deployment.Current.Dispatcher` property to the `ObserveOn()` method to get thread-safe access to the current Dispatcher and use it to update visual elements on the phone. The use of a single `ObserveOn()` method is significantly easier than dealing with the Dispatcher's `Invoke` method, which is a common way to update UI in multi-threaded Silverlight and WPF applications.

Adding an Animation that Plays as Flickr Images Load

You can further enhance the Flickr image search application by adding a simple animation that will play while the web pages with the results of your image search are loading. To do that, you will create a simple animation in Expression Blend for Windows Phone, subscribe to the Navigated event of the WebBrowser control, and play the animation in code.

Follow these steps to add this feature to your project.

1. Still in Visual Studio for Windows Phone, add a textblock to the phone's design surface and place it between the "Searching for..." textblock and the WebBrowser control. Name that textblock lblLoading, set the caption to "Loading Images," and set its Visibility property to Collapsed.

Microsoft Expression Blend for Windows Phone is a powerful application for creating and editing graphics and animations for Windows Phone 7 devices. You have used it in the first part of this book to style controls and for other graphical tasks.

2. To launch Expression Blend and load it with the Flickr project, right-click MainPage.xaml in Visual Studio and select Open in Expression Blend. Microsoft Expression Blend launches with your solution open and ready to edit.

Your animation will be a progress bar in the form of a rectangle that will grow in width as the time passes. This animation will loop indefinitely, so that when it reaches maximum allowable size, the rectangle will go back to its beginning and the animation will be repeated.

3. In Expression Blend, select a Rectangle from the Toolbox, draw a very narrow, almost invisible rectangle right next to the "Loading Images" textblock, and set its Fill color to red.

Now, you will create what is called a timeline animation in Expression Blend. Timeline animations are created with the use of the storyboards, so you will create a new storyboard in this step.

4. In the Objects and Timeline window, click the "New" button (shown in Figure 18–5), name the storyboard loadingImages, and click OK.

The Objects and Timeline panel will now change to display a timeline, and Blend is ready to record your animation.

5. Select the rectangle that you placed on the Windows Phone design surface and click the "Record Keyframe" button, as shown in Figure 18–6.

6. Next, move the Animation Playhead (the yellow vertical line in the Timeline) to about 1.5 seconds, as shown in Figure 18–7. Click the "Record Keyframe" button again, and then resize the rectangle to be close to the full phone screen width.

Now you will now set the animation to loop as long as it is active.

7. In Objects and Timeline, click and select the loadingImages storyboard name. Common Properties for the Storyboard dialog appears. Select "Forever" in the Repeat Behavior property of this storyboard.

With the animation now complete, you are ready to show it when the user performs a search for Flickr images.

Figure 18–5. Creating a new storyboard animation in Expression Blend

8. Save everything in Expression Blend (File ➤ Save All) and switch back to Visual Studio.

Now what you will do is add code to first show the animation when the search for images is initiated, and then stop the animation once that search is complete.

To start the animation you have just created once the user initiates search for Flickr images, you will call the Begin method of the loadingImages animation.

In MainPage.xaml.cs, change the code that creates an Observer for the KeyUp event to the following:

```
keys.ObserveOn(Deployment.Current.Dispatcher).Subscribe(evt =>
{
    if (txtSearchTerms.Text.Length > 0)
    {
        lblSearchingFor.Text = "Searching for ..." + txtSearchTerms.Text;
        lblLoading.Visibility=System.Windows.Visibility.Visible;
        loadingImages.Begin();

webResults.Navigate(new Uri("http://www.flickr.com/search/?q=" +
txtSearchTerms.Text));
    }
});
```

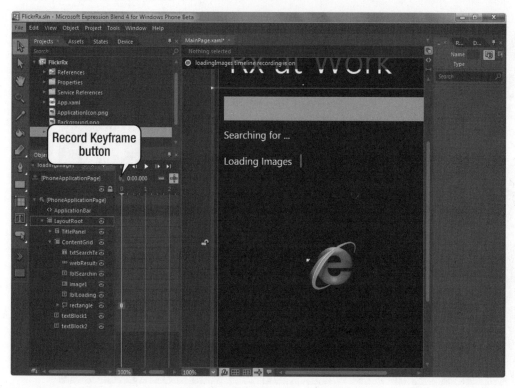

Figure 18–6. *Beginning of the "Loading Images" timeline animation*

Once the images load in the WebBrowser control, you will stop the animation by calling the Stop method of the loadingImages animation. To accomplish this, you will use Rx.NET to subscribe to the web browser's Navigated event. Once this subscription receives data, you will stop the animation. The following code accomplishes these tasks.

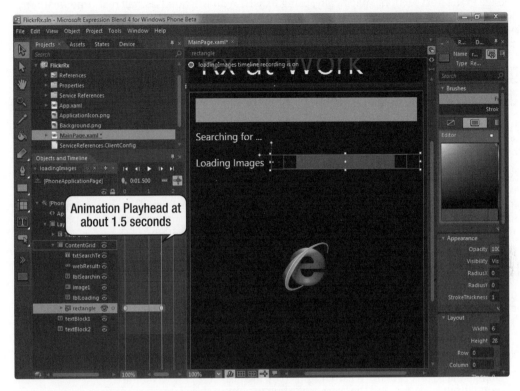

Figure 18–7. *End of the "Loading Images" timeline animation*

9. Paste the following code at the end of the `MainPage` constructor.

```
var browser =
Observable.FromEvent<System.Windows.Navigation.NavigationEventArgs>(webResults, "Navigated");

        browser.ObserveOn(Deployment.Current.Dispatcher).Subscribe(evt =>
        {
                loadingImages.Stop();
lblLoading.Visibility = System.Windows.Visibility.Collapsed;
        });
```

You are now ready to run the application.

10. Press F5, type a keyword into the text box, and observe the animation while the images are being loaded into the browser.

While we have only scratched the surface of Rx.NET and its applications, you can already see how powerful this framework is. Using Rx.NET, you can think of virtually any event as an observable data source, whether it's a location service that generates coordinate values (which you can think of as an observable set of position values) or accelerometer data, or key press events, or web browser events, such as those already demonstrated. Now that you have seen how to create `Observable` data sources from events using the `FromEvent<T>` keyword and how to subscribe to those events, we will expand upon this knowledge in the next section. Specifically, using Rx.NET, you will build a small real-time weather application that will use a publicly available web service to asynchronously retrieve current weather and show a small picture representing current weather for the zip code provided.

Using Rx.NET with Web Services to Asynchronously Retrieve Weather Data

In this section, you will use a publicly available weather web service located at www.webservicex.net/WCF/Default.aspx to retrieve and display current weather for a given zip code within the United States. In addition to weather services, there are many other useful web services available at this location, including zip code validation and currency conversion. As an exercise in the usage of Rx.NET, you are encouraged to build useful, functional applications that take advantage of these services.

From the development point of view, the weather application will consist of (1) asynchronously capturing user input—zip code, and (2) asynchronously calling the web service and then displaying the current weather for a given zip code. Let's go ahead and create the application.

Creating a Windows Phone Project

First, you will create a new project, import all of the libraries and create service references necessary to make the weather application work.

1. Launch Visual Studio 2010 Express for Windows Phone and create a new Windows Phone Application project. Name it "WeatherRx."

2. In MainPage.xaml, change the name of the application to "WeatherRx" and change the page title to "Weather App" (you are also certainly welcome to name the application and the page according to your preference).

3. Since you will be using Rx.NET to build this application, add a reference (by right-clicking and selecting Add Reference) to Microsoft.Phone.Reactive and System.Observable assemblies.

You need to add a Service Reference to the weather service already mentioned. The weather service is an .asmx web service hosted at www.webservicex.net.

4. To add a reference to this service, right-click the Project Name and select Add Service Reference. In the dialog that comes up, enter the following value in the Address Textbox: http://www.webservicex.net/WeatherForecast.asmx. Press the "Go" button.

5. The WeatherForecast service should appear on the left. Click the arrow next to it, make sure to select WeatherForecastSoap service, and then rename the namespace to "svcWeather."

6. Your final Add Service screen should look like Figure 18–8.

7. Press the OK button.

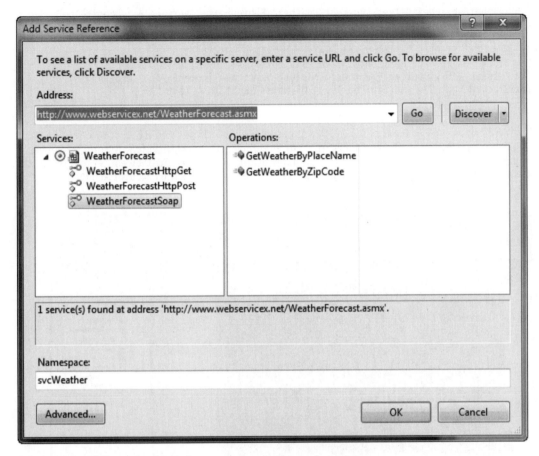

Figure 18–8. Adding a Service Reference to the weather web service

Creating a User Interface

For the application, your goal is to create a screen that looks like the one shown in Figure 18–9. To assist in that objective, the XAML for visual elements that appear after the page title is pasted here. You can also copy and paste this XAML from the sample code available in the downloads for this chapter.

1. Open `MainPage.xaml` and add the following code:

```
<!--ContentPanel - place additional content here-->
        <Grid x:Name="ContentGrid" Grid.Row="1">
            <TextBox Height="72" HorizontalAlignment="Left" Margin="0,51,0,0"
Name="txtZipCode" Text="" VerticalAlignment="Top" Width="480" />
            <TextBlock Height="53" HorizontalAlignment="Left" Margin="6,13,0,0"
Name="lblLegend" Text="Enter Zip Code Below for Current Weather" VerticalAlignment="Top"
Width="462" />
            <TextBlock Height="30" HorizontalAlignment="Left" Margin="6,129,0,0"
```

```
Name="lblWeatherFahrenheit" Text="Current Weather, Fahrenheit " VerticalAlignment="Top"
Width="435" />
            <Image Height="150" HorizontalAlignment="Left" Margin="241,213,0,0"
Name="imgWeather" Stretch="Fill" VerticalAlignment="Top" Width="200" />
    <TextBlock Height="30" HorizontalAlignment="Left" Margin="6,162,0,0"
Name="lblCelsius" Text="Current Weather, Celsius" VerticalAlignment="Top" Width="435" />
    <TextBlock Height="30" Margin="6,379,39,0" Name="lblStatus" Text=""
VerticalAlignment="Top" />
        </Grid>
    </Grid>
```

Notice that in addition to the textblocks that will hold the current weather information, the XAML also creates an image control that will show a visual representation of the current weather (e.g., sunny, raining, snowing, etc.). Notice also that the last </Grid> statement closes the LayoutGrid element, not shown in the preceding fragment.

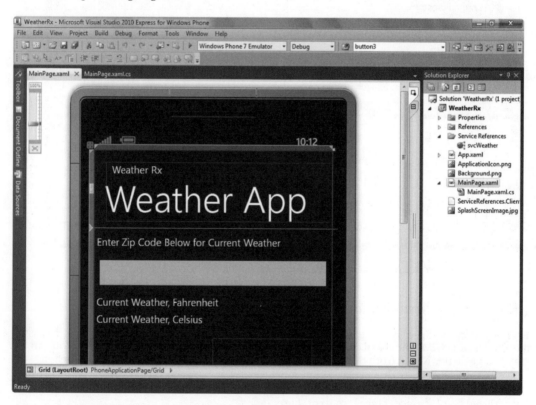

Figure 18–9. WeatherRx design layout

Adding Logic to Get Weather Information

With design elements and proper references in place, you are ready to add code to the application. In this walkthrough, you will split the code into multiple functions for enhanced readability.

1. Open `MainPage.xaml.cs` (by clicking `MainPage.xaml` and selecting View Code) and add the following using statements to the top of the page:

```
using Microsoft.Phone.Reactive;
using System.Windows.Media.Imaging;
```

2. Add the following code after the `InitializeComponent()` statement of the `MainPage()` constructor:

```
WireUpWeatherEvents();
WireUpKeyEvents();
```

Here, you are wiring up web service events and keystroke events in separate functions, a technique that will become very useful in the subsequent sections of this chapter when you deal with error recovery.

3. Create the `WireUpWeatherEvents` function and its supporting `GetWeatherSubject` function by pasting the following code. Note how you have created a separate function (`GetWeatherSubject`) to return an `Observable` collection from the weather web service event.

```
private void WireUpWeatherEvents()
{
    var weather = GetWeatherSubject();
    weather.ObserveOn(Deployment.Current.Dispatcher).Subscribe(evt =>
    {
        if (evt.EventArgs.Result.Details != null)
        {
            lblWeatherFahrenheit.Text = "Current Weather, Fahrenheit: " +
evt.EventArgs.Result.Details[0].MinTemperatureF.ToString() + " - " +
evt.EventArgs.Result.Details[0].MaxTemperatureF.ToString();
            lblCelsius.Text = "Current Weather, Celsius: " +
evt.EventArgs.Result.Details[0].MinTemperatureC.ToString() + " - " +
evt.EventArgs.Result.Details[0].MaxTemperatureC.ToString();
            imgWeather.Source = new BitmapImage(new
Uri(evt.EventArgs.Result.Details[0].WeatherImage, UriKind.Absolute));
        }
    },
        ex => { lblStatus.Text = "Sorry, we encountered a problem: " + ex.Message; }
    );
}

private IObservable<IEvent<svcWeather.GetWeatherByZipCodeCompletedEventArgs>>
GetWeatherSubject()
{
    var weather =
Observable.FromEvent<svcWeather.GetWeatherByZipCodeCompletedEventArgs>(weatherClient,
"GetWeatherByZipCodeCompleted");
    return weather;
}
```

4. Create the `WireUpKeyEvents` function that will create an Observable collection from the KeyUp events and create subscription to that collection by adding the following code:

```
private void WireUpKeyEvents()
{
      var keys = Observable.FromEvent<KeyEventArgs>(txtZipCode,
"KeyUp").Throttle(TimeSpan.FromSeconds(1)).DistinctUntilChanged();
      keys.ObserveOn(Deployment.Current.Dispatcher).Subscribe(evt =>
      {
          if (txtZipCode.Text.Length >= 5)
          {
              weatherClient.GetWeatherByZipCodeAsync(txtZipCode.Text);
          }
      });

}
```

5. Press F5 to run the application. You should see a screen prompting you to enter the US zip code to retrieve the current weather for. If you enter your zip code, you should get a reasonable estimate of your current weather, both on the Fahrenheit and Celsius scales. You should also see a small picture with a visual representation of the current weather conditions. Figure 18–10 shows sample output for the Jacksonville, FL area (zip code of "32202").

Let's spend some more time dissecting the tools you used to build this application. First, you used Rx.NET to create an `Observable` collection from the asynchronous responses to the weather web service calls. You used the following statement to create that collection:

```
var weather =
Observable.FromEvent<svcWeather.GetWeatherByZipCodeCompletedEventArgs>(weatherClient,
"GetWeatherByZipCodeCompleted");
```

You then defined an `Observer` for this data source, so that when the data is pushed from the web service to `Observers`, you take action by displaying that data in the User Interface.

Next, you created an `Observable` collection of the KeyUp events in the `txtZipCode` text box and created an `Observer` for that collection. As a result, whenever users pause their typing for one second, the `Observer` on the keys data source will validate whether five or more digits have been entered in the Zip Code field. Then, it goes ahead and calls the function `GetWeatherByZipCodeAsync`, which in turn invokes an asynchronous request to the weather web service.

It's important to note the asynchronous nature of all these calls—if you had other functionality built into the application, you could continue using it while the asynchronous request completes. The asynchronous processing is an area that Rx.NET was specifically designed to address.

If you have done some form of asynchronous programming prior to Rx.NET, you can certainly appreciate that foregoing single code line. Prior to Rx.NET, in an asynchronous method design pattern in .NET, two methods were provided. The first method started the computation, and the second method acquired the results of the computation. If there was more than one asynchronous operation, even just the simple ones we have illustrated in the weather example, the management of those multiple methods quickly became a headache. The fact that Rx.NET also attempts to parallelize asynchronous requests across all available cores is a hefty bonus to an already generous benefits package of clarity and powerful querying of Observers.

Figure 18–10. Sample output of WeatherRx application for zip code 32202

Handling Errors in Rx.NET

In the world of asynchronous programming, and especially in the world of distributed asynchronous programming, errors are a fact of life and should be expected. Rx.NET Observers provide a separate OnError event handler to deal with unforeseen errors that may arise. For instance, to make the WeatherRx application more robust, let's add an OnError handler to the weather.Subscribe call. The resulting code would look like this:

```
weather.ObserveOn(Deployment.Current.Dispatcher).Subscribe(evt =>
        {
                if (evt.EventArgs.Result.Details != null)
                {
                    lblWeatherFahrenheit.Text = "Current Weather, Fahrenheit: " +
evt.EventArgs.Result.Details[0].MinTemperatureF.ToString() + " - " +
evt.EventArgs.Result.Details[0].MaxTemperatureF.ToString();

lblCelsius.Text = "Current Weather, Celsius: " +
evt.EventArgs.Result.Details[0].MinTemperatureC.ToString() + " - " +
evt.EventArgs.Result.Details[0].MaxTemperatureC.ToString();
```

```
imgWeather.Source = new BitmapImage(new Uri(evt.EventArgs.Result.Details[0].WeatherImage,
UriKind.Absolute));
                }
            },
    ex => {
    Deployment.Current.Dispatcher.BeginInvoke(() => lblStatus.Text = ex.Message);
            }
    );
```

Note the somewhat cryptic (it's a lamda expression and it uses a lambda expression within its own body) use of the `Deployment.Current.Dispatcher.BeginInvoke` statement to get around cross-thread access issues discussed previously. In the preceding code, the `OnError` handler simply displays the exception text, but there is nothing stopping you from dissecting an error thoroughly and providing a possible corrective action. For instance, if the web service is not available at the address specified, you may retry your call to a different location of the web service. Rx.NET also has exception handling operators `Catch`, `Finally`, `OnErrorResumeNext`, and `Retry`, which aid in recovering from errors. You will explore some of those in the next section as we discuss some potential ways of handling intermittently available data connections on the phones.

Handling Data Connection Issues with Rx.NET

On a phone, slow or lost data connections are a fact of everyday life. Ideally, phone applications should detect such connections and provide a recovery mechanism to deal with them. Two potential ways to deal with slow or lost connectivity on the phone are: (1) let the user decide whether the application should retry what it was doing before the connection timed out or lost, and (2) provide an automated retry mechanism.

Rx.NET can aid in both of those scenarios. Furthermore, Rx.NET includes a special Timeout operation that will generate a timeout error if it does not receive data, such as a web service callback, from its `Observable` within a user-specified interval. Let's take a look at the Timeout operation in action. Let's change the `WireUpWeatherEvents` function to time out if it does not get any data for two seconds:

1. Replace the `WireUpEvents()` function of the `WeatherRx` application with the following code:

```
private void WireUpWeatherEvents()
{
    var weather = GetWeatherSubject();
    weather.ObserveOn(Deployment.Current.Dispatcher)
        .Timeout(TimeSpan.FromSeconds(2))
        .Subscribe(evt =>
    {
        if (evt.EventArgs.Result.Details != null)
        {
            lblWeatherFahrenheit.Text = "Current Weather, Fahrenheit: " +
evt.EventArgs.Result.Details[0].MinTemperatureF.ToString() + " - " +
evt.EventArgs.Result.Details[0].MaxTemperatureF.ToString();
            lblCelsius.Text = "Current Weather, Celsius: " +
evt.EventArgs.Result.Details[0].MinTemperatureC.ToString() + " - " +
evt.EventArgs.Result.Details[0].MaxTemperatureC.ToString();
            imgWeather.Source = new BitmapImage(new
Uri(evt.EventArgs.Result.Details[0].WeatherImage, UriKind.Absolute));
        }
    },
```

```
        ex => {
              Deployment.Current.Dispatcher.BeginInvoke(() => lblStatus.Text =
ex.Message);
            }
        );
    }
```

Now run the application and notice how after two seconds, it immediately times out and displays the timeout exception text on the emulator. What happened? You did not even get a chance to specify the zip code to show the weather for.

Our code needs a little refactoring, or changing around. In the code so far, you subscribed to the web service's events immediately on application launch, and since you did not get any data two seconds after the launch of the application, that subscription timed out. The change that you need to make is to subscribe to the web service's events right before you invoke that web service, yet you have to be careful to create this subscription just once.

2. Remove the call to WireUpWeatherEvents from the MainPage constructor and place it within the WireUpKeyEvents function to make that function look like the following:

```
private void WireUpKeyEvents()
{
        var keys = Observable.FromEvent<KeyEventArgs>(txtZipCode,
"KeyUp").Throttle(TimeSpan.FromSeconds(1)).DistinctUntilChanged();
        keys.ObserveOn(Deployment.Current.Dispatcher).Subscribe(evt =>
        {
            if (txtZipCode.Text.Length >= 5)
            {
                WireUpWeatherEvents();
                weatherClient.GetWeatherByZipCodeAsync(txtZipCode.Text);
            }
        });

    }
```

Now the timeout feature should work properly. Notice, however, that it will most likely take slightly more than two seconds to return a valid response from the Weather service.

Rx.NET also provides a Retry method that optionally takes a parameter for the number of times to retry to re-subscribe to the Observable collection. If you don't specify that parameter, Rx.NET will try to re-subscribe to the Observable collection indefinitely. One way to deal with an absent or slow connection is to retry the subscription two or three times, and then, if unsuccessful, give the user the option to either retry once more or cancel. You will see how to give the user that option in the next section.

Revising WeatherRx to Manage Slow Data Connections

To modify the WeatherRx application, you will first add buttons to the UI to allow the user to either retry the failed connection or to exit gracefully. Then, you will add code to the application to react to the events on these new User Interface elements.

To add the new elements to the WeatherRx UI, do the following:

1. Open MainPage.xaml and add two buttons right below the lblStatus textblock, as shown in Figure 18–11. Name the first button btnRetry and set its Content property to "Retry." Name the second button btnQuit and set its Content property to "Quit." Set the Visibility of both buttons to Collapsed.

Figure 18–11. Weather application with error recovery elements

On retry, you will recreate the Observable connection to the weather web service, if it's needed, and then invoke the web service again.

2. Double-click the "Retry" button and add the following handler code to the btnRetry_Click function:

```
private void btnRetry_Click(object sender, RoutedEventArgs e)
{
    btnQuit.Visibility = System.Windows.Visibility.Collapsed;
    btnRetry.Visibility = System.Windows.Visibility.Collapsed;
    lblStatus.Text = "";

    WireUpWeatherEvents();
    weatherClient.GetWeatherByZipCodeAsync(txtZipCode.Text);
}
```

If the user selects Quit, let's simply hide the buttons and the exception text.

3. Double-click the "Quit" button and add the following code to the btnQuit_Click function:

```
private void btnQuit_Click(object sender, RoutedEventArgs e)
{
    btnQuit.Visibility = System.Windows.Visibility.Collapsed;
    btnRetry.Visibility = System.Windows.Visibility.Collapsed;
    lblStatus.Text = "";
}
```

Finally, you will need to ensure there is only one subscription to the weather web service at any given time.

4. To ensure that there's only one subscription, first declare a module level variable by adding the following statement:

```
IObservable<IEvent<GetWeatherByZipCodeCompletedEventArgs>> _weather;
```

5. Next, change the GetWeatherSubject function to the following:

```
private void GetWeatherSubject()
{
    if (_weather == null)
    {
        _weather =
Observable.FromEvent<svcWeather.GetWeatherByZipCodeCompletedEventArgs>(weatherClient,
"GetWeatherByZipCodeCompleted");
    }
}
```

6. Finally, change the WireUpWeatherEvents method to look like the following (notice how the timeout value is now set to a more reasonable five seconds as well):

```
private void WireUpWeatherEvents()
{
    GetWeatherSubject();
    _weather.ObserveOn(Deployment.Current.Dispatcher)
        .Timeout(TimeSpan.FromSeconds(5))
        .Subscribe(evt =>
        {
            if (evt.EventArgs.Result.Details != null)
            {
                lblWeatherFahrenheit.Text = "Current Weather, Fahrenheit: " +
evt.EventArgs.Result.Details[0].MinTemperatureF.ToString() + " - " +
evt.EventArgs.Result.Details[0].MaxTemperatureF.ToString();
                lblCelsius.Text = "Current Weather, Celsius: " +
evt.EventArgs.Result.Details[0].MinTemperatureC.ToString() + " - " +
evt.EventArgs.Result.Details[0].MaxTemperatureC.ToString();
                imgWeather.Source = new BitmapImage(new
Uri(evt.EventArgs.Result.Details[0].WeatherImage, UriKind.Absolute));
            }
        },
        ex =>
        {
```

```
                        Deployment.Current.Dispatcher.BeginInvoke(() => lblStatus.Text =
ex.Message);
                        Deployment.Current.Dispatcher.BeginInvoke(() =>
btnQuit.Visibility=System.Windows.Visibility.Visible);
                        Deployment.Current.Dispatcher.BeginInvoke(() => btnRetry.Visibility =
System.Windows.Visibility.Visible);
                }
            );
        }
```

This walkthrough illustrates one approach to handling connection issues on Windows Phone 7 devices: you specify a timeout period, and if you don't get a response within that period, you prompt the user to retry or to quit.

Handling Multiple Concurrent Requests with Rx.NET

So far, the weather application that you have created is sending as many requests for weather data as the user types in zip codes. When the data comes back from the weather web service, the order that this data comes back in is not guaranteed. For example, if the user first types in "32207" (Jacksonville) and then types in "10001" (New York City), the weather results for Jacksonville may come in behind New York City, yet the user would not realize that she's seeing Jacksonville's weather when New York's zip code still remains on the screen. It would be great if there were a solution that gave an application the power to cancel out all weather requests that occurred prior to the latest one, i.e., in our example, a request for Jacksonville weather is canceled as soon as request for New York City weather is made.

Rx.NET provides such a solution. There are two operators in Rx.NET—TakeUntil() and Switch—that allow for cancellation of operations that occur prior to the latest operation and are still "in-flight" so to speak, or are still pending the return values. Through the use of an elegant LINQ query, these operators tie together Observable collections, as you will see shortly. But first, there is some bad news: in the current implementation of .NET framework on Windows Phone 7, it is impossible to link the beginning of the asynchronous web service invocation to the end of that invocation. The root of the problem is the exclusion of the CreateChannel method implementation in the Windows Communication Foundation libraries on Windows Phone 7. Microsoft had to slim down and optimize .NET framework on the phone, and the loss of this method for the time being seems to be due to those optimization efforts.

Nevertheless, the technique for canceling "in-flight" requests still applies to the clients with full .NET framework installed (Windows Forms and WPF applications) and to the Silverlight platform. For the weather application, we will demonstrate the technique of canceling those requests by creating a new Observable collection for the weather service each time a user types in a new zip code. Note, however, that the Observable subscriptions that you will be creating listen for any completed weather service requests, and not the specific ones. In other words, each one of these subscriptions would process both Jacksonville and New York City weather from the example, and the order that this weather data comes in would be irrelevant. This is due to the limitation that we have discussed in the current implementation of Windows Phone 7 framework—at present, you cannot link the beginning of the web service call to the end of that service call on this platform.

To make the cancellation of operations on the Observable collections possible while those operations are "in-flight," you will change the code around to expose Observable collections to LINQ queries.

Follow these steps to make operation cancellation possible:

7. At the top of the MainPage class (right above the constructor), paste the following code to declare a module-level Observable collection for the KeyUp events of the zip code text box:

```
IObservable<IEvent<KeyEventArgs>> _keys;
```

8. Expose the `Observables` for both the `KeyUp` event of the zip code text box and for the web service callback by adding the following two methods to your code:

```
private IObservable<IEvent<GetWeatherByZipCodeCompletedEventArgs>> GetWeatherSubject()
{
        return
Observable.FromEvent<svcWeather.GetWeatherByZipCodeCompletedEventArgs>(weatherClient,
"GetWeatherByZipCodeCompleted");
}

private void GetKeys()
{
        if (_keys == null)
        {
                _keys = Observable.FromEvent<KeyEventArgs>(txtZipCode,
"KeyUp").Throttle(TimeSpan.FromSeconds(1)).DistinctUntilChanged();
        }
}
```

The magic that makes the cancellations work appears in the next code snippet. Pay particularly close attention to the LINQ query; it establishes the relationship between the `Observable` collection for the `KeyUp` events and the `Observable` collection for the web service callbacks. Note that had Windows Phone 7 framework supported what is referred to as the Asynchronous pattern for web service calls (with the use of `BeginXXX`/`EndXXX` methods), you could have established a direct relationship between key sequences and web service invocations. However, with the following code, you have only a loose or indirect relationship between those two, since each subscription listens for any and all responses from the weather web service, and not just for specific ones. Right after the LINQ statement, there is a `Switch()` operator that instructs the application to dispose of the old subscription to the weather web service once there is a new key sequence awaiting in the _keys Observable collection.

9. Add the following code to the application:

```
private void WireUpWeatherEvents()
{
        GetKeys();
        var latestWeather = (from term in _keys
                        select GetWeatherSubject()
                            .Finally(() =>
                            {
Deployment.Current.Dispatcher.BeginInvoke(() => Debug.WriteLine("Disposed of prior
subscription"));
                            })
            ).Switch();

        latestWeather.ObserveOnDispatcher()
            .Subscribe(evt =>
        {
            if (evt.EventArgs.Result != null)
            {
                lblWeatherFahrenheit.Text = "Current Weather, Fahrenheit: " +
evt.EventArgs.Result.Details[0].MinTemperatureF.ToString() + " - " +
evt.EventArgs.Result.Details[0].MaxTemperatureF.ToString();
                lblCelsius.Text = "Current Weather, Celsius: " +
evt.EventArgs.Result.Details[0].MinTemperatureC.ToString() + " - " +
evt.EventArgs.Result.Details[0].MaxTemperatureC.ToString();
```

```
                    imgWeather.Source = new BitmapImage(new
Uri(evt.EventArgs.Result.Details[0].WeatherImage, UriKind.Absolute));
                }
        },
            ex => {
                        Deployment.Current.Dispatcher.BeginInvoke(() =>lblStatus.Text =
ex.Message);
                }
        );
    }
```

Notice the .Finally statement in the code. Its purpose is to print a "Disposed of prior subscription" message into the Output windows when one Observable collection is being removed and replaced with the newer one. That occurs when there is a new event in the _keys module-level Observable collection.

Finally, you need to make some minor changes to the WireUpKeyEvents function, namely, the Observable sequence generation for the KeyUp event on the zip code has been moved into a separate GetKeys method.

10. Replace the WiredUpKeyEvents() function with the following code:

```
private void WireUpKeyEvents()
{
    GetKeys();
    _keys.ObserveOn(Deployment.Current.Dispatcher).Subscribe(evt =>
    {
        if (txtZipCode.Text.Length >= 5)
        {
            weatherClient.GetWeatherByZipCodeAsync(txtZipCode.Text);
        }
    });
}
```

You are now ready to run the application.

11. Press F5 and observe that the application behavior is virtually unchanged from the previous walkthroughs: you still type in the zip code and receive weather information for that zip code. However, behind the scenes, you will notice the messages printed in the Output window indicating that there are Observable sequences being disposed of in accordance to the new data (zip codes typed in) available in the key sequence observable collection.

Perhaps in the very near future, you will see a CreateChannel method available on the Windows Phone 7 platform. Once that happens, you could very easily enhance the foregoing walkthrough with the code linking the beginning and end of an asynchronous web service call through the Observable.FromAsyncPattern method. For right now, however, you can still take advantage of this extremely powerful feature of Rx.NET in Silverlight or on clients running the full version of .NET framework.

Summary

In this chapter, you received a general overview of Reactive Extensions for .NET and their implementation of the Observer pattern. You built three applications that demonstrated the features of Rx.NET, including event representation as Observable data sources and seamless concurrent asynchronous processing and error handling. You have also observed techniques for managing unreliable data links and the principles of cancellation of "in-flight" operations using the Rx.NET framework. As concurrent programming becomes more and more the norm, Rx.NET provides a powerful framework for asynchronous and parallel programming, including programming for the cloud. While we have touched on the subject of Rx.NET lightly, we hope that you have gained an appreciation for this technology and will take the initiative to learn (and, most importantly, practice!) Rx.NET development techniques on your own.

In the next and final chapter of this book, we will discuss how to make your Windows Phone 7 applications more secure. We will go over the common threats to mobile devices, as well as the steps you must take to protect yourself and your customers from unwanted and potentially harmful attention.

CHAPTER 19

■ ■ ■

Security

Because everything about the design and operation of Windows Phone 7 targets consumers, it is only natural that Microsoft has carefully thought through the ways to protect consumers from both intended and unintentional harm. Windows Phone 7 ships with a compelling set of built-in security features that go towards accomplishing that goal. The capabilities of the Windows Phone 7 platform allow the data to be protected both in transit and on the device. Because of the centralized application certification process, consumers gain confidence that no malicious applications are downloaded and installed on their devices. And should the phone be lost or stolen, each device comes with a free web-based tool that allows you to remotely control the phone, including locking and wiping all data on that phone.

In this chapter, you will learn how the Windows Phone Marketplace certification process acts as a gatekeeper and allows only legitimate applications to be present on the device. Then you'll look at the ways you can ensure that your Windows Phone 7 application can receive, transmit, and store sensitive data in a secure manner. Finally, you'll take a look at the free support for remote lock and wipe that Microsoft provides to protect lost or stolen Windows Phones.

We will lead you through an analysis of Windows Phone 7 security features along the following four domains: application security, network security, data security and device security. You will learn about each domain as we introduce it, and then the tools Windows Phone 7 platform has to address specific security concerns associated with each domain.

Understanding Application Security

Ideally, all Windows Phone 7 applications would come from legitimate sources and behave like good citizens. However, experience shows that many applications break those rules and that safeguards must be put in place to prevent these kinds of behavior. On the application security front, Windows Phone 7 platform includes the safeguards to verify the identity of the author of the application and sandboxes the execution of each mobile application. In the next few sections, you will explore these safeguards in detail.

Windows Phone Marketplace

The early years of Windows XP were not happy ones at Microsoft. The whole world was upset with the company for allowing its operating system to be exploited by multiple malicious programs. Even though Windows XP shipped with safeguards that could prevent those exploits, their activation was left up to the user, and that activation rarely happened. What Microsoft quickly learned from that experience was that it must take a lot of responsibility to protect its user base from both known and potential malicious attacks.

Because mobile devices contain huge amounts of personal information and by their nature are frequently lost or misplaced, application monitoring is all the more necessary. For Microsoft to assume this responsibility for Windows Phone 7 applications, it must have as much control as possible over the applications built and deployed onto its platform, while still encouraging developer creativity as much as possible. To facilitate this dual goal of being autocratic and democratic at the same time, Microsoft has created a Windows Phone Marketplace. Windows Phone Marketplace is the single online distribution point for all Windows Phone 7 applications. The objectives of Windows Phone 7 Marketplace and the way it achieves those objectives are described in the following sections.

Non-repudiation: Proof of the Integrity and Origin of Data

The first objective of Windows Phone Marketplace is to confirm the identity of an application's author. In the Internet era, attempts to claim false identity are extremely common—think about millions of e-mails processed daily that claim to come from an online bank or an African prince. In a similar fashion, without a centralized approval mechanism, any malicious Windows Phone 7 application could claim to be genuine and capture the user's personal information. In software security, the concept of *non-repudiation* refers to the guarantee that the application indeed came from the source it claims to have come from. On the Windows Phone 7 platform, the origin and safety of applications are confirmed during the application certification, a required step for all Windows Phone 7 applications. During application certification, the developer submits her application to the Windows Phone Marketplace and pays a fee, at which point Microsoft runs a series of automated and manual tests to confirm application safety and, to some extent, reliability.

Currently, no application can be loaded onto the phone without going through Windows Phone Marketplace. While there is a possibility that this policy will be revisited in the future to allow enterprise customers to bypass Windows Phone Marketplace, at the time of this writing it is only a possibility. All Windows Phone 7 developers must sign up for the marketplace and must provide legitimate proof of their identity to the marketplace before any of the applications they create are available for installation on users' phones. Once their identity is verified, application developers receive a code-signing certificate.

This digital certificate verifies that the application was created by the specified company or individual, fulfilling the concept of non-repudiation mentioned previously.

Intellectual Property Protection

Software piracy is a huge problem affecting both giants of software development like Microsoft as well as small one-person shops trying to building mobile applications. To help safeguard from piracy, Microsoft requires that a valid application license issued by the Windows Phone Marketplace be present on the Windows Phone 7 device before it allows the execution of an application. This means that even if somebody figures out how to load an application onto the device without going through Windows Phone Marketplace, the application will not run since the license key for that application will not be available.

Safe Application Behavior

The Windows Phone Marketplace application approval process includes a suite of certification tests to prohibit risky applications from being loaded onto users' phones. Risky applications may contain malware or viruses themselves, or they may contain code constructs that could allow malicious code execution.

All applications submitted to Windows Phone Marketplace will be subject to malicious software screening, which will attempt to confirm that applications are free from viruses and malware. After successful completion of those tests, additional tests are performed to confirm that an application is written using only type-safe Microsoft Intermediate Language (MSIL) code. Writing applications in MSIL avoids "public enemy #1," as software buffer overruns were called in the book *Writing Secure Code*, by Michael Howard and David LeBlanc. In addition, an application must not implement any security-critical code, since Windows Phone Application Platform does not allow an application to run security-critical code. You will revisit MSIL and security-critical code on mobile devices at the end of this chapter.

To get a better idea of how the Windows Phone Marketplace submission process helps improve the security of a user's device, let's walk through the steps involved in submitting an application to the marketplace.

Submitting an Application to Windows Phone Marketplace

In this walkthrough, you will prepare a package for your application to submit to Windows Phone Marketplace and learn about the steps involved in successfully publishing an application to the marketplace, beginning with the creation of an XAP file. Let's get started.

Generating an XAP Submission File

The submission file that Windows Phone Marketplace requires is an XAP file that gets generated when the Windows Phone 7 application is built. An XAP file is a zip file containing all elements an application needs to run. To generate an XAP file, you must first build your application, as described in the following steps.

1. Open your Windows Phone 7 application project inside Visual Studio Express for Windows Phone.

2. Set the Solution Configuration option to "Release" if it presently isn't, as shown in Figure 19–1.

3. In Solution Explorer, right-click the name of the solution and select "Build." At this point, if the build succeeds, Visual Studio creates the `ProjectName.xap` file, where `ProjectName` is the name of your solution.

4. Locate the `SolutionName.xap` file you created in Step 3. Open Windows Explorer and navigate to the project's directory and the `bin/Release/` folder. You should find there a file named `ProjectName.xap`. This is the file that you will upload to the marketplace.

The next step is to log in to Windows Phone Marketplace and submit the XAP file you just created.

Uploading the XAP File to Marketplace

Before uploading files to Windows Phone Marketplace, you must create Windows Phone Marketplace login credentials at `http://developer.windowsphone.com/`. To do that, once you open the Marketplace web site, click the "Register for the Marketplace" link and follow the step-by-step wizard to create your username and password for the Marketplace. With login credentials created, follow the following step-by-step guide to submit your application to the marketplace.

1. Login to Windows Phone Marketplace (`http://developer.windowsphone.com/`) and create a new application submission.

2. When prompted, locate the XAP file that you created in the previous section (remember, it's in the `bin/Release/` folder of the project's directory) and follow instructions to upload it to the Marketplace.

3. Enter a description for your application, select its category and upload an icon for it.

4. Next, choose the countries that you would like your application to be available in and set the pricing.

5. While you are busy entering application details (description, category, pricing), Marketplace is at work validating the XAP file. This is the step that confirms that the XAP file is valid and can be passed on for further testing of its reliability and security.

   - If basic XAP file validation fails, you will get a failure notification and will have to start the process over.

   - If validation succeeds, you will be presented with a screen that lets you make your application available to customers right away or wait until you decide to publish.

6. The automated process within Windows Phone Marketplace opens up the submitted XAP file and updates the application manifest file (WMAppManifest.xml) with a unique product identifier and which hub (for example, Media + Video hub) this application belongs to. In addition, the header file called WMAppPRHeader.xml is created, and it will be used to protect digital rights to your application. Finally, an additional update to the application manifest file listing all of the security capabilities of an application is performed and the application is repackaged into a new XAP file. This new XAP file is then deployed to the actual Windows Phone 7 device at the Marketplace for certification testing.

Figure 19–1. Before deploying your application, make sure to set Solution Configuration to Release.

Certification testing consists of both manual and automated verification that the application complies with the rules set by Microsoft regarding content, security, performance, and reliability of Windows Phone 7 applications. If an application violates any of these provisions, it is not published and you get a failure report with details of the problem-causing behavior.

If the application successfully passes certification tests, the XAP file is signed and becomes available for installation from the Windows Phone Marketplace according to the option you selected in Step 6.

■ **Note** When you update your application, you will have to go through the same certification steps as the original application.

Sandboxed Execution and the Execution Manager

"Sandboxed Execution" refers to the concept that each application runs in its own environment, or sandbox, and that it has no access to applications running in different sandboxes on the same device. Applications running on the same Windows Phone 7 device are isolated from each other and must communicate with services provided by the Windows Phone 7 platform by using a well-defined standard mechanism. System files and resources are shielded from user applications. To store and retrieve application and configuration data, applications must use Isolated Storage, which is designed to be protected from access by any application other than the currently running one. For in-depth information on working with Isolated Storage, please refer to Chapter 13.

To further ensure security and responsiveness of the Windows Phone 7 platform, Microsoft has built in separate provisions to make it even more secure. These provisions include the use of the Execution Manager, as well as granting only the rights an application absolutely requires to function.

The Execution Manager monitors application resource usage in accordance with certain defined conventions. For instance, the Execution Manager may terminate an application in the background if it deems that an application in the foreground is not very responsive. Similarly, the Execution Manager may dismiss an application if it makes an excessive number of requests for phone resources.

The Windows Phone Application Platform also tries to minimize the number of privileges granted to an application. For instance, if an application does not require the use of the location services library, Windows Phone will create a custom execution environment for the application that does not include the rights to that library. This way, the number of potential exploits against the application is minimized.

Implementing Network Security

If your application accesses sensitive data over the network, it is critical that this data is encrypted during transit from the remote location to the Windows Phone 7 device. Similarly, if your application requires authentication, it is important to implement a secure authentication mechanism within your application. Windows Phone 7 platform allows you to accomplish both of these objectives. Any time you have to transmit sensitive data from a remote location, you should use Secure Sockets Layer (SSL) protocol, an industry standard for encrypting data. And if your environment requires secure authentication, it is possible to use digital certificates on a Windows Phone 7 device for that authentication, eliminating the need for user names and passwords.

In the next sections, you will walk through establishing SSL connections and configuring a certificate for secure authentication on a Windows Phone 7 device.

Securing Connections with SSL

Secure Sockets Layer protocol is a sophisticated way of securing connections between the client (Windows Phone 7 device) and cloud service, and it utilizes the concepts of asymmetric cryptography and certification authority (CA) hierarchies. When a Windows Phone 7 device initiates a secure connection to the remote service, it requests that service's certificate. That certificate is checked and the certification authority that issued that certificate is determined. Once the CA of the certificate is known, Windows Phone 7 client then checks its own installed list of certification authorities. If it finds a certification authority in its list, that implies that a trust relationship between the Windows Phone 7 device and the CA has been previously established, and that a secure connection between the phone and the remote server can be created.

Windows Phone 7 devices come with several certification authorities pre-installed. This means that, most of the time, establishing an SSL connection will be a seamless experience. As long as the remote service obtained its certificate from a very well-known certification authority (such as VeriSign, for example), SSL connections can be created both from Internet Explorer on the phone, as well as from application code. The following walkthrough demonstrates how to test if you can establish a secure connection to the remote server (PayPal) that has a certificate issued by a well-known CA (VeriSign).

Testing and Opening an SSL Connection

In this brief walkthrough, you will test if you can establish a secure connection to a remote server (PayPal), and then you will write a small Windows Phone 7 application that programmatically loads secure content from the PayPal web site.

1. The quickest way to test whether a connection to a secure web site can be established is to open up Internet Explorer on Windows Phone 7 Emulator or a Windows Phone 7 device and type the URL of a secure remote server. Launch Windows Phone 7 Emulator by clicking Start ➤ All Programs ➤ Windows Phone Developer Tools ➤ Windows Phone 7 Emulator. Once the emulator loads, click the Internet Explorer icon and type in "`https://www.paypal.com`" to go to the secure PayPal site. You should see the main screen of the PayPal web site.

■ **Tip** It may get quite tiresome having to click all of the keyboard buttons on the emulator. To enable the use of computer keyboard in the emulator window, you can press the PgUp key once the emulator loads up. To discontinue using the keyboard in the emulator, press the PgDn key.

---

2. Now, you will create a small Windows Phone 7 application that will access the PayPal site via a secure connection. You could access any secure remote service in a similar manner, but only if that service has a certificate issued by a CA that Windows Phone 7 device trusts. In the next section of this chapter, you will go through creating, exporting, and installing the self-signed certificates, which is a bit more complicated.

3. As usual, launch Visual Studio 2010 Express for Windows Phone and create a new Windows Phone 7 Application project. Name that project `SSLConnection` and click OK. `MainPage.xaml` is presented in the Designer.

4. From the toolbox, drag and drop the WebBrowser control onto the design surface. Make the width and height of that control to be the full width and height of available design surface on MainPage.xaml.

5. Switch to code view (right-click MainPage.xaml and select View Code) and add the following code to the MainPage() constructor. This code will create a WebClient object, register the callback function for that object (you will write in in the next section), and create a request to retrieve the contents of paypal.com securely.

```
WebClient client = new WebClient();
client.OpenReadCompleted += new
OpenReadCompletedEventHandler(HandleResponse);
client.OpenReadAsync(new Uri("https://www.paypal.com"));
```

6. Write the HandleResponse callback function for the request. This function will display the contents of whatever was returned as a result of the previous request to https://www.paypal.com.

```
void HandleResponse(object sender, OpenReadCompletedEventArgs e)
{
    StreamReader reader = new StreamReader(e.Result);
    string res = reader.ReadToEnd();
    webBrowser1.NavigateToString(res);
}
```

7. Press F5 to run the application. You should see the PayPal page displayed in the web browser window.

As you can see from the previous example, establishing a secure connection to the remote service is fairly straightforward if a remote service has a certificate issued by a major CA with whom Windows Phone 7 has an existing trust relationship. Just remember to use Apress Standard Book Blank.doc instead of Apress Standard Book Blank.doc when accessing a remote web service securely. But certificates issued by a major certification authority can be expensive, and may not be necessary if all users of remote service trust that the service is legitimate. In addition, you may want to experiment or test your secure service without spending a lot of money on the certificates. Self-signed SSL certificates offer the same degree of data protection in transit (data is encrypted using SSL), without the expense of using the certification authority. There is a slight administrative overhead in issuing and installing those certificates, but you will easily tackle it in a few steps in the next walkthrough.

There are three steps to enabling the use of self-signed certificates on Windows Phone 7 device: first, you have to create a self-signed certificate; second, you have to export that certificate for installation on the mobile device; and third, you have to install that certificate on the Windows Phone 7 device. Creating and exporting the self-signed certificate steps occur on the server where the secure service resides. Installing the certificate, of course, happens on each device that will need to establish a secure connection to the service using a self-signed certificate.

Creating a Self-Signed Certificate

Internet Information Services (IIS) is the web server software written by Microsoft. IIS has evolved significantly over the years, and the most current version in production as of this writing is IIS version 7. With IIS 7, creating self-signed certificates and enabling SSL using those certificates is much easier than with previous versions of IIS. IIS 7 comes with Windows 7 by default, and the following walkthrough assumes that you are using IIS7 installed on a Windows 7 machine. The walkthrough also assumes that both the server and the Windows Phone 7 client (the emulator) reside on the same machine.

1. Open IIS Manager by clicking Start ➤ Control Panel ➤ Administrative Tools ➤ Internet Information Services (IIS) Manager.

2. Create a new web site by right-clicking the Sites node on the left and choosing "Add Web Site." Name the site "WP7Server" and fill in the rest of the web site properties as shown in Figure 19–2.

■ **Note** The physical path on your computer may certainly be something else, but be sure to make the Port setting something other than the default "80," otherwise IIS might complain that port 80 is already taken.

Figure 19–2. IIS 7 new web site properties dialog

Next, you will issue a self-signed certificate.

3. Click the root machine node on the left, and then click the Server Certificates node, as shown in Figure 19–3. This should bring up a dialog listing all of the certificates currently registered on the machine.

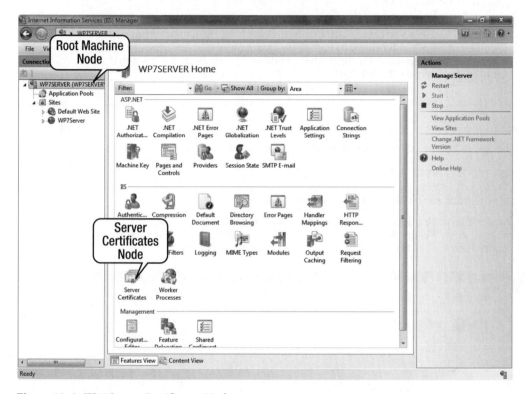

Figure 19–3. *IIS 7 Server Certificates Node*

4. Click the "Create Self-Signed Certificate" link on the right-hand side of the dialog. Then, specify a name for that certificate when prompted—for example, "wp7cert."

Next, you will enable SSL on the web site by creating a binding of that web site to the https protocol.

5. In the list of sites, click the "WP7Server" and then click "Bindings" on the right-hand side, as illustrated in Figure 19–4.

6. To create an HTTPS binding for the site, so that traffic to and from the site can be encrypted using SSL, click "Add Binding." When the dialog shown in Figure 19–5 comes up, select https type binding and select the "wp7cert" certificate from the certificates list. This certificate will be used to encrypt traffic between the web site and your Windows Phone 7 client application.

Finally, you need to create some content to browse to on the secure web site. In the real world, this would most likely be the service returning some sort of sensitive data, such as financial information. However, for this walkthrough, you will simply create an HTML file and save it onto the server.

421

7. Open Notepad and paste the following HTML into it:

```
<html>
<h1>Hello, Windows Phone 7</h1>
</html>
```

8. Save the HTML file you created to the physical path for the web site that you specified in Step 2 (referenced in Figure 19–2) and name the file index.html. For example, if you kept your Physical Path setting as "C:\WP7Server\" in Step 2, then you will save the HTML file as "C:\WP7Server\index.html."

■ **Note** You may be getting a "Permission Denied" error when you try to save the HTML file (we did). In that case, make sure that the currently logged-in user has permissions to write to that folder and try again.

You are now ready to test out your self-signed certificate.

1. Open Internet Explorer and navigate to https:/*machinename*/, where machinename is the name of your computer (for example, wp7server). You should see the "Hello, Windows Phone 7" message in the browser.

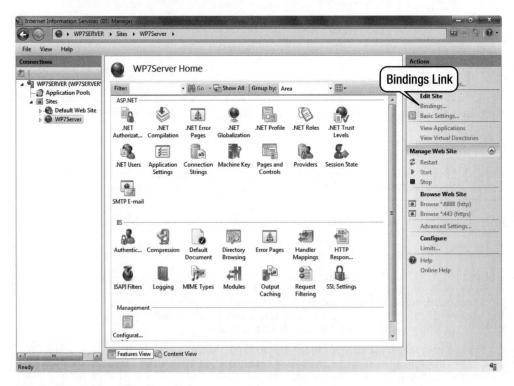

Figure 19–4. Web site bindings link

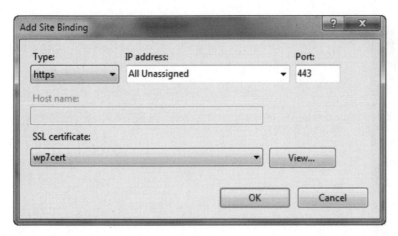

Figure 19–5. Adding https site binding

You can also start testing accessing secure data from your Windows Phone 7 application.

9.   From your Windows Phone 7 emulator, navigate to `https:/machinename/`. The very first time you start up the emulator, you will see a screen like the one shown in Figure 19–6, the absence of trust relationship error message. If you click Continue, however, you will be able to establish SSL connections to the web server from both the browser on the Windows Phone 7 device and the applications.

Exporting a Self-Signed Certificate

It is possible to establish secure connections to Microsoft Exchange from the Windows Phone 7 device using self-signed certificates.

The first step in establishing an Exchange connection secured by a self-signed certificate between the client and the server is to export the certificate from the server. The next walkthrough shows you how to do that. This walkthrough assumes that you are using Internet Explorer 8 to export certificates.

1.   On the server, open Internet Explorer, and click Tools ➤ Internet Options. If the menu bar with Tools menu option is not visible, press the Alt key.

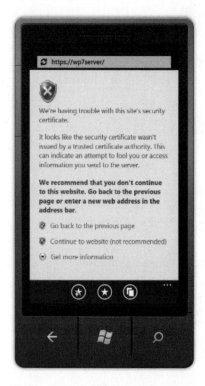

Figure 19–6. Certificate authority error on the Windows Phone 7 Emulator

2. In the window that comes up, click the Content tab, and then click the Certificates button. In the dialog that comes up, select the Trusted Root Certification Authorities tab. The self-signed certificate that you created should be listed in this tab—you can scan the Friendly Name column and look for the "wp7cert" name to find it, as shown in Figure 19–7.

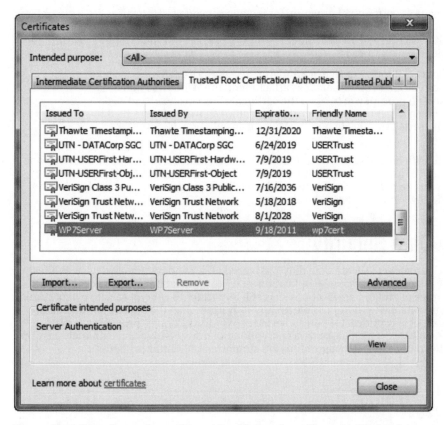

Figure 19–7. List of trusted root CAs, with self-signed certificate highlighted

3. Click on the "Export…" button, then click the Next button. On the next screen, select "No, do not export the private key" (the default option) and click Next.

4. On the next screen, choose the DER Encoded binary X.509 format (default option) and click Next. Finally, select the folder, name the file "wp7cert" (make sure to put it somewhere you can find it later!), click Next, and then click Finish. You should get a message notifying you that the export was successful.

With the certificate exported, you are now ready to finalize the trust relationship between the Windows Phone 7 device and the server secured by a self-signed certificate. You will do that in the next section.

Installing Self-Signed Certificate on Windows Phone 7

The easiest way to install a self-signed certificate on Windows Phone 7 device or emulator in the first release of Windows Phone 7 framework is to simply e-mail it. Then, let the built-in Windows Phone 7 features recognize the certificate file and install it on the device. The next few steps will guide you through this process.

5. Open or navigate to your e-mail program; for instance, if you use Hotmail as your default e-mail, log in to Hotmail.com and create an e-mail message to yourself. In that e-mail, add an attachment—the `wp7cert.cer` file you created previously. Send e-mail to yourself.

6. From the Windows Phone 7 device or emulator, access the e-mail message you just sent. Once you click the `wp7cert.cer` attachment, the Windows Phone 7 framework should prompt you to open the certificate file. Go ahead and click (or tap) the screen to get the Install Certificate prompt shown in Figure 19–8. Then, click the Install Certificate button. After the installation, click the OK button.

You are now familiar with how to secure data in transit from a remote service to the Windows Phone 7 device. You have seen how to use SSL with both trusted third-party certificates from established certification authorities and self-signed certificates. In the next section, you will take a look at securely storing data on your Windows Phone 7 device by encrypting it.

Implementing Data Security

In this section, you will learn how to secure data that gets stored on a Windows Phone device. While the data in Isolated Storage is sandboxed for each application—i.e., an application cannot access the contents of Isolated Storage of another application—it is still important to encrypt sensitive data stored on the device. Encrypting data makes it impossible for anybody other than the data owner to read that data, something that is especially critical for enterprise users. Windows Phone 7 provides a powerful subset of .Net encryption classes, which make data encryption not only possible, but extremely easy on this device. The following data encryption algorithms are supported on Windows Phone 7:

- AES

- HMACSHA1

- HMACSHA256

- Rfc2898DeriveBytes

- SHA1

- SHA256

As you will see shortly in the next walkthrough, many of these algorithms complement each other to provide a robust data encryption strategy for Windows Phone 7 devices. But first, let's briefly review the purpose of each of the supported encryption algorithms.

AES (stands for Advanced Encryption Standard) is a symmetric encryption algorithm. That means that it uses the same key (password) to encrypt and decrypt data. Since the key used to encrypt/decrypt data could be easy to guess by iterating through words in a dictionary in an automated manner, an additional secret key is added during the encryption process.

Figure 19–8. Installing certificates via e-mail

This key is called *salt* and is usually a random set of bits, such as an employee identification number, that is used to make the AES-encrypted message harder for intruders to decrypt.

HMACSHA1 and HMACSHA256 algorithms both generate a unique message authentication code (MAC) from the data and password supplied. Both algorithms use the same approach to generating MAC: they take data and hash it with the secret key using standard hash function SHA1 and SHA256 correspondingly. The difference between HMACSHA1 and HMACSHA256 lies in the strength of the message generated: HMACSHA1 output is 160 bits long, while HMACSHA256 has output 256 bits in length.

Finally, Rfc2898DeriveBytes is an algorithm that relies on the HMACSHA1 function to generate a strong key, using the password and salt values supplied, to be used to encrypt and decrypt data. In the following walkthrough, you will see how the Rfc2898DeriveBytes algorithm is used to generate a set of keys for the AES-based encryption.

■ **Note** Do not store password or salt values in application code. It is extremely easy to peek at compiled .NET code using tools such as Ildasm.exe or even a simple text editor and retrieve the value of the password/salt.

In the first data security walkthrough, you will experiment with HMACSHA1 and HMACSHA256 algorithms to observe the keys that those algorithms generate from the input and password/salt values supplied. In the second walkthrough, you will encrypt and decrypt data on the device using the AES algorithm.

Using HMACSHA1 and HMACHSHA256

Both HMACSHA1 and HMACSHA256 functions are one-way: once the message authentication code is generated using either of those functions, it is impossible to recreate the original message from the generated MAC. This makes those functions ideal for storing values of security codes: the only way to produce a match of the MAC on those values is to supply a valid password and security code. The following walkthrough demonstrates how to generate HMACSHA1 and HMACSHA256 messages.

Creating a User Interface

The application interface will consist of textboxes to accept a message and password to create a MAC from, and it will show the MAC generated using both HMACSHA1 and HMACSHA256 algorithms.

1. Open Visual Studio Express for Windows Phone and create a new project called HMACTest.

2. Make `MainPage.xaml` look like Figure 19–9. For reference, the XAML of this page is pasted here (and don't forget that you can also download all code samples for this book):

```xml
<!--LayoutRoot contains the root grid where all other page content is placed-->
<Grid x:Name="LayoutRoot" Background="Transparent">
    <Grid.RowDefinitions>
        <RowDefinition Height="Auto"/>
        <RowDefinition Height="*"/>
    </Grid.RowDefinitions>

    <!--TitlePanel contains the name of the application and page title-->
    <StackPanel x:Name="TitlePanel" Grid.Row="0" Margin="24,24,0,12">
        <TextBlock x:Name="ApplicationTitle" Text="MY APPLICATION"
Style="{StaticResource PhoneTextNormalStyle}"/>
        <TextBlock x:Name="PageTitle" Text="HMAC Test" Margin="-3,-8,0,0"
Style="{StaticResource PhoneTextTitle1Style}"/>
    </StackPanel>

    <!--ContentPanel - place additional content here-->
    <Grid x:Name="ContentGrid" Grid.Row="1">
        <Button Content="Generate" Height="72" HorizontalAlignment="Left"
Margin="149,437,0,0" Name="button1" VerticalAlignment="Top" Width="160" Click="button1_Click"
/>
        <TextBox Height="72" HorizontalAlignment="Left" Margin="149,23,0,0"
Name="txtMessage" Text="" VerticalAlignment="Top" Width="317" />
        <TextBlock Height="99" HorizontalAlignment="Left" Margin="21,216,0,0"
Name="textBlock1" Text="TextBlock" VerticalAlignment="Top" Width="445" TextWrapping="Wrap" />
        <TextBlock Height="114" HorizontalAlignment="Left" Margin="24,321,0,0"
Name="textBlock2" Text="TextBlock" VerticalAlignment="Top" Width="442" TextWrapping="Wrap" />
```

```
            <TextBlock Height="30" HorizontalAlignment="Left" Margin="21,44,0,0"
Name="textBlock3" Text="Message:" VerticalAlignment="Top" Width="122" />
            <TextBlock Height="30" HorizontalAlignment="Left" Margin="21,129,0,0"
Name="textBlock4" Text="Key:" VerticalAlignment="Top" />
            <TextBox Height="72" HorizontalAlignment="Left" Margin="149,101,0,0" Name="txtKey"
Text="" VerticalAlignment="Top" Width="246" />
        </Grid>
    </Grid>
```

Coding the Application Logic

The next step is to add logic that takes advantage of the cryptography classes on Windows Phone 7 to show Message Authentication Codes.

1. Add the following using directive to the top of the page:

```
using System.Security.Cryptography;
```

2. Because you want all of the encryption logic to happen on the button click, add an event handler to the Click event of the Generate button. To do that, double-click the "Generate" button and paste the following code inside the handler. Note how after declaring the HMACSHA1 and HMACSHA256 classes, all of the magic happens in the ComputeHash function, which returns an array of bytes that you convert to the hexadecimal string.

```
string message = txtMessage.Text;
string key = txtKey.Text;

System.Text.UTF8Encoding encoding = new System.Text.UTF8Encoding();

byte[] keyByte = encoding.GetBytes(key);

HMACSHA1 hmacsha1 = new HMACSHA1(keyByte);
HMACSHA256 hmacsha256 = new HMACSHA256(keyByte);

byte[] messageBytes = encoding.GetBytes(message);
byte[] hashmessage = hmacsha1.ComputeHash(messageBytes);
textBlock1.Text = ConvertToString(hashmessage);

hashmessage = hmacsha256.ComputeHash(messageBytes);
textBlock2.Text = ConvertToString(hashmessage);
```

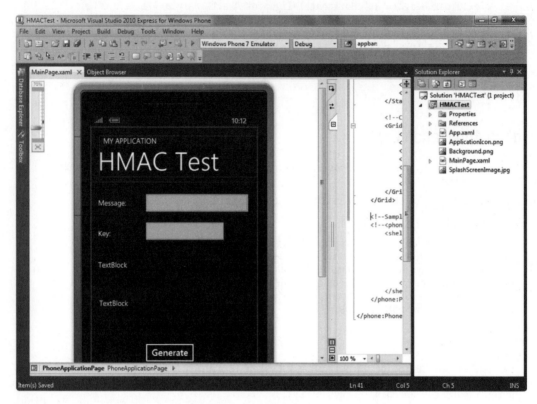

Figure 19–9. User interface for the HMACTest application

3. Finally, paste the contents of the ConvertToString helper function that converts a
    byte array passed in to the hexadecimal string.

```
public static string ConvertToString(byte[] buff)
{
    string sbinary = "";

    for (int i = 0; i < buff.Length; i++)
    {
        //hex-formatted
        sbinary += buff[i].ToString("X2");
    }
    return (sbinary);
}
```

Press F5 to run the application. Enter some message text (for example, "Hello, World") and key (for
example, "test") and observe the MAC values generated using the HMACSHA1 algorithm (top TextBlock)
and HMACSHA256 algorithm (bottom TextBlock). Notice that not only does the length of the MACs
differ, but the MACs themselves are completely different from each other.

In the next walkthrough, you will encrypt and decrypt data using AES.

Using Rfc2898DeriveBytes and AES to Encrypt Data

To encrypt data from prying eyes on a Windows Phone 7 device, you need a strong encryption mechanism that, in turn, relies on the strong key to make encryption withstand all of the known attempts to break it. The Rfc2898DeriveBytes algorithm, available on Windows Phone 7, creates a very strong key for use in AES encryption from the password and salt values passed in. The next walkthrough demonstrates how to use both of those algorithms on a Windows Phone 7 device.

Creating a User Interface

The interface will prompt the user for data to encrypt and for a password and salt to use for that encryption. The interface will also have two buttons—one for encryption and the other one for decryption of data.

1. Open Visual Studio Express for Windows Phone and create a new project called AESEncryption.

2. Make the MainPage.xaml page look like the one shown in Figure 19–10. For convenience, the XAML of this page is pasted here:

```
<!--LayoutRoot contains the root grid where all other page content is placed-->
<Grid x:Name="LayoutRoot" Background="Transparent">
    <Grid.RowDefinitions>
        <RowDefinition Height="Auto"/>
        <RowDefinition Height="*"/>
    </Grid.RowDefinitions>

    <!--TitlePanel contains the name of the application and page title-->
    <StackPanel x:Name="TitlePanel" Grid.Row="0" Margin="24,24,0,12">
        <TextBlock x:Name="ApplicationTitle" Text="CLASSIFIED" Style="{StaticResource
PhoneTextNormalStyle}"/>
        <TextBlock x:Name="PageTitle" Text="AES Encryption" Margin="-3,-8,0,0"
Style="{StaticResource PhoneTextTitle1Style}"/>
    </StackPanel>

    <!--ContentPanel - place additional content here-->
    <Grid x:Name="ContentGrid" Grid.Row="1">
        <TextBox Height="65" HorizontalAlignment="Left" Margin="6,41,0,0"
Name="txtDataToEncrypt" Text="" VerticalAlignment="Top" Width="462" />
        <TextBlock Height="30" HorizontalAlignment="Left" Margin="20,21,0,0"
Name="textBlock1" Text="Data to encrypt" VerticalAlignment="Top" Width="419" />
        <TextBox Height="72" HorizontalAlignment="Left" Margin="6,334,0,0"
Name="txtPassword" Text="" VerticalAlignment="Top" Width="462" />
        <TextBlock Height="30" HorizontalAlignment="Left" Margin="20,310,0,0"
Name="textBlock2" Text="Password" VerticalAlignment="Top" Width="346" />
        <TextBox Height="72" HorizontalAlignment="Left" Margin="6,426,0,0" Name="txtSalt"
Text="" VerticalAlignment="Top" Width="462" />
        <TextBlock Height="36" HorizontalAlignment="Left" Margin="21,403,0,0"
Name="textBlock3" Text="Salt" VerticalAlignment="Top" Width="304" />
        <Button Content="Encrypt" Height="72" HorizontalAlignment="Left"
Margin="20,504,0,0" Name="button1" VerticalAlignment="Top" Width="160" Click="button1_Click"
/>
```

```
            <Button Content="Decrypt" Height="72" HorizontalAlignment="Left"
Margin="296,504,0,0" Name="button2" VerticalAlignment="Top" Width="160" Click="button2_Click"
/>
            <TextBlock Height="30" HorizontalAlignment="Left" Margin="24,101,0,0"
Name="textBlock4" Text="Encrypted Data" VerticalAlignment="Top" Width="432" />
            <TextBox Height="72" HorizontalAlignment="Left" Margin="8,123,0,0"
Name="txtEncryptedData" Text="" VerticalAlignment="Top" Width="460" />
            <TextBlock Height="27" HorizontalAlignment="Left" Margin="21,197,0,0"
Name="textBlock5" Text="Decrypted Data" VerticalAlignment="Top" Width="435" />
            <TextBox Height="72" HorizontalAlignment="Left" Margin="13,221,0,0"
Name="txtDecryptedData" Text="" VerticalAlignment="Top" Width="460" />
        </Grid>
    </Grid>
```

Coding the Application Logic

AES encryption in the .NET Framework is implemented via a class called AesManaged. The following code uses this class, together with the Rfc2898DeriveBytes class to encrypt the data.

Add the following using directive to the top of the page:

```
using System.Security.Cryptography;
using System.IO;
using System.Text;
```

1. Code the Encrypt method. The Encrypt method takes data to encrypt, password and salt as parameters, and returns a string. Notice how the Encrypt method creates the Rfc2898DerivedBytes class and uses that class to generate a strong key from the password and salt combination; that key is later used by the AesManaged class to encrypt data.

```
public string Encrypt(string dataToEncrypt, string password, string salt)
{
    AesManaged aes = null;
    MemoryStream memStream = null;
    CryptoStream crStream = null;

    try
    {

//Generate a Key based on a Password and Salt
        Rfc2898DeriveBytes rfc2898 = new Rfc2898DeriveBytes(password,
Encoding.UTF8.GetBytes(salt));

        //Create AES algorithm with 256 bit key and 128-bit block size
        aes = new AesManaged();
        aes.Key = rfc2898.GetBytes(aes.KeySize / 8);
        aes.IV = rfc2898.GetBytes(aes.BlockSize / 8);

        memStream = new MemoryStream();
        crStream = new CryptoStream(memStream, aes.CreateEncryptor(),
```

```
CryptoStreamMode.Write);

                byte[] data = Encoding.UTF8.GetBytes(dataToEncrypt);
                crStream.Write(data, 0, data.Length);
                crStream.FlushFinalBlock();

                //Return Base 64 String
                return Convert.ToBase64String(memStream.ToArray());
            }
            finally
            {
                //cleanup
                if (crStream != null)
                    crStream.Close();

                if (memStream != null)
                    memStream.Close();

                if (aes != null)
                    aes.Clear();
            }
    }
```

2. Code the Decrypt method. The Decrypt method is the inverse of Encrypt: it takes data to decrypt, password and salt as parameters, and returns an input string. Since AES is a symmetric algorithm, the same password and salt values must be used to decrypt data as were used to encrypt it. The Decrypt method initializes the Rfc2898Bytes key and uses it to create Decryptor for data.

```
public string Decrypt(string dataToDecrypt, string password, string salt)
{
    AesManaged aes = null;
    MemoryStream memStream = null;
    CryptoStream crStream = null;

    try
    {
        Rfc2898DeriveBytes rfc2898 = new Rfc2898DeriveBytes(password,
Encoding.UTF8.GetBytes(salt));
        aes = new AesManaged();
        aes.Key = rfc2898.GetBytes(aes.KeySize / 8);
        aes.IV = rfc2898.GetBytes(aes.BlockSize / 8);

        memStream = new MemoryStream();
        crStream = new CryptoStream(memStream, aes.CreateDecryptor(),
CryptoStreamMode.Write);
        byte[] data = Convert.FromBase64String(dataToDecrypt);
        crStream.Write(data, 0, data.Length);
        crStream.FlushFinalBlock();

        byte[] decryptBytes = memStream.ToArray();
        return Encoding.UTF8.GetString(decryptBytes, 0, decryptBytes.Length);
    }
    finally
```

```
            {
                if (crStream != null)
                    crStream.Close();

                if (memStream != null)
                    memStream.Close();

                if (aes != null)
                    aes.Clear();
            }
        }
```

3. Add code to call the Encrypt method when the user clicks the Encrypt button. Double-click the Encrypt button in MainPage.xaml and add the following code to the click event handler:

```
txtEncryptedData.Text = Encrypt(txtDataToEncrypt.Text, txtPassword.Text,
txtSalt.Text);
```

4. Finally, add code to call the Decrypt method when the user clicks the Decrypt button. Double-click the Decrypt button in MainPage.xaml and add the following code to the Click event handler:

```
    txtDecryptedData.Text = Decrypt(txtEncryptedData.Text, txtPassword.Text,

            txtSalt.Text);
```

Press F5 to run the application. Enter some data (for example, "Classified Information"), a password (for example, "test"), and salt (note that it must be at least 8 characters long, otherwise AES classes will throw an exception), and observe the values being encrypted in the Encrypted Data textbox. Press Decrypt and you should see the original text in the Decrypted Data field. Note that if you enter the password or salt values that are different between encryption and decryption, the application will raise an error.

Now that you understand the cryptography framework on the Windows Phone 7, it's time to take a look at the physical security of the device.

Figure 19–10. *User interface for the AESEncryption application*

Understanding Device Physical Security

With Windows Phone 7, customers rarely have to worry about sensitive data ending up in malicious hands if the device is lost or stolen. That is because several standard features that come complimentary with the phone (i.e., no extra charges) make it possible to feel confident about the security of the device. In this section, we will walk you through the Windows Phone 7 physical security safeguards that Microsoft provides.

Map It

From an individually customized web site, Windows Phone 7 users will be able to see the location of their phones using Bing maps.

Ring It

From that same web site, you can instruct the phone to ring for 60 seconds using a special ringtone, even if the ring tone has been turned off.

Lock It and Display a Message

You can also lock the phone from the web site and display a custom message to instruct people who may have found your phone on how to get in touch with you.

Erase It

Finally, if all is lost and there is no hope of recovering the phone, you can remotely wipe all of the data from that phone and reset it to factory settings.

As you can see, the Windows Phone 7 security story is very compelling, especially for the first generation of this device. You can expect this story to only become better and more feature-rich in the very near future. Certainly, more and more features from the full .NET framework will find their way onto the phone, which should further contribute to the security of the device.

Capability List

Windows Phone Marketplace fully discloses to the user whether an application is relying on any of the following services for proper operation:

- Gamer Services

- Location Services

- Media Library

- Microphone

- Networking

- Place Phone Calls

- Push Notifications

- Sensors

- Web Browser

These capabilities are requested on a Windows Phone 7 device when an application developer submits her application for certification. Only the requested capabilities are granted, protecting device users from unexpected behavior of potentially privacy-intruding applications.

Meeting Certification Requirements

Microsoft documentation on security in Windows Phone 7 lists explicit requirements regarding application code that gets rejected during the certification phase of an application. In the few remaining pages of this chapter, you will gain an understanding of what types of application behavior are not tolerated by Microsoft.

Application Must Implement MSIL Code

Microsoft imposes a requirement on Windows Phone 7 application developers to use managed code to construct their applications. Strong typing, bounds checking and memory management features of managed code help minimize the most common types of attacks (also referred to in the security community as "attack vectors") on both the application and the Windows Phone 7 application platform.

Generally, if you use C# language with its default settings, you will be in compliance with this restriction imposed by Windows Phone Marketplace. The problems will arise, however, if you venture into unsafe C# code territory, which can be enabled by using the unsafe keyword in a method signature. In addition to the unsafe keyword, applications with unsafe code must be compiled with a special switch, as shown in Figure 19–11. As an example of unsafe code, consider the following code, which uses a simple SquarePtrParam function to accept a pointer variable (non-MSIL code) and perform pointer arithmetic on it:

```
public partial class MainPage : PhoneApplicationPage
{
    unsafe public MainPage()
    {
        int i=5;
        InitializeComponent();
        SquarePtrParam(&i);
        PageTitle.Text = i.ToString();
    }

    // Unsafe method, using a pointer to square the number
    unsafe static void SquarePtrParam(int* p)
    {
        *p *= *p;
    }
}
```

The good news for Windows Phone 7 developers is that while the foregoing code is a perfectly valid .Net code, the Windows Phone 7 templates in Visual Studio disable the option to compile unsafe code. This option is generally found under Project ➤ Properties ➤ Build tab, and the check box "Allow Unsafe Code" is grayed out on Windows Phone 7 templates, making the option of writing unsafe application for Windows Phone 7 a challenging exercise. And even though it is possible to work around this limitation by modifying the project file (.csproj) using a text editor and specifying the <AllowUnsafeCode> attribute, it is certainly not worth the trouble because Windows Phone Marketplace will reject the application anyway.

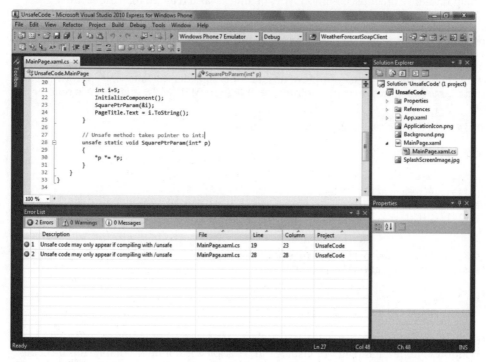

Figure 19–11. *Applications that implement unsafe code must be compiled with a special switch.*

Application Must Not Implement Any Security-Critical Code

With .Net version 4.0, Microsoft has moved away from the complexities of its Code Access Security (CAS) model and towards a simpler model it calls the Transparent Security model. The first transparency rule set was initially introduced in .Net 2.0 and then expanded to Transparency Level 2 in .Net 4.0. With Transparency Level 2, code is segregated into three types: transparent code, security-safe-critical code, and security-critical code, which are discussed in the following sections.

Transparent Code

In the transparent category, there are applications that run in a sandbox, which are pretty much all of the Windows Phone 7 applications that you ever write, and these applications have a limited permission set granted by the sandbox. That means that as a developer you do not have to be concerned about checking security policies when you write your applications, as long as you don't try to perform any operation deemed not accessible by the transparent code. For reference purposes, here is the list of tasks that transparent applications are not permitted to perform:

- Directly call critical code

- Perform an Assert operation or elevation of privilege

- Contain unsafe or unverifiable code

- Call native code or code that has the SuppressUnmanagedCodeSecurityAttribute attribute

- Call a member that is protected by a LinkDemand

- Inherit from critical types

Security-Safe-Critical Code

In the security-safe-critical category, there is code that is fully trusted but is still callable by transparent code. It exposes a limited surface area of full-trust code. Correctness and security verifications happen in safe-critical code.

Security-Critical code

Finally, there is a category of code that can't be called by transparent code. This is usually security-critical code that typically implements system-level functionality and has unlimited access to Windows Phone resources, making it a perfect place to embed malicious behavior. Therefore, Microsoft disallows this type of code, and to successfully pass Windows Phone Marketplace certification criteria, applications must not implement any security-critical code. In addition, applications must not invoke native code via PInvoke or COM Interoperability.

You will most likely never have to worry about the ins and outs of the Transparent Security model when you program for Windows Phone 7. But in case you decide to try to implement unsafe or security-critical code in your application, remember that Marketplace certification tests will quickly uncover this type of behavior and deny entry to your application.

Summary

In this last chapter of the book, you've seen how the Windows Phone 7 platform provides the facilities to secure data in transit and data on devices, as well as how it imposes a set of rigorous tests to confirm the identity of the application developer. The Windows Phone 7 device also provides security for the device itself, giving users the ability to remotely find, ring, or erase all data from the phone. Windows Phone 7 has already implemented a strong set of security features, and those features will only get better and better.

Index

■■■

You Need the Companion eBook

Your purchase of this book entitles you to buy the companion PDF-version eBook for only $10. Take the weightless companion with you anywhere.

We believe this Apress title will prove so indispensable that you'll want to carry it with you everywhere, which is why we are offering the companion eBook (in PDF format) for $10 to customers who purchase this book now. Convenient and fully searchable, the PDF version of any content-rich, page-heavy Apress book makes a valuable addition to your programming library. You can easily find and copy code—or perform examples by quickly toggling between instructions and the application. Even simultaneously tackling a donut, diet soda, and complex code becomes simplified with hands-free eBooks!

Once you purchase your book, getting the $10 companion eBook is simple:

❶ Visit **www.apress.com/promo/tendollars/**.

❷ Complete a basic registration form to receive a randomly generated question about this title.

❸ Answer the question correctly in 60 seconds, and you will receive a promotional code to redeem for the $10.00 eBook.

233 Spring Street, New York, NY 10013

Offer valid through 4/11.